THE GREAT LAKES FRONTIER

THE

An Epic of
the Old Northwest

THE **BOBBS-MERRILL** COMPANY, INC.
A SUBSIDIARY OF HOWARD W. SAMS & CO., INC.
Publishers • INDIANAPOLIS • NEW YORK

GREAT LAKES
FRONTIER

by JOHN ANTHONY CARUSO

Maps by FRANCIS J. MITCHELL

Books by JOHN ANTHONY CARUSO

The Liberators of Mexico

The Appalachian Frontier

The Great Lakes Frontier

Copyright © 1961 by John Anthony Caruso
Printed in the United States of America

First Edition
Library of Congress Catalog Card Number: 60-12631

For

MY BROTHER PAUL,
HIS WIFE HELEN,
AND THEIR SON ALEX

Table of Contents

THE GREAT LAKES FRONTIER

The Illinois Country

In June 1673 seven men descended the Mississippi in two birch-bark canoes. At the bow of the first canoe stood the leader of the expedition, his alert look falling on each new object as his two companions paddled down the wide and swift river. He was a large, sinewy young man with dark eyes and beard. The French authorities of Canada, Talon and Frontenac, had sent him from Quebec to explore the mighty river often described by the Sioux. Quite different was the unoccupied man in the other canoe. He was a delicate, careworn ascetic clad in a shapeless and frayed black robe. His deeply sunken eyes and his thin, clean-shaven face bespoke excessive vigils. He was a Jesuit, a worthy successor to those priestly martyrs of the frontier—Jogues, Garnier and Brébeuf. While the rough fur trader in the first canoe often scanned the riverside with apprehension, the gentle missionary in the other canoe burned only to suffer, even to die, in the service of Jesus and the Virgin. Very opposite were the personalities of the first known explorers of the Illinois country, Louis Jolliet and Jacques Marquette.

No sign of mankind relieved the terrible silence of their voyage. Father Marquette startled at something that bumped into his canoe. His companions threw in a net and caught a sizeable spadefish. Presently they saw herds of buffalo grazing on the lush prairie that skirted the river. Father Marquette could not forget the old bulls staring fiercely through half-blinding manes.[1]

The expedition owed its origin to Jean Talon, who for several years had served as the King's intendant at Quebec. As the officer in charge of the financial, police and judicial affairs of the province, he was the most important person in Canada next to Count Frontenac, the governor. Ambitious and energetic, Talon had done much to develop the commerce and industries of New France. In 1670 he prevailed upon Louis XIV to lay claim to all the territory in North America traversed by French explorers, missionaries and traders, and to assert supremacy over all its Indian tribes. In June 1671 Simon François Daumont, Sieur de Saint-Lusson, a soldier of fortune who had crossed to Canada on the same ship with Talon, led the pageant of possession to Sault Ste. Marie, the French missionary center at the head of the Great Lakes. Swinging aloft his sword in the presence of awed Indian allies, Saint-Lusson proclaimed the sovereignty of France of "all the countries, rivers, lakes and streams . . . both those which have been discovered and those which may be discovered hereafter, in all their strength and breadth, bounded on one side by the seas of the North and the West, and the other by the South Sea." The Indians, greatly impressed by the boom of musketry, the shouts of "*Vive le Roi!*" and the splendid pageantry that celebrated the power of their white ruler, yelped joyously as they returned to their villages.[2]

Talon next took steps to hasten the discovery of the Mississippi. He quickly enlisted the support of the French government. "Since nothing is so important for the colony as the discovery of a passage to the South Sea," wrote one of the King's ministers to Talon, "his majesty wishes you to give this your attention." Talon forthwith chose Jolliet to lead the expedition. No other man was better qualified. One of his countrymen, who knew him well, summed up his career with a Gallic epigram: "He has courage to dread nothing where everything is to be feared." As a student in the Jesuit college in Quebec, where he was born in 1645, Jolliet distinguished himself in surveying and cartography. He also became a competent musician; in later years he beguiled idle hours by playing the organ in the cathedral of his native city. He took minor orders and served as clerk in the church, a drudgery which may have caused him to yearn for a life of adventure. Relinquishing his plans to enter the priesthood, he became a fur trader and explorer. Yet he remained all his life a close friend of the Jesuits, who "regarded him as their special representative in the field of discovery." In 1669, at the age of twenty-four, he accompanied the Sulpician fathers Casson and Galinée in their successful missionary and exploratory venture on the Great Lakes. Two years later he was present with Saint-Lusson at Sault Ste. Marie.[3]

The French government had several reasons for wanting to undertake the expedition. Having settled on the lower St. Lawrence,

The Illinois Country 13

French explorers and traders quickly traced that river to its source in the Great Lakes, which on early maps they called the "sweet seas." Around Lake Superior French traders and trappers met Indians from several tribes, who spoke of the great river beyond the lake. The French hoped to outflank the Spaniards, who had described the Mississippi as flowing through North America into the Gulf of California or into the Pacific Ocean, then known as the South Sea. The French also planned to hem in the English colonists on the Atlantic slope with a chain of strongholds and trading posts connecting the fur centers on the Mississippi with those on the St. Lawrence. Furthermore, they wanted to extend the fur trade and to discover mines of gold, silver, copper and lead. Last but not least, they planned to Christianize the Indians.[4]

In October 1672 Jolliet left Quebec, probably alone, in a birch-bark canoe. He was bound for the mission station of St. Ignace, on the northern shore of the narrow Strait of Mackinac, which Father Claude Dablon, Superior of Missions for the Lakes, called "the key and the door for all the peoples of the south." There its founder, Father Marquette, had been teaching the Word of God to the Huron refugees from Pointe du St. Esprit and to a band of Ottawas who had joined them. Jolliet was to carry to the missionary an order from Frontenac and Talon—doubtless written with Father Dablon's blessing—to join the expedition. Jolliet toiled through the turbulent Ottawa and Mattawan rivers, across the dangerous portage path to Lake Nipissing, and down the French River, Georgian Bay and, finally, Lake Huron to his destination. He reached St. Ignace on December 8, the day on which the Catholic Church celebrates the Immaculate Conception of the Blessed Virgin.[5]

Father Marquette received word of his new mission with joyous gratitude. For the past two years—ever since his arrival in St. Ignace —he had constantly invoked the Blessed Virgin to obtain from God the grace of being able to visit the tribes who dwelled along the Mississippi. He had spent eighteen of his thirty-five years as a Jesuit. Arriving in Quebec from his native France in 1666, he was sent to the trading post at Tadoussac, on the mouth of the Saguenay, where, in preparation for missionary work, he mastered difficult Indian tongues taught by Father Gabriel Druillettes. Two years later he undertook his first mission at Sault Ste. Marie, in the country of the Ottawas, only to succeed Father Claude Jean Allouez at the mission of Pointe du St. Esprit on lonely and land-locked Chequamegon Bay. Here he remained until 1671, when the Sioux drove out the Hurons and Ottawas, many of whom he had converted.

Father Marquette fled with the refugees to St. Ignace, where, assisted by Indians and a few fur traders, he performed his priestly duties in "a rude and unshapely chapel, its sides of logs and its roof of bark." But Father Marquette was dissatisfied. He yearned to extend the kingdom of Jesus Christ and to make Him known and adored by the Illinois who, when he was at St. Esprit, had begged him very earnestly to bring the Word of God among them. Thanks to Divine intercession, his chance now had come.[6]

The voyagers traveled very lightly. Provided with smoked meat and Indian corn, they embarked on May 17, 1673, with five men in two canoes. Paddling westward, they passed the Strait of Mackinac, crossed the northern section of Lake Michigan and reached a village of the Menominee or Green Bay Indians, who, unwilling to lose their position as middlemen in the fur trade, did their utmost to dissuade them from their journey with tales of natives "who never show mercy toward strangers," of "horrible monsters, which devoured men and canoes together" and of heat "so excessive that it would inevitably cause our death."

Undeterred, they pushed on to the south end of Green Bay, entered the Fox River, dragged their canoes up the long and noisy rapids, crossed Lake Winnebago and drifted down the lower Fox to the Mascouten and Miami village, which stood on a height between the Fox and the Wisconsin rivers and which Dablon and Allouez had visited several years before. Father Marquette was delighted to find that the village was "beautiful and very pleasing; for, from an eminence upon which it is placed, one beholds on every side prairies, extending farther than the eye can see, interspersed with groves or with lofty trees." But what delighted him more was

. . . a handsome Cross erected in the middle of the village, and adorned with many white skins, red belts, and bows and arrows, which these good people had offered to the great Manitou (this is the name which they give to God). They did this to thank him for having had pity on them during the winter, by giving them an abundance of game when they most dreaded famine."[7]

As soon as the voyagers reached the village, they called a meeting of the chiefs and elders. Frontenac, they said, had sent them to discover new countries and to illumine the people "with the light of the holy Gospel." The chiefs and elders received their message with attention and offered them guides to show them the way to the Wisconsin River. Two Miami helped them across the short portage,

then bade them farewell. Thus the voyagers "left the waters flowing to Quebeq, four or five hundred leagues from here, to float on
those that would thenceforward take us through strange lands." On
June 17 they entered the Mississippi "with a joy," wrote Father
Marquette, "which I cannot express."[8]

For a week they saw nobody. Then on June 25 they found footprints and a path on the western bank. Landing—probably close to
the mouth of the Des Moines River—and leaving their men and
canoes behind, Jolliet and Marquette followed the path, which
eventually took them to an Indian village. Its inhabitants swarmed
from their huts, while four chiefs announced that they were Illinois
and passed around calumets decorated with feathers, which everybody smoked. Then explorers and Indians went to another village
nearby, where, in a lodge of the principal chief, Marquette addressed the Illinois in the Algonquin tongue, saying that he came
from God and extolling the glory of Count Frontenac. The chiefs
feasted the explorers and presented them with a young male slave,
whom they felt obliged to accept. In the morning six hundred of
the Indians escorted the white men to their canoes. Father Marquette promised the chiefs that he would return in the following
year and instruct the people in the true faith.[9]

Past the mouth of the Illinois and just above where the city of
Alton, Illinois, now stands, the voyagers came in view of what the
French called the "Ruined Castles," a group of rocks which wind
and wave had chiseled into odd forms. What they saw on the flat
face of a high rocky bluff doubtless convinced Father Marquette
that the Devil was undisputed master of the wilderness. Painted in
red, black and green was a pair of monsters, each as large as a calf
with horns like a deer and beard like a tiger. The face, while resembling that of a man, grimaced frightfully; the eyes were red; the
body was covered with scales; and the tail was so long it wound
between the legs and around the body and head, ending like the
tail of a fish.[10]

Scarcely had the explorers recovered from their fright when they
plunged into real danger. At its mouth the tumultous Missouri,
descending from countless prairies, bore down huge masses of driftwood across the width of the Mississippi and hurled a torrent of
yellowish mud at the canoes, compelling the men to seek safety off
the eastern bank. Escaping injury, the explorers proceeded southward on the rapid current, passing by the present sites on which
St. Louis and Kaskaskia later stood.[11]

The river by now had become as broad as an inland sea. On its marshy banks, which were often covered with thick cane, the voyagers sometimes came on Indians from various tribes; but Father Marquette, by offering kind words and holding aloft the plumed calumet which the Illinois had given him as a parting gift, always succeeded in allaying their suspicions and averting their possible attacks.

Once a group of braves moved close to the riverbank and, entering a canoe, made signs to the strangers to approach. To avoid possible danger Jolliet obeyed. The Indians strung their bows and the white men cocked their guns, but Father Marquette offered gifts, which immediately obviated trouble. Seeing that the white men meant no harm, the Indians invited them to supper, offered them shelter for the night and promised to escort them in the morning to a more populous village eight leagues down the river.[12]

The Indians were as good as their word. Ten of them got into a canoe, went a short distance ahead of the white men to the village and interceded for them. The village, which lay on the eastern bank of the river just above the Arkansas, sent out a welcoming committee in two canoes. When the Frenchmen landed, one of the warriors held forth a calumet, presented Marquette and Jolliet with tobacco and a loaf of corn bread, and "sang very agreeably."

The chief escorted the white men to his lodge, where clean rush mats had been spread for them. Elders, braves, women and children gathered around Marquette as he addressed them and gave them gifts. Through a brave who spoke the Illinois tongue, Marquette tried to explain the Christian creed, which he urged them to accept. Then he asked about the sea. Their spokesman replied that it was only ten days' journey away. He added that the land bordering the Mississippi was full of hostile Indians who were armed with guns bought from the Spaniards and that their enemies forbade them to trade with the white men. They explained that they had obtained what few hatchets, knives and beads they had from the Indians to the East and from an Illinois village. Unable to hunt wild cattle for any distance up or down the river, they lived principally on corn, and because they were weak, they were poor.[13]

Though they were apparently friendly, a few of them schemed to kill and plunder the white men during the night, but the chief forbade them. The strangers were his guests; he had dined and smoked with them; he would, therefore, protect them. Early in the morning he came with an interpreter and warned them of their danger. To emphasize his words he danced with the calumet, then presented them with the sacred pipe.[14]

The voyagers soon held a conference. Should they continue down the river, or should they return to Canada with the information they had obtained? Because they had traveled south and not west, they concluded that the Mississippi River flowed into the Gulf of Mexico, not into the Gulf of California. They further agreed that, if they continued southward, they might fall into the hands of the Spaniards and that their maps and carefully kept records, which would clear the way for all subsequent explorers, might be destroyed. Moreover, wrote Father Marquette,

We saw very plainly that we were not in a condition to resist savages allied to the Europeans, who were numerous, and expert in firing guns, and who continually infested the lower part of the river. Finally, we had obtained all the information that could be desired in regard to this discovery. All these reasons induced us to decide upon returning.[15]

Day after day, week after week, they toiled under the parching sun against the fierce sweep of the river, landing only to hunt and sleep. Exhausted by the voyage, Father Marquette easily contracted a severe attack of dysentery. Unable to help in any labor, he lay in the canoe praying fervently to the Virgin for strength. At last they reached the mouth of the Illinois and, on the advice of a friendly Indian, entered that river. The prairie teemed with buffalo and deer, and the silver streams reflected the blue of a cloudless sky. Despite his illness, Father Marquette felt as though he had wandered into some forgotten corner of paradise.

Well up the river on its western bank they halted at Kaskaskia, a name later given to another village at the junction of the Kaskaskia and Mississippi rivers. The Illinois received them warmly. Father Marquette wanted to remain to instruct them but had to bow to the wishes of Jolliet, who was anxious to return to Canada. So the voyagers turned their battered canoes homeward, following the Illinois and the Des Plaines rivers and then going by portage to the Chicago River. Eventually they reached Lake Michigan, paddled up its western shore and late in September reached the mission of St. François Xavier on Green Bay, where Jolliet wrote a report and made a map of his explorations. The voyagers had been gone for four months and had covered over 2,500 miles.[16]

In the following month Jolliet resumed his journey. Just above Montreal, however, his canoe overturned during a gale. His report and map were lost, and two of his men and the Indian slave boy were drowned. He was himself injured and lay unconscious for hours. He wrote Frontenac an ironical letter in which he said that he had escaped every peril from the Indians and had passed forty-two rapids without accident only to find that, at the point of joy at his success after so long and difficult a journey, he had nothing left save his life. When he finally reached Quebec, however, he was not neglected. Frontenac received him warmly, had a *Te Deum* chanted in the cathedral and rewarded him with the island of Anticosti.[17]

Desperately ill with dysentery, Father Marquette remained all that winter and the following spring and summer at the mission of St. François Xavier in Green Bay. He prayed constantly to God to restore his strength so that he could return to the waiting Illinois with his message of salvation; and at last, in the autumn, his prayers were answered. At the command of Father Dablon he left the mission on October 25, 1674, leading an expedition composed of ten canoes, two servants—Pierre and Jacques—and a number of Indians which gradually increased as he journeyed southward. They followed the east shore of Green Bay to the head of Sturgeon Cove, whence they proceeded by portage to Lake Michigan.

Always in the hands of God, Father Marquette made little of the November storms which often whipped the lake. They were more than a month feeling their way south through snow and chilly winds along the desolate shore to the mouth of the Chicago River. They found it deserted and dreary and wrapped in all the somberness of winter. With infinite patience and labor they coaxed their canoes for two leagues through the ice that already coated the narrow stream. Here Father Marquette suffered a severe hemorrhage. The party, unable to press forward with so sick a man, reluctantly encamped on the frozen ground. Then, on a snow-covered plain near what is now known as the South Branch, Pierre and Jacques built a rude hut in which they all remained for the rest of the winter.[18]

While the others hunted with success, Father Marquette spent his time praying that he might be spared to continue his work. And by the end of March 1675 he was able to resume his toilsome journey. Leaving the miserable hut, now partly covered with water, they paddled through knee-deep water and mud across the portage leading to the Des Plaines River. In a ceaseless downpour they swept down the surging current, past leafless woods and prairies half under water until they arrived at the broader Illinois, down which they made rapid progress toward the large Indian village of Kaskaskia, near where Utica, Illinois, now stands.

The Indians, wrote Father Dablon, received Marquette "like an angel from heaven." Instantly forgetting his ailment, he passed with Jesuit zeal from wigwam to wigwam, preaching of God and the Virgin, of paradise and hell, of angels and demons. When he thought they were ready to accept the faith, he summoned them to a large meadow near the village. Around him gathered several hundred savages, chiefs and elders, youths and warriors, women and children. Displaying four large pictures of the Blessed Virgin that had survived flood and storm and were now attached to pieces of Chinese taffeta and raised on long poles, he preached again of the divine mysteries and exhorted them to accept the true God. They not only received his message with enthusiasm but begged him to remain in the village and tell them more of his wonderous faith.[19]

But his malady had returned. Believing that he was dying, he decided to return to Canada. He celebrated Easter with his Indian friends, then departed, accompanied on the river by a large group of them as far as Lake Michigan, where they bade him farewell. With faithful Pierre and Jacques he journeyed along the eastern bank of the lake, bound for the mission of St. Ignace. On May 19, fearing that his end was near, he asked them to land near the mouth of a small river, now called the Pere Marquette, at the mouth of which stands the present city of Ludington, Michigan. Obeying his wishes, they built a hut of bark on the rising ground near the bank and carried him to it. With the casual air of a man engaged in trivial conversation he told them how he wished to be buried, asked their forgiveness for the trouble he had caused them, heard their confessions and thanked God for permitting him to die a Jesuit. Seeing that they were tired, he told them to get some sleep; when the end approached, he said, he would call them. Within a few hours he feebly summoned them and asked for holy water and his reliquery. Removing the crucifix from around his neck, he begged one of the servants to hold it before his eyes. He prayed aloud. Then, as though he were intimately conversing with God, he whispered: "*Sustinuit anima mea in verbo ejus,*" and, a moment later, "*Mater Dei, memento mei.*" One of the servants, believing him to be near his end, called aloud: "Jesus, Mary!" "Jesus, Mary!" repeated Father Marquette distinctly, raised his eyes to his crucifix and died. Near the hut Pierre and Jacques sorrowfully dug a grave and buried the priest in accordance with his wishes. Resuming their journey, they paddled to St. Ignace, where they informed the missionaries of his death.[20]

Two years later a group of Kaskaskians who had been hunting on Lake Michigan decided upon their return home to take the remains of Father Marquette with them. They opened his grave, washed and dried his bones, and placed them carefully in a box of birch bark. Then, singing funeral songs, they bore the remains to St. Ignace in a procession of thirty canoes. Priests, Indians and traders thronged to the shore, received Father Marquette's bones with solemn ceremony and buried them beneath the floor of the little chapel where he had instructed and converted so many of his beloved children of the wilderness.

2

Two years passed before another exploratory party appeared in the Illinois country. This time its leader bore the most famous French name in the history of the region: Réné-Robert Cavelier, Sieur de la Salle, who may have been the first European to explore Lake Michigan and the mouth of the Ohio. Certainly no other man accomplished as much as he in the development of New France.

La Salle was born in Rouen, Normandy, of wealthy parents. He was muscular and unusually tall. Educated as an ardent Catholic under the guidance of the Jesuits, he may have derived from the missionary zeal of that Order the inspiration to seek his fortune in the New World. From the first time he landed in Canada in 1666 at the age of twenty-three, his imagination never ceased to travel beyond the French frontier to that limitless expanse of wilderness in the West. Three years later he realized his dream when he repudiated comfort and property to devote himself to exploration in the name of his king.

His is a sad, heroic story of constant struggle, not only against the countless dangers of frontier life but also against the unrelenting conspiracy of his own countrymen, who misunderstood him. A weaker man would have surrendered to his increasing difficulties, but La Salle battled grimly to the end, a brave, pathetic figure writing his name indelibly across the epic of the Old Northwest.

He became great because he was misunderstood. Though a few men, like Tonti and La Forest, clung to him with passionate devotion, the majority of his followers regarded him as distant, tyrannical, arrogant. He failed to inspire confidence in his equals and superiors alike. He never applied the strategic force of conciliation.

He disdained to win over the merchants of Canada to his plans, though these included lucrative privileges in the fur trade. And yet he, like all men, yearned for friendship, which he held inviolate. The truth was that this fiercely courageous man, this Ulysses of the wilderness, repelled by his excessive timidity. His fear of meeting people was so great that he sought the solitude of the wilderness rather than the associations of civilized society. Out of his own diffidence he fashioned a great career. Unfortunately, few knew him as well as he knew himself. To a friend he once wrote:

As for what you say about my look and manner, I myself confess that you are not far from right. But *naturam expellas*; and if I am wanting in expansiveness and show of feeling toward those with whom I associate, it is only through a timidity which is natural to me, and which has made me leave various employments, where without it I could have succeeded. But as I judged myself ill-fitted for them on account of this defect, I have chosen a life more suited to my solitary disposition; which, nevertheless, does not make me harsh to my people, though, joined to a life among savages, it makes me, perhaps, less polished and complaisant than the atmosphere of Paris requires. I well believe that there is self-love in this; and that, knowing how little I am accustomed to a more polite life, the fear of making mistakes makes me more reserved than I like to be. So I rarely expose myself to conversation with those in whose company I am afraid of making blunders, and can hardly help making them.[21]

La Salle, perhaps in October 1679, first saw the Illinois country somewhere along Lake Michigan and within the limits of present Lake County, Illinois. A series of colorful events had brought him there. In France he gained the support of Louis XIV to plant the lilies of France on the western frontier. Returning to Canada, he built a small ship which he christened *Le Griffon* and, gathering a crew, launched his plans. His purpose was clear, his ideal a truly great one. He dreamed of establishing a chain of forts which would connect fur posts in Canada with those at the mouth of the Mississippi. Had he been permitted to realize his ideal, had he been loyally supported by the Canadian authorities, he doubtless would have changed the course of frontier history.

In August 1679 the towering Norman set sail in *Le Griffon*, the first sail ship to navigate on the waters of the Great Lakes. When he arrived at Green Bay, he loaded *Le Griffon* with furs and sent her back east under her captain with orders to return to the head of Lake Michigan as soon as she had discharged her cargo. La Salle with fourteen men, who included Father Louis Hennepin, started southward in four canoes for the mouth of the St. Joseph River.[22]

They were more than a month paddling down the shore of the present state of Wisconsin. Despite gales that almost wrecked their canoes and the constant threats of his men to desert, La Salle advanced doggedly toward his destination. One day while they were feasting on some wild grapes, they found a number of human footprints on the sand. That night while La Salle and his followers slept and the sentinel sought shelter from the cold rain, a group of Outagamis stole up to their camp. Eventually discovered, the Indians came reluctantly forward, protesting their friendship; but in the morning La Salle's servant discovered that the savages had stolen a number of articles. La Salle, his pistol ready, went forthwith into the forest, seized a young warrior and led him prisoner to camp. Then he went to the chief in the nearby village, threatening to kill the hostage if the stolen goods were not returned. The Indians, being strong in numbers, prepared to fight. Three Flemish friars and eleven Frenchmen, guns in hand, found themselves facing one hundred twenty yelling Indians! Yet neither side attacked. Instead, they agreed to a parley that ended with the return of most of the stolen goods.[23]

Continuing their journey around the south shore of Lake Michigan, the voyagers reached the mouth of the St. Joseph, as La Salle called the River of the Miamis, on November 1. Here he expected to find his friend and lieutenant, Tonti, who had sailed with him on *Le Griffon* to Green Bay and who had agreed to come down the eastern shore of the lake with twenty men. Tonti had not yet arrived. He, too, awaited the arrival of *Le Griffon* with twenty recruits from France. To divert his men from mischievous thoughts La Salle put them to work building a fort that would serve both to protect *Le Griffon* in port and as a storehouse for her cargo. The men, seeing flakes of ice already appearing on the river, began to despair: they would starve, they complained, if they failed to reach the Illinois villages before the tribe scattered for the winter hunt. La Salle was too loyal to what very few friends he had—and especially devoted to Tonti—to heed their fears. He told them that even if they all deserted, he with the three friars and his Indian hunter would remain to wait for Tonti. The men grumblingly obeyed him. Less than three weeks later Tonti arrived.[24]

Henri de Tonti—to give the proper spelling of his name—was a French soldier of Italian parentage. As Governor of Gaeta his father, Lorenzo Tonti, had taken part in Masaniello's unsuccessful conspiracy in Naples and had fled to France, where he found service under the Prince de Conti and where he established the form of insurance called the Tontine. His son Henri, who was born probably near Naples, entered the French army in his late teens, became an officer and took part in seven campaigns. In one of these, the Sicilian Campaign, a grenade carried away his right hand. Tonti replaced the loss with an artifical hand that prompted his awed Indian friends to nickname him Iron Hand. After the Treaty of Nymwegen in 1678 when his regiment was disbanded, he returned to Versailles, where the Prince de Conti presented him to La Salle. The two men soon became fast friends. In ensuing years La Salle was to learn that Tonti was worth more than all the arms, money and men he had secured at the French court. Tonti stuck by him through every danger, toil, misfortune and calumny. And his friendship endured after La Salle's death. After La Salle's assassination Tonti made every effort to carry out his friend's plans, to restore his good name and to secure his fame and fortune.[25]

Tonti brought no reassuring news of *Le Griffon.* The ship, he said, had never reached Michilimackinac. Even the Indians had no word of her, though they came from all parts of the lake. Tonti, moreover, came with only half of his men. His provisions had failed, and the rest of his party had been left thirty leagues behind to sustain themselves by hunting. La Salle told him to return and hasten them forward. Tonti left with two men but encountered a storm, lost his canoe and returned to La Salle. All the truant hunters save two who deserted soon rejoined the party.[26]

Fearing that the gathering ice on the rivers would block his passage, La Salle resumed his voyage early in December. The party, which according to Tonti now included twenty-nine white men in eight canoes, paddled through floating ice on the St. Joseph as far as the present city of South Bend, Indiana, where it took the short portage to the Kankakee River. Floating along a swamp down this narrow and wild stream and on into the broader Illinois, they reached the site of present Ottawa, Illinois, where they saw on several small islands a large number of Indian lodges, whose occupants were absent on their winter hunt.[27]

Borrowing thirty *minots* of corn from a supply hidden in the ground, La Salle continued downstream. On New Year's Day 1680 they landed and heard Mass. Father Hennepin made what he called a "touching" speech in which he wished a happy new year first to

La Salle and then to the other men. Five days later they arrived at Peoria Lake. Making their way along its northern bank, they soon reached the site of modern Peoria, where they camped.

Next morning, when they arrived at the point where the lake narrows into the Illinois River, they discovered about eighty Illinois wigwams on both banks. La Salle prepared for possible trouble. They let their canoes drift toward the Indians and took up their guns and made for the shore. With Iron Hand on his left and his other men around him, La Salle leaped to the shore, an act which intimidated the Indians, who offered the white men calumets. The council that ensued resulted in pledges of mutual friendship. Yet the Indians objected to La Salle's plans. Believing that the French were allies of their deadly enemies, the Iroquois, they wanted no French fort built in their country. They told the white men to go home. Eventually La Salle won them over by pledging himself to defend their village against possible Iroquois raiders.[28]

Turning from this disheartening problem, he faced another. One night six of his men, among whom were two of his best carpenters, deserted into the woods, doubtless with the intention of joining those vagabond hunters who, even at that early day, were beginning to appear in Indian villages. Another man put poison into La Salle's kettle. Soon after breakfast he began to suffer violent pains, but an antidote saved his life.[29]

To protect himself and what men remained from possible Iroquois attacks and to prepare for a journey down the Mississippi, La Salle built another fort. This rose on a low hill or knoll with a ravine on either side and a swamp in front, had a stockade of pointed logs twenty-five feet high and a foot thick and enjoyed the added protection of being surrounded by a high earthen embankment. Inside the fort were two barracks and a little cabin that served as living quarters and chapel for the priests. Father Hennepin lamented the lack of wine that prevented him from celebrating Mass, "but every morning and evening he summoned the men to his cabin to listen to prayers and preaching, and on Sundays and fete days they chanted vespers."[30]

They named the new fort Crèvecoeur, not from the heartbreak they experienced there as Father Membré believed and with whom most historians concur, but in honor of that Dutch stronghold which fell to Marshal Turenne in July 1672 when Henri de Tonti served as one of his minor officers.[31]

La Salle next undertook the vexing task of building a ship with which to explore the lower Mississippi. Late in February when the ship was half finished, he sent Father Hennepin and two other men to explore the Mississippi from the mouth of the Illinois northward. These men never returned to the Illinois country. They were captured by the Sioux and taken to what is now the state of Minnesota, where they were rescued by Frenchmen. Father Hennepin returned to France and published an untrue account of his journeys that became popular and brought La Salle's name before the reading public for the first time.

In the following month La Salle departed for Canada to ascertain the whereabouts of *Le Griffon* and to secure needed supplies for his intended expedition down the Mississippi. Leaving Fort Crèvecoeur under Tonti with sixteen men, he started with five men and two canoes on a journey that, fraught with a thousand privations, attests to his incredible physical vigor and moral courage. In an unusually severe winter he and his men dragged their canoes through the dreary woods for more than fifteen miles until they finally discovered a current sufficiently rapid to keep the stream clear of ice. Launched again, they were constantly blocked in their passage upward by masses of wedged ice, which compelled continual portage. Cold rain fell in torrents while temperatures remained so low that the clothes froze on their bodies. One snow storm was so severe that it forced them to halt for three days. Ten more days of terrible exertion and privation brought them to Buffalo Rock.[32] The same distance we now cover by rail in less than two hours.

One day they met Chassagoac, principal chief of the Illinois, who in exchange for a red blanket, a kettle and some knives and hatchets, promised to send Tonti a load of corn. Leaving two of his men and a canoe to take the promised corn back to Fort Crèvecoeur, La Salle with the others in a single canoe pressed on up the river through thickening ice. When they were unable to proceed farther they hid the canoe on what has since been named Treat's Island, just above the junction of the Du Page and Illinois rivers, and advanced on foot. Carrying their load of supplies, they plunged through marsh country which brought them to the Little Calumet where with great difficulty they built a raft. When this floundered, they crossed the river, wading in deep ice. At last on March 24 they reached the fort which La Salle had built in the previous year at the mouth of the St. Joseph.[33]

They found two Frenchmen whom La Salle in the previous year had sent from this place to Michilimackinac to search for *Le Griffon*. The two men reported that they had looked in vain for the ship in every section of the lake. They also repeated a rumor that

La Salle's Canadian creditors, headed by his brother, had seized all his property. Ordering the two men to Fort Crèvecoeur, La Salle with his five companions crossed the river on a raft, then, seeking a river that would take them to Lake Erie, began to walk across unexplored southern Michigan. The woods, wrote La Salle, "were so interlaced with thorns and brambles that in two days and a half our clothes were all torn, and our faces so covered with blood that we hardly knew each other." But then they found the woods more open and the game abundant; for several days they feasted on roasted venison or turkey. The region through which they were now passing was battleground for several tribes. The shots they fired and the carcasses they left behind soon brought Indians on their trail. On the evening of March 28 when they found themselves surrounded, they took to trees with their guns. Fortunately for them, the Indians mistook them for a strong force of Iroquois and ran off without shooting their arrows. La Salle encouraged the delusion by leaving on trees charcoal drawings of slaves and scalps and prisoners with which the Iroquois usually commemorated their victories. He also left traces of campfires but obliterated the marks of his route by burning the grass. In this way he and his men got through the region without difficulty.[34]

During all this time they continued to seek a river that would take them to Lake Erie. Eventually they found a small one, probably the Huron. Two of the men fell sick, but their companions made a canoe of elm bark, which at that time of the year had to be loosed from the wood with hot water. Down the river they paddled until impeded by a barricade of floating trees. The men who had been sick were now able to walk again, and they all pushed eastward on foot through the forest. In a short time they reached the Detroit River.

Unwilling to believe that *Le Griffon* was lost, La Salle had two of his men make a canoe and go to Michilimackinac to obtain possible information of her whereabouts. With the remaining men he crossed the Detroit River on a raft, then walked along the north shore of Lake Erie. Through torrents of rain, through flooded woods, they pressed doggedly toward Niagara, carrying in a canoe La Salle's Indian hunter and a Frenchman who had come down with pneumonia. On Easter Monday 1680 they reached the French fort at Niagara Falls.

Here he received depressing news. *Le Griffon* had never returned and her fate was unknown. Moreover, another ship, *St. Pierre*, had sunk at the mouth of the St. Lawrence with a consignment of goods valued at twenty-two thousand livres sent to him from France. The new intendant, Jacques Duchesneau, who hated him and his friend Frontenac, had detained sixteen of the twenty hired men on their way to join him. The remaining men, believing maliciously fostered gossip that he had died in the wilderness, had returned to France.[35]

On May 6 he reached Fort Frontenac, where even more disheartening news awaited him. Two voyagers brought him a letter from Tonti, who wrote that most of his men had mutinied, wrecked Fort Crèvecoeur, torn down its palisade, pillaged its storehouse, thrown into the river all arms and ammunition—save those they could carry away—and fled, leaving Tonti with five men, two of whom were friars. A few days later two traders informed La Salle that they had met the deserters whose number was now increased to twenty by recruits from Michilimackinac and Niagara. They had demolished the fort at the mouth of the St. Joseph, stolen from Michilimackinac a large number of furs belonging to La Salle and pillaged the storehouse at Niagara. Here they had separated, twelve of them heading for Fort Frontenac to kill La Salle as the surest way of escaping punishment.[36]

La Salle took nine men with him on the brigantine which was to carry him back to the Illinois country and sailed in search of the deserters. Concealing the ship at a wooded cape opposite Gull Island, he got into a canoe with five other men and began to patrol the shore. At sunrise they saw two canoes approaching. When the first canoe, which contained five men, drew near, La Salle darted from the cape and called on them to surrender. Completely surprised, they threw down their guns. The two men in the next canoe also surrendered. La Salle took the seven prisoners to Fort Frontenac and the next day returned to patrol the lake for the remaining five deserters who, their comrades disclosed, were following in a third canoe. At six o'clock that afternoon La Salle saw this group of deserters across the lake and ordered his men to give chase.

Seeing them coming, the deserters paddled madly to the shore and, protecting themselves from among rocks and trees, began to fire on their pursuers. La Salle kept four men to guard the shore and sent the rest farther down the cape to surprise the deserters from the rear. The deserters ran back to their canoes and in the growing darkness attempted to escape. La Salle ordered them to halt. Instead they fired on their pursuers, who, returning the volley, killed two of them and captured the other three. They, too, were imprisoned at Fort Frontenac.[37]

Having removed this danger to his person, La Salle on August 1 started westward to rescue Tonti, whom he regarded as his only abiding hope for the future. Within a few months he had surmounted every monetary obstacle and every opposition of his enemies to enlist the services of François Daupin de La Forest with twenty-five men including a surgeon, ship's carpenters, joiners, masons, soldiers and laborers. Journeying by way of the Great Lakes he reached Michilimackinac, where he left La Forest to gather a store of supplies and to follow with it as soon as possible. With ten Frenchmen, two Indian hunters and a small number of dogs La Salle pushed southward in canoes. On November 4 he reached the demolished fort at the mouth of the St. Joseph, where he left five men with supplies for La Forest. With the remaining men La Salle ascended the St. Joseph, crossed the portage to the Kankakee and followed that river to the northern branch of the Illinois.

They now approached friendly ground. Soon they would see the great Illinois village; soon its inhabitants would greet them with a whooping salute. But as the familiar landscape opened before them, as they landed that evening on the site of the village, their faces grew ashen and their eyes widened with dread. The village had disappeared. In its place was devastation and death. Gone were the numerous arborlike lodges with their coverings of rush mats. In their place stood remnants of their framework—charred poles and stakes on which hung human skulls. Wolves tore at pieces of flesh, and crows and buzzards picked at the skulls. When the astonished voyagers approached, the wolves fled and the crows and buzzards circled in the sky or perched on branches in the nearby forest. The corn in the fields hung on parched stalks or lay in charred heaps on the ground. The graves were rifled and the bodies of illustrious chiefs and warriors were flung down from the scaffolds where, in accordance with the custom of this tribe, they had been buried. The trenches in which the Illinois were accustomed to hide their belongings during their absence were broken open, and their kettles and pots all shattered. In all this La Salle and his companions recognized the fiendish work of the Iroquois. The blow which had so long threatened had fallen at last. The peaceful Illinois tribes had been wiped out.[38]

Stunned and horrified, La Salle could entertain only one thought: what had become of Tonti and his few loyal men? He searched the ghastly corpses, turning them over one by one, but all of them were Indian. Evening overtook his task. Crouched around their campfire, he and his companions kept vigil through a seemingly endless and dreadful night. In the morning La Salle continued the search for his lost friend. Near the riverbank he discovered six posts painted red. On each was a rude drawing in black paint depicting the figure of a man with bandaged eyes. Believing that these represented six French prisoners alive in the hands of the Iroquois, La Salle turned his canoes down the river in relentless pursuit.

So desperate was this venture that in the hope of preserving lives he again divided his little band. Three men he hid on an island with strict orders to put out their fires at night and not to fire their guns. With the other men in a single canoe he set forth undaunted on his perilous adventure. Each man was armed with a gun, a pistol and a sword. Each man realized that, if he fell into the hands of the Iroquois, his fate would be death by torture. Yet none hesitated. They swept past the silent shores, witnessing everywhere fresh evidences of savage cruelty.

They passed a number of deserted camps. On the site of every Illinois village across the river they recognized the more recent camping ground of pursuing Iroquois. The facts were plain to see: as the Illinois had fled in their canoes, the Iroquois had as rapidly followed on foot. Below Peoria Lake La Salle and his men reached demolished Fort Crèvecoeur. Though the hull of La Salle's unfinished ship was still intact, the Iroquois had somehow pulled out the iron nails and spikes. On one of the boards had been scribbled: "*Nous sommes tous sauvages: ce 15, 1680*"—perhaps the work of one of the deserters. The surrounding plain was one vast graveyard. Here and there along the riverbank the voyagers saw hideous blackened figures tied to stakes. All of them were bodies of women and children. Apparently the Illinois warriors and older men had fled, leaving their families to their doom.[39]

The Frenchmen looked constantly for Tonti and his comrades but found no sign of them. At last La Salle saw flowing before him the great river which had long been the object of his passionate striving. But now, ironically, it meant little to him: all his thoughts he reserved for his lost friend. The latitude and the flora and fauna of the surrounding country; the river's course; the bluff at the mouth of the Illinois which afforded an ideal location for a fort; the fertility of the surrounding plain, so inviting to settlers: what were all these compared with such a friend as a man can have once in a lifetime? His men attempted to rally him by offering to go with him to the sea. He refused. Instead he buried some hatchets and knives and addressed Tonti a letter explaining how these could be found and informing him that he had returned to the ruined village. The letter and a board on which he made drawings of himself and his men sitting in a canoe he hung on a tree. He hoped that some friendly Indian would see the letter and sign and would deliver them to Tonti.[40]

Day after day, night after night, they toiled at their paddles, spanning the two hundred fifty miles to the village in just four days! They found the river frozen. While they waited for a thaw, they harvested the corn from the charred stalks. One night they saw a brilliant comet appear above the rim of the prairie. At that moment it was terrifying the whole world, but La Salle, having been all his life surrounded by danger and death, "could afford to remain calm about something so impersonal as a comet." He coolly sat down and made notes of the phenomenon for the scientists in Paris.[41]

On December 28 they resumed their journey. Nine days later they reached the juncture of the Des Plaines and Kankakee rivers. A slight distance up the river stood a rude log cabin. Within its walls La Salle saw an object that cheered him with a gleam of hope. It was just a piece of wood, but it had been cut with a saw. Could Tonti and his party have passed that way, escaping the carnage behind them? Leaving two men to guard the stores, he pushed with the others directly overland toward the fort at the mouth of the St. Joseph. Here they found La Forest and his men, who, however, had received no news of Tonti.[42]

La Salle knew no rest. His thoughts were filled with plans for the future. He must relieve the men he had left behind; he must explore the Mississippi; he must colonize the Illinois country, where he planned to build a fort to protect the Algonquin tribes against any possible Iroquois attack.

To realize his plans he needed allies. These were close by. A band of Abnaki and Mahican whom the Puritans had defeated in King Phillip's War had fled from New England to friendly French country near the St. Joseph. In the region, too, were some Miamis who had lately suffered at the hands of the Iroquois. Through his Indian hunters La Salle negotiated with the three tribes and eventually won their enthusiastic support. With fifteen men he returned to the Illinois country to obtain supplies and bring back the men he had left behind. On snowshoes they glided in bright and cold weather over the glaring prairie for so many miles that La Salle and a few others became snow blind. In extreme pain La Salle camped at the edge of a forest and sent out a man to gather some pine needles for making a decoction useful in relieving his ailment. The man followed fresh Indian tracks to a camp of Foxes, who told him that they had seen white men among the Potawatami. The white men were traveling from the Illinois country northward toward Green Bay, keeping alive with elderberries and wild onions which they grubbed up out of the snow. This information greatly cheered La Salle. Tonti and his men were alive! While La Salle with his loaded canoes had been coming down the east coast of Lake Michigan, his good friend had been ascending the opposite shore![43]

The blind men soon recovered. La Salle returned with his men to the St. Joseph, where he put them to work planting corn and vegetables while he completed negotiations with his New England and Miami allies. Then, late in May 1681 he traveled up Lake Michigan to Michilimackinac, where he found Tonti, who had arrived from Green Bay the day before.

Tonti explained that the Iroquois had captured him and his comrades and prepared to put them to death, but that an Onondaga chief who knew La Salle had saved their lives and permitted them to ascend the Illinois without supplies. Finding that their canoe was leaking, they stopped to repair it. One of the friars, Father Gabriel Rebourde, strolled with a breviary in his hand to a grove for an hour of meditation. His comrades never saw the good old man again. A band of Indians, perhaps Kickapoo, had seized him, knocked him on the head and danced merrily around his scalp. The rest of the party abandoned their worthless canoe and set out on foot for Lake Michigan to seek help from the friendly Potawatomi on Green Bay. During their journey they would have starved to death had not a group of Kiskakon Ottawas seen the smoke of their fire and carried them to a Potawatomi village, where they found five Frenchmen and where they were kindly received. Tonti's horrible experiences by no means dampened his ardor for fresh adventure. Seeing his friend as determined as ever to explore the Mississippi, he immediately agreed to accompany him. So they set out for Fort Frontenac to obtain the fresh supplies they needed for the expedition.[44]

In this endeavor La Salle once more was successful. Though his estate was already mortgaged, he obtained men, supplies and even funds from Count Frontenac and a wealthy relative. In Montreal he made his will in favor of a cousin and once more set out for the west. This time he assumed personal command of his followers.

December saw him again at the mouth of the St. Joseph, where he chose eighteen of his Indian allies to accompany his party of twenty-three Frenchmen. Some of the Indians took their squaws and children with them, swelling the entire company to fifty-four persons. Tonti and Father Membré led the way in six canoes, leaving La Salle with a few men to cache supplies they could not take along. Because the familiar route by the Kankakee River was frozen, they crossed Lake Michigan to the Chicago River, where La Salle joined them a few days later. When they found even the Chicago covered with ice, they made sleds, strapped their canoes and supplies on them and, in a straggling procession, dragged them wearily mile after mile over the glistening surface until open water below Peoria Lake permitted them to take to their canoes. On February 6, 1682, they reached the Mississippi.[45]

They traveled down the river in rain and sunshine over water gradually changing from brackish to brine, past the Missouri and the Ohio, through country of tall canebrakes and cypress forests, through lands of friendly tribes who feasted and entertained them and areas where grew exotic flowers and the alligators on whose musky flesh they sometimes dined. On April 9 they came to their journey's end. Before them spread the Gulf of Mexico. On dry ground near the mouth of the river La Salle planted a large rough column which bore the King's arms cast from the copper of a kettle. While the New England Indians and their squaws looked on in awed silence, the Frenchmen mustered their arms, chanted the *Te Deum*, the *Exaudiat*, and the *Domine salvum fac Regem*. Then, amid volleys of musketry and shouts of *"Vive le Roi,"* La Salle took formal possession of the vast country which became known as Louisiana Territory.[46]

On his return journey La Salle became very ill with a disease symptomized by high fever. He sought rest at Fort Prudhomme, which he had built at Chickasaw Bluffs on his way down the river. Leaving Father Membré as nurse, Tonti continued his journey to Michilimackinac, whence he sent news of the recent exploration to Canada. In September La Salle joined his friend and sent him back to the Illinois country to build Fort Saint Louis, which stood on a rock rising out of the Illinois River to the height of one hundred twenty-five feet. Though still weak from his recent illness, La Salle wanted to return to Quebec to take ship for France, but, hearing that the Iroquois planned to attack the Illinois country again, he rejoined Tonti instead. The Iroquois never struck.

That fall La Salle returned to Canada to find that his friend Frontenac had been recalled. Learning that the new governor, Antoine le Fevre de la Barre, was hostile to him, La Salle sailed for France to obtain the King's support for what was to be his crowning enterprise. This was to establish at the mouth of the Mississippi a colony which would prevent the English from seizing the region and to fortify the upper reaches of the river to hold it for France. In his quest he was successful; but, ironically, it proved his undoing. In February 1684 he sailed with four ships and four hundred men. After a stormy voyage he missed the mouth of the Mississippi and landed instead at Matagorda Bay. Here, in the present state of Texas, he established Fort Saint Louis of Texas, where he and his party suffered innumerable privations and where all of his ships were wrecked. On March 19, 1687, while he marched northward to obtain supplies in Canada, one of his rebellious followers murdered him.

The founder of French dominion in the Mississippi valley gave to his country a claim to the interior of the continent, while a later generation of his countrymen realized his dream by building a chain of forts connecting Louisiana with New France. From New Orleans northward to the Illinois country French settlements sprang up during the next twenty years. Thousands of settlers, some from Canada, some from Louisiana, planted themselves along the Mississippi valley and established a number of villages, some of which were to figure prominently in the history of the Old Northwest. By the middle of the eighteenth century La Salle's dream of an unbroke empire stretching from New Orleans to Quebec had begun to be realized.

3

In those days the Illinois country extended from the Miami and Wabash rivers westward to the Mississippi and from the Illinois southward to the Ohio. It was rich land of countless praires, some level, some rolling, some long, some narrow, some as broad as a day's riding across them. Alluvial bottoms, densely covered with trees and underbrush, ran along the rivers. Here and there copses of woodland lay like islands in endless seas of tall, waving grass, which abounded with wild game. From time immemorial bear, elk and deer dwelt in the groves around the borders, and herds of buffalo, wandering in long files and beating deep but narrow trails, thundered across the prairies in all directions.

Scattered over this vast expanse of green desert was a number of small French villages which included St. Philippe, Prairie du Rocher, Vincennes, Cahokia, Fort de Chartres and Kaskaskia. The first three of these were the smallest. St. Philippe, located five miles from Fort de Chartres on the road to Cahokia, had sixteen houses and a small church; Prairie du Rocher, located fourteen miles from Kaskaskia, had twenty-two houses; and Vincennes, established in 1722 but not settled until 1734, on the east bank of the Wabash and a hundred fifty miles from its mouth, boasted eighty to ninety families.[47]

The oldest of the six villages, Cahokia, founded in 1699, stood fifteen leagues from Fort de Chartres and six leagues below the mouth of the Missouri. In its palmiest days it had a church and forty-five houses occupied mostly by Canadian hunters who had married Indian women. Dominating the village was the mission of St. Sulpice with its busy plantation and mill. The untilled fields that surrounded the village disclosed its preoccupation with the fur trade.[48]

Fort de Chartres, named for the Duc de Chartres, son of the Regent, was founded in 1720 by Major Pierre Dugue Boisbriant. Coming up the Mississippi with one hundred men, he built a wooden fort which was one in the chain extending from Quebec to the Gulf of Mexico. It was rebuilt thirty-six years later and had the reputation of being the most commodious fortification in America, but its garrison was always small. In 1747 it had one hundred thirty-five men and thirteen officers; in 1751 it had six companies numbering three hundred men. The officers, many of whom were the scions of noble families and all of whom belonged to the French gentry, represented the highest social caste in the Illinois country. Their long, multicolored coats, their embroidered vests and their knee breeches brightened the primeval surroundings, and their wives with their elegant finery, quadrilles and gavottes and their vivacious chatter lent to the banks of the Mississippi the air of a miniature Versailles. The illusion vanished, however, with a look at the soldiers in their ragged uniforms. Poorly paid and supplied, these scarecrows preferred to arm themselves with attractive sticks rather than rely on their outmoded guns.[49]

The most important of the six villages, Kaskaskia or Notre Dame de Cascasquios, stood on the west bank of the river of the same name and about six leagues from its mouth. The population was composed of about five hundred whites and an equal number of Negroes. To this place came in 1721 the enterprising young adventurer, Pierre Renault, with two hundred miners and five hundred slaves, whom he had brought from Santo Domingo to work the mines he expected to discover. The enterprise faded, but Kaskaskia remained. It soon became a parish, and in 1722 its commandante issued the first land warrant in the Illinois country.

The village grew rapidly. The Jesuits established a college and a monastery. To the visitor Kaskaskia presented a peaceful and orderly appearance with an air of permanancy unusual in so bleak a region. The houses of the prosperous inhabitants were usually built of stone quarried from the bluffs and sported broad verandas and large low-ceiling rooms with high mantel pieces and molded doors. The other dwellings were built upright hewn logs with concave sides forming a rounded space filled with clay, straw and stones. At one end of each house—sometimes at both ends—was a large chimney with a generous fireplace. A painted roof, thatched or bark, extended over the porch or gallery. Around each property ran a white picket fence enclosing flower beds, a small orchard of fruit trees, a vegetable garden and the slave cabins and a barn.[50]

The streets were narrow and emanated from large grass-covered squares. Here stood the church and the picketed fort which served as asylum in case of Indian attack. The church was an extremely awkward and ungainly old pile with projecting eaves, walls of hewn timber perpendicularly planted and interstices stuffed with mortar. Its old-fashioned spire and its dark, storm-beaten casements swathed it with romantic charm. Its walls were rudely plastered with lime and decorated with a few dingy paintings. The floor was of loose, rough boards and the ceiling was arched with oaken panels. The altar and the lamp suspended above it were very old.[55]

The French frontiersmen were largely descendants of immigrants originally from Picardy and Normandy. They spoke a jargon of French. Some had drifted down long waterways from distant Canada, pausing often as they voyaged, and others had found passage up the Mississippi from New Orleans. The common people were beginning to give up the practice of reckoning time by months and years. Like the Indians, they dated events from such natural phenomena as floods, the maturing of green corn or the ripening of strawberries.[52]

The population was divided into two social groups, the upper class or gentry, and the lower class known as *habitants*. The gentry was composed of the officers, the holders of large tracts of land and the richer merchants. They lived in comfort. The Jesuits in Kaskaskia owned a wooden house one hundred twenty feet long, another building divided "into many low apartments," Negro cabins, cowsheds, a barn, a mill run by horse power, a stable and a dovecote. Sixty-eight Negroes served them as farmers, black-smiths, carpenters, brewers, and masons. In addition to their farm-land the Jesuits owned a large farm on the bluffs across the Kas-kaskia River. Some private families were even more affluent. In 1765 a member of the Bauvois family owned eighty slaves. He furnished to the royal magazine eighty-six thousandweight of flour, which was only a part of one year's harvest.[53]

The homes of wealthy merchants were as large and comfortable as those of some English landowners in the East. The typical house contained twelve or fourteen rooms divided by a hall that ran from front to back. It was relatively well furnished: small services of plate could be seen on the sideboards. The walls were hung with religious pictures and French mirrors with gilt frames. Some families could boast billiard tables.[54]

But the dwellings of the *habitants* were poorly equipped and the furniture was frequently handmade. The American pioneers of Vincennes said that the French women could neither sew nor spin nor make butter and that they were inveterate gossips who left their houses dirty and in disorder.[55]

The classes dressed in accordance with their position in society. The officers wore the French uniform of the day. The costume of the fur trader was a luxurious raiment including a richly trimmed coat, embroidered waistcoat with "diamond" buttons, silken hose and silver buckles. The relatively wealthy, both men and women, imitated as far as possible the styles of Paris as they were passed up the river from New Orleans.

The costumes of the *habitants* showed the influence of their environment. Too poor and too remote from civilization to obtain fabrics, the men wore buckskin in winter and pantaloons made of coarse blue cloth during the summer. Over shirt and long vest fell a flannel cloak or *capote* with a hood that could be drawn over the head on cold days and thrown back on the shoulders on warm. Madras cotton handkerchiefs covered their heads instead of hats or caps. *Voyageurs* and hunters wore headgear of blue cloth folded in the form of a turban. At balls and other affairs the women donned fancy headdresses often tastefully trimmed with ribbons and ornamented with gay flowers. The dress of the matron, though plain and short-waisted, was frequently varied according to the taste of the wearer. Women as well as men wore moccasins which they decorated for public occasions with shells, beads and ribbons. In the summertime they often went barefooted.[56]

Life seemed to bubble with eternal youth. On summer evenings some of the citizens would gather in the broad squares and dance and sing and gossip merrily, while others, sitting on their cool balconies, would watch the gay spectacle below as they chatted volubly over their wine. In the carnival season, which began on January 6, young and old, rich and poor, danced the cotillion and *rigaudon*, the reel and minuet night after night on the puncheon-floored cabins. The village priest himself shared in their bonhomie. While he chided them for neglecting their crops and livestock, he joined them enthusiastically in every one of their numerous festivals.[57]

People of primitive, uninhibited feeling, they permitted themselves the sins of their environment. They were often patient in performing their daily chores, usually prompt in meeting their obligations. They were faithful to their friends and revengeful toward their enemies. And they were afflicted with a thirst that could be quenched only by plentiful and sometimes profuse quantities of the heady wine they made from wild grapes. Drunkenness and an addiction to cards often kept them in debt.[58] Yet their records show no excessive amount of crime. On the contrary, they were lovers of peace and order; respecting the wisdom of their judges, they ran to them with every dispute. They were proverbially French in that they were thrifty.

4

The French government always maintained that the welfare of the Illinois country rested on its agriculture; therefore, it never overlooked an opportunity to encourage settlers to develop the land. This was successful despite the fact that the population was small and the people never expert farmers. Many of them were simple tillers of the soil. Their agricultural methods were those of a century earlier. Clumsy wooden plows drawn by oxen turned the rich soil. They knew no fertilizer. The cattle, deprived of proper care and food, grew smaller and leaner. Hogs roamed the forest in large, noisy groups.[59]

A large part of the land in each village was reserved for common use and was known as the common field. This was usually a large patch of enclosed prairie, part of which was cultivated and part of which served as a pasture for cattle. The part of the common field set aside for agricultural purposes was divided into strips of one arpent in front by forty in depth, and one or more strips was allotted to each inhabitant according to his skill and industry as a cultivator. The arpent as used by the French of the west was a rather rough measure of surface, less in size than an acre. Farms held by private ownership likewise ran back in long strips from a narrow front that usually lay along some stream. Several of them generally lay parallel to one another, each including something like a hundred acres but occasionally exceeding this amount.

Near the town grew orchards of gnarled apple trees, planted by their forefathers when they came from France, and old pear trees of a kind known to Americans; but the fields lay often untilled while the owners lolled in the sunshine smoking their pipes. In consequence, they were sometimes brought to sore distress for food, and often they were obliged to pluck their corn while it was still green. Each village had water mills for grinding corn and sawing boards, and gristmills which were operated with horses or water power.[60]

The chief products were oats, hemp and tobacco. Melons, potatoes and squashes grew abundantly in the gardens, and apple, peach and pear trees flourished in the house yard.

Game was so plentiful that some of it found market in New Orleans. Both white men and Indians hunted game as well as furs. The products shipped to New Orleans included bear meat and grease, venison, hides and buffalo wool.[61]

The great business rival of agriculture in the Illinois country was the fur trade. In Canada the French government had made vain efforts to regulate the trade. It then tried the expedient of leasing the trade to various posts. While this monopolistic method relieved the government of many annoyances, it resulted in many complaints from the Indians. The Mississippi Company naturally exercised some control over the trade. On the pretext that traders encouraged intertribal war for the purpose of obtaining Indian captives as slaves, it issued an ordinance in 1720 prohibiting individuals from carrying trade with the Indians on territory under its jurisdiction. The commandante, Boisbriant, granted so many permits that Canadian officials complained of being unable to correct the abuses of the *coureurs de bois*.[62]

The search for furs led the Illinois far afield. Many of them explored the Missouri northward. Ambitious to reach the Santa Fé and enter there into a profitable business with the Spaniards, Pierre and Paul Mallet with six companions in 1739 followed the south fork of the Platte River, then struck southward through the present state of Colorado. The fur trade of the Illinois country thus reached the southern spurs of the Rockies.[63]

For decades New Orleans was the most accessible market for the products of the Illinois country. Yet the port was unsatisfactory because the heat there spoiled a large part of the furs. So the fur traders maintained a connection with the northern ports. Detroit and Machilimackinac became emporiums of the trade.

Most of the articles sold in the Illinois country were imported from New Orleans. The established price was a hundred per cent higher than that of France. In small purchases beaver was used as a measure of value, but other furs passed as currency at a price fixed in relation to this most esteemed pelt. The river craft plying trade between the Illinois country and New Orleans were of three kinds: birch-bark canoes, pirogues and bateaux. The birch-bark canoes were used least of all on account of the danger from snags. In the absence of portages their light weight was of no advantage. The pirogues, made by hollowing trunks of trees, were in more general use though they were heavy and unfit for sails. Most of the merchants traveling the Maumee-Wabash portage from Canada substituted these heavier craft for the canoes as soon as they reached Ouiatenon.[64]

The first convoy of the year usually left New Orleans in late winter or early spring, and the second in August. In the summer when the water was low, the current forced the boats to use every stretch of backwater formed by the numerous bends of the river; but the boats were much safer when the river was high and over-flowed its banks. The return voyage against the current was hard and laborious under any circumstances; seventy days and sometimes much longer were required to reach home. The voyage down was, of course, less of a hardship and much more rapid.

Private boats often passed up and down the river along with the royal convoys. Sometimes merchants would combine for protection, making a sizable fleet. The safest boats were those which were guarded by soldiers commanded by an officer of the marine. Merchants naturally preferred to ship their merchandise in such boats or at least to place their own boats under the command of the convoy captain, a position that gave ample opportunity for graft.[65]

5

The first governor of Louisiana, Pierre le Moyne, Sieur d'Iberville, regarded the Illinois country as lying within his jurisdiction. And so it remained, irrespective of its formal local administration. In 1712 Kaskaskia became the provincial capital.

In the ensuing years the governor of Louisiana abandoned his quest for nonexistent gold and lead mines. Instead, he encouraged agriculture, a policy aimed at making the Illinois country the granary and the breeding ground for cattle for the army and the civilian population. At the same time France faced the danger of losing her lucrative fur trade to the British. Aggressive and enterprising traders from Virginia, the Carolinas and Pennsylvania annually sent trains of pack horses into the Illinois country. The tribes, bribed with plentiful gifts, killed Frenchmen and even attacked the French stronghold at Detroit. In 1743 the French authorities captured on the Mississippi four Englishmen and a Dutchman carrying a route map, a passport and a trade permit from "a judge in Albany." The Pennsylvania traders under their aggressive and able leader, George Croghan, who had migrated to America from Dublin in 1731, eventually dominated the trade of the Illinois country. From his center at Logstown, Pennsylvania, Croghan moved first into the Ohio country, then into the region of the Wabash and the Maumee rivers and finally to the Mississippi, "bringing anxiety into the hearts of the best French officials, who felt the potential power of English influence even in the distant Illinois country."[66]

Despite this threat France during King George's War maintained her dominion. By the Treaty of Aix-la-Chapelle, which ended the war in 1748, each nation restored its conquests in Asia, Europe and America. Nevertheless, France in the years of peace visualized greater danger than in the years of war. The great army of British fur traders continued to march into French domain. They came now mainly from Virginia, Maryland and Pennsylvania, spreading out like the sticks of a fan along the banks of every stream on the frontier and defying the orders of the French authorities to remove themselves from territory which France claimed by right of exploration.

In 1749 these incursions prompted La Galissonière, the governor of New France, to send Pierre Joseph Céloron de Blainville to renew possession of the vital Ohio country. Céloron descended the Ohio and at important points along the river buried lead plates claiming the region for France. In addition he left with the Indian chiefs messages for the British governors warning them against future trespasses of French territory. When the governors ignored these warnings, the French established a number of forts in western Pennsylvania, which Virginia claimed by right of her ancient charter.

The building of these forts resulted in clashes that precipitated the French and Indian War. In this conflict the Illinois country played an important part. The French commander at Kaskaskia, Major de Makarty-Mactingue—or simply Major MacCarthy, as he sometimes spelled his name—was a militant Irishman who wasted no time in furnishing the commanders at Fort Duquesne with ample supplies. One convey was composed of 120,000 hundredweight of flour and 40,000 of pork. Its leader was Captain Coulon de Villiers who, anxious to avenge the death of his brother Jumonville in a skirmish with young George Washington at Great Meadows early in the conflict, had asked Makarty for active service. On July 13, 1756, Villiers set out with twenty-two men, who were later reinforced by thirty-three Indians, to attack Croghan's stockade on Aughwick Creek near its confluence with the Juniata River at the site of modern Shirleysburg, Pennsylvania. Losing his way he came unexpectedly on Fort Granville, which he attacked and under cover of darkness set on fire. The commander was killed and the garrison of thirty-eight men surrendered. Among the captives were three women and seven children whom Villiers saved from the vengeance of the Indians and conveyed to Fort de Chartres, where some of them were taken in by French officers and *habitants*. The others were sent to New Orleans.[67]

Makarty continued to send expeditions to Fort Duquesne until it fell to the English in 1758. By this time Makarty's convoys had almost drained the provincial treasury: during a period of eight months he had spent almost six hundred thousand livres. The most conspicuous figure of these convoys was Charles Philippe Aubry, who later became the last acting governor of Louisiana. Makarty, learning that the British were planning to send a war party to the Mississippi by way of the Tennessee River, ordered Aubry, who was leading a convoy which included one hundred fifty men, to build a fort on the Ohio. This fort, called first Ascension and later Massiac, was completed in June 1757 and served as the springboard for George Rogers Clark's invasion of the Illinois country twenty-one years later.[68]

In the last five years of the French and Indian War England wrested victory from France—thanks to the sleepless efforts of William Pitt. In 1758 she captured Fort Frontenac. In 1759 Wolfe won his great victory over Montcalm on the Plains of Abraham, and subsequently English troops took Quebec, Le Boeuf, Machault and Niagara. In the following year the fall of Montreal yielded all Canada. As the war drew to a close, Spain entered it on the side of France, only to lose Cuba and the Philippine Islands.

By the definitive Treaty of Paris signed on February 10, 1763,

France surrendered to England all her possessions in North America east of the Mississippi save the Island of Orleans and two fishing posts in the Gulf of St. Lawrence. France compensated Spain for her loss of Florida by ceding Louisiana west of the Mississippi and the Island of Orleans. The French and Indian War drove the French from North America and opened the vast and fertile Mississippi Valley to American frontiersmen.

British forces soon took possession of the frontier strongholds at Detroit, Michilimackinac, Sandusky, Miami, Ouiatenon, St. Joseph, Green Bay and Sault Ste. Marie. But before they could reach Fort de Chartres in the Illinois country the great Ottawa chief, Pontiac, launched his conspiracy to drive the "red-coated dogs" into the sea. Hitherto the tribes had employed the simple diplomacy of playing France off against England. In earlier days their fear of French military power had inclined them toward the more commercially minded English. But England's refusal to distribute the accustomed gifts, her rapacious traders and the encroachments of her backwoods settlers caused many tribes to listen eagerly to the fiction of French traders that their Great Father in France had been sleeping but was now awake and ready to help them wipe the English "from the face of the earth." Encouraged by this assurance of aid, Pontiac in 1761 and 1762 created a confederacy which included all the tribes of the Great Lakes region and even one of the Six Nations. In May 1763 the Indians struck.

The English were completely surprised. General Jeffrey Amherst, commander in chief of British forces in America, had such a contempt for the Indians that he expected to hold the western country with a few soldiers scattered among widely separated posts. The result of this foolish policy was that the Indians, through treachery or force, captured Michilimackinac, St. Joseph, Miami, Ouiatenon, Sandusky and a number of smaller forts within a few weeks. Only Detroit, Fort Niagara and Fort Pitt withstood the triumphant Indians and proved rallying points of ultimate British victory.

Amherst retaliated quickly. He sent out two expeditions: one, under Captain James Dalzell, marched along Lake Erie to relieve Detroit; the other, under Colonel Henry Bouquet, a native of Switzerland, thrashed the Indians at Bushy Run—near the present site of Turtle Creek, Pennsylvania—lifted the siege of Fort Pitt, then set out for a town on the Tuscarawas, in the present state of Ohio, where he dictated harsh terms to the Shawnee and the Wyandots.

Greatly dejected by his defeats and by the failure of the French to come to his aid, Pontiac in October 1764 fled to the Illinois country, which the English had not yet occupied and where he hoped to organize a new campaign. Unfortunately for him, most of his followers had already deserted him. In the spring of 1765 the Delawares met Sir William Johnson, British superintendent of Indian affairs, at his home near Johnstown, New York, and signed a treaty of complete surrender. Later in the spring the Shawnee surrendered at Fort Pitt.[69]

England had long before organized the territory she had acquired. The Proclamation of 1763, which George III signed on October 7, divided the territory ceded by Spain into the provinces of East Florida and West Florida and organized the Canadian possessions into the Province of Quebec. A governor with full power was appointed over each of these provinces, whose inhabitants were guaranteed the same civil rights as those enjoyed by the thirteen English colonies. The three provinces were also promised the same type of representative government as that which existed in the crown colonies.

One of the salient features of the Proclamation was calculated to appease the Indian tribes and to protect them in their rights. England's old policy of allowing each colony to supervise its relation with the Indians had given unscrupulous traders ample opportunity to cheat them of their furs and speculators to rob them of their lands. The Proclamation endeavored to eliminate the possibility of such recurrences. It set off the vast region west of the Allegheny Mountains as an Indian reservation which was divided roughly at the Ohio River into two departments with an Indian superintendent over each. Here no white man could settle or buy land, and no white settlements could remain. Thus the Illinois country was legally closed to American frontiersmen.

For several years Pontiac's conspiracy cut off the Illinois country from the East, delaying British occupation. The French flag continued to fly from the ramparts of Fort de Chartres until 1765, when Croghan, now a deputy under Sir William Johnson, arrived in the Illinois country to restore order among the tribes and to open the region to the British. With his keen sense of business and his sympathy toward the Indians he had easily detected in the Proclamation of 1763 grave defects which, during a business trip to London, he urged the British government to remedy with a plan of his own. Under the Proclamation the provincial governors alone issued licenses to the fur traders, who often irritated the Indians by their trickery or dishonesty. The two Indian superintendents were powerless to stop their abuses.

Croghan's plan, which enjoyed the support of the two Indian superintendents, Sir William Johnson and Colonel John Stuart, and which the British government adopted, gave the Indian departments complete control of all public Indian affairs. The northern department, which included the Illinois country, was divided into three subdistricts under deputy superintendents. These in turn were divided into thirteen areas, one for each tribe in the department. Each tribal area maintained a number of trading posts where the superintendent was represented by a commissary, an interpreter and a blacksmith. The commissary was empowered to set prices, supervise bartering and protect the Indians from dishonest traders and speculators and aggressive settlers. Hereafter military officers and governors could hold meetings with the Indians only with the approval of the Indian superintendents. Though the traders still obtained their licenses from the governors, they were "obliged to name the posts or Indian towns where they intended to trade, and to give bond that they would abide by the regulations." As soon as a trader entered the Indian country he was subject to the supervision of the Indian department and was compelled to show his license to the commissary of the post. The Plan of 1764 forbade to the Indians rum, swan shot or rifle-barreled guns and credit in excess of fifty shillings.[70]

For his efforts in their behalf the Indians regarded Croghan as a friend and on his arrival in the Illinois country received him warmly, though a party of Kickapoo had mistakenly taken him prisoner as he passed the mouth of the Wabash. As soon as the Indians had released him and had apologized for their error, Croghan went down the Wabash, where he met Pontiac, who was coming to Fort Ouiatenon with a large following. Arm in arm the two men returned to the fort, where, in council, Pontiac denounced the French for deceiving him and pledged that he would no longer war against the English. With this promise he threw aside his rank and henceforth supported himself by hunting. News of the treaty eventually reached Fort Pitt, where a hundred men under Captain Thomas Stirling had been holding themselves in readiness to relieve Fort de Chartres. They immediately set out to meet Croghan. On October 9, 1765 they arrived in the Illinois country and on the following day the fleur-de-lis of France dropped from the ramparts of Fort de Chartres and in its place went the Union Jack of Great Britain.[71]

In the ensuing years Croghan, in association with the Philadelphia firm of Baynton, Wharton and Morgan, launched one of the most elaborate trading schemes in colonial American history. The junior partner, George Morgan, built stores at Vincennes, Kaskaskia, Cahokia and Fort de Chartres, where *habitants* and Indians could buy, or barter fur skins for the articles they needed. But unlucky circumstances doomed the expected trade. The "Grand Illinois Venture," as Croghan's trading scheme was called, overreached itself; it consumed huge sums of money without realizing a profit. The fur-bearing animals had been practically exterminated. Baynton, Wharton and Morgan was not only undersold by the rival firm of Franks and Company but the French inhabitants preferred to buy for less from their own countrymen across the river in St. Louis, which Pierre Laclède, the representative of a firm in New Orleans, had established in 1764. Baynton, Wharton and Morgan suffered still another setback when in 1768 Amherst's successor, General Thomas Gage, stopped the gifts which the Indians had been receiving annually under the Plan of 1764. By the end of 1768 the Grand Illinois Venture had failed.[72]

Meanwhile the French inhabitants were becoming increasingly dissatisfied with English rule. The authorities had considered the region neither a part of Louisiana nor of Canada and had, therefore, placed it under military rule. Thus deprived of civil government, the people had no access to courts or other offices of justice. Though the Proclamation of 1763 had guaranteed them a representative government, it barred them from holding office because of their religion. The English commanders took advantage of their isolated positions to enrich themselves at the expense of the inhabitants. They charged exorbitant fees for issuing writs and similar documents and for receiving oaths of allegiance. Rather than abide this tyranny, many of the best French families had sold their property and moved across the Mississippi to St. Louis and St. Genevieve.[73]

By 1774 the British government realized that it could conciliate the French inhabitants, preserve the region from anti-English intrigue, stop white settlement and fraudulent speculation and remedy the disorganized fur trade only if it revised its frontier policy. In June it passed the Quebec Act, which placed the Illinois country under the jurisdiction of Quebec by extending the boundaries of that province to the Ohio and the Mississippi. To discourage new settlers, nearly all of whom were Protestants and used to democratic government, the Act extended the French civil law to the Illinois country and granted complete religious freedom to its

Catholic inhabitants. At the same time it preserved the fur trade for the Scotch merchants of Montreal and their French employees. These merchants had developed the trade in the Old Northwest, were determined to keep it and had brought their influence to bear on the British government. On the Canadians the Quebec Act had the desired effect. When the American Revolution broke out in the following year, they remained loyal to Great Britain.

The English colonists, however, denounced the Quebec Act as a great injustice. Virginia, which claimed the western country by right of her ancient charter, denied that the British government had the right to award it to a colony alien in law and population. Speculators and traders naturally cursed the Act. Young Alexander Hamilton attacked it in one of his earliest political speeches. In the colonial mind it was associated with the "Intolerable Acts," which soon led to Lexington and the beginning of the American Revolution. It doubtless provided George Rogers Clark, whose exploits we are about to follow, with the primary emotional motivation to conquer the Illinois country.

George Rogers Clark

SPORTING A NEW COAT AND A NEW LINEN SHIRT, GEORGE ROGERS Clark on December 10, 1777, presented himself to His Excellency, Patrick Henry, Governor of Virginia. He had arrived more than a month before in Williamsburg from the Kentucky frontier, his new home, to lay before the governor a plan for the conquest of the Illinois country and eventually the British post at Detroit.

In the past year Clark had given careful thought to his project. His aim was twofold: to stop the Indian allies of the British from crossing the Ohio River and attacking the Kentucky settlements, which in the past two years he had done much to defend; and to drive the British from the Illinois country and secure it for the United States. Kentucky, he realized, was in a desperate position. Surrounded by Indian tribes and separated by two hundred miles of wilderness from the nearest Eastern town, her settlers could easily be conquered, be forced to make peace with the British at Detroit and allow themselves to be carried off to that post. This evil possibility would accompany an even greater one. By conquering Kentucky the Indians would be in a position to strike anywhere, forcing the states to rush to the assistance of the pioneers with supplies and soldiers instead of the pioneers rushing to the assistance of the states. Clark realized the impossibility of marching an army through great distances against the Indian towns, even granting that these could be found. On the other hand, the Kentucky settlers, if they could be supported and encouraged, would be in a position to march to the succor of any distressed settlement. Nothing, then, could be of greater service than their defense. Clark was firmly convinced that his patriotic duty demanded capture of the French towns in the Illinois country as the only means

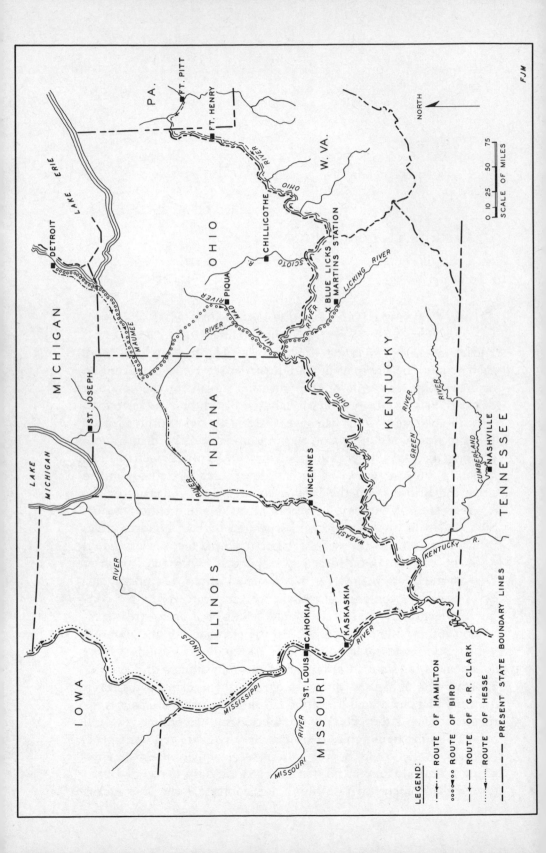

LEGEND:

————————— ROUTE OF HAMILTON

ooooooooo ROUTE OF BIRD

————→ ROUTE OF G. R. CLARK

·············· ROUTE OF HESSE

— — — — PRESENT STATE BOUNDARY LINES

SCALE OF MILES

0 10 25   50   75

NORTH

FJM

of stopping the British commanders north of the Ohio from exciting the Indians against the settlers south of the river.[1]

Such a plan, so bold in its conception, so packed with peril in its implications, called for the utmost secrecy. Not a word must be breathed to anyone. Not even to Samuel Moore and Benjamin Linn, two young men whom Clark sent to the Illinois villages to ascertain general conditions there. Disguised as hunters, Moore and Linn left Harrodsburg on April 20, 1777, and returned on June 22 of that year. Though they had been discovered, accused of spying and forced to flee, they furnished Clark with much of the information he sought. They reported that, although the British had no idea of any American campaign against the Illinois country, they kept their soldiers in readiness for any surprise attack, and that they took the greatest pains to inflame the French inhabitants against the Americans.[2]

Clark relayed this information to Governor Henry, pointing out that the British commanders sent Indian tribes and encouraged Indian forays against the Kentucky settlements. Kaskaskia, moreover, fed the garrison at Detroit and, by controlling navigation on the Mississippi and the Ohio, prevented Americans from securing Spanish provisions with which to carry on the Indian trade. The Americans, he concluded, must either capture Kaskaskia or send an army against the Indian tribes on the Wabash, a task which would be costly and would be much less effective.[3]

Realizing that he could never conquer the Illinois country with the meager force on the frontier, he decided to appeal to Governor Henry in person for support. The journey to Williamsburg, which began on October 1, proved full of dramatic incidents. Before setting out he bought a horse for £12. When he reached the Holston, he showed his shrewdness in horseflesh by swapping horses with Isaac Shelby and making £10 on the deal. On the Wilderness Trail his horse strayed; further on, he traveled in company with a large party of men, women and children who, disheartened by the Indian ravages, were returning to the safety of the East. They marched from fourteen to twenty miles a day, driving beeves along for food. On the tenth day of the journey he met a company of fifty men and two families going to Boonesboro; on the nineteenth day, finding himself in an unpeopled wilderness, he accelerated his progress. Then he fell in with a Captain Campbell, who was his companion for a week. Before he arrived at his father's house, he had swapped horses again and had sold his gun for £15. Altogether he had traveled six hundred twenty miles.[4]

Arriving in Williamsburg on November 2, he found its inhabitants greatly excited over recent news of Burgoyne's surrender. Another man would have availed himself of this circumstance to press his plans; but Clark was in no hurry. He mingled with friends and strangers, taking in everything he saw and heard that might aid him to ascertain "the disposition of those in power." He also settled his account with the state auditors for his services as major of the Kentucky militia. He wrote in his diary: "Nov. 18 Setled with the Auditors drew the Money of the treasurer £726. Bought a piece of Cloth for a Jackote Price £4.15 Buttons & Morehair 3/."[5] After leaving the cloth and buttons with his tailor to make his "jackote" during his absence, he visited his father again. On December 6 he returned to Williamsburg. Two days later he put on his new clothes and went to see Governor Henry.

The Governor was impressed with Clark's plans, but he hesitated to order an expedition in such a distant country. He had grave doubts that it would succeed. First of all, would Virginia, whose domains the states were already urging Congress to claim as the common property of all, profit by the conquest? And what about Spain and France? Would Spain allow the United States to grow stronger on territory adjacent to Louisiana? On the contrary, she wished to secure the region for herself, an endeavor in which she had France as her secret and powerful ally.[6]

On the other hand, Virginia might profit from the enterprise if it showed any possibility of succeeding. Kentucky was proving a veritable paradise for settlers—her rich soil had already attracted a number of Virginians, many more contemplated moving there once peace was restored. Moreover, western Virginia had thousands of acres with rich mineral deposits, while the country north of the Ohio was even more valuable. Unless the British were driven from the French villages, all these regions would probably be lost to the state, and the Indians would still be free to continue their depredations along the whole inner frontier.

If he laid his plan before the assembly, he would deprive it of all secrecy and would defeat his purpose. Thomas Jefferson, George Mason and George Wythe, before whom the project was presented, advised the assembly and council that it be carried out and, as an added inducement, promised to use their influence to secure from the assembly three hundred acres of conquered land for each man enlisting in the expedition. The assembly and council were impressed, and on January 2, 1778, they gave consent on the ground that the expedition was designed as a defense of Kentucky.[7]

Clark received two sets of written instructions, one public and the other secret. The public instructions authorized him to enlist seven companies to "proceed to Kentucky and there obey such orders and directions as you shall give them, for three months after their arrival at that place, but to receive pay in case they remain on duty a larger time."[8] From such instructions the volunteers would gather that they would go only as far as Kentucky. In the secret instructions, which followed substantially all of Clark's plans, he was directed to "attack the British post at Kaskaskia; to take especial care to keep the true destination of your force secret"; and to treat British captives humanely.[9] He was given £1,200 to defray the expenses of the expedition.[10]

2

Clark was by temperament and training well fitted to undertake the expedition. He was born November 19, 1752, in beautiful Albemarle County, Virginia, about twelve miles east of the Blue Ridge Mountains. His father, John Clark, a planter of considerable means, desired to provide his children with the best education he could afford. He sent George Rogers and his brother Jonathan to a school conducted by their uncle, Donald Robertson, a noted Scotch educator who was probably a graduate of the University of Edinburgh. George Rogers, however, had little taste for books; he preferred outdoor life, which gradually molded his physical and mental make-up. Hunting alone on the frontier, for example, taught him the importance of discipline, close observation of men and nature, self-reliance, courage and endurance. His father always encouraged him to strive for self-sufficiency. When George Rogers was fifteen, his father bought him clothes and other articles and charged them against the crop of tobacco the boy was raising. Next year he raised both corn and tobacco and sold them for nearly £30, a sum which today has the purchasing power of over $500.[11]

In 1773 George Rogers left his father's home to make his fortune on the frontier. He was then a tall, slender, blue-eyed lad of nineteen with clear complexion and reddish hair. He went with a companion down the Ohio in a canoe, observing everything and jotting down the names of the creeks and rivers they passed. The young explorers went as far as the mouth of the Great Kanawha, whence they returned home across the mountains. Two months later he returned to the frontier and established himself with his father and two Negro slaves on Fish Creek, in present Marshall County, West Virginia, where he raised a crop of corn.[12]

At the same time Clark spent much time surveying the lands of settlers who were pouring into the region. When the settlements spread to the mouth of the Scioto, Clark, eager to obtain as much rich land for himself as he could, set out with a company of Virginians to explore Kentucky. He accompanied them for a part of the journey, then, perhaps because he needed funds for land entry, returned to the East. In the fall he went back to his settlement on Fish Creek to harvest his crop of corn.[13]

Early in the spring of 1774 Clark with ninety men gathered at the mouth of the Little Kanawha, on the site of present Parkersburg, West Virginia, and descended the Ohio to Kentucky. While he was exploring, he was interrupted by signs of Indian war. Most of his associates abandoned their clearings and fled across the mountains. Clark and a few friends, bent on organizing for retaliatory attacks on Indian villages, ascended the river to Pittsburgh, where they selected Michael Cresap as their leader. But Cresap pleaded for peace and went with them to Wheeling to learn what was taking place. There they learned from Dr. John Connolly, Governor Dunmore's representative at Fort Pitt, that hostilities had begun.[14]

In the ensuing struggle, known as Lord Dunmore's War, Clark served as captain of militia. With him were Joseph Bowman, Leonard Helm and William Harrod, all of whom were to give him notable assistance in his conquest of the Illinois country.

Defeated at Point Pleasant, the Shawnee in the Treaty of Camp Charlotte promised Lord Dunmore that they would henceforth stay out of Kentucky. Clark availed himself of this treaty to accompany Colonel Hancock Lee to central Kentucky. They soon laid out the town of Leesburg, in the outskirts of modern Frankfort. Clark soon learned that the Transylvania Company under Judge Richard Henderson and his associates, all of whom were North Carolinians, had bought from the Cherokee for £10,000 in goods a tract of land which comprised nearly all of present Kentucky and a large portion of present Tennessee. But the proprietors soon incurred the displeasure of many of the settlers by raising the price of land and by engrossing the best acres for themselves.

When Clark, a loyal Virginian, learned of this situation, he decided to contest their shady claims to Transylvania. Hearing, during a visit to Virginia, that her leaders shared his views, he returned to Kentucky, where he visited the settlements and camps, acquainting himself with the problems of the settlers and winning their confidence and friendship by his attractive personality and enterprising spirit. He planned to hold on June 6, 1776, a meeting of the settlers at Harrodsburg, the center of the discontent, for the purpose of having two agents appointed to appeal to the Virginia assembly for redress of grievances and, should this fail, for the establishment of an independent state. But when on the appointed day Clark reached Harrodsburg, he learned that the settlers had appointed two delegates, himself and a lawyer named Gabriel Jones, to present to the Virginia assembly a petition asking that the Kentucky section of Transylvania be taken in as a separate county, detailing their distressed and defenseless condition and begging for relief and protection. Within a few days Clark and Jones set out for Williamsburg.[15]

Though they learned that the assembly had adjourned, Clark held an interview with Governor Patrick Henry, who advised him to appeal to the Council and wrote a letter of recommendation to that body. Clark knew that the Council would be obliged to assert control over the region if he could persuade it to grant him a supply of ammunition. Therefore, he lost no time asking the Council for five hundred pounds of powder to defend Kentucky. The Council agreed to lend him the ammunition as to a friend in need and asked him to assume responsibility for it. Clark flatly rejected the offer on those terms, saying that "if a Cuntrey was not worth protecting it was not worth Claiming." Whereupon the Council, fearing that the Kentuckians would seek protection elsewhere as Clark intimated, acquiesced. Later the assembly declared Henderson's purchase of Transylvania null and void and established the County of Kentucky on its Virginia portion.[16]

From Williamsburg Clark and Jones went to Pittsburgh, where the ammunition was to be forwarded. With eight men in a small boat they proceeded with the powder down the Ohio, narrowly escaping capture by Indian scouting parties. Finding on their arrival at the mouth of Limestone Creek that they were still pursued, they hid their ammunition, set their boat adrift and departed on foot for Harrodstown to obtain a force sufficiently strong to take the ammunition safely to its destination. At the Blue Licks, where they stopped to rest, they met four men who told them that Colonel John Todd with a group of men was in the vicinity and that, if they could find him, he would surely assist them. Leaving Jones and the other men to await his return, Clark with two men pushed forward. No sooner were they gone when Todd arrived at the Blue Licks and agreed to go with ten men to fetch the ammunition. On their way back, they bumped into Indians who killed Jones and another man and took two men prisoner. The others fled. Early in January 1777 a force of thirty men took the powder to Harrodsburg, where it was distributed among the settlements, which had been fighting off Indian attacks instigated by British officials in Detroit. As major of the Kentucky County militia, Clark led the settlers in a number of retaliatory expeditions. And while he quieted their fears with assurances of aid from Virginia, he secretly planned to relieve their suffering by conquering the Illinois country north of the Ohio.[17]

3

Clark left Williamsburg early in January 1778 and spent the rest of the month traveling to Fort Redstone, the site of present Brownsville, Pennsylvania, on the Monongahela River, whence persons from across the mountains usually took boats to Pittsburgh. At Redstone he found William Harrod, whom he commissioned captain and requested to recruit a company. He had given similar tasks to Captain Leonard Helm and Captain Joseph Bowman and requested them to meet him in Redstone at a designated time. To Captain William Bailey Smith went the more difficult assignment of recruiting four companies in the Holston settlements. Smith and his men were to meet Clark in Kentucky.[18]

Clark received discouraging news from the start. Helm wrote that he had encountered difficulties in his recruiting efforts because the Virginia assembly had told the Holston people that it was unacquainted with the kind of service he sought. Clark himself complained of frustration. In those days both Virginia and Pennsylvania claimed the region around Pittsburgh, and each of these states had its rabid supporters. Each group damned what the other praised. Clark found his problem intensified by the fact that his public instructions authorized him to raise men for the defense of the country while his real instructions remained secret. Why should men be drawn off at so critical a time for the defense of a few detached settlements in a remote region? Why not remove the settlers to a safer place? Such were the questions men everywhere asked. The longer Clark remained in Redstone, the worse his position became. He realized now that his ultimate aim of marching against Detroit would fail. He resolved, therefore, to depart for Kentucky with what men he could gather.[19]

Late in May he arrived in Pittsburgh. Its commander, General Edward Hand, welcomed him warmly and offered him the provisions he needed. Joined by a group of immigrants and their families, he sailed down the Ohio River to Point Pleasant at the mouth of the Great Kanawha. The settlers, who had just fought off one

Indian attack, were anticipating another and begged him to remain; but he stayed only a day or two, then continued down the river to the mouth of the Kentucky. Believing that Smith had by then reached the Ohio, he sent him word to march immediately for the Falls of the Ohio. To his great disappointment he soon learned that Smith had not arrived and that, indeed, all of that officer's men, save a part of a company under Captain Thomas Dillard, had been stopped by the mixed threats and adverse criticism of the Holston settlers.

The thought of failure only increased Clark's determination to succeed. The more he reflected on his position, the more he was pleased with the enterprise. Proceeding to the Falls, he viewed his position from every angle. Since his real instructions were as yet unknown and since he could not determine what might result when he disclosed them, he concluded that he must strengthen his position as much as he could. Observing that Corn Island, opposite the site of modern Louisville, was seldom flooded, he took possession of it, fortified it and divided it into gardens for the immigrant families that had followed him from Pittsburgh.[20]

Now he disclosed to Bowman the real object of his expedition. All of his officers and men received it with enthusiasm save the Holston men. Having been reared in the forest, they were too free to fall under the spell of Clark's personality. They expressed fear in the undertaking; the enemy's country, they said, was too far away from home; even if they succeeded in reaching their destination, they might be attacked in their posts without a possibility of escape. Some of them, therefore, schemed to return to their homes by swimming or wading the channel opposite their camp. Before daybreak, Hutchins, their leader, led them to the opposite side of the river before they were discovered by the sentinels. To discourage any other attempt at mutiny, Clark ordered a strong force of cavalry and infantry to pursue the fugitives and to execute every one of them who refused to surrender. The fugitives were overtaken about twenty miles from the island, on the trace to Harrodsburg; seven were captured, the rest "scattered in the woods." The captives were brought back to the island, and the escapees "suffered most severely every species of distress." The settlers of Harrodsburg resented their conduct to the extent that they refused them food and kept them out of the fort for several days. Hutchins they burned in effigy.[21]

Despite this episode Clark was in a more cheerful mood. From Pittsburgh he received word that France had in the previous February acknowledged the independence of the United States, and that the two countries had joined in a military alliance. This, of course, was very heartening news. He quickly perceived that it should render him great service in the event of success against Kaskaskia.

On June 23 the men spent the day amusing themselves. Then, during a total eclipse of the sun—which many of them interpreted as a good omen—Clark shot the Falls with about one hundred eighty men and officers, most of whom were Virginians and all of whom were in the Virginia service. They double-manned their oars and went on day and night until they ran into the mouth of the Tennessee River. Here they landed on a tiny island, from which Clark prepared to march against Kaskaskia. Soon after they landed, they came upon a few American hunters who had recently come from Kaskaskia and who furnished Clark with valuable information. Moreover, the hunters furnished direct aid, for they requested and received permission to take part in the expedition as guides.[22]

Down the river they dropped ten miles to abandoned Fort Massiac, where they hid their boats, and struck off through the wilderness toward their destination, a hundred twenty miles away. Each man carried only such equipment as he needed for a journey calculated to last four days. They advanced singly in order to make as few tracks as possible. Each wore moccasins, a coonskin cap, and a fringed buckskin hunting shirt belted with a decorated broad leather strap from which hung a tomahawk. Some wore leather breeches; others, boots and leggings made of coarse woolen cloth, On their shoulders hung shot bags, powder horns and clumsy flintlock rifles.[23]

In three days they had toiled through fifty miles of forest. As they reached level prairie, John Saunders, a hunter who served as chief guide, filled them with confusion by losing his way. Clark, fearing discovery by spies or attack by Indians, grew suspicious: was the fellow leading him and his men into a trap? His anger grew with his fear; he began to grill Saunders, who begged for permission "to go some distance into the plain"; he might, he said, discover "whether or not he was right." Clark sent a few men with him to prevent his possible escape and threatened to kill him should he fail to take them to the right road. Within two hours he came to a place he knew perfectly, and Clark, his anger allayed, realized that the poor fellow had merely been bewildered.[24]

For two more days they marched without food. Then on July 4 they arrived within three miles of Kaskaskia. Halting until dark and out of sight of the town, Clark sent spies ahead. They returned with the news that, before the men could reach Kaskaskia, they had to cross the river of the same name. At nightfall they marched to a farmhouse on the south shore of the river, made its occupants prisoners and obtained boats in which they rowed to the other side. Clark ordered one group of men to surround the village, while he with the other broke into the fort and captured its commander, Philip François de Rastel, Chevalier de Rocheblave, who was in bed asleep. Quickly aroused, Rocheblave sprang up half-dressed and rushed to the door, only to find Clark, who informed him that he was a prisoner of the Americans. Clark also seized dispatches in which the governors of Detroit, Quebec and Michilimackinac had requested Rocheblave to incite the Indians against the Americans and offered them great rewards for scalps.[25]

Loud huzzas by one group answered by shouts from the other signified that neither had encountered resistance and that the village was theirs. In fifteen minutes Clark had every street secured. Clark's runners ordered the people on pain of death to keep close to their houses, where they were all disarmed before daybreak. Guards in every street prevented any escapees from giving alarm to the other villages.[26]

After a few days Clark granted an interview to Father Pierre Gibault and five or six other elderly gentlemen. The appearance of Clark and his men shocked them more than did the sudden capture of their village. To them the Americans with their dirty, torn clothing and their lacerated faces looked like a band of savages. The Frenchmen were so astonished that for a few minutes they were speechless. Then their spokesman, Father Gibault, told Clark they could reconcile themselves to the loss of their property, but they hoped that he would not separate them from their families and that the women and children would be permitted to keep their clothes and some food. The Frenchmen explained that their conduct had been influenced by their commanders, that they had had no opportunity to become acquainted with the American way of life and that they had shown as much favor toward Americans as discretion permitted.[27]

Clark had no reason to doubt their words. Moreover, he had no intention of maltreating the villagers. Realizing that if he incurred their hostility he could not hope to hold them with his small force, he resolved to convert them into supporters of his plans. Above all, he wanted to bring them to a submissive position.

With a show of insulted pride he asked them whether they thought they were speaking to savages. Did they think that the

Americans meant to strip their women and children and take the bread out of their mouths? Did they think the Americans warred on women and children? What an idea! The purpose of the war, he explained, was simply to stop Indian depredations provoked by British commanders and agents. He would leave, he said, as soon as he obtained his object. Then, to their great relief, he then told them that the King of France had lately joined the Americans and that this alliance would hasten the end of the war. He invited them to choose one side or the other without any dread of losing their property or having their families mistreated. To all those who took the oath of allegiance to the United States he granted all the privileges of citizens. To all those who preferred to leave the country with their families he granted complete freedom.[28]

His speech had the desired effect. Their despair suddenly changed to great joy. They no longer bewailed their fate; they welcomed it as a gift. Just one thing more troubled Father Gibault and his flock: would they, he asked, be permitted to worship God according to their ancient faith? Clark replied that he had nothing to do with the Church save to defend it from insult and that, by the laws of the United States, the Catholic religion enjoyed the same privileges as any other. "This statement," says Theodore Roosevelt, "removed from them the last and strongest obstacle to their complete loyalty; they immediately became devoted and effective champions of the American cause."[29] In their joy they turned their village into a large carnival. They adorned the streets with flowers and the squares with multicolored flags and buntings. And they sang the old songs of Brittany and Normandy in the streets.

Only Philip Rocheblave scorned American liberality. When Clark invited him to dinner, he refused in an insulting manner. Whereupon Clark sent him to Virginia as a prisoner of war and sold his slaves for £500, which sum he distributed among his soldiers as prize money.[30]

Meanwhile he had sent Bowman, now a major, with a small force against Cahokia. Word of the capture of Kaskaskia, of the attitude of its inhabitants and of the alliance between France and the United States won that village for Clark almost overnight. Father Gibault performed a similar service for Clark in Vincennes, which he placed under the command of Leonard Helm.[31]

4

Despite Clark's initial successes his position remained insecure. He had won the region, but could he hold it? Could he count on the continued loyalty of a population alien in creed and language while he conducted a campaign against the British? Could he control the Indian tribes so deeply embittered against all Americans? The nearest American troops were hundreds of miles away; he could hope for no reinforcements, no advice, no instructions for a good many months, perhaps for a year. He saw clearly that for continued success he must rely entirely on his own resources and upon his own responsibility.

His men, having completed their time of service, wished to return to their homes. His first task was to persuade them to remain. By offering them presents and promises he managed to hold a hundred of them for eight months longer. He resolved next to test the loyalty of the people. Alleging that he rested entire confidence in their ability to defend themselves, he pretended departure for the Falls. The ruse confirmed his expectations: with one voice they begged him to remain, saying that, as soon as he left, the British would surely try to retake the region. With a show of reluctance he yielded. He would stay, he said, with two companies; if they needed more, he could call them from the Falls. This stratagem rewarded him handsomely: so many young Frenchmen joined him that in a short time he had enough to add four companies to his original force. Discipline soon converted them into fine soldiers.[32]

At the same time Clark strengthened his position by winning the friendship of the Spanish commanders of the scattered villages across the Mississippi. Always hostile to the English, they welcomed the opportunity to befriend the Americans. Especially helpful was Fernando de Leyba, governor of Upper Louisiana, with headquarters in St. Louis. The two men on meeting liked each other and soon became good friends. Clark had never met a Spanish gentleman and had entertained the frontier fallacy that Spaniards in general were haughty and formal. He was surprised to find that Leyba was democratic and much more gracious and hospitable than his fellow Virginians. The governor offered him all the force he could raise in case of an Indian attack from Detroit.[33]

Clark also showed great tact in dealing with Gabriel Cerré, a principal merchant who had been on excellent terms with the English. A group of Frenchmen, anxious to win favor with Clark, had informed him that Cerré was an inveterate enemy of the Americans and that he had lately returned from Quebec to St. Louis with a large quantity of goods. Clark immediately suspected that Cerré's accusers were indebted to him and wished to ruin him. Therefore, he refrained from committing himself until the merchant returned to Kaskaskia, when his accusers refused to repeat the charges against him. By this tact Clark not only gained the confidence and support of a leader but of his followers who were among the chief men in the village and on whose generosity Clark was dependent for supplies for his men.[34]

Clark received supplies and money from many sources. The Italian merchant, Giuseppe Francesco Vigo, who had served as an officer in the Spanish army and was De Leyba's partner in the Indian trade, furnished Clark with large supplies from his own stores and even paid for goods which Clark bought from local French merchants. Clark once realized $1,290 by renting his pack horses to a Major George Slaughter, who used them to carry his men's baggage across the Allegheny Mountains. At another time a William Harrison paid Clark $540 in rental fees for the use of his boats in transporting flour to Pittsburgh. In the winter of 1779 a squaw furnished Clark's men with provisions on "our way to attack Governor Hamilton." Clark later compensated her with a bushel of corn and five pounds of pork.[35]

But the bulk of his supplies came from Oliver Pollock, a wealthy merchant of New Orleans. This ardent patriot, whom historians have shamefully neglected, was a Roman Catholic and a native of Ireland. He wrote:

From the opening of the Revolution, my soul panted for the success of the American arms, nor could I omit any opportunity of manifesting the sincerity and ardor of my feelings, when it was in my power to be useful either to the public interest or to any individuals who had embarked their fortunes and their lives in an enterprise so hazardous and so glorious.[36]

Placing his fortune at the disposal of the Revolutionary authorities, Pollock became a member of the Commercial Committee of the Continental Congress, acting in the double capacity of agent for the state of Virginia and "commercial agent" for the United States. Availing himself of his influence with the Spanish governors in New Orleans, in the summer of 1776 he obtained from Governor Ungaza ten thousand pounds of powder, most of which was used for the protection of Wheeling and Fort Pitt. Pollock was also instrumental in persuading Governor Gálvez to aid the Americans with arms, ammunition and provisions for the frontiers of Pennsylvania and Virginia, all of which aid amounted to $70,000.[37]

Following instructions, Pollock gave Clark all possible assistance. He purchased goods on the best terms, chartered vessels or bought them if necessary, was responsible for the safe arrival of the cargoes and paid for the goods or arranged for his friends to pay them. Clark was indebted to him from the very outset of his expedition. Pollock had supplied the goods which Clark had received from General Edward Hand in Pittsburgh and Wheeling. In the ensuing months his ammunition, clothing, sugar, liquor and many other articles came in large part from Pollock.[38]

After the fall of Kaskaskia Clark, finding himself without funds, began to draw drafts on the Treasurer of Virginia and on Pollock. Because Pollock received and paid such bills at their face value in silver, merchants and traders were happy to accept them. On July 18, 1778, Clark wrote Pollock that he had so far succeeded in his campaign and he hoped the merchant would accept the drafts drawn on him. Pollock complied with Clark's request. Pollock wrote to the Commercial Committee,

You'll see he is in possession of the Illinois and that he has drawn bills on me with the expectation of my honoring them for the State of Virginia. There is to the amount of 1,000 Dollars already come to hand which I have accepted payable in January next, and if any more are presented I shall accept them payable at the same time as I hope before that you'll have it in your power to furnish me with sufficient funds to wipe off the whole.[39]

Pollock interpreted the capture of the Illinois forts as a step toward the opening of the Mississippi to American trade and securing control of the river posts and possibly Pensacola. In this manner he hoped to be relieved from the burdens he had assumed on behalf of the American cause.

Routine documents throw much light on the numerous items Clark needed during his campaign. These are typical passages: "Let this man Have 4 lb. of pork for the people that are going down the River to Traverse the Horses"; "Please to issue for the use of the Kaskaskias Indians 40 weight of flour"; "The Commissary of Issues is amediately ordered to prepair one Thousand Relations to have them Ready to Imbark by 12 o'clock"; "Furnish Mr. Edward Murray with five gallons of whiskey he having agreed to accept that Quantity in full for his pay as Express for this place"; "As there is a Party of militia going after a Party of Indians as have done mischief you will be pleased for to let me have one Pound of Powder and two Pound of Lead we haveing not a Sufficient quantity for to Persew them."[40]

To meet such necessities Clark drew orders on Pollock in favor of Cerré for $619, another for $2,000 and a third for $1,273; in favor of A. Chouteau for $2,100; in favor of Laffont for $1,000; in favor of a score of other well-known villagers for various sums. From the first the Charleville brothers, three in number, had co-operated to the full with Clark. The first draft on Pollock received by Charles Charleville was for $200. The next one was for ten times that sum. The Charlevilles, together with the Lachances and the Janises, traders whose boats plied between the Illinois country and New Orleans, had favored the American cause even before Clark's arrival.[41]

Though Pollock was without present resources to meet these obligations, he assured Clark that "the cause in which we are embarked urges me to strain every nerve, and luckily having a number of good Friends have hitherto enabled me to serve my Country. In consequence of this I have accepted your bills." At this time he was already obligated to pay $42,500 which he had accrued on behalf of the general government. This was in addition to the large sum he had secured from Governor Gálvez to supply the frontiers of Pennsylvania and Virginia with arms, ammunition and supplies.[42]

5

In dealing with the regional tribes Clark faced his most difficult task. He solved it with rare psychological skill.

His sudden appearance had filled the Indians with consternation. Not that they expected the Big Knives, as they called the Virginians, to take them by the hand. But they were greatly concerned over the friendship that the French and the Spanish showed toward the Americans. What should the Indians do? They asked the French, who advised them to make peace with the Big Knives. So chiefs and warriors from every regional tribe, including Chippewa, Ottawa, Potawatomi, Sauk, Fox, Miami—some of whom came as far away as five hundred miles—gathered in Cahokia for a powwow with Clark, who treated them as the occasion demanded—kind, conciliatory or severe—though he confessed his apprehension "among such a lot of devils." While he assumed an air of bravado, he took every precaution against the possibility of trouble with them.[43]

A band of Puans and other Indians schemed to abduct Clark. One night they attempted to overpower the guards stationed at his house, but the sergeant detected them and alerted the villagers, who frustrated the plot and, at Clark's request, marched the chiefs of the Puans off to prison in irons. Clark had so far treated the Indians well; he had spared them the brutality which had often embittered them against the English; but now he knew he must be firm. The prisoners protested their innocence, insisting that they were only trying to ascertain if the French were really friendly toward the Americans; they begged to be released. Clark refused to let them speak to him. Though he slept in the same room as before, he took care to conceal fifty armed men in an adjoining room and alerted the guard for any eventuality. When the other chiefs tried to intercede for the prisoners, Clark declared that his course would be the same whether they were friends or foes. This attitude puzzled Indians and Frenchmen alike. Clark showed his indifference by assembling "a Number of Gentlemen and Ladies" and dancing with them "nearly the whole Night."[44]

Next morning he released the prisoners and requested them to attend a great council of all the tribes. They performed the elaborate ceremonies which always accompanied such an important council and then submitted to Clark with dignified language. They had taken up the bloody belt against the Big Knives, they said, only on the insistence of the British. But they promised to pay no more heed to English agents, "those bad birds flying through the land." They hoped that the Great Spirit would incline the Big Knives to accept them as friends. And they took down and tramped upon the flags and belts of wampum they had accepted from their former allies.

Clark replied that, though he had taken in all they said, he would keep his answer until tomorrow, when he hoped they would open their hearts as well as their ears to the truth. And he forbade them to give their hands to the Americans until they would give their hearts also. They seemed pleased as they left the council, agreeing among themselves that Clark's sentiments were those of man who speaks with but one heart and one tongue.[45]

The next day Clark summoned them and addressed them:

Men and warriors! Pay attention! You informed me yesterday that the Great Spirit had brought us together, which you hoped was good, as He is good. I also have the same hope, and whatever may be agreed to by us, . . . I expect that each party will strictly adhere to, whether for peace or war, and henceforward prove ourselves worthy of the attention of the Great Spirit. I am a man and a warrior, and not a councillor. [I] carry in my right hand war and peace in my left. . . . I was sent by the great Council Fire of the Big Knife and their friends to take possession of all the towns that the English possession in this country, and to remain here watching the motions of the red people; to bloody the paths of those that continued the attempt of stopping the course of the river, but to clear the roads that lead from us to those that wish . . . to be in friendship with us, that the women and children might walk without anything being in the way of them to strike their feet against; but to continue to call on the Great Fire for a sufficient number of warriors to darken the land of the [enemy], so that the inhabitants should hear no sound in it but that of birds that live on blood.

A mist, he continued, had gathered before their eyes, but he would dispel it so that they might see clearly the cause of war between the Big Knives and the English. They would then judge for themselves who was in the right. And he unfolded the causes that led up to the Revolution in this fashion:

In the beginning the Big Knives knew no better than the red men how to make blankets, powder, and clothing. So they bought these articles from the British and lived chiefly by raising corn and hunting and trading. But in time the Big Knives grew more numerous than the trees. They needed so much food that the land became impoverished and the animals became scarce. As they saw their children half naked, the women in their distress learned how to make clothes and even provided their husbands with blankets. And the men, on their part, learned how to make guns and powder, so that they no longer needed to buy these articles from the British. This prosperity angered the Great White Father across the sea: he put up strong garrisons everywhere; he forbade the women to make clothes and the men to make powder; henceforth, he decreed, they must buy from him alone. Furthermore he asked two bucks for a blanket that used to cost one buck and ordered the Big Knives to obey all his wishes. This, continued Clark, made the Big Knives angry and they warred on the Great White Father. Victory brought them freedom.

The Great Spirit, continued Clark, had become angry because the Indians had aided the tyrant. And the Great Spirit had caused their older Great White Father, the French king, and other nations to join the Big Knives and fight with all their enemies. And the English became like deer running in the woods.

From this, he concluded, the Great Spirit had caused the Indian waters to be troubled: if their women and children cried, they must blame themselves for it, not the Big Knives. He said:

You can now judge who is in the right. I have already told you who I am. Here is a bloody belt and a white one. Take which you please. Behave like men and dont let your pre[sent] situation,—being surrounded by the Big Knife,—cause you to take up the one belt with your hands, when your hearts drink up another. If you take the bloody path, you shall go from this town in safety and join your friends the English; and we will try like warriors who can put the most stumbling blocks in the roads and keep our clothes the longest perfumed with blood.

Since he was convinced, he said, that they had never heard the truth, he would not ask them for an answer until they had discussed the matter among themselves. And he proposed that the meeting be interrupted and not resumed until they were ready to speak with "one heart and one tongue." With these words he dismissed them. In the morning they returned, protested that they had been misled, and promised that they would never fight the Big Knives again.[46]

Clark, nevertheless, declined to free all the Puan prisoners. He told those he released that they were only "old women and too mean to be killed by a Big Knife; but, as they ought to be punished for putting on breech-cloth like men, th[ose] should be taken from them and plenty of provisions given to [take them] home, as women dont know how to hunt." They were much ashamed. After some time they rose and, advancing toward Clark with a belt and a pipe of peace, began to make a speech; but the American leader broke the pipe with a sword that lay on the table and told them that the Big Knives never treated with women and ordered them to sit down and amuse themselves with gossip—as women did.

The Puans conferred and decided to offer him two young braves as propitiation for their conduct. The two young men were selected and advanced to the middle of the floor, sat down, and flung their blankets over their heads to receive the tomahawk. Clark was deeply moved. This, he wrote later, "prejudiced me in their favor and, for a few seconds, I was so agitated that I would have killed the first man who harmed them." He told the two braves to go in peace, forgave the Puans and, on the following day, feasted and befriended them. Thereafter they regarded him as a great warrior, a great orator, and a great diplomat. His influence over them endured for many years. Once when the United States was endeavoring to make a treaty with the Indians of the region, the Puans refrained from speaking to any general or commissioner while Clark was present.[47]

6

To Lieutenant Colonel Henry Hamilton, British commander of Detroit, whom the Indians called the Hair Buyer General, word of the capture of Kaskaskia and Cahokia fell like a bolt of lightning in his own backyard. Abandoning his plans to attack Fort Pitt, which had fallen to the Americans, he prepared an immediate expedition against Clark. To the Wabash he sent French agents, ordering them to incite the Indians against the Americans. To the commanders at Michilimackinac and St Joseph he sent messages asking them to obtain the support of the Lake Indians. And he himself feasted the loyal Ottawa, Chippawa and other tribes, while he disclosed to them his plans against Clark.[48]

He spent the entire month of September 1778 in feverish pursuance of his aim. Every day, nearly every night, he employed every man in Detroit mending boats, making biscuit, packing provisions, preparing artillery, until he had fifteen "large pirogues, capable of transporting from eighteen hundred to three thousand lbs. each." In letters to his superior, General Frederick Haldemand, commander-in-chief of Canada, he alternated between confidence in the success of his plans and bitter denunciation of the French for having joined the Americans:

The Spaniards are feeble and hated by the French; the French are fickle and have no man of capacity to advise, or lead them; the rebels are enterprising and brave, but want resources; and the Indians can have their resources but from the English, if we act without loss of time in the present favorable conjuncture.[49]

On October 7 he was ready to march. He drew up his troops, which numbered about 177 whites and sixty Indians, in the commons, where the venerable Father Pathier blessed those of the Catholic faith who promised to abide by their oath of allegiance. Then Hamilton led them out of town on a journey which, covering six hundred miles of wilderness, was packed with incredible hardships. They paddled down the mouth of the Detroit River and toward the mouth of the Maumee in a midnight gale that sometimes furiously rocked their boats and finally beached them on an oozy flat. The shallow water forced them to pole slowly against the current until, on October 24, they reached a large Indian village on the portage to the mouth of the Wabash, where they held conferences with several tribes. Then they carried their boats and supplies nine miles to the Wabash. This shallow river would have halted their progress had not beavers deepened it by a dam four miles below the landing. By cutting a passage through the dam, they were able to get their boats through. Even then swamps delayed them and forced them, in several places, to build dams through which they floated their boats.[50]

Winter meanwhile overtook them. Deep ice cut their hands as they dragged their boats and supplies over the shoals and rocks. Undaunted they passed from Indian village to Indian village, holding conferences and giving presents, until they reached a Wea village, where they met several Wabash chiefs who, though they had made peace with the Americans, promptly returned to the allegiance of the King. Resuming his march toward Vincennes, Hamilton sent ahead Indian parties to surround the village and to intercept any messages that Clark might have sent either to the Falls or to the Illinois. When Hamilton came within two days' travel of Vincennes his men captured a few men whom Helm had sent out to reconnoiter. One of them was carrying a note from Helm to Clark warning him that the British were approaching. On December 17, just seventy-one days since he left Detroit, Hamilton reached Vincennes. By now his force numbered five hundred men.[51]

Deprived of his spies, Captain Helm was uncertain of Hamilton's whereabouts until they were within three miles of Vincennes. At the sight of the redcoats the French turned their backs to Helm who, left with only one American to guard the fort, was forced to surrender. The militia readily surrendered their commissions; the fort lowered its flag; and Vincennes returned to the British.[52]

Had Hamilton desired to push against Kaskaskia and Cahokia he doubtless would have been successful. But such a task seemed to him insurmountable for the present. Not that he feared the inhabitants. Control of the fort gave him control of the town. But realizing his stock of provisions was inadequate for that time of the year and fearing that his march might be delayed by floods, he decided to wait until spring, when he expected Indian allies, troops from Pensacola, and reinforcements of regular and militia from Detroit. He sent his militia home and permitted the Indians to return to their villages.[53]

7

Meanwhile, in Kaskaskia, Clark learned that General Lachlan McIntosh planned to march from Fort Pitt against Detroit. But in

December, 1778, when he expected to learn that McIntosh had captured the post, he heard instead that the general had abandoned the expedition. At the same time Clark learned of Hamilton's capture of Vincennes. He promptly planned to arrest his advance. He set out for Cahokia to ascertain the attitude of its leaders in case it should be forced to surrender. Three miles out of Kaskaskia and nine to Prairie du Rocher he and his guard of six or seven men and several wealthy Frenchmen in "chairs," as their creaking wooden carts were called, narrowly escaped capture by a band of Ottawas and Canadians who lay in ambush and who had come from Vincennes. That evening the inhabitants of Prairie du Rocher honored them with a ball. At midnight, while Clark was dancing, he received a message informing him that Hamilton was within three miles of Kaskaskia with eight hundred men and that he planned to attack the town during the night. Clark vividly describes the memorable night:

I never saw greater confusion among a small assembly than . . . at that time,—every person having their eyes on me, as if my word was to determine their good or evil fate. It required but a moments hesitation in me to form my resolutions. I communicated them to two of my officers. . . . I ordered our horses saddled, in order if possible to get into the fort [at Kaskaskia] before the attack could be made. Those of the company that had recovered their surprise, so far as to enable them to speak, begged me not to attempt to return, saying that the town was certainly in possession of the enemy and the fort warmly attacked. Some proposed conveying me to the Spanish shore,—some one thing and some another. I thanked them for their care . . . of my person and told them it was the fate of war; that a good soldier never ought to be afraid of his life where there was a probability of his doing service by venturing it, which was my case; that I hoped that they would not let the news spoil our diversion sooner than was necessary; that we would divert ourselves until our horses were ready; forced them to dance, and endeavored to appear as unconcerned as if no such thing was in agitation.[54]

On his return to Kaskaskia Clark found the town "as calm as we could expect." Though nobody believed that Hamilton was coming, Clark took every precaution against a surprise. He tore down the buildings near the fort and prepared to make a stand if Hamilton appeared. As soon as the people saw the buildings burn they grew panicky. Clark assembled them and asked them whether they should defend the town or abandon it, leaving only a small guard at the fort. While they begged Clark to believe that they favored the Americans they expressed doubt that he could withstand an attack by Hamilton's superior forces and suggested that he take refuge with his men across the Mississippi. Clark wrote:

I very seldom found but I could govern my temper at pleasure, but this declaration of theirs and some other circumstances put me in a most violent rage; and, as soon as I could curb my passion, [I gave] them a lecture suitable for a set of traitors, although I could not conceive the whole of them to be such.[55]

The next day their fears subsided when Captain Bowman arrived with his company and a company of volunteers from Cahokia. Clark now saw that the inhabitants were ashamed of how they had behaved. They expected him to treat them with some severity but instead he showed them the greatest kindness and granted all their requests. And in a few hours his influence over them was greater than ever: they condemned their own behavior and admitted that he had treated them as they deserved. Clark was convinced that "had Mr. Hamilton appeared we should have defeated him with a good deal of ease." Hamilton never appeared to give them an opportunity to display their talents. And Clark, seeing no prospect of a storm, sent Bowman back to Cahokia.[56]

But what should he do? Wait or advance? Within a few days Vigo brought him the answer. Finding himself in Vincennes when Hamilton captured that post, the Italian merchant was imprisoned and then discharged on agreeing to do nothing injurious to British interests on his way back to St. Louis. His agreement fulfilled, he hurried to Kaskaskia where, on January 29, 1779, he told Clark that Hamilton had eighty men in garrison with three pieces of artillery, but that in the spring he intended to gather a very large force to take the offensive.[57]

Clark, realizing the precariousness of his position, resolved to strike first. At that moment, he said, he would have been happy to become a slave for five hundred troops. This was a vain wish. Governor Patrick Henry had sent him not a man, not even "a scrape of a pen." Yet his confidence in the eventual success of his plan was unshaken. His enthusiasm, his encouraging words, soon electrified the people; girls, becoming interested in the expedition, persuaded their sweethearts to join it. Clark then equipped a row-gallery with two four-pounders, a nine pounder, and four swivels and christened her the *Willing* in honor of Captain James Willing, whom the

Commerce Committee of the Continental Congress had commissioned to secure supplies which Pollock's men had deposited at New Orleans and take them to Fort Pitt. Clark sent the *Willing* off with a crew of forty men under his cousin, Lieutenant John Rogers, down the Ohio to patrol the river and to prevent any boat from descending the Wabash, by which route the British might attempt to escape in case of defeat.[58]

On February 5 Clark, mounted on a magnificent stallion from New Mexico and at the head of one hundred and thirty men—nearly half of whom were French volunteers—began his heroic and dramatic expedition against Vincennes. His route, over a hundred and eighty miles in length, lay through a well-watered country of beautiful groves and prairies. The weather was unseasonably mild and the ground was covered with water from frequent rains. Clark shared every hardship, every labor, with his men. He encouraged them to hunt and to feast in the fashion of the Indian war-dancers, each company inviting the others to smoke and to cook and enjoy the meat. At night they built large campfires, around which they feasted on bear's ham, buffalo hump, elk saddle, venison haunch, and the breasts of wild turkeys, while they sang songs of love and war and the hunt or danced after the manner of French *coureurs de bois* and trappers.[59]

On February 13 they reached the first branch of the Little Wabash. Vincennes was now only twenty miles distant, but how far away the village seemed! The intervening ground was covered with water. The two branches of the river, which normally were a league apart, now formed a single channel five miles wide. Such a barrier would have stopped any group of men lacking the determination of Clark and his men. He built a canoe and had his men and stores ferried across the main stream; he built on the foreside of the channel a scaffold on which the baggage was lifted until pack horses could haul it away. Then they toiled to the second branch and crossed it in the same manner. They were now so close to Vincennes that they could hear the morning gun at the fort. Still the guerdon seemed remote. Neither ford nor dry ground lightened their burden. At last they found the water receding from a small, almost submerged hillock, and there they huddled, hungry and shivering from the cold, through black and drizzly night. The next morning they plodded downstream to the Wabash, where they remained for two days. Clark set his hungry, drenched, and dispirited men to build pirogues in which they hoped to cross the river.[60]

They had not had a meal for several days. Many of the French volunteers began to despair and talked of returning to their homes. Clark expressed his problems in a letter to George Mason:

If I was sensible that You would let no Person see this relation I would give You a detail of our suffering for four days in crossing these waters, and the manner it was done; as I am sure that You would Credit it, but it is too incredible for any Person to believe except those that are as well acquainted with me as You are, or had experienced something similar to it.[61]

Confident that his Americans would remain loyal to him Clark paid no heed to the complaints of the volunteers. He laughed at their fears and told them to go out and try to shoot a deer. They grumblingly remained.

Soon Clark received heartening news. His men captured five Frenchmen who were coming down from Vincennes in a small canoe. They told Clark that affairs in Vincennes were unchanged and that Hamilton had no suspicion that the Americans were so close. That evening the men killed a deer and ate their first meal in several days.

Dawn on February 21 brought a heavy rain. This enabled Clark to ferry his troops to a hillock on the eastern bank of the Wabash, upon which stood Vincennes nine miles away. All the ground around them was under water save a few hillocks here and there. Clark and his men plunged into the water, which sometimes rose to their shoulders, reached another hillock, and rested for the night. In the morning they resumed their march. While the strong men waded through the water, shouting and singing and laughing at the jokes and antics of the drummer boy as he floated on his drum, the exhausted and famished men rode in canoes. At one place they found the water so deep that they feared they would drown. Whereupon Clark, with admirable awareness, blackened his face with gunpowder, gave a war-whoop, and, springing forward into the icy water, waded straight to the deepest point. The men followed him in silence. At Clark's order the men nearest him began to sing one of their favorite songs, which the whole line immediately took up and which greatly shortened the distance to the point they feared. Here Clark intended to ferry his men but one of them felt that his feet were in a path. They cheerfully followed it and came to a hillock which had once been a maple sugar camp. Without food and drenched through, they camped for the night, six miles from their destination.

The night brought a heavy frost. Though the morning dawned

bright, ice formed an inch thick in and around the edges of the smooth water. In burning words Clark told his stiffened, famished, half-frozen followers that evening would surely see them at their destination. Without waiting for an answer he plunged into the water. In Indian file they followed with huzzas. Before the third man had entered the water Clark halted and told one of his officers, Bowman, to close the rear with twenty-five men and to put to death any man who refused to march. More huzzas greeted this order.[62]

Then came the most trying time of the whole march. Shortly after sunrise they reached Horse Shoe Plain. Stretching four miles under water varying from knee-high to breast-high and bordered on its furthest end by a dense woods, it posed an almost insurmountable obstacle. But it failed to impede Clark's progress. Plunging into deep water with fifteen or twenty of his strongest men, he led them slowly to the middle of the plain. But to the weaker men it was impassable; cold and exhausted, they had to be helped into canoes and then carried to a piece of ground, where the water was shallow, to prevent them from drowning. The others advanced to the woods, where the water rose to the shoulders of the tallest man. As they reached it, the shorter and weaker men had to hug the trees to keep from falling or had to float on logs until they were picked up by the canoes. Reaching a spot of dry land, some of them built fires, but these failed to revive the weak men, each of whom had to be placed between two stronger men and run up and down by the arms until he recovered.[63]

After this ordeal their fortunes brightened. They saw nearby an Indian canoe paddled by squaws and children. Overtaking it, the soldiers found a quarter of buffalo and corn, tallow, and kettles. They revived the weak by serving them broth, and restored their spirits with jokes and encouraging words. In brighter weather they resumed their advance. Crossing a deep but narrow lake in their canoes and then marching a short distance, they came to a copse of timber from which they could clearly see the town less than two miles away. The sight of the prize erased from their memory all they had suffered. Their dogged despair blossomed to a radiant confidence.[64]

Between them and the town lay a plain glimmering with little pools around which some mounted hunters were shooting ducks. At a command from Clark a small group of French soldiers captured one of the hunters, who informed the American leader that Hamilton had no idea of an impending attack. The hunter, however, advised him that several hundred Indians had just arrived in town.[65]

This information annoyed Clark. The number of trained men in town, including British, French, and Indians were now four times his own; they were heavy odds to face; even with the advantage of a surprise, he had little chance of success. From this information, however, he derived one ray of hope: the captured hunter told him that the French were lukewarm in their allegiance to the British; they would certainly avoid fighting if they could. Weighing these circumstances carefully, Clark resolved to overcome his disadvantage by a bold stroke. He addressed to the villagers a letter which he believed would encourage his friends while it would confuse and confound his enemies. The letter, delivered by the hunter, said:

Gentlemen: Being now within two Miles of Your Village with my Army determin'd to take your Fort this Night and not being willing to surprize you I take this step to request of such of you as are true citizens and willing to enjoy the liberty I bring you to remain still in your house, and those (if any there be) that are friends to the King, will instantly repair to the fort and join the Hair Buyer General and fight like Men and if any such as do not go to the fort, shall be discovered afterwards, they may depend on being well treated and I once more request they shall keep out of the streets for every person I find in arms on my arrival I shall treat him as an enemy.[66]

When the villagers read this letter they were so surprised that none dared tell Hamilton. Meanwhile Clark about sunset had marched against the village with drums beating and colors flying. The slight elevation of land proved an invaluable ally of which he quickly availed himself. Realizing that only the flags could be seen in the town, he marched his men to and fro, giving the impression that a large force was approaching.[67]

As night deepened he reached the town in two divisions, one led by himself and the other by Bowman. At his orders a small force immediately attacked the fort. Hamilton, completely unaware of his approach, believed that the rifle shots were those of drunken Indians until one of his men was wounded. Then he investigated, but too late.[68]

The villagers received Clark joyfully. They presented him with supplies of ammunition they had hidden while a chief of the Piankashaw offered him the services of a hundred warriors of his tribe. He declined them.[69]

Clark detached fifty of his men to guard against the possibility of outside attack and with the rest assaulted the fort. All night long each side fired continually. At one o'clock the setting moon allowed Clark to throw up an entrenchment outside rifle-shot of the strongest battery, which consisted of two guns. By sunrise both guns were silenced, and Clark summoned the fort to surrender. While he awaited a reply, he and his men ate breakfast—their first meal in six days. Instead of surrendering Hamilton proposed a three days' truce. Clark immediately rejected the proposition and resumed firing, which lasted several hours. Then Hamilton sent word that he would surrender on honorable terms. "Immediate surrender!" demanded Clark. The negotiations continued.[70]

Then occurred an incident that hastened capitulation. A band of Indians under French officers returned from a successful scalping party. Ignorant of what was taking place, they marched triumphantly into town. Some of Clark's men attacked them, scalping two, capturing six and wounding several who tried to escape. One of the prisoners was the son of one of Clark's French officers. His father persuaded Clark to spare his life. To show the Indians that their British allies were powerless to aid them, Clark condemned the rest of the captives to death. He had them tomahawked within view of the fort and had their bodies thrown into the river.[71]

That decided matters for Hamilton. In the afternoon he sent out another flag, met Clark in the Catholic church and, after exchanging recriminations, they agreed on terms. The garrison, seventy-nine strong, was to become prisoners of war and its supplies surrendered.[72]

Clark had won a remarkable victory. Without artillery, without cavalry, without supplies, he had taken a stockade which Hamilton had fortified with heavy cannon and swivels and had garrisoned with trained and equipped men. But Clark himself possessed an invincible weapon in his consummate knowledge of human nature, which enabled him to master his own troops and to keep the French and Indians neutral despite his insignificant force and unimpressive arms. And he believed in the sacredness of his cause. His zeal in marching against Hamilton and his cohorts matched that of Geoffrey de Bouillon in marching against the Moslems during the First Crusade. To Clark Vincennes was the Jerusalem which he felt he must liberate from political and social heresy.

8

No sooner had Hamilton surrendered than Clark sent Captain Helm and his men up the Wabash in boats armed with the captured swivels to intercept a convoy which the British commander had expected from Fort Ouiatenon. Helm captured seven boats loaded with provisions and Indian goods valued at $6,000, booty which he divided among his soldiers. Two days later Clark sent Hamilton with his officers and some civilian prisoners—twenty-seven men in all—to Williamsburg. There the Hair Buyer General was accorded much less hospitality than he had received from Clark. The new governor, Thomas Jefferson, charged him with instigating Indian cruelties and punished him by having him put in chains for a time. Later he was paroled and allowed to return to England.[73]

Meanwhile, on February 28, the *Willing* returned to Vincennes. Its crew was bitterly disappointed to learn that it had not been privileged to participate in the capture of the village. On her way up the Wabash the *Willing* took on a messenger bearing dispatches from the governor of Virginia, who promised Clark reinforcements in the spring. Among the dispatches was a resolution of the Virginia assembly commending Clark and his men for their courage and perseverance in capturing Kaskaskia and thanking them for "the important services thereby rendered their Country." The governor enclosed an act of the assembly, dated December 12, 1778, creating the new county of Illinois and stating that Captain John Todd had been appointed civil governor of the region with the title of Colonel and County Lieutenant. This was the first American government in the Great Lakes Frontier and the only one recognized there until, five years later, Virginia ceded the region to Congress.[74]

Todd's appointment was highly pleasing to Clark. Not only was Todd an old friend with whom he had shared adventures in Kentucky and in Lord Dunmore's War, but he admired Todd's athletic prowess and his skill in Indian fighting. He was in addition a seasoned politician. In 1777 he had served with ability as a delegate to the Virginia House of Burgesses from the county of Kentucky.[75]

On May 12, 1779, Clark assembled the Kaskaskians at the door of the church, where he had a proclamation of the new government read to them in French. In this he promised that, as soon as he could, he would grant them the liberty and protection enjoyed by all Americans. He told them that the new government was kind and that, once they understood it, they would bless the day on which they espoused it. "You may be persuaded," he said, "that we desire nothing so much as to render you happy and procure for you all the help possible." With this he presented Todd, who, he told the assembled citizens, was the only person in the state he wished to fill the post. "I am fully persuaded from my knowledge of his capacity and diligence that he will render you justice and at the same time make you happy." At Clark's request the villagers exercised their first rights as citizens by electing judges whom they believed were best qualified to carry out the provisions of the new government. At the head of the county court was Gabriel Cerré, now one of Clark's stanchest supporters.[76]

But the harmony between governors and governed proved only a chimera. Just two weeks after the inauguration of the new government the justices of Kaskaskia swamped Todd with protests against the conduct of American troops. They had killed plow oxen and milch cows for food and had sold Negro slaves without permission of their owners. And they continued to speculate in land and to sell firewater to the Indians. Captain Richard McCarty let his hogs run wild to destroy the crops on some of the French farms. When these animals were killed, the irate captain petitioned Todd for redress:

I don't see yet through the Designs of a few Despicable Inhabitants who say they are authorized by you to parade themselves in the fields Destroying My property when there is Numbers of other hogs in the Same place that are as fauctious as Mine. . . . Indeed unless there is soon a change made for the Better me nor my Soldiers will have no Business hear, neither can we stay half naked, what we are paid with call'd down by the Civil Power; with what can we get our necessaries of Life; Neither do I kno' the Laws you have Established.[77]

When his petition was ignored he wrote to a friend that "Colo. Todd's Residence here will spoil the people intirely for the Inhabitants no more Regard us than a Parcel of Slaves. . . . I think it would be a happy thing could we get Colo. Todd out of the Country for he will possitively Sett the Inhabitants and us by the Ears."[78]

The French merchants were unwilling to part with goods and food without assurance of payment in something more substantial than the depreciated currency, which in the language of the time was "not worth a continental damn." Captain John Williams complained that he could secure neither clothing nor provisions without pelts. Since Pollock's private resources were exhausted, the bills which Clark and other officers drew on him came back protested. Colonel John Montgomery added to Todd's difficulties by telling the Kaskaskians to get their guns ready, for he was about to take by force what food he needed for his soldiers. At last Todd in disgust gave up his post to a deputy, Richard Winston, and in November 1779 left the Illinois country forever.[79]

During this period of strife Clark made preparations to march against Detroit. To this end the governor of Virginia promised him five hundred soldiers but instead sent a hundred fifty shoeless and half-starved men under Colonel John Montgomery. With them Clark marched from Kaskaskia to Vincennes, where Colonel John Bowman promised to meet him with three hundred Kentuckians. When he arrived he learned that Bowman, instead of coming to Vincennes, had decided to win laurels for himself by leading his men against the Shawnee in their capital at Chillicothe. Bowman burned the town but the Indians took refuge in a blockhouse from which they succeeded in driving the Kentuckians away. By this time most of Bowman's men had served the period of their enlistment and had returned home. When Bowman finally joined Clark, he had only thirty men left. Clark, of course, desponded pitifully: "Never was a person more mortified than I was," he wrote, "to see so fair an opportunity to push a victory; Detroit lost for want of a few men."[80]

Abandoning his cherished plan for the present, Clark distributed most of his troops among Vincennes, Kaskaskia and Cahokia. With the remaining men he went to the Falls of the Ohio, at the site of modern Louisville, Kentucky, where he had built a fort and where presumably he believed he could buy supplies with paper money. Soon Governor Jefferson ordered him to build another fort near the mouth of the Ohio. Both men agreed that such a stronghold would serve as the gateway of trade with the West, would control the warlike Chickasaw and the English posts on the Mississippi and would facilitate intercourse with New Orleans, now that Spain had entered the war against England. At the "Iron Banks," five miles below the mouth of the Ohio, Clark built Fort Jefferson.[81]

Clark's failure to march against Detroit had encouraged the regional tribes to align themselves again with the English. Availing herself of this change of heart, England planned four campaigns to reconquer the entire West. The first, under a trader named Emanuel Hesse, was to strike against the Spaniards in St. Louis and the Americans in Cahokia. The second was to conquer the plains between the Wabash and the Mississippi. The third, under intrepid Captain Henry Bird, was to "amuse" Clark in the fort at the Falls, then surprise the settlements in central Kentucky. The last and most formidable was to come by sea, conquer Spanish Louisiana and unite with Hesse up the Mississippi.

Somehow the Cahokians learned of Hesse's approach and sent Clark a message asking for his assistance. De Leyba in St. Louis and Montgomery in Kaskaskia also informed Clark that Hesse was com-

ing with a force of nine hundred fifty traders, servants and Indians
under the Ottawa chief, Matchikuis, whom the British had won
over by conferring on him the title of general and permitting him
to wear a scarlet coat with epaulets. When Hesse arrived before
Cahokia in May, 1780, Clark was there to greet him with cannon
shot. Awed more by Clark's presence than by his fire, the Indians
after a brief skirmish forced Hesse and his men to cross the river to
St. Louis. Here they suffered defeat, especially the Winnebagos,
who tried to fight their way through the village. Hesse then retreated with them to the countryside, where they killed and
wounded and captured many poor people "who had no other arms
than those of the good faith in which they lived." Fearing that
Clark was at his heels Hesse hastily withdrew with his followers to
Michilimackinac, his starting point. Two other campaigns fizzled
out. In the south the British suffered defeat at the hands of Governor Gálvez, who captured Baton Rouge, Natchez, Pensacola and
other posts and reduced all West Florida to Spanish control. On
receiving word of these defeats the force sent to conquer the plains
between the Wabash and the Mississippi retired in canoes and two
other vessels. It was composed largely of Sioux and Foxes. To punish them Clark sent a motley army of regulars, French volunteers
and Spaniards from St. Louis against their villages on the Rock
River. When Montgomery found the villages deserted, he burned
them to the ground and returned to the Illinois country.[82]

Of the four English expeditions only the one led by Captain Bird
achieved any measure of success. Journeying by water through
Shawnee country, Bird gathered seven hundred warriors and set
out to attack the fort at the Falls before Clark could reach it. But
when he arrived to within a hundred miles of his goal, the Indians,
harkening to false rumor that Clark was already there, became so
terrified that they persuaded their leader to lead them instead to
Licking Valley. There they attacked Ruddell's Station, whose
inhabitants were Pennsylvania Germans, and forced it to surrender.
Bird gave his promise, which the Indians confirmed, that he would
spare their lives and take them to Detroit as prisoners. But the
minute the settlement gave up, the Indians rushed into the cabins,
"tore the poor children from their mothers' breasts, and killed a
wounded man and every one of the cattle, leaving the whole to
stink." They repeated such atrocities in three other stations before
Bird, seeing the uselessness of trying to restrain them, decided to
return with three hundred prisoners to Detroit. On the way the
Indians tomahawked so many of them that Bird was constrained to

march the women and children twenty miles a day over high mountains in order to get them as quickly as possible to safety. Even so, only a hundred fifty prisoners remained when Bird reached Detroit.[83]

Meanwhile, Clark had learned of Bird's intentions and had resolved on retaliatory measures. On June 5, 1780, he paddled with a few men to Fort Jefferson. To avoid danger he and two companions disguised themselves as Indians and in a raft they made by binding logs with grape vines journeyed to Harrodsburg by way of the Tennessee and Kentucky rivers. He called for volunteers, but most of the settlers, being more interested in acquiring choice land than in fighting Shawnee, ignored his summons. Whereupon Clark angrily closed the land office. When some of the settlers threatened to return to the East, Clark commandeered their horses, guns and ammunition. These measures proved effective. Clark soon gathered a thousand men at the mouth of the Licking and led them across the Ohio to the Shawnee capital at Chillicothe. When the Indians fled, he burned their town and crops and pursued them to Piqua, a village on the upper Miami. With a small cannon he had brought on horseback, he battered the fort in which they had taken refuge and brought them to submission. Clark's cousin, Joseph Rogers, who had been a prisoner of the Shawnee for two years, made his escape and ran toward the Americans shouting, "Don't shoot! I am a white man!" but Clark's men, mistaking him for an Indian, shot him down. He died in Clark's arms. Clark burned to subdue the entire Shawnee country, but lack of provisions forced him to return to the Licking where he disbanded his force.[84]

He now returned to his plan to capture Detroit. In this he received encouragement from Governor Jefferson, who believed with George Washington that the Kentucky settlements would never have peace and security as long as the post remained British. Hearing that the British planned another expedition against Kentucky in the spring, Jefferson appealed successfully to Washington to furnish Clark with powder from continental arsenals. In addition Washington ordered General Daniel Brodhead, commander at Fort Pitt, to give Clark the supplies he needed and to allow the regiment under Colonel John Gibson to take part in the expedition. At about the same time, in January 1781, Washington commissioned Clark brigadier general, and Virginia promised him two thousand men, who were to meet at Pittsburgh and journey in canoes down the Ohio and up the Wabash just as soon as the rivers thawed.[85]

Difficulties appeared and thickened almost as soon as promises began to be translated into realities. The militia of Berkeley, Frederick, Hampshire, Greenbriar and Monongalia counties refused to leave their homes to join Clark in such a remote campaign and threatened to mutiny should they be forced to do so. Colonel Brodhead heard that the Indians planned an attack from Detroit and Niagara and from the Delaware. Seeing here an opportunity to win laurels for himself, Brodhead grew jealous of Clark and kept Gibson's regiment in Pittsburgh, and all the while he continued to convey his assurances of co-operation to Clark. Clark then appealed to President Joseph Reed of Pennsylvania, but Pennsylvania politicians were so jealous of Virginia that they thwarted her attempt to raise men. When Dr. John Connolly prepared to march from Lake Ontario against Pittsburgh, they excused themselves by pointing out the inexpediency of stripping the state of men for a remote expedition. On August 4, five months later than the date set for the march on Detroit, Clark arrived in Wheeling with only four hundred troops, hardly enough to guard the supplies accumulated for the two thousand men Virginia had promised him. There he waited for Colonel Archibald Lochry, who had promised to join him with about one hundred men from Westmoreland County, Pennsylvania. But Clark's men deserted in such large numbers that on August 8 he felt he could wait no longer. Leaving a message for Lochry to follow, he journeyed with his remaining men toward the Falls. Just a few hours after Clark's departure Lochry arrived in Wheeling, found his message and obeyed his instructions. But the great Mohawk chief, Joseph Brant, waylaid and killed him and six of his officers and thirty of his men.[86]

On his way down the river Clark's men continued to desert. When he reached the Falls, his ranks were so depleted that he gave up his military plans. He never had another chance to resume them. In the West the situation looked dark for the Americans, but in the East the tide had turned against Great Britain. On October 19, 1781, her unsound strategy of waging war for three years with divided forces resulted in Cornwallis' surrender at Yorktown.

In the West the war continued for about two more years. Unable to finance another expedition, Virginia adopted the more economic policy of defending Kentucky by garrisoning the Falls, the mouth of the Kentucky, the mouth of the Licking and the mouth of Limestone Creek. Governor Benjamin Harrison entrusted this task to Clark, who was unable to obtain the necessary men and supplies for all four forts. He decided, therefore, to concentrate his main force at the Falls, where he had built a stronger fort named in honor of Governor Thomas Nelson. He made Fort Nelson the key to his whole system of defense, sending crews in gunboats up and down the Ohio to warn the interior settlements of Kentucky should Indian raiding parties approach. The patrol proved defective. On August 15, 1782, a small body of British rangers and three hundred Wyandots and Lake Indians succeeded in crossing the Ohio and in storming Bryant's Station. The settlers beat off the attack, then pursued their enemies to the Blue Licks. That master of Indian fighting and psychology, Daniel Boone, urged the Kentuckians to delay until they should receive the reinforcements they expected, but they ignored his advice and rushed headlong into ambush where sixty of them, including Colonel John Todd, were killed and twenty captured or badly wounded. To conceal their lack of judgment the surviving Kentuckians deluged Governor Harrison with letters blaming the disaster on Clark's failure to build the prescribed forts, on what they regarded as his faulty strategy of concentrating his main force at Fort Nelson and on his alleged addiction to alcohol. The governor, having neglected repeated warnings of the dangers that threatened the Kentucky settlements, feared that he himself would be blamed for the disaster until the Kentuckians attributed it to Clark. Then he asked Colonel William Fleming, who was going to Kentucky, to investigate the charges against Clark. Fleming found nothing to censure either in Clark's personal or in his general conduct. Indeed, he and his colleagues endorsed Clark's military plans, approved his accounts and in many other ways showed their esteem for him.[87]

Meanwhile Clark, in retaliation for the disaster at the Blue Licks, had again marched against Chillicothe with a thousand Kentucky volunteers. The Shawnee, warned of his approach, fled from the town. Clark burned it and five other Indian villages and destroyed ten thousand bushels of corn and quantities of provisions. Though he failed to entice the Indians to a general engagement, his rigorous measures cowed them to the extent that they never again attempted an invasion of Kentucky. This was Clark's last military success. In the fall of 1782 a preliminary treaty between the United States and Great Britain ended hostilities in the West. This left Virginia without an adequate command for Clark. On July 2, 1783, he resigned.[88]

By the definitive Treaty of Paris, signed on September 3, 1783, Great Britain ceded the Old Northwest to the United States. The diplomatic papers dealing with the treaty make no mention of Clark's conquest as a factor in determining this cession. Yet most of the older historians, persuaded more by fervent patriotism and admiration than by historical evidence, have given Clark full credit for it. "The inference," wrote Roosevelt, "is strong that we got what we did only because we had won and held it." The best biographer of Clark, James Alton James, supported this view, but his arguments are obscure and unconvincing. Still another historian of this school was Claude H. Van Tyne, who wrote that

Clark would have pushed on to capture Detroit also but want of sufficient reinforcements compelled him to be content with holding Vincennes, Cahokia and Kaskaskia. These posts, however, were sufficient to insure the American hold upon the Northwest until, in the peace negotiations of 1782, the military prowess of Clark was followed by the diplomatic triumph of Jay.[89]

This statement controverts accurate historical evidence. In the winter of 1780-1781 Clark withdrew the garrisons of Vincennes and Kaskaskia to strengthen Fort Jefferson. Clarence W. Alvord accurately summed up the situation as follows:

The summer of 1779 marked the zenith of Virginia's power north of the Ohio; from that date, there was steady decline. . . . For a year more there were a score of soldiers in those posts, acting as scouts; but even these were recalled in the following winter, and the villages were left to shift for themselves. . . . Virginia had really only weakened the hold of the mother country on a small corner of the disputed territory.[90]

This view is corroborated by the findings of Samuel Flagg Bemis, one of the best authorities in the diplomatic history of the American Revolution. Bemis states that Rayneval, private secretary to the Comte de Vergennes, French minister of foreign affairs, asserted in a memorandum that Clark's excursions in the Illinois country could not seriously be advanced as an American claim. "So far as the documents relating to the entire negotiation reveal," writes Bemis, "such a claim was never made on the basis of Clark's conquests. As a matter of fact he had at this time withdrawn his garrisons to the falls of the Ohio River, and the Northwest was 'no man's land.'" He adds that "by far the greater part of that territory was more subject to the influence of British garrisons at Detroit and Michilimackinac than to Clark's at Fort Nelson."[91]

How, then, did the United States acquire the Old Northwest? The credit for it should go to Benjamin Franklin and Lord Shelburne, prime minister of Great Britain. Franklin pointed out to Shelburne that the frontiersmen, "being far removed from the eyes and control of their respective governments, are most bold in committing offenses against neighbors, and are forever occasioning complaints, and furnishing matter for fresh differences between their states." In view of these circumstances, he strongly urged generosity, which, he said, would lay a strong foundation for eternal amity between England and America. Impressed by the wisdom of these arguments, Shelburne raised almost no objection when the American commissioners, following instructions, asked for the Mississippi and the Great Lakes as boundaries. Their success in the Treaty of Paris must be attributed, therefore, "in large measure to the idealism of the prime minister of Great Britain. He yielded to the United States the Old Northwest, although the greater portion of it was occupied by British troops and Indians."[92]

These historic revaluations do not in any way undermine Clark's enviable niche in the Valhalla of American heroes. Only those who attempt to make science out of the art of historiography and who read cause and effect in almost every event in order to fit it into the pattern of a prescribed theory would discredit Clark on the ground of these revaluations. He remains as secure as such magnificent failures as Hannibal and Napoleon and Robert E. Lee. He lives for us, not because of any materialistic achievement—which is often transitory—but because of such inspiring qualities as his consummate knowledge of human nature, his undying determination and his matchless courage in the face of the most discouraging obstacles.

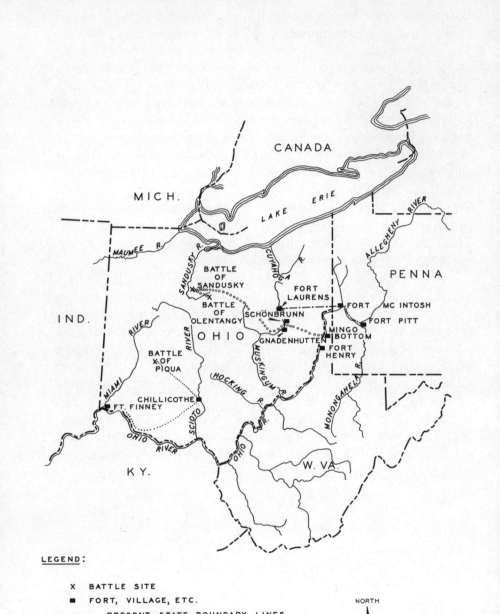

CANADA

MICH.

LAKE ERIE

MAUMEE R.

SANDUSKY R.

CUYAHOGA

R.

ALLEGHENY RIVER

PENNA

BATTLE
OF
SANDUSKY

FORT
LAURENS

SCHÖNBRUNN

FORT MC INTOSH

FORT

FORT PITT

IND.

RIVER

BATTLE
OF
OLENTANGY

OHIO

GNADENHUTTEN

MINGO
BOTTOM

RIVER

MUSKINGUM R.

FORT
HENRY

BATTLE
X OF
PIQUA

HOCKING R.

MONONGAHELA R.

MIAMI

CHILLICOTHE
FT. FINNEY

SCIOTO

OHIO RIVER

OHIO

KY.

W. VA.

LEGEND:

X   BATTLE SITE
■   FORT, VILLAGE, ETC.
– – – –   PRESENT STATE BOUNDARY LINES
–·–·–   CAMPAIGN OF GEN. MC INTOSH
··········   CAMPAIGN OF GEORGE ROGERS CLARK
oooooooooo   CAMPAIGN OF COL. CRAWFORD

NORTH

0 5   25   50   75
SCALE OF MILES

FJM

The Ohio Country

THE GREAT SPIRIT MADE THE OHIO COUNTRY FOR THE INDIANS, NOT for the white men. So Chief Shendeta of the Wyandots, a wise and eloquent man, grimly reminded his people when soon after the Revolution their ancient country was threatened by an avalanche of Americans. The chiefs of the regional tribes agreed. The Wyandots, the Shawnee, the Delawares, and the Miami loved this land of gleaming rivers and gently rolling hills; its rich soil had always yielded a superabundance of berries, nuts and corn, and its endless forests teemed with game of every description. In their jealous contentment they had repeatedly guarded it against white encroachment even when they quarreled among themselves, and during the Revolution they had resisted successfully every attempt on the part of the Americans to take it. They claimed with pride that they had never honorably negotiated a treaty in which they consented to give up an inch of their forest domain. Now, with the coming of peace, they planned to improve their lot. The Delawares in eastern and the Shawnee in southern and central Ohio were about to transfer their towns to the more fertile banks of the upper Muskingum, Scioto and Great Miami rivers, while the Wyandots and the Miami, feeling crowded at home in northwestern Ohio, planned to move to the more spacious and better watered lands in the south. These tribes were, therefore, determined that the Ohio River should separate them forever from the white men.[1]

Sir John Johnson, British superintendent of Indian affairs, encouraged them to fortify this determination by forming themselves into a confederacy. Meeting their chiefs at Sandusky in the fall of 1783 and winning their friendship with a lavish distribution of gifts, he told them that the King, his and their common father, had made peace with the Americans and had given them the Ohio country as well as other lands. But he had not given them the Indian lands. The Ohio was still the boundary between themselves and the Americans, whom they must never permit to pass and return in safety. But since war between England and the United States was over and since the Indians had entered it out of love for their king and not from any quarrel of their own, he would remove the tomahawk from their hands. But he would not take it away; he would merely lay it by their side, so that they could pick it up in case the Americans invaded their country and molested their rights and their property.[2]

They accepted his advice with boastful joy. The leader of the confederacy was Joseph Brant, chief of the Mohawk, a man of unusual military gifts and political acumen. His Indian name was Thayendanegea and his father was a full-blooded Mohawk who had dwelled in the Ohio country. On becoming a widow his mother had returned to the Mohawk country with her children, Joseph and Mollie, and had settled at Canajoharie, where she married an Indian whose name was Carrihogo but who was known to the British as Nickus Brant, because he had the habit of carrying a brant or brand to light his way in his nocturnal wanderings. Joseph and Mollie assumed their stepfather's name.[3]

Joseph was a likable fellow with a fierce countenance. He was tall and slender and spoke with a soft voice unless aroused by anger. His costume was that of the Mohawk chief: moccasins elegantly trimmed with beads, leggings and breech cloth of superfine blue, short green coat with two silver epaulets and a small laced round hat. A mounted silver cutlass hung by his side. Over his shoulders he wore a blue blanket gorgeously decorated with a red border. When he sat down he let his blanket drop to display his epaulets.[4]

Brant owed his rise to Sir William Johnson, Sir Guy Johnson's uncle and also his predecessor as superintendent of Indian affairs, who, enchanted by Mollie's beauty and expert horsemanship, had taken her as his Indian wife. Sir William used his influence to enter Joseph in Dr. Wheelock's School in Lebanon, Connecticut, where he proved a brilliant student, especially in Indian tongues. Sir William employed him as interpreter at £83 a year with other payments for extra services. Later, when Sir Guy Johnson succeeded his uncle in 1774, he made Brant his secretary, commissioned him captain and took him to England. Brant was presented at court, met such notables as Boswell and Dr. Johnson and sat in Mohawk regalia for his portrait to George Romney. Returning to America, he plunged into the Revolution and soon became a terror throughout New York, especially in the Mohawk Valley. In the St. Leger expedition he commanded the Indians with rare skill. At the Battle of Oriskany he displayed desperate courage and surrounded the Americans under General Nicholas Herkimer, though he failed to win a victory over them.[5]

2

In the two years between Cornwallis' surrender and the formation of the Confederacy, Indian resentment had increased with the number of American atrocities in the Ohio country.

The most shocking of these was the massacre of the Christian Delawares at Gnadenhutten in present Tuscarawas County, Ohio. Under the guidance of the Moravian missionaries David Zeisberger and John Heckewelder these Indians had built, on the banks of the Tuscarawas River, the villages of Salem, Gnadenhutten, and Schönbrunn, where they dwelt in peace and justice, raising crops and livestock, abstaining from firewater and schooling their children.

When the Revolution began, their leaders advised them to adopt the wise policy of neutrality. This, however, was impossible. Lying between the American settlements on the southeast and the "British" Indians—Wyandots, Shawnee and Delawares—around Sandusky, the Moravian villages were stopping places at which war parties often refreshed themselves either on their way to attack the Kentucky or western Pennsylvania settlements or on their return home with scalps and plunder. Regarding their peaceful kinsmen as traitors, the warring Delawares often tried to embroil them in attacks on the settlements. Sometimes a few of the Moravian Indians would join the war parties, thereby arousing the suspicions of the Americans. At the same time Zeisberger sympathized with the Americans and, whenever he heard of an impending British attack, would forewarn Colonel Brodhead at Fort Pitt, a hundred miles away.

Learning of Zeisberger's sentiments and fearing that the Americans might use the Moravian villages as points from which to attack Detroit, the British decided to move the Christian Delawares to the Upper Sandusky where a stricter watch could be kept on them. In September 1781 Captain Matthew Elliott led a force of about two hundred fifty Indians, chiefly Wyandots, to the Moravian villages and forced their inhabitants to accompany him to the Upper Sandusky where he left them to fend for themselves. Zeisberger and Heckewelder were taken to Detroit for trial but were released when no accuser appeared against them. That winter the refugee Indians suffered greatly from cold and hunger. In February 1782 eighty-six of them received permission from the British to return to the deserted villages to harvest the corn they had left in the fields.[6]

At about the same time a band of Shawnee took advantage of unusually fine weather to invade the settlements of western Pennsylvania. Near Buchanan Fort they killed John Fink while he and his father were sledding rails on their farm. The old man unlinked the chain that fastened his horse to the sled and galloped away. He reached home safely and immediately took his family to the fort.

On February 8 another band of Shawnee attacked Robert Wallace's home in Washington County, Pennsylvania, during his absence and took his wife and three children prisoners. A few days later another Indian party seized John Carpenter, who escaped and told the surrounding settlements that two of his captors were Christian Indians who spoke German.[7]

Satisfied with this identification of their enemies, about a hundred fifty mounted militia under Colonel David Williamson took the direct trail to the villages of the Christian Indians. On the way they found Mrs. Wallace's body impaled on the sharpened trunk of a sapling. Finding her youngest son troublesome, the Indians had tomahawked and scalped him before they reached the Ohio. The other children they took to Sandusky, where the older of them died. The survivor lived with the Wyandots for two and a half years, then returned home.[8]

Enraged by the ghastly murders, the whites quickened their pace. On March 6 they arrived at Gnadenhutten, where they rounded up the unsuspecting Indians in two houses, the men in one and the women and children in the other. At a council the majority of Williamson's officers voted to put their captives to death. When the Indians heard of the fate that awaited them they requested a little time in which to prepare for death. They begged one another's pardon for whatever wrong they might have done, prayed, kissed one another farewell and, as the murderous soldiers attacked them, sang hymns of praise to God. Thus they all died, within the very wall where they had been imprisoned.[9]

The massacre of Gnadenhutten aroused all the Ohio tribes, even those friendly to the Americans, to a bitter war of revenge. They intensified their attacks on the Virginia and the western Pennsylvania, stealing, kidnaping and murdering.

The Americans, of course, struck back. In May 1782, four hundred eight mounted men under Colonel William Crawford gathered at Mingo Bottom, near present Steubenville, Ohio, and rode straight to the chief town of the Wyandots, where most of the marauding parties originated.

Crawford found the town deserted. Indian scouts had watched the Americans gather at Mingo Bottom and had informed the Wyandot chief Half King, who had sent runners to Detroit for help. That implacable hater of Americans, Chief Pipe of the Delawares, responded with two hundred braves, while the formidable war chief of the Wyandots, Zhaus-sho-toh, gathered many more. In addition the Shawnee promised to send two hundred braves from their towns in present Logan County, Ohio, and Butler's Rangers prepared to march from Detroit with two field guns and a mortar.[10]

On June 4 as Crawford and his men struck out into an open prairie only two miles from Half King's capital, they saw a force of Indians approaching from a considerable distance. In the vanguard were the Delawares under Captain Pipe with his lieutenant Wingenund and the renegade Simon Girty. Behind them were Zhaus-sho-toh's reinforcements. Crawford, seeing the Indians taking possession of a grove and detecting the advantage of their position, ordered his men to charge on foot. In a short time they drove the Indians out of the grove and into open prairie. At this moment, however, Pipe and his men flanked Crawford to the right, then attacked him in the rear. The Americans, turning quickly, fought them off.

Though Crawford was left in possession of the field, his enemies were far from discouraged. They planned to renew the battle as soon as the Shawnee and Butler's Rangers arrived. The next afternoon while the Americans, fatigued or sick from their march in the torrid sun, rested in a small copse, they saw the enemy sweeping down on them. Among the Indians were Butler's Rangers.

As soon as he discerned their uniforms Crawford lapsed into utter gloom, for he realized now that victory was impossible. He held a council of war at which his officers decided to retreat. They wasted no time. By now the Shawnee "kept pouring in hourly from all directions." As the Indians came closer and closer, the Americans, who had been retreating in good order, became a confused, noisy mass of men. Soon the Delawares and Shawnee fell upon them, shooting many of them down on their horses and scattering the rest into a swamp. The next day a small group of them under Colonel Williamson made a stand at Olentangy, in modern Crawford County, and were utterly routed. Meanwhile Crawford and Dr. John Knight, the force's physician, had fallen into an ambuscade of Delawares headed by Wingenund, who took them to his camp.[11]

There, in the presence of Elliott, Girty, Pipe and an exulting group of Delawares and Wyandots, Crawford, as the "Big Captain" of the invading army, was condemned to be burned at the stake. Wingenund's men stripped him naked, made him sit down and beat him with sticks and their fists. Then they tied him at the ligature around his wrists to the foot of a post fifteen feet high. The rope was long enough to permit him to sit down or walk around the post once or twice and return in the same way. Pipe made a speech to the Indians, who yelled a hideous and hearty assent to all he said. They took up their guns and shot over seventy loads of powder at Crawford from his feet up to his neck. Then they crowded around him, lopped off his ears, and stuck him in the ribs with burning hickory poles. The dying man begged Girty to shoot him, but the renegade replied with a laugh that he had no gun. At last Crawford, able to endure his suffering no longer, lay down on his stomach. A Delaware lunged at his head with a tomahawk and threw the scalp at Knight's face. The Indians piled hickory sticks around Crawford's blackened body and danced around it as flames and smoke rose to the evening sky.[12]

Knight was more fortunate. The Shawnee, wanting to burn him in one of their own towns, delivered him up to a tough-looking fellow named Tutelu, who started for a destination fifty miles away. The mounted Indian drove his prisoner before him. Tutelu tied him when they rested and released him when they resumed their journey. One morning Knight got behind his captor and whacked him on the head with a dogwood pole. The mighty Tutelu ran howling away. Knight took his horse and rode back to the settlements.[13]

3

The Indian successes occurred before Brant formed the Indian confederacy and greatly encouraged the Indians to hold out for the Ohio River boundary. By the Treaty of Paris, which ended the Revolution, the Ohio country as part of the Northwest Territory became American. But though the British gave up the Old Northwest, they made every effort to retain the lucrative fur trade in it. They, therefore, refused to comply with American demands to surrender the posts at Oswego, Michilimackinac, Niagara and Detroit. The last was especially important as the center of intrigue with the Indians. The Americans, unable to force the British to evacuate the posts and to put down Indian warfare, faced serious danger to their prestige in the Ohio country. In such circumstance Congress had no choice but to offset its weakness by passing aggressive legislation. It enacted the Ordinance of October 15, 1783, which wrested from the Indians all of their lands between the Ohio River and Lake Erie east of the Great Miami and the Maumee rivers.[14]

The Indians regarded the Ordinance as nothing less than an open declaration of war. It stated that they had forfeited their right to the lands by breaking their pledges of neutrality and by joining the British during the American Revolution. But it added that the United States preferred clemency to rigor because the Indians "could not be restrained from acts of hostility and wanton destruction." Instead of compelling them to retire beyond the lakes, the United States would "supply their wants and partake of their Trade . . . from motives of compassion . . . and establish a boundary line between them and us, beyond which we will restrain our citizens from hunting and settling." This conciliatory gesture was aimed at discouraging the confederacy from starting a general war against the whites. The Iroquois had already declared that, though they stood for peace, they would take the warpath should the United States threaten to conquer their lands.[15]

In accordance with the Ordinance, Congress appointed five commissioners to treat with the Indians. Three of these, Oliver Wolcott, Richard Butler and Arthur Lee, were assigned to Fort Stanwix, where the proposed treaty with the Iroquois was to take place. Brant wanted to treat only with the United States, but when New York persisted in making arrangements for her own treaty, he acquiesced, though he refused to discuss matters of importance with the state commissioners. When the New York commissioners met him at Fort Stanwix in September, he told them that "the Voice of our Chiefs and their Confederates" demanded "that We should first meet Commissioners of the Whole Thirteen States and after that if any Matters should remain between Us and any particular State, that we should then attend to them." The state commissioners remonstrated with Brant in vain. The conference broke up.[16]

In October the three United States commissioners arrived at Fort

Stanwix. They found that most of the tribes had become impatient for their arrival and had returned home. The only western
Indians present at the conference were the Iroquois and a few
Shawnee. Since the entire confederacy was not represented, Brant
announced that a treaty would be invalid.

Nonetheless, the commissioners insisted on signing a treaty with
the Iroquois. To remind them that George III had yielded to the
United States "all pretentions, and claims, whatsoever, of all the
country South, and West of the Great Northern Rivers, and Lakes,
as far as the Mississippi," the commissioners on October 11 read the
Treaty of Paris to the assembled warriors. As a gesture of generosity the commissioners then invited the Indians to propose a boundary line that would "be just for you to offer, and honorable for
the United States to agree to."[17]

To the Iroquois a just boundary was that upon which they had
agreed in the Treaty of Fort Stanwix of 1768. They confessed
naïvely that Great Britain had deserted them and that their only re-
liance was the Great Spirit. The Seneca chief, Cornplanter, said
that the Indians loved their land and that they, being a hunting people, needed it to range in. He proposed a boundary line not much
different from that drawn by the earlier Treaty of Fort Stanwix and
expressed hope it would remain as long "as the sun rolls over from
day to day."

To this plea the commissioners were indifferent. The Indians,
they said, were mistaken if they supposed

. . . that having been excluded from the United States and the King
of Great Britain, you are become a free and independent nation,
and may make what terms you please. It is not so. You are a sub-
dued people; you have been overcome in a war which you entered
into with us, not only without provocation, but in violation of most
sacred obligations. The great spirit who is at the same time the
judge and avenger of perfidy, has given us victory over all our
enemies. We are at peace with all but *you*, *you* now stand out
alone against our *whole force*.

When we offer you peace on moderate terms, we do it in mag-
nanimity and mercy. If you do not accept it now, you are not to
expect a repetition of such offers. Consider well, therefore, your
situation and *ours*. Do not suffer yourselves to be again deceived
so as to raise our arm against you. You feel the sad effects of having
refused this counsel before—beware how you do it again. . . .

We shall now, therefore, declare to you the condition, on which alone you can be received into the peace and protection of the United States.[18]

So saying, the commissioners dictated terms. Cornplanter, having no choice, rose and said: "You have this day declared your minds to us fully, and without disguise. We thank you for it; this is acting like men, for thus men speak."

By this treaty the Iroquois relinquished their historic claims to lands west of the states of New York and Pennsylvania. As compensation for their loss the commissioners promised them a quantity of goods "for their use and comfort." Six of the Indian delegates agreed to remain as hostages until the Iroquois delivered up all the prisoners they had taken in the American Revolution. Brant considered this act so dishonorable that he suspended all preparations to visit England and bent all his efforts toward gaining the release of the hostages by returning the prisoners, many of whom preferred Indian life. The Iroquois then dealt with the New York and Pennsylvania commissioners, who quickly appropriated most of the hunting grounds within the boundaries of their respective commonwealth.[19]

From Fort Stanwix Arthur Lee and Richard Butler journeyed to Fort Pitt, where they picked up another commissioner, George Rogers Clark. The three then proceeded to the American military headquarters for the Ohio country, Fort McIntosh, a stronghold with four bastions of well-hewn logs located at the mouth of Beaver Creek in extreme western Pennsylvania. The commissioners found the Indians angry with the Iroquois for signing the Treaty of Fort Stanwix. This pleased the commissioners who, bent on destroying the confederacy, planned to deal only with the Wyandots, the Delawares and a few roaming Ottawas and Chippewa, all of whom had agreed at Sandusky in 1783 not to cede any lands except with the consent of the confederacy.

At the council Captain Ebenezer Denny counted about four hundred Indians, "a very motley crew—an ugly set of devils all—very few handsome men and women." Their tempers were as uncomfortable as their countenances. The chiefs asserted that the lands which the United States claimed under the Treaty of Paris were their own. But the commissioners held their ground. On January 8, 1785, they read to the Indians the treaty of alliance between the United States and France and pointed out that Louis XVI had renounced forever any claim to land in the United States. The commissioners then read the Treaty of Paris to their irate listeners and solemnly informed them that it contained nothing that could be construed as favorable to any Indian tribe which fought against the Americans during the Revolution. "You are therefore left to obtain peace from the U. States," said the commissioners, "& to be received under their government and protection, upon such conditions as seem proper to Congress, the Great Council of the U. States." The commissioners strengthened this argument by concluding that the Iroquois had surrendered at Fort Stanwix and that, therefore, the confederacy was broken.[20]

Confused by this explanation the Indians became submissive and began to plead for their lands. Their only argument was that they resided on lands handed down to them by their forefathers. "I think as the old men in former times did," said a Delaware. "They are old, I am young; nevertheless, I think that the grant was good, and that the country is mine. And as our children grow up, we tell them that the country is ours." Words which the Wyandots strongly endorsed: "Attend to what my nephew [the Delaware] has said to you. Believe him; for he has spoke the truth . . . I set him down in *this land. The rest belongs to the Wyandot.*"[21]

To these pleas the commissioners remained indifferent. They told the Indians that

You have been particular in describing to us the claim and title of each particular tribe. . . . The detail of these claims and title may appear to be of consequence among yourselves. But to us & to the business of the Council Fire to which we have called you, they have no relation; *because* we claim the country by conquest; and are to give not to receive. It is of this that it behooves you to have a clear and distinct comprehension.[22]

With these arguments the commissioners on January 21, 1785, dictated the terms of the treaty, which the Indians accepted. It was falsely declared to be "between the commissioners plenipotentiary of the United States, of the one part, and the sachems and warriors of the Wyandot, Delaware, Chippewa and Ottawa nations, of the other." The new boundary line began at the mouth of the Cuyahoga and ran to the Tuscarawas portage, to a crossing above Fort Laurens, west to the Indian village of Pickawillany on the Miami, over the portage to the Maumee, to Lake Erie and back to the starting point. The land beyond this boundary was to belong to the Wyandot, Delaware and Ottawa tribes, who were to enjoy the protection of the United States but who were to surrender the posts of Detroit and Michilimackinac to the United States for trading purposes. Henceforth the Indians could punish as they saw fit any white man who trespassed on any part of their domain, while they in turn promised to surrender to the nearest American post for punishment any Indian who robbed or murdered a white man. The last article of the Treaty stated that the commissioners, "in pursuance of the humane and liberal views of Congress," would deliver goods to the tribes "for their use and comfort."[23]

4

In its many conflicts with the Indians, Congress saw clearly the need of adopting a policy capable of attracting to the Ohio country a sturdy and numerous population which would uphold American rights. Hitherto the conflicting claims of the states in this region prevented the realization of such a policy. Four states—New York, Virginia, Massachusetts, and Connecticut—claimed portions of the Old Northwest. New York rested her claims on her former guardianship over the Iroquois, who had asserted control of the land by right of conquest. The other three states based their claims on charters. The claims of Massachusetts and Connecticut had no more substance than the paper on which they were written. They were purely theoretical—no foreign power would have honored them; they were no more in hand than are a group of birds in a tree. And they would remain valueless until they could be reduced to possession either by act or by action of the states and the nation.

Of the four states only Virginia could justify her claims on practical grounds. Clark's recent conquest of the Illinois country had enabled her to occupy some portions of the region. This lion's share had aroused the envy of less affluent states. Maryland, having no western lands at all, was particularly bitter. She asserted that Virginia's claims were void. She argued that Virginia could not cede to the federal government what she did not own. She advocated that all western lands should be declared a part of the federal domain. Her attitude signified a disguised fear of her neighbor. She was afraid of Virginia's power, wealth, population; she was afraid her own citizens would migrate to the western lands; she was afraid she would grow weaker while Virginia grew stronger. The other states shared some of this insecurity. In those days each colony or state regarded another as a possible commercial and even military rival. Implacable jealousy and distrust divided each state indubitably more than did geographical boundaries.

Several times Congress had intervened to prevent an open break between the have and the have-not states. To obtain greater national solidarity and to acquire the western lands, it sought, at the same time, a solution to the irksome land problem. It needed to sell the western lands in order to reduce the Revolutionary War debt and to meet a part of the national expenses. But it realized that the problem was an emotional one and that, therefore, it could not be solved by reasoned argument. One emotion is often dispelled, however, by a nobler one. Congress appealed to that of nationalism. On this ground it persuaded the states with western claims to surrender certain points until each came to a common agreement.

New York led the way; in 1780 she abandoned her claims. Congress was quick to seize upon this surrender as an argument by which to move the other states to follow suit. It discussed neither its own rights nor those of the states; it simply followed its policy of appealing to their sense of nationalism. It announced that it would divide the western lands into districts which, as soon as they were properly settled, would be admitted as states.

The other states reluctantly followed the example set by New York. Early in 1784 Virginia ceded to Congress all of her western lands northwest of the Ohio save a small region which she retained as a military reserve for the use of her soldiers. The following year Massachusetts gave up her claims to land lying west of the present boundary of New York. In 1786 Connecticut made a similar cession, retaining, however, a tract of about five thousand square miles in present northern Ohio, which became known as the Western Reserve.

Hard pressed for funds, the government wanted to sell its western lands as quickly as possible. What plan should it adopt? As early as 1781 a lawyer named Pelatiah Webster had suggested in a pamphlet that Congress divide the public domain into square townships and sell each of them at the rate of a dollar an acre. Congress turned down the proposal. Four years later, however, it advocated a similar plan. The public domain was to be divided into townships seven miles square and sold at a dollar an acre to united groups of settlers. These suggestions were modified and incorporated into the Land Ordinance which Congress adopted on May 20, 1785.[24]

This law provided for division of the public domain into townships six miles square and for subdivision of these townships into thirty-six numbered sections, each of which contained one square mile or six hundred and forty acres. Alternate townships were to be sold either entire or in sections, thereby satisfying New Englanders who needed large pieces of land and southerners who needed less. The lands were to be sold at auction in every eastern state at the minimum of a dollar an acre. Congress reserved four sections in each township for future disposal and every sixteenth section for educational purposes. The Ordinance stated that the Northwest Territory was to be surveyed on an east and west base line running from where the western boundary of Pennsylvania crossed the Ohio River and on a north and south range line running southward from this to the Ohio. The first seven ranges of townships were to be opened to settlers as soon as they were surveyed.[25]

The Land Ordinance of 1785 ended the prevailing confusion in regard to the public domain. Now a settler could buy a piece of ground that could be definitely located. Yet the Ordinance proved impracticable. Years of laborious surveying would be required before these lands could be sold and perhaps years more before pioneers could be persuaded to buy located lands in preference to choice lands selected by themselves. And that was only half of the difficulty. The Ordinance, by limiting sales to auctions in eastern states and by forbidding purchase of less than six hundred and forty acres, defeated its own purpose. Few settlers needed so much land, and few could afford to spend so much money.[26]

Congress soon sent Captain Thomas Hutchins, geographer for the United States, to survey the first seven ranges of the Ohio country. He was amply suited for his task. As a young man in General Forbes's march to Pittsburgh he had acquired indispensable knowledge of the trails and waterways of western Pennsylvania. Six years later while serving as a captain in the Sixtieth Royal Regiment and engineer in the Ohio expedition of Colonel Bouquet, he had intoduced "the simplest of all known modes of survey." Two years later a hydrographical survey he made of the Ohio River gave him intimate knowledge of its source. Now with characteristic enthusiasm and promptness he began to survey the basic east and west Geographer's Line. Indian warfare soon interrupted his work, yet he succeeded in collecting the material for an elaborate report to Congress on the topography, quality and adaptability of different crops in the federal domain he had surveyed. In the summer of 1786 he resumed his survey, and again his work was hampered by inadequate military protection and supplies. But in six months he had completed the survey of the first four ranges.[27]

5

Instead of stopping the Indian depredations in the Ohio country, the Fort Stanwix and Fort McIntosh treaties only increased them. The Ohio tribes denounced the Iroquois for surrendering hunting grounds which were not theirs, and the Shawnee rendered the Treaty of Fort McIntosh useless by refusing to sign it. This disharmony among the Indians provided Kentuckians with the excuse to swarm across the Ohio and settle on forbidden lands. At the same time bands of ruffians, outlaws and adventurers from Virginia and western Pennsylvania elbowed their way into peaceful Indian villages and "tomahawked" many land claims in the region between Pittsburgh and the Muskingum River. The commissioners, fearing an Indian war, requested Colonel Josiah Harmar, commander of federal troops in the Northwest, to expel the white troublemakers by force of arms. Harmar found such a task impossible. Not only was his force too small but the whites, whom Harmar called "banditti," had organized a government with an elected governor. When told to move on, one of their leaders, John Amberson, posted a notice which proudly asserted that

. . . all mankind, agreeable to every constitution formed in America, have an undoubted right to pass into any vacant country and there form their constitution, and that the Confederation of the whole United States Congress is not impowered to forbid them; neither is Congress impowered from the Confederation to make any sale of the uninhabited lands to pay the public debt, but the Confederation has prescribed a particular mode for the payment of all public debts, which is by tax levied and lifted by authority of the legislatures of each state.[28]

Hoping to stem their advance, Congress requested Harmar to build at the mouth of the Muskingum a fort to which he gave his name. Even this failed to stop the onrush of settlers. More embarrassed than Harmar were the commissioners who, having dealt with the Iroquois, Delaware, Wyandot, Chippewa and Ottawa tribes, now turned their attention to the Shawnee to persuade them to a cession of their land. Brant had gone to England to enlist the support of the government in his plans. Availing themselves of his absence, Butler, Clark and Samuel Holden Parsons sent runners to invite the Shawnee to a conference at the mouth of the Great Miami. After hesitating a month a few Wyandot and Delaware chiefs straggled in, but the Shawnee remained aloof. While the commissioners were waiting for them, they built a new fort which they named Fort Finney in honor of Captain Walter Finney, whom Harmar had sent to the designated place of the conference with orders to establish fortified winter quarters.[29]

At last on January 8, 1786, an officer brought word that one hundred fifty Shawnee were coming. Later in the day arrived nearly four hundred fifty other Indians including a hundred thirty Delawares and Wyandots. Six days later the Shawnee approached the fort, saluting with three rounds for each of their men. At the order of his superior, Captain Ebenezer Denny had twelve of his men return the salute by parading while they fired three rounds of musketry. Led by a chief who was beating a drum, the Shawnee, men and women, came up in single file singing songs of their nation. The commissioners, remembering that the Shawnee were an exceedingly proud people, extended them the same honors. Thus the soldiers cooked and served food to the old women of the tribe.[30]

A week later arrived Bohongehelas, one of the most celebrated chiefs of the Delawares. The Americans saluted him in the same manner. As the stately chief sat down, he saw George Rogers Clark. Admiring him as a great warrior, Bohongehelas rose and saluted him. Instead of shaking hands, the two men affectionately gripped each other right-handedly near the shoulders and joined left hands underneath right arms. Then Bohongehelas spoke:

Not as a King, but as a warrior, I Bohongehelas address you. You are the head of a great nation, as I am of mine. To the Great Spirit I give thanks for having preserved us till this day when we have opportunity of speaking together. Three weeks are gone since I assigned the hatchet into the hands of my kings. Since that time I have ceased to war and have now come to this council fire with my chiefs, our women and children, to promote the work of peace. At this council fire I am glad to see you present, because I hope that you will assist your great men, as I will mine, to settle every matter which is to be transacted. Brother, General Clark, again as a warrior I tell you I am glad to see you and thank the spirits above who on this morning have brought us together.[31]

To which the mighty warrior of the Illinois country replied that he was glad to see Bohongehelas and his party and that his own endeavors to promote and complete the good work which had begun would not be wanting.[32]

That evening the Shawnee entertained the small American group with social dances and war dances. One of the social dances especially pleased the Americans. A fairly large group of young men, encircling a fire, moved and danced while they sang love songs. At length a group of girls who had been looking on rose one after another and seized a partner. Clinging to each other, the couples danced and went through a variety of gestures while they exchanged dresses and jewelry as tokens of their regard.

The war dance, performed at the request of the American officers, involved eight or ten of the most vigorous young men. Painting their bodies and faces, they stripped to their breechcloths, armed themselves with tomahawks and knives and danced in a circle to a mournful tune. Then, giving a horrifying war whoop, they all sat down and bowed their heads in silence. Suddenly one of them jumped up and danced and capered madly while he recited his exploits and injuries and exhorted his comrades to be strong and rise and avenge their wrongs. Aroused by this exhibition, they rose one by one and began yelling and jumping and gesticulating in imitation of shooting, scalping and tomahawking. Then at a signal they gave way to a brooding silence. At last one of them brought the ceremony to a close with a brief speech.[33]

These entertainments by no means dispelled the danger which surrounded the commissioners. The Shawnee greatly outnumbered the Americans. When the time came for them to sign a treaty, would they reply with pen or tomahawk? For several days the commissioners discussed the methods which they thought best in dealing with the Shawnee and carefully worked out a bold program. In handling them Butler and Parsons doubtless made use of Clark's superior experience.

The commissioners decided to leave the Shawnee to the last. They gathered the Delawares and Wyandots and explained to them the wishes of the United States. Then they carefully weighed and wrote down the words they wanted to address to the Shawnee. Butler agreed to deliver the speech.

The commissioners next held a private conference with the Shawnee chiefs and explained that they were about to deliver a speech so worded that their young men would understand what harm they had caused their own people. By this policy the commissioners hoped to induce the young warriors to listen to the advice of their chiefs. And the chiefs themselves would be flattered and prepared for the strong language that the commissioners were ready to use in the public council.

On the following day, January 28, Butler called a meeting of the
Shawnee, Wyandots and Delawares at which Telapaxi, the Delaware chief, informed the Shawnee that he had laid down the
hatchet forever and invited them to follow suit. Then Butler began
his address to the Shawnee, recapitulating the numerous times they
had broken their treaties with the United States, the trouble they
had caused American citizens and the distress in which they had
involved their people by their conduct. Then he told them that
they were at the mercy of the United States and demanded a reply.
They promised to give it after they had discussed and considered
what he had said.[34]

Butler gave them three days, then summoned them and explained
to them the new boundary line between themselves and the United
States. It was to begin where the south line of the Treaty of McIntosh crossed the Miami and run down the river to the next fork below Pickawillany, then due west to the west fork of the White
River and then to the Wabash. The commissioners also demanded
that the Shawnee surrender all their white prisoners and, until this
was done, that they leave three hostages. This requirement of hostages surprised and angered them. While they were willing to
secure an advantage by making promises they had no intention of
keeping, they flatly refused to deliver any member of their tribe to
their bitterest enemies. Their fiery orator and war chief, Kehen-
epelithy, rose and said:

Brothers! By what you said to us yesterday we expected everything past would be forgotten; that our proposals for collecting the
prisoners were satisfactory, and that we would have been placed
on the same footing as before the war. Today you demand hostages
till your prisoners are returned! You next say you will divide the
lands! I now tell you it is not the custom of the Shawnees to give
hostages. Our words are to be believed. When we say a thing we
stand to it; we are Shawnees! As to the lands, God gave us this
country! We do not understand measuring out the lands. It is all
ours! You say you have goods for our women and children. You
may keep your goods and give them to other nations. We will have
none of them.

Brothers, you seem to grow proud because you have thrown
down the King of England; and as we feel sorrow for our past
faults, you rise in your demands on us. This we think hard. You
need not doubt our words. What we have promised we will perform. We told you that we have appointed three good men of our

nation to go to the town and collect your flesh and blood. They shall be brought in. We have never given hostages, and we will not comply with this demand![35]

So saying he angrily flung down upon the table a white and a black belt—the white meaning an offer of peace; the black, one of war. The commissioners were to choose which they would have. Unwilling to risk possible massacre by insisting on their demands, the commissioners conferred a short time on their answer. They resolved they would not recede from any of their demands. Butler then addressed the Shawnee:

You have addressed us with great warmth. We think the answer unwise and ungrateful. In return for just and generous proposals, you have not only given us improper language, but asserted the greatest falsehoods. You say you cannot give hostages for performance of your promises, as it is contrary to your usages, and that you never break your word. Have you forgot your breach of treaties in the beginning of the late war with Britain, between the United States and your chiefs in '75 & '76? Do you think us ignorant of these treaties? Do you think we have forgot the burning of our towns, the murder and captivity of our people in consequence of your perfidy? or have you forgot them? Don't you remember, when Col Bou[quet] came to Tuscarawas that you there gave him hostages? Do you forget that you gave hostages to L[d] Dunmore? Do you forget that, when he had agreed to send people to collect the prisoners, that you were like to have been murdered in your towns? Recollect, and you must know that these are treaties [by which] you gave to both these great men hostages. . . .[36]

Butler then told them that their speeches were insincere. And he added that since they had joined the British against the Americans, they must share the fortune of the defeated. The British have "cast you off and give us your country, and Congress, in bounty and mercy, offer you a country and peace. We have told you the terms on which you shall have it." If the Shawnee refused the terms, he said, he would provide them with supplies to depart in peace. No man should touch them for three days, but when that time expired the United States would take the most effective measures to protect American citizens and to distress their enemies. "It rests with you," Butler told them and went on to conclude: "The destruction of your women and children, or their future happiness, depends on your present choice. Peace or war is in your power. Make your choice like men and judge for yourselves."[37]

As he spoke Butler picked up the white Shawnee belt from the table and threw it down. Clark, who was sitting, coolly brushed it off the table with his cane and then, rising, stepped on it, whereupon the council broke up with great commotion. The Indians, conferring angrily among themselves, talked of war and peace in the same breath. Eventually cooler tempers prevailed among them and they requested another meeting with the commissioners. When this was granted, their old king, Molunthy, made a short speech during which he presented a white string to show that he removed all that the war chief had said. And the war chief had no choice but to apologize for his action:

Brothers, you have every thing in your power—you are great, and we see you own all the country; we therefore hope, as you have everything in your power, that you will take pity on our women and children . . . and we agree to all you have proposed, and hope, in future, we shall both enjoy peace, and be secure.[38]

The Shawnee returned home, but they had no intention of keeping their promises. In the strong measures which had forced them to sign the Treaty of Fort Finney they saw justification for repudiating it. They assumed an attitude of proud belligerency which soon transformed into open warfare on their white enemies. In addition frontiersmen accused them of tolerating Mingo and Cherokee raids on a number of white settlements. George Rogers Clark charged them with breaking the treaty and in the fall of 1786 led a thousand men up the Wabash Valley against their villages, but low water, lack of discipline and wholesale desertions forced him to retreat to Vincennes. At about the same time an expedition of Kentuckians under Colonel Benjamin Logan crossed the Ohio to the headwaters of the Mad River, burned seven villages, killed ten chiefs, destroyed much corn and livestock and took a goodly number of prisoners. One of these was Molunthy who, though friendly to the Americans, was shot down while he displayed the Thirteen Stripes and held out a copy of the recent treaty.[39]

This disgraceful incident made the Shawnee all the more determined to deliver their people from white aggression. From that time until the Battle of Tippecanoe twenty-seven years later they were rabid supporters of the confederacy, which rejected the Fort

Stanwix, Fort McIntosh and Fort Finney treaties as false and requested the United States to reopen the boundary line issue. By this time Joseph Brant had returned from England. In the fall of 1786 Logan's invasion prevented the Mohawk chief from trying to assemble the confederacy at Wakatomika to discuss the possibility of a new treaty with the United States. But in December he succeeded in assembling the confederacy at a Huron village near the mouth of the Detroit River. Armed with assurances of British friendship, which he had secured during a visit to England, he was adamant in his insistence of the Ohio as the boundary line between the confederacy and the United States.[40]

Brant's keynote speech at the opening of the great council is one of the strongest and most eloquent ever made in defense of Indian union. Recalling to the assembled tribes the history of the Indian race in America since the coming of the white man, he told them that their continual retreat had resulted from their inability to unite against the common enemy. Before the white man came to America, he said,

. . . we were the Sole Lords of the Soil! . . . the Great Spirit placed us there! and what is the reason why we are not Still in possession of our forefathers birth Rights? You may Safely Say because they wanted that Unanimity which we now So Strongly and Repeatedly recommend to you. . . . Therefore let us . . . be unanimous, let us have a Just sense of our own Value and if after that the Great Spirit wills that other Colours Should Subdue us, let it be so, we then Cannot reproach our Selves for Misconduct. . . . The Interests of Any One Nation Should be the Interests of us all, the Welfare of the one Should be the Welfare of all the others.[41]

To these eloquent exhortations the tribes replied with an address to Congress. It expressed their displeasure at having been ignored in the Treaty of Paris and at the unwillingness of the United States to deal with the united tribes. It asked for a new treaty council and requested Congress to withdraw its surveyors from the Ohio country. It submitted these proposals as reasonable and threatened war if they were rejected.[42]

For obvious reasons Congress played for time. Not until 1788 did it call for the council which the confederacy had requested. Meanwhile, so many whites filled the Ohio country that a reconsideration of terms was futile. By the time Congress agreed to a new council with the Indians the first settlements in the Ohio country were firmly established.

6

In the fall of 1787 Congress decided to open for immediate settlement the four ranges which Hutchins had surveyed. Its first auctions, held in New York City in the fall of 1787, brought few buyers; it realized only $117,108 in depreciated currency—a paltry sum which only made the national debt seem larger. One thing was certain: the land system in operation was a failure. It would have to be revised, and revised quickly, if Congress hoped to meet its financial obligations.

In fact Congress had already made the change. On July 13, 1787, it had unanimously passed the great Northwest Ordinance. This law is linked with the absorbing story of the Ohio Company of Associates, one of the most important land organizations in American history and the one responsible for the first settlement in the Northwest Territory.

In June 1783 while the veterans of the Revolutionary War were in camp waiting for the Treaty of Paris to send them home, two hundred eighty-eight officers petitioned Congress for a land grant in the West. The petition, drawn up by Colonel Timothy Pickering, contained certain provisions of government essential to the required grant. Pickering turned the petition over to his close friend, General Rufus Putnam, who as an experienced surveyor had much knowledge in laying out the western country. Putnam fashioned and elaborated the so-called Newburgh Petition in which he represented the pressing need of populating the Ohio country "to which we are entitled . . . and also for all Officers and Soldiers who wish to take up these lands in this quarter." Putnam forwarded the petition to George Washington, requesting him to lay it before Congress with his recommendation. Though Washington gladly complied with Putnam's request, Congress, engaged with the claims of the various states to the western lands, was in no position to take action.[43]

Undaunted, Putnam persuaded General Benjamin Tupper to join the surveyors of the Seven Ranges to choose a suitable spot for a colony. While assisting the surveyors, Tupper made several exploratory journeys in the surrounding country. As the location for the colony he chose the Muskingum Valley, a fertile region protected by Fort Harmar and adjacent to the Seven Ranges.

Several months later he returned home with such a glowing description of the region that Putnam was enthralled. The two men wasted no time in inserting "A Piece called Information" in the

Massachusetts newspapers asking all Revolutionary War officers and soldiers interested in establishing an association "by the name of the Ohio Company" to send delegates to

... the Bunch of Grapes Tavern in Boston, on Wednesday the first day of March [1786] at ten o'clock A.M. then and there to Consider and determine upon a general Plan of Association for said Company—which plan, covenant or agreement being published, every person (under condition therin to be provided) may by Subscribing his Name, become a Member of the Company.

The eleven delegates who gathered on that day enthusiastically endorsed the project. They formed an organization entitled Ohio Company of Associates, pledged themselves to sell $1,000,000 worth of stock for continental certificates and agreed to settle on the Ohio lands purchased with that sum.[44]

By the end of the year enough shares had been subscribed to justify further proceedings. Another meeting of the Ohio Company, this time at Brackett's Tavern in Boston on March 8, 1787, resulted in the appointment of Putnam, General Samuel Holden Parsons, Dr. Manasseh Cutler and General James Mitchell Varnum as directors. They were requested to apply immediately to Congress "for a private purchase of lands and under such descriptions as they shall deem adequate to the purposes of the Company."[45]

For this particular task the directors chose General Parsons, who in May petitioned Congress for lands on the Scioto, which he preferred to those on the Muskingum; but that body lacked a quorum and could take no action. When Parsons reported his failure to the directors, Putnam, still determined that the proposed colony should be located on the Muskingum, sent Dr. Cutler to make another attempt to close a deal with Congress.[46]

Manasseh Cutler was a courtly and impressive man of forty-four with a ready wit, a gargantuan capacity for food and drink and the gift of driving home the subject of his conversation, whatever it may be, with apt simile and metaphor. His hunger for knowledge, which was as insatiable as his appetite for food, had driven him from profession to profession, in each of which he quickly distinguished himself. As a young graduate of Yale, he read law and was admitted to the Massachusetts bar. Shady prospects in his profession, however, troubled his Puritan conscience, which he expiated by studying theology. Ordained at Ipswich, Massachusetts, he preached there until he entered the Revolutionary War as a chaplain. But while he admonished and exhorted and consoled, he yearned for military glory. It was nearer than he knew. With his baptism of fire he won his spurs, and the colonel of his regiment rewarded him with a fine horse which had just been captured from the British. By now he was sick of bloodshed—or perhaps he wanted to get away while his skin was still whole. He returned to his parish, only to plunge into the study of medicine. Taking his M.D., he brimmed the next several years with attempts to save bodies as well as souls. When this cloyed, he traveled deeper into the realm of science, into astronomy, into meteorology, into botany, winning the friendship of Benjamin Franklin and Benjamin Rush and memberships in the American Academy of Arts and Sciences and in other learned societies. He wrote articles for scientific journals; he classified over three hundred fifty species of plants found in his region; he became the Linnaeus of the New World. He became increasingly famous—and increasingly poor. He was unable to provide his family with the barest necessities. He wrote:

I had suffered exceedingly in y[e] war, and after it was over, by paper money and y[e] high price of articles of living. My salary small and family large, for several years I thought y[e] people had not done me justice, and I meditated leaving them. Purchasing lands in a new country appeared to be y[e] only thing I could do to secure a living to myself, and family in that unsettled state of public affairs.[47]

He had found a new endeavor which, as we shall see, he pursued with his usual enthusiasm and skill.

Armed with letters of introduction to a good many members of Congress, Cutler appeared before that body in New York City early in July 1787. His two weeks' stay was to him a glorious round of dinners. He wrote that at one of these his host, Colonel William Duer, Secretary of the Board of Treasury, served fifteen different kinds of wine, "and after the cloth was removed . . . excellent bottled cider, porter, and several other kinds of strong beer." He won much respect for his appetite and his learning but little support for his scheme. Some of the New England members of Congress frowned on the land company; it would result, they averred, in depriving the region of some of its most enterprising citizens. Massachusetts wanted to turn the tide of emigration northward to her lands in the present state of Maine. So Cutler, more disgusted than discouraged, prepared to return home.[48]

Destiny detained him. As Secretary of the Board of Treasury,

Colonel Duer was in charge of all the land sales for the government. Calling on Cutler, he disclosed that a number of "the principal men of the city"—he carefully refrained from implying that most of these were congressmen—were interested in seeing the Ohio Company secure the grant it sought. They, too, desired to buy shares in western lands but could not because they held positions in the government. They would, however, buy them in secret. Cutler, whose business acumen equaled his alimentary and intellectual endowments, readily understood. Over an "elegant" dinner of oysters "cooked in every possible form" at Stone House Tavern in the nearby village of "Brookline," the two men formed one of the largest speculative companies in American history.[49]

Duer and his friends wanted Cutler to apply to Congress for one and a half million acres for his Ohio Company, which was to be paid in two installments, one when the sale was made and the other when the surveys were completed. At the same time Cutler was to purchase an additional five million acres for Duer and his friends, who were to organize a separate Scioto Company and pay for their land in six installments. In return for this service Duer agreed to advance the Ohio Company the money to meet its first installment and to take in Cutler and one of his associates, Major Winthrop Sargent, as partners in the Scioto Company. Of the Scioto Company's thirty-two shares, Cutler and Sargent were to receive thirteen, or over two million acres, Duer and his friends an equal amount and the remaining six shares were to be sold in France at a profit large enough to enable the company to meet a few installments until such time as it could sell its option to some other speculative company.[50]

Among the "principal men" interested in the Scioto Company were General Arthur St. Clair, president of Congress, who yearned for the governorship of the Northwest Territory as a stepping stone to higher office. Through his influence and that of some of his colleagues, Congress passed the land sale and on July 27 directed the Board of Treasury "to take order and close the contract." Cutler then played his part in the bargain. He recommended St. Clair as governor, General Parsons as one of the three judges and Sargent as secretary, of the Northwest Territory. These three men were duly appointed to office.[51]

All this constituted only a part of Cutler's work. During his negotiations with Congress he warned that it could expect no profitable sales unless it provided the territory with an orderly government, suggestions for which he was prepared to submit.

When Congress balked at his proposals he threatened to break off negotiations and return home. Congress promptly adopted substantially all of his suggestions. Three days later the famous Northwest Ordinance became law.[52]

As the instrument of government for the frontier the Ordinance has won the admiration of many statesmen and scholars. To be regarded as its author was a signal honor, though it is really the composite work of several men. Article 6, which prohibited slavery in the Northwest Territory, was especially esteemed. In 1830 Daniel Webster named Nathan Dane as its author and eulogized him. Robert Y. Hayne and Thomas Hart Benton claimed it for Thomas Jefferson. Dane claimed it for himself. Rufus King, William Grayson and Richard Henry Lee were contenders for the honor. In 1837 an Ohio panegyrist delighted his audience by telling them that the ancient Romans would have ascribed the composition of so blithe a document to the nymph Egeria. One of the best scholars of the Ordinance, Thomas C. Pease, wrote that its "sanctity" would "still prevail beyond all doubt" even though the "devil's advocate" were "allowed to say everything in its disfavor."[53]

The sober truth is that the document is defective in its style as well as in some of its provisions. Its crabbed, inverted phraseology points like a reprimanding finger at its hasty authors. Its obscure clauses have provided ground for innumerable controversies. The political myopia of some of its clauses has caused objective scholars to doubt its wisdom and its sincerity. It permits only a limited number of voters to participate in the choice of government. It invests the territorial governor with absolute veto power even in the second stage of territorial government. It requires property for the suffrage and for holding office. It dismisses American treatment of the Indians with pious platitudes. It shows that the politicians who labored on its passage were not always high-minded and disinterested. With some justifications its critics have argued that its section on the prohibition of slavery was dictated by an unholy wedding of Yankee prejudice with Dixie self-interest which had no intention of allowing slave-grown tobacco in the Northwest Territory to compete with that produced in the Old South.

And yet its virtues far outweigh its vices. Or rather some of its vices may be construed as virtues. With admirable foresight it takes into account the independent, freedom-loving spirit of the frontiersmen. The Scotch-Irish and German immigrants of the older Appalachian Frontier by showing a hatred for any form of despotism had set a precedence for American democratic principles. The Regulators of the back country of North Carolina, the settlers of Henderson's grant in Transylvania and the Wataugans of the lost state of Franklin—all had rebelled against the authoritarian policies of the mother states. Both Virginia and North Carolina had lost control of their frontiersmen by refusing them, among other things, proportional representation and protection from Indian attacks. Even Amberson's squatters in the Ohio country disdained the demands of the government to remove themselves from forbidden lands. In the face of these experiences Congress saw clearly that the frontiersmen would accept nothing less than the same privileges accorded to the thirteen original states. These privileges were embodied in statehood, which the Ordinance promised to every region that should meet its requirements as set forth in three stages of territorial government.

On the other hand, Congress realized that the frontiersmen needed central control. Without strong government they might either drift into an alliance with Great Britain or Spain or, by some act of lawlessness, involve the infant United States in a disastrous war with either or both of these powers. They might, too, slip into possible anarchy and allow their trade outlets to the south and north to fall under the control of Spain or England. Standing as they did on a pivot between the older states to which they were tied by blood and political principles, the frontiersmen apparently could profit more from the great empires to the north and to the south than from the weakling United States.

In this light the Northwest Ordinance is a document of give and take. Though it was hastily delivered, it cannot be said to have been hastily conceived. It was the product of a long evolution going back to the Resolution of October 10, 1780, which promised to form separate states from the western lands, and to Jefferson's abortive Ordinance of 1784. It was, therefore, a compromise of varying points of view, deriving its great strength from practical provisions. "Together with the Ordinance of 1785," wrote Bond, "it made possible the orderly settlement and development of the Northwest Territory, including of course the Ohio country."[54]

The Ordinance erected the "Territory North West of the Ohio" into one temporary district but authorized Congress to divide it eventually into not less than three and no more than five territories. It established three stages of government for each territory in its progress toward statehood. The first stage, during the confusion of establishing the first settlements, was necessarily an arbitrary one under a governor, a secretary and three judges appointed by the President to enforce laws and control the militia. When a territory attained a fair degree of stability, as evidenced by a population of five thousand free white males of voting age, it reached the second stage of government, which permitted it to have a legislature consisting of a House of Representatives elected by the people and a Council of five members elected by Congress on nomination of the territorial House of Representatives. At this stage a territory could also send a delegate to Congress, who could participate in the deliberations of that body but could not vote. Finally, when a territory attained sixty thousand people, a number which the Ordinance considered an established society, it reached the third and final stage of government. It would then frame a constitution and apply for admission to the Union "on an equal footing with the original states in all respects whatever."[55]

The Ordinance granted religious freedom, guaranteed trial by jury and declared that "schools and the means of education shall forever be encouraged." The sixth and last article of the Ordinance declared that the Northwest Territory should forever be free of slavery or involuntary servitude, "otherwise than in the punishment of crimes whereof the party shall have been duly convicted." This article, however, carried a proviso that stamps it as a compromise: "Provided always, that any person escaping into the same, from whom labor or service is lawfully claimed in any one of the original States, such fugitive may be lawfully reclaimed, and conveyed to the person claiming his or her labor or service aforesaid."[56]

With the Northwest Ordinance Cutler struck a "great bargain" with the United States, which immediately took steps to colonize the Ohio country with the "best men" of Connecticut and Massachusetts. The Ordinance determined the character and politics of the Ohio country for a generation.

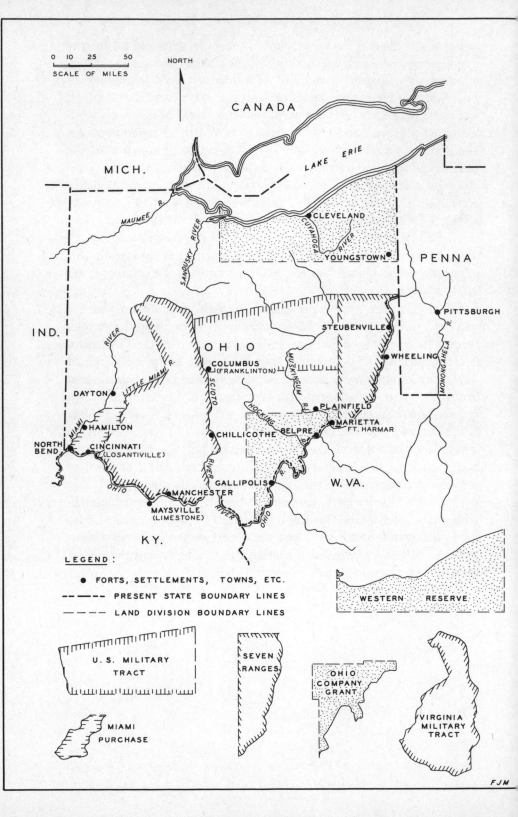

SCALE OF MILES
0 10 25   50

NORTH

CANADA

MICH.

LAKE ERIE

MAUMEE R.

SANDUSKY RIVER

CUYAHOGA RIVER

CLEVELAND

YOUNGSTOWN

PENNA

IND.

MIAMI RIVER

LITTLE MIAMI R.

OHIO

SCIOTO

MUSKINGUM R.

COLUMBUS
(FRANKLINTON)

DAYTON

HAMILTON

NORTH
BEND

CINCINNATI
(LOSANTIVILLE)

OHIO

MANCHESTER

MAYSVILLE
(LIMESTONE)

KY.

CHILLICOTHE

HOCKING

SCIOTO RIVER

BELPRE

GALLIPOLIS

OHIO R.

PLAINFIELD

MARIETTA
FT. HARMAR

STEUBENVILLE

WHEELING

PITTSBURGH

MONONGAHELA R.

W. VA.

LEGEND:

● FORTS, SETTLEMENTS, TOWNS, ETC.
--- PRESENT STATE BOUNDARY LINES
--- LAND DIVISION BOUNDARY LINES

WESTERN   RESERVE

U. S. MILITARY
TRACT

SEVEN
RANGES

OHIO
COMPANY
GRANT

VIRGINIA
MILITARY
TRACT

MIAMI
PURCHASE

FJM

Early Settlements in Ohio

ON THE BRIGHT, COLD MORNING OF DECEMBER 3, 1787, TWENTY men grouped around a covered wagon drawn by oxen marched briskly and confidently westward from Dr. Manasseh Cutler's house in Ipswich, Massachusetts. The large, white letters in his own handwriting on the wagon's black canvas cover announced to the world this remote and perilous destination: FOR THE OHIO COUNTRY. The men were boatbuilders and their assistants who composed one of the two parties that Rufus Putnam, superintendent of the expedition, had hired to assist him in establishing the first permanent settlement west of the Ohio River. Putnam himself was not present. He was in Hartford assembling the other party, which he planned to lead to the Ohio country in person. Earlier in the morning the members of the first party had paraded to Cutler's house and received his blessing with bowed heads. Now, as they departed for Danvers, Massachusetts, their first objective, where Major Haffield White was to assume command, they commemorated the great adventure they were about to undertake by firing three volleys from their rifles.[1]

Between them and the Muskingum Valley lay eight hundred miles of rough roads, unchartered trails, swollen rivers and the hazardous wilderness of the Allegheny Mountains—all of which they must traverse in the bleakest weather. So great were the risks that their wives and children were forbidden to accompany them. Especially dreaded were the possible Indian raids during and at the end of their journey.

Why did Cutler and his associates choose a hilly section of the Ohio country when they knew that the first settlers, being mostly farmers, would prefer a level one? Their reasons were numerous and sound. The Muskingum country was the only one to which the United States had clear title. Connecticut still claimed the Western Reserve, and Virginia still claimed the land lying between the Scioto and the Little Miami rivers. Since the region lying west of the Little Miami was too far from the settled part of the country, Cutler and his associates had no choice but to accept the southern section.[2]

The Muskingum country, too, afforded a number of advantages to prospective settlers. Cutler and his associates learned from surveyors and cartographers that the region abounded in salt and coal. They may have been influenced by the following entry in Christopher Gist's journal:

The land from the Muskingum is rich and broken. Upon the north side of Licking Creek, about six miles from its mouth, were several salt licks, or ponds formed by little streams or drains of water, clear, but of a bluish color, and salt taste: The Traders and Indians boil their meat in this water, which, if proper care is not taken, will make it too salt to eat.[3]

The presence of salt in a region always attracted early settlers. They needed it to preserve their meat and to give taste to their otherwise unsavory diet. In making preparations to move westward the pioneer often had to overcome the difficulty of providing himself with an adequate supply of this vital article. It was very expensive, often costing as much as $20 a bushel, because it could be bought only on the seacoast and had to be transported for a considerable distance. Small wonder that the presence of salt in "Putnam's Paradise," or "Cutler's Indian Heaven," as people skeptical of the venture called the Muskingum Valley, was an added inducement for settlement.[4]

To these reasons the Ohio Company of Associates added several others of no less importance. The Ohio and Muskingum rivers with their limitless supply of fish greatly lessened the need of having to hunt in forests possibly infested with hostile Indians. The Muskingum country, moreover, was closer to New England; it lay on what was then the greatest thoroughfare of western travel; it was protected by Fort Harmar; and it could enlist the support, if needed, of the settlement founded by Isaac Williams on the Virginia side of the Ohio, opposite the mouth of the Muskingum. Finally, Cutler and his associates had accepted Thomas Hutchins' opinion that the Muskingum country was "the best part of the whole of the Western Country."[5]

The advance party made rapid progress to Danvers, from which place Major White led it southward, then southwestward through Pennsylvania over stage coach roads, mountain trails and paths it blazed as it advanced. On January 23, 1788, the little group reached Sumrill's Ferry—now West Newton, Pennsylvania—on the Youghiogheny River, thirty miles southwest of Pittsburgh. There they began to build boats which they hoped to have ready to proceed down the Ohio by the time Putnam arrived with the other party.[6]

Meanwhile, on New Year's Day, the superintendent had assembled four surveyors and twenty-two assistants. At the last minute business at the War Office in New York detained him, but he ordered the party, under Colonel Ebenezer Sprout, to depart for Swatara Creek, between Lebanon and Harrisburg, Pennsylvania, where he promised to join it.

The superintendent had all the qualities necessary to lead the expedition. His whole life had been a gradual triumph over the bitterest discouragement. When he was nine years old, his father died and his mother remarried. His stepfather deprived him of education and substituted hard work. For six years, he recalled, "I was made a ridicule of and otherwise abused for giving my attention to books, and attempting to write and learn arithmetic." Then he was apprenticed to a millwright who proved so abusive that Rufus ran away and sought adventure in the English army. Though he yearned for glory in battle, he found only the old drudgery of the mill. Leaving the army in disgust, he turned to farming and surveying. At the beginning of the American Revolution he was appointed military engineer and, as the conflict progressed, constructed fortifications at West Point, which he suggested as the place for a military academy. At the end of the Revolution he retired with the rank of brigadier general and returned to farming and surveying. Congress appointed him surveyor of the Seven Ranges, but he resigned to survey lands in Maine for his own state of Massachusetts. At his recommendation Tupper was sent to the Ohio country in his stead.[7]

Putnam's salary as superintendent of the enterprise was $40 a month. His expenses were also paid. For this paltry consideration he undertook a task requiring much imagination, patience, fortitude and energy. He drew the plans of a city to be built at the mouth of the Muskingum. It was to have wide streets and public parks and houses for as many as four thousand persons!

To realize this program he enlisted the services of four surveyors and twenty-two assistants, six boatbuilders, four house carpenters, one blacksmith and nine laborers. Each man was required to provide himself with a rifle, a bayonet, six flints, a powder horn and pouch, a half pound of powder, one pound of balls and one pound of buckshot. The salary of each surveyor was $27 a month and that of each laborer was $4 a month and board.[8]

Late in January Putnam joined his party. Finding that the ice on Swatara Creek was too thin to support his wagons, he set his men to cutting an opening in the stream so that it could be forded. While they were so occupied a heavy snowfall blocked the roads and made travel difficult. Eventually they arrived at Cooper's Tavern, near the foot of Tuscarora Mountain, where the deep snow forced them to abandon their wagons and build sleds on which to carry their baggage and tools. The men walked ahead to break a path, and the horses followed, pulling the sleds in single file. Two weeks of such travel brought them to Sumrill's Ferry, where they joined the first party.[9]

Putnam found that the rigorous weather had greatly impeded the boatbuilders in their work, but his invigorating presence and his mechanical skill endowed them with new life. Under the immediate supervision of a seasoned sea captain, Jonathan Devoll, the flotilla was ready by the first day of April. Their chief boat was the *Adventure Galley*, a name which they soon changed to *Mayflower* in memory of those earlier pioneers who had landed nearly one hundred sixty-eight years before on the coast of New England. It was forty-five feet long, twelve feet wide and fifty tons burden. Constructed of heavy timbers and furnished with a deck roof and curved bows, it was typical of the many flatboats which carried emigrants down the Ohio. Another flatboat of three tons burden, the *Adelphia*, meaning "brothers," and three large canoes completed the flotilla.[10]

On April 1 Putnam sent the horses, oxen and wagons overland to Buffalo Creek, on the present site of Wellsburg, West Virginia. Next day he floated with his men down the Youghiogheny to the Monongahela. At Pittsburgh he swung out into the Ohio and arrived on April 5 at Buffalo Creek, where he boarded the horses, oxen and wagons and had his men gather the lumber with which to build huts on their arrival in the Muskingum country. Resuming their journey, they arrived two days later at Kerr's Island. "I think it time to make an observation, we must be near the mouth of the Muskingum," said Captain Devoll to Putnam; but when they neared Fort Harmar they did not see it because of the overcast sky and because the tall sycamores extended their branches over the riverbank. When they discovered their mistake, they were beyond the fort. Its garrison, however, had seen the boats and its commander had immediately dispatched a few mounted soldiers with ropes to tow them back. About noon on April 7 they landed a little distance above the mouth of the Muskingum.[11]

They found about seventy Delawares on hand to welcome them. The Indians had come a few days before with their chief, Captain Pipe, to trade peltries with the garrison at Fort Harmar. The erstwhile bitter enemy of the white men now took the settlers by the hand and assured them that his people would live in peace with them.[12]

How vastly different from New England was this primeval forest! The weather was mild; the trees were in leaf. The pea vines and the buffalo grass, which rose nearly knee-high, afforded rich pasturage for their horses. Around them stretched an endless forest of poplar, sycamore, maple, oak, hickory and elm. One venerable sycamore had a trunk measuring forty-one and a half feet in circumference; six horsemen could ride abreast in it and it could contain eighty-four men! The land was amazingly fertile. That summer one settler was to boast that "the corn had grown nine inches in twenty-four hours, for two or three days past."[13]

Another settler wrote to a friend in Worcester, Massachusetts, that the region

... for fertility of soil and pleasantries of situation, not only exceeds my expectations, but exceeds any part of America, or Europe, I ever was in. The climate is exceedingly healthy; not a man sick since we have been here. We have started twenty buffaloes in a drove. Deer are as plenty as sheep with you. Beaver and otter are abundant. I have known one man to catch twenty or thirty of them in two or three nights. Turkies are innumerable; they come within a few rods of us in the field. We have already planted a field of one hundred and fifty acres of corn.[14]

Bears, panthers, wildcats and wolves were a menace to livestock. Schools of fish made so much noise flapping against the boats that the men could not sleep on board. One settler caught a black catfish that weighed ninety-six pounds; another settler did even better with a pike that was six feet long and weighed almost a hundred pounds![15] For fishermen this was truly Putnam's Paradise and Cutler's Indian Heaven.

As soon as they arrived, these practical settlers of English stock went to work, building temporary huts for shelter and their provisions and a hempen marquee in which Putnam for several months resided and transacted the business of the little colony. While one detachment cleared four acres of land at the junction of the rivers, another surveyed the city lots. Then they plowed the ground, shaped commons or public squares, built cabins and laid out the streets, which were ninety feet wide, lined with elms, and ran with the course of the river. Some of the settlers called the town Muskingum, others preferred Adelphia; but on July 2, when the directors and agents held their first meeting, they agreed on Marietta, a contraction of the words Marie Antoinette, Queen of France, whose country had aided the Americans in their fight for independence. Showing veneration for their classical training they bestowed Roman names on their squares and streets: Campus Martius was the public square on which the local stockade was to be built; another important square, Quadranaou, connected with the Via Sacra, a broad, graded road running to the Muskingum; and the Capitolium and Cecelia were smaller squares from which emanated important avenues.[16]

At their first meeting the officials adopted a number of regulations known as the Marietta Code, which served for the welfare of the community until Governor Arthur St. Clair and the territorial judges issued a more legally constituted code. The Marietta Code provided for a board of police, created city lots for the use of the directors and the officers at Fort Harmar and planned a stockade on Campus Martius.[17]

The celebration of Independence Day opened at dawn with a federal salute of thirteen guns from Fort Harmar. The settlers, gathering merrily, read the Marietta Code, which was clearly written in longhand and posted on the smooth bark of a huge beech tree. Then they collected under a bowery that stretched along the Muskingum and sat down to a sumptuous dinner of fish, venison, bear meat, buffalo and roast pig. Especially delicious was the fish, which included a pike so large that when two tall men lifted it by a pole to their shoulders, its tail dragged on the ground. Fishing from a canoe around the mouth of the Muskingum, Captain Devoll and his son Gilbert had worn down the pike after a long chase and had caught it with a gig.[18]

Among the guests was Judge James Mitchell Varnum, who a month earlier had come down with forty persons from his native Rhode Island. Though gravely ill with tuberculosis he had worked indefatigably with St. Clair on the laws of the territory and had written a speech for the Independence Day celebration. This abounded in the involved rhetoric and sentimental apostrophes fashionable in that romantic age. Anticipating St. Clair's arrival, Varnum exclaimed:

We mutually lament that the absence of his excellency will not permit us, upon this joyous occasion, to make those grateful assurances of sincere attachments, which bind us to him by the noblest motives that can animate an enlightened people. May he soon arrive. Thou gentle flowing Ohio, whose surface, as conscious of thy unequaled majesty, reflecteth no images but the grandeur of the impending haven, bear him, oh, bear him safely to this anxious spot! And thou beautifully transparent Muskingum, swell at the moment of his approach, and reflect no objects but of pleasure and delight!

Judge Varnum then turned his florid cadences upon his "fair auditors":

We are happy . . . in expressing our admiring attachments to those elevated sentiments which inspired you with the heroic resolution of attempting the rude passage of nature's seeming barrier, to explore, in the rugged conditions of the field, the paradise of America. Gentle zephyrs, and fanning breezes, wafting through the air ambrosial odors, receive you here. Hope no longer flutters upon the wings of uncertainty. Your present satisfaction, increasing by the fairest prospects, will terminate in the completion of all your wishes.

Amiable in yourselves, amiable in your tender connections, you will soon add to the felicity of others, who, emulous of following your bright example, and having formed their manners upon the elegance of simplicity, and the refinements of virtue, will be happy in living with you in the bosom of friendship.[19]

The celebrants drank fourteen toasts including the United States, Congress, "the new Federal Constitution," Captain Pipe, "patriots and heroes" and the "amiable partners of our delicate pleasures." The celebration closed with a beautiful illumination of Fort Harmar.[20]

Eleven days later Marietta held an even more significant celebration. Governor Arthur St. Clair, escorted by a detachment of troops from Fort Harmar, crossed the Muskingum in a twelve-oared barge. Three days later Putnam, the three territorial judges and the citizens greeted him at the bowery "with the most sincere

and unreserved congratulations." The governor, a gouty gentleman
of fifty-four years, bowed stiffly and thanked his audience with a
few formal words, whereupon Winthrop Sargent, Secretary of the
Northwest Territory, read the Ordinance and the commissions of
the governor and of the officers. The governor then delivered an
address in which he instituted territorial government. Though
stilted and pompous, the speech glowed with a sincere eloquence
evoked by the place and purpose of the meeting. In the course of
his speech he said:

The subduing a new country, notwithstanding its natural advantages, is alone an arduous task; a task, however, that patience and
perseverance will at last surmount, and these virtues, so necessary
in every situation, but peculiarly to yours, you must resolve to exercise. Neither is reducing a country from a state of nature to a state
of civilization irksome as it may appear from a slight or superficial
view; even very sensible pleasures attend it; the gradual progress of
improvement fills the mind with delectable ideas; vast forest converted into arable fields, and cities rising from places which were
largely the habitations of wild beasts, give a pleasure something like
the attendant of creation. If we can form an idea of it, the imagination is ravished, and a task communicated of even the "joy of God
to see a happy world."[21]

During the speech, says an emotional contemporary writer, "a
profound veneration for the elevated station and exalted benevolence of the speaker . . . called forth all the manly emotions of the
human heart!" When he was finished, "peals of applause rent the
surrounding air, while joyful echo reverberated the sound." To
shouts of "Long live the Governor!" the townsfolk dispersed to
begin life under the protection of the United States.[22]

Eight days later St. Clair issued a proclamation creating Washington County. It was the first county in Ohio and had an area
comprising more than the eastern half of the present state. In the
following month Marietta became the county seat.[23]

To these typical New Englanders school and church were first
and foremost. Their first minister was Dr. Daniel Breck, chaplain
of the Ohio Company. On July 20, 1788, he preached to an audience of about three hundred persons composed of citizens, families
from the Virginia side of the Ohio and soldiers from the garrison
at Fort Harmar. As his text he took Exodus 19:5-6: "Now, therefore, if you will obey my voice indeed, and keep my covenant, then
ye shall be a peculiar treasure unto me above all people; for all the

earth is mine. And ye shall be unto me a kingdom of priests, and an holy nation." St. Clair was pleased with the sermon, for it was appropriate to a people just beginning to lay the foundation of a society in the wilderness. But he was particularly pleased with the singing which, says a contemporary writer,

. . . far exceeded any thing of the kind he had ever heard. Indeed it was enchanting! The grave, the solemn, the tender, and the pathetic were so happily blended, as to produce a most perfect harmony, and to melt the soul in sympathetic effusion of gratitude and adoration to the great Author of our religion, and had listening angels tuned their harps, they would have paused for a moment at the melodious sound.[24]

Despite this auspicious beginning Dr. Breck, for reasons known only to himself, did not stay in Marietta. After his departure on August 18 for his home in Massachusetts the Ohio Company passed a resolution to employ an instructor "eminent for literary accomplishments" and for the "virtue of his character" to teach the youth and to promote public worship among religiously indifferent settlers. The post went to the Reverend Daniel Story, who arrived in Marietta from his native Massachusetts in the spring of 1789. Story continued to preach on Campus Martius and in the blockhouse at the stockade until the close of the Indian War. Later he occasionally risked his scalp by venturing in a canoe down the river to preach in neighboring settlements.[25]

On the day after Dr. Breck's departure Marietta welcomed Manasseh Cutler. He had traveled with gay companions overland through Pennsylvania and then down the Ohio in a big flatboat which had on board forty-eight other persons. He was as awed with what he saw as is a tourist in an exotic land. He hiked up the Muskingum with General Putnam, expressing his astonishment at the broad cornfields, the giant trees, the ubiquitous deer and the oversized "clam cohog [quahaug] shells." He had "a genteel dinner" with St. Clair at Fort Harmar, where he was delighted with the grapevines, the flower garden and Mrs. Harmar's good looks. He graced every social affair with wit and knowledge, preached three rousing sermons at Campus Martius, munched apples as he sauntered in the forest and visited several groups of friendly Indians. One day he and Putnam killed a large rattlesnake and got a severe dousing during a shower. So enthralled was he with the country that he stayed for three weeks, enjoying countless dinners, punch and wine and—Mrs. Harmar's good looks.[26]

On September 2 he witnessed the formal opening of the first court in the Northwest Territory. "With all the dignity and impressiveness of his prototype the sheriff of Middlesex at a Harvard commencement," Ebenezer Sprout, sheriff, led the parade of citizens, which now numbered one hundred thirty, past the governor, the territorial officers and the militia to Campus Martius while Indians of the neighborhood watched with mingled curiosity and awe. Dr. Cutler offered a prayer before Sprout read the commissions of the judges and of the officers. Then the sheriff shouted the usual proclamation for the occasion: "Oyez! A court is opened for the administration of even-handed justice to the poor and the rich, to the guilty and the innocent, without respect of persons; none to be punished without trial by their peers, and in pursuance of the law and evidence in the case."[27]

A week later Dr. Cutler left Marietta. Taking a lengthy adieu of his friends and kissing Mrs. Harmar's hands again and again, he boarded Francesco Vigo's comfortable flatboat, which bore him homeward. During the journey upstream, he and his companions caught a huge catfish and shot pigeons and squirrels, plucked bunches of grapes along the riverside and feasted like kings. In the middle of September he reached Ipswich, exuding pride for his handiwork on the remote Muskingum and regaling his friends with tales of his fishing prowess.[28]

In the remaining months of 1788 the little settlement progressed rapidly. Putnam wrote that "upwards of seven thousand have gone down [the Ohio] since we began our settlement" and that "we are continually erecting houses, but arrivals are faster than we can possibly provide Convenient Covering." Grateful for "Benefits received, & to implore [God's] superintending Care & Providence for future Blessings," the townsfolk coaxed St. Clair to institute a New England ideal by setting aside Thursday, November 25, 1788, as "a day of solemn Thanksgiving & Praise." The decree ordained

... that the People may with one Voice & sincere Hearts express their grateful Sensations, & consecrate themselves to the Will & Pleasure of their divine Benefactor   And, that together with their Acknowledgments, they may unite in humble Supplications to Almighty God, that he would be graciously pleased to prosper this Infant Settlement, & the whole Territory, in their Husbandry, Trade, & Manufactures, and by his own nurturing Hand, mature & bring to Perfection all Seminaries of Learning, & the Promotion & Enlargement of Piety & true Religion amongst all the Nations of the Earth.

And I do prohibit all Servile Labour on that Day.[29]

But the new year brought only sorrow and suffering. On January 11, 1789, Marietta was saddened by the death of Judge Varnum. Later in the month a boat on its way to Kentucky put on shore a man sick with smallpox. He infected his nurse, who in turn infected her husband; she proved hardier than the two men and recovered. Soon much of the town was down with the disease. The healthy settlers hastily built a hospital where they confined the sick and where two doctors inoculated the others. This expedient stopped the spread of the disease, though six old women died from the shock of the needle.[30]

Scarcely had the town recovered from the epidemic than it experienced a famine. In October a heavy frost scared the corn as it stood in its "milk" or succulent stage. It was quickly cribbed and stored with the intention of converting it into bread when it became fairly dried. But the corn spoiled; it sickened animals and people with symptoms similar to those produced by "fungus grain" or sick wheat. The price of corn rose from 50¢ to $1.50 and $2 a bushel. The poorest corn sold for $1 a bushel.[31]

By the middle of May 1790 Marietta faced starvation. The scarcity of cows and hogs and the absence of sheep intensified the general misery. The forest, which in the previous year had teemed with game, was now as empty as an old settled country. In their efforts to discourage the settlers, hostile Indians had driven away nearly all the deer within twenty miles of Marietta. The settlers had no kettles in which to boil maple sap, which would have provided a valuable food in the general scarcity.[32]

In these adverse circumstances the frontiersmen showed their sterling qualities. Those who had food and clothing to spare shared them with the needy. Occasionally hunters brought in a turkey or a piece of bear meat which the settlers boiled up with hominy or coarse meal. The river furnished them with a variety of fish and the pigeonberry offered its tender shoots, which they boiled with a little flour. They searched every field for nettle tops and potato tops; they plucked every spicebush of its berries; they dug for sassafras roots, which provided them with drink in place of tea or coffee. The Ohio Company assisted poor families with small loans, and emigrants on their way to Kentucky sometimes left them small quantities of grain. In this manner Marietta struggled along until summer came to its rescue with a bumper crop of the vegetables and grain planted in the previous spring.[33]

Despite the famine the town grew steadily. During the year one hundred fifty-one men arrived, about a third of whom brought their families. By this time settlement had spread westward as well as northward along the Ohio. Acting on the reports of exploring parties, forty men journeyed from Marietta to the rich bottom lands south of the town and founded Belpre. Another Marietta group of thirty-nine men laid out, on the fertile lands up the Muskingum, the town of Plainfield, a name changed later to Waterford, where, near the mouth of Wolf Creek, Major Haffield White with two companions built a dam, a sawmill and a gristmill that furnished Marietta with most of its flour. Further extension from Marietta stopped when the Indians, aroused by the Treaty of Fort Harmar and by the advance of the frontiersmen, threatened to wipe out the settlements beyond the protection of Fort Harmar. Early in January 1791 the Wyandots and Delawares made good their threat. Striking at Big Bottom, thirty miles north of Marietta, they killed several settlers and set fire to many cabins. Alarmed by news of this attack, all Plainfield gathered in Fort Frye, a triangular palisade with the usual blockhouses at each angle. The fort defended itself successfully with the loss of only a few cattle.[34]

Imitating the example of Plainfield, the settlers living along the riverbank at Belpre quickly built thirteen cabins, six in one row and seven in another, which they enclosed with a formidable palisade. Here in Farmers' Castle, as they called the place, they lived for several years, plowing their fields, which were several miles away, and amusing themselves with dances, ball games, foot races, wrestling and leaping contests. Sometimes young couples from Marietta would come down with Vansan (or Vincent), a French violinist from Gallipolis, and dance with them all night long in the wide street between the two rows of cabins. Sometimes, "in the pleasant moonlit evenings of summer," the unmarried girls of the Castle, numbering about twenty, would steal into a canoe, push silently up the Ohio and risk the possibility of being kidnaped or killed by tomahawk to serenade the young men who happened to be serving as sentinels on the towers.[35]

So the settlements of the Ohio Company progressed and prospered, thanks to its careful plans and its strict adherence to the Northwest Ordinance. Some of its leaders, too, were men of education, who, adhering to the traditions of their forefathers, insisted on recognition of cultural values. Washington extolled their fine qualities and regretted that old age prevented his joining them. Perhaps Thomas Carlyle had them in mind when he wrote the following in a letter to his friend, Ralph Waldo Emerson:

How beautiful to think of lean, tough Yankee settlers, tough as gutta-percha, with most occult, unsubduable fire in their belly, steering over the Western mountains, to annihilate the jungle, and bring bacon and corn out of it for the posterity of Adam. The pigs in about a year eat up all the rattlesnakes for miles around; a most judicious function on the part of the pigs. Behind comes Jonathan with his all-conquering plowshare—glory to him, too![36]

2

The next area of settlement lay between the two Miamis in present southwestern Ohio. This was known as the Miami Purchase. Its sole agent and guiding spirit was John Cleves Symmes, an associate judge of the Supreme Court of New Jersey and a member of the Continental Congress, which provided him not only with the impetus to establish a colony in the Ohio country but also with the political influence and friendship he needed to realize his plans.

But he derived his main urge from another source—the glowing reports given him by one Benjamin Stites.

Benjamin Stites was a Revolutionary War veteran who migrated from his native Short Hills, near Morristown, New Jersey, to Redstone Old Fort, at the present site of Brownsville, Pennsylvania, where he set up as a merchant. In the spring of 1786 he loaded a flatboat with flour and whisky and descended the Ohio to sell these articles at Limestone, now Maysville, Kentucky. Thence he proceeded a few miles westward to the settlement of Washington, where he found its inhabitants in an uproar because Indians had stolen some of their horses. Stites forthwith helped to organize a posse and rode with it across the Ohio and up the valley of the Little Miami for about sixty miles to the villages of the horse thieves, whom, however, they found too strong to attack. Turning westward from the futile chase, the posse crossed a plateau which took them to the Great Miami, whence they returned to the Ohio and home.[37]

By this time Stites had lost all thought of the stolen horses and even of his trade. Instead he thrilled at the rich, rolling country he had just seen: what an ideal spot for a colony! Fascinated by his brain child, which grew more attractive with age, and hoping to interest somebody of sufficient wealth and influence to undertake a settlement on his newly discovered paradise, he hastened to New York, where Congress was in session. Soon he met Judge Symmes, who quickly succumbed to his rapturous appeal. Himself a bubbling optimist and a weaver of roseate dreams, Symmes envisioned a teeming and prosperous colony over which he would rule like a maharajah. He resolved to see the Miami country with his own eyes. Accordingly, in the following spring he descended the Ohio as far as Louisville and then ascended the Wabash, where, above Vincennes, he decided to plant the colony. To attract Kentuckians to his plans he addressed them a preliminary circular in which he gave these instructions:

With a considerable detachment of citizens from New Jersey and other parts of the United States when it will be expected that all those who intend to honor [me] with their company into the federal country will rendezvous at Louisville with such supplies as provisions, arms, ammunition, and implements of husbandry and tools for mechanism as they may have it in their power to provide.[38]

He promised to provide artillery and military stores for their protection and suggested that they leave their children and wives in Vincennes "until a lodgement be effected and a town fortified at the first eligible tract of country above that place."[39]

But the flighty judge soon saw the folly of establishing a colony in a country which was as remote from transportation as it was replete with hostile Indians. Instead, he wisely chose the region between the two Miamis, which was the only ungranted region remaining north of the Ohio and which promised rich agricultural reward to patient industry. To the north it commanded the most accessible route to Lake Erie and Detroit. To the south the Licking River led easily to the rich Blue Grass region of Kentucky. To the east and west the Ohio opened a broad avenue of commerce.[40]

Once he had decided on this site, Symmes eagerly made plans for actual settlement. Returning to the East, he organized the Miami Land Company, which counted twenty-four members including Stites, Elias Boudinot and Jonathan Dayton. Then he opened negotiations with the Board of Treasury for the purchase of two million acres between the Miamis. Before the Board of Treasury had tentatively agreed to the grant, Symmes in November 1787 issued his Trenton circular in which he extolled the beauty and fertility of the land he hoped to purchase and stated the terms on which it could be bought. Even more roseate was the advertisement he printed in two influential New Jersey newspapers. The Miami country, he wrote, was the best of the Federal lands:

Horses, cattle and hogs can live well in the woods, where there is abundance of food through the winter, which are very moderate: Every kind of grain and vegetable raised in the middle states grows here, with the addition of cotton and indigo, which may be raised in sufficient quantities for family use. The land is generally free from stone and a rich, easy soil for tillage. There are no mountains and few hills, so that the country for the most part is level! It is extremely well watered throughout, and surrounded on three sides by rivers navigable in the boating seasons: Vessels may be built here of two hundred ton burden, and being fully freighted may be navigated with safety to New York, or any other sea-port. The finest timber of every kind known in the middle states, with many other sorts of more southerly production, grow in plenty here, but there is very little underwood or brush. Millstones and grindstones are found in some of the hills. Wild game and fish may be taken in abundance. Salt is now made to any quantity, in Kentucke, opposite this tract on the south-east side of the Ohio, where seven counties are already considerably settled and where any number of meat-cattle may be had very cheap.[41]

The timeliness and mood of this description brought an enthusiastic response. Scores of veterans, paid for their services in currency that commanded only a small portion of its face value, eagerly sought western lands as the only stable commodity. In six months Symmes had collected and turned over to the Board of the Treasury more than $83,000 in military bounties and Continental certificates. Having by now reduced his grant to half of the original number of acres, Symmes felt the sum sufficed and issued a notice to that effect. Then, on July 1, he set out from his home in Morristown for his new colony. In the previous February Congress had enhanced his position as a colonizer by appointing him a judge of the Northwest Territory.[42]

His party consisted of some sixty persons including members of his own family. In the entourage were six heavy wagons, a stage-coach, a "chair" cart, thirty-one horses, three carpenters and a stonemason. The journey over narrow Pennsylvania trails upset Judge Symmes's usual good humor. In a letter to Jonathan Dayton he complained that he had "broken seven axel-trees on the road, had much rain, the roads bad, and my people a little ungovernable." At times he was obliged to be "a little austere." His daughter Mary, nicknamed Polly, perturbed him by succumbing to such "passions" as hope, fear, sorrow and joy. "Bad roads and sometimes good company," he thought, "has made her tour a mere comic-tragedy." On August 20 they arrived in Pittsburgh, where the people received them with "great hospitality." Polly found the ladies of the town "extremely polite & agreeable," and regretted that she had to leave them so soon.[43]

From Pittsburgh they all proceeded to Wheeling, where they took boats for Limestone. After stopping with the Harmars for a few days they resumed their journey and reached their destination on the last day of August. Judge Symmes still dwelled on the difficulties he had encountered in Pennsylvania. He regretted he had not used his oxen which, he said, "are cheaper by one-half in the first purchase, not so much exposed to accidents—the Indians have never disturbed them in any instance and after long service they are still of their original value."[44]

At Limestone, where he secured "a tolerable house" for his family, Symmes met Matthais Denman, a Revolutionary War veteran from New Jersey; Colonel Robert Patterson, one of the founders of Lexington, Kentucky; and John Filson, a surveyor and schoolmaster from near Brandywine, Pennsylvania. In 1783 Filson had migrated to Kentucky and in the following year published a pamphlet, *The Discovery, Settlement, and Present State of Kentucky*, whose vivid descriptions of the Blue Grass region attracted many settlers there. To these men Symmes sold eight hundred acres opposite the Licking and persuaded them to assemble a party of Kentuckians to help him explore the Miami Purchase. On September 22, 1788, Symmes and Israel Ludlow, chief surveyor of the Miami Company, floated down the Ohio to about the site of present Cincinnati, where they met Denman, Patterson and Filson, who had come by land with about fifty Kentuckians. After helping Ludlow survey along the riverbank, Symmes with the Kentuckians rode into the interior for about forty miles and arrived near a Shawnee encampment, where they dismounted to pick plums. Spying the encampment, the Kentuckians immediately wanted to attack it, but Symmes, anxious to preserve peace, forbade such a foolhardy act. Whereupon about half of the Kentuckians, including Filson, deserted him and turned homeward. Three hours later Filson, wandering in the woods, met death, probably at the hands of a single Indian. The poet of the Miami country, W. H. Venable, immortalized Filson in prophetic quatrains as a martyr of American progress:

> By lurking foes his steps are dogged,
> A yell his ear appalls!
> A ghastly corpse upon the ground,
> A murdered man he falls.

> The Indian, with instinctive hate,
> In him a herald saw

Of coming hosts of pioneers,
The friends of light and law;

In him beheld the champion
Of industries and arts,
The founder of encroaching roads
And great commercial marts;

The spoiler of the hunting-ground,
The plower of the sod,
The builder of the Christian school
And of the house of God.

. . .

John Filson had no sepulchre,
Except the wildwood dim;
The mournful voices of the air
Made requiem for him.[45]

Symmes soon returned to Limestone and made no immediate attempt to establish a colony on the land he had purchased. Unwilling to establish a settlement in the wilderness without military protection, which neither Harmar nor St. Clair could provide for the present, he occupied himself in making his family more comfortable in their new home.[46]

No such apprehension deterred Benjamin Stites, who in the summer had landed at Limestone with a number of Pennsylvanians and was ready to take possession of the land he had bought from Judge Symmes. Heedless of the floating ice on the Ohio, on November 16 he drifted down that river with twenty-six persons including four women and two small boys. A little after sunrise on November 18 they approached the mouth of the Little Miami at the present suburb of Columbia in the city of Cincinnati. Stites sent his brother Hezekiah and two friends in a canoe to the shore to ascertain whether Indians were encamped there. By landing they signified that all was well. The settlers then landed their flatboats and climbed a steep bank to a pawpaw thicket, which they cleared of its underbrush so that the women and children could sit down. Posting sentinels around the thicket, the settlers sang a song of praise to God and, kneeling, gave thanks for past and prayer for future protection. While a few of the men stood guard, the remaining began to build a small blockhouse near the riverbank. Made of round logs, each about the size of a man's body, it gave them adequate protection until Stites built three more blockhouses near it and then enclosed all of them with a stockade that gave them the appearance of a square fort. Then Stites set his followers to building log cabins whose doors and floors were made from the planks of the dismantled flatboats.[47]

The Indians, who were then gathering at Fort Harmar to negotiate a treaty with St. Clair, let the settlers alone. But during the winter the little group suffered from lack of provisions. Wild game and fish they had in abundance, but they soon used up their salt and flour. In this extremity they relied on roots, especially bear grass, which they found covering Turkey Bottom and which they boiled, washed and dried on smooth boards and then pounded into a kind of all-service flour. So they pulled through to the more promising days of March, when the thaw permitted the men to plow the fertile bottoms of the Little Miami and plant their first corn and vegetables. Elijah Stites, brother of Benjamin and Hezekiah, grew enough corn to feed the entire settlement for a year.

The settlers called their village Columbia, more in poetic homage to the Union than in honor of the discoverer of America. By 1790 it was a thriving little community boasting fifty cabins, a gristmill and a subscription school which seems to have specialized in English and classical languages and literatures. And the grateful settlers remembered God. In March 1790 Elder Stephen Gano visited relatives in Columbia and there organized the first Baptist church in the region. Stites, who belonged to that denomination, happily donated both lot and building. Judge Symmes sent a sergeant with six men to protect the village, which continued to grow until it eventually became a part of neighboring Cincinnati.[48]

The second settlement in the Miami Purchase began life on December 28, 1788, when at least twenty-three men under Colonel Robert Patterson landed opposite the mouth of the Licking. In the party were Patterson's partners, Matthais Denman and Israel Ludlow, who had acquired Filson's share in their eight hundred-acre tract. The settlers clambered up an embankment to a wooded terrace, where they built rude huts from the boards of the flatboats they had dismantled. Surveyor Ludlow ran his line among the trees to lay out streets and lots for the new settlement. They called it Losantiville, a name which Filson in a pedantic moment had concocted from the initial letter of the word Licking, the Latin word *os* for mouth, the Latin word *anti* for opposite, and the French word *ville* for town. When read backward the word means the town opposite the mouth of the Licking.[49]

Encouraged by the successful settlement of Losantiville, by the arrival in Limestone of forty-eight soldiers under Captain Kearsey, who had been sent to protect the new settlements, and by letters from Stites informing him of the frequent visits of Indians to the blockhouse in Columbia and of their great desire to see him, Judge Symmes decided to go to his grant without delay. Before he departed down the Ohio, he despatched a letter of friendship to his new Indian neighbors:

Brothers of the Wyandot and Shawnee! Hearken to your brother, who is coming to live at the Great Miami. He was on the Great Miami last summer, while the Deer was yet red, and met with one of your camps; he did no harm to anything which you had in your camp; he held back his young men from hurting you or your horses, and would not let them take your skins or meat, though your brothers were very hungry. All this he did, because he was your brother, and would live in peace with the Red people. If the Red people will live in friendship with him, and his young men who come from the great Salt ocean, to plant corn and build Cabins on the land between the Great and Little Miami, then the White and Red people shall all be brothers and live together, and we will buy your Furs and Skins, and sell you Blankets and Rifles, and Powder and Lead and Rum, and everything that our Red Brothers may want in hunting and in their towns. . . .

Brothers! I send you a string of white beads, and write to you with my own hand, that you may believe what I say. I am your brother, and will be kind to you while you remain in peace. Farewell![50]

Late in January 1789 a rise in the river cleared it of ice and permitted Symmes to float down the Ohio with his family and his furniture and the soldiers under Captain Kearsey. His intention was to establish a colony on the site of Fort Finney, but he gave this up when he found all of Columbia under water except one house which stood on high ground. The soldiers had been driven from the ground floor of one of the blockhouses to the loft and from the loft to the only boat that the ice had spared. Symmes spent the night at Columbia, then pulled up at Losantiville, where the water had begun to ebb, though it had not damaged the village. At three o'clock on the afternoon of February 2 he landed in the most northerly bend of the Ohio between the Muskingum and the Mississippi and fittingly called it North Bend. His description of his first home there presents a vivid picture of the hardships he and his family endured during the rest of the winter:

. . . we raised what in this country is called a camp, by setting two forks of saplins in the ground, a ridge-pole across, and leaning boat-boards which I had brought from Limestone, one end on the ground and the other against the ridge-pole: encloseing one end of the camp, and leaving the other open to the weather for a door where our fire was made to fence against the cold which was now very intense. In this point I lived six weeks before I was able to erect myself a log-house & cover it so as to get into the same with my family and property.[51]

Meanwhile Captain Kearsey, displeased because Symmes had established his colony at North Bend instead of at Fort Finney and because he had no tools to build another fort, had departed with all but five of his men for the Falls at Louisville. Fortunately for Symmes the Indians had accepted his message of peace. Once a chief visited him and asked him whether the Thirteen Fires had sent him. Answering in the affirmative, Symmes displayed the Stars and Stripes and, pointing to Kearsey's parading soldiers, informed the chief that they were warriors whom the Thirteen Fires kept in readiness to avenge wrongdoing. The United States, he added, desired peace but was ready to punish any aggressor. By way of demonstrating what he meant, he showed the chief the seal of his commission, which bore the American eagle. He explained that the branch of a tree it held in one of its claws was an emblem of peace and that the sheaf of arrows it held in the other denoted its power.

The chief studied the device, then replied through his interpreter that the eagle, if peacefully inclined, should be represented with its wings folded as in rest, not with its wings spread as in flight. Fur-thermore, asked the chief, how can a tree be considered an emblem of peace? Are not rods, which are made from the boughs of trees, used to correct or punish? The chief insisted that the American eagle, with its large whip in one claw and its sheaf of arrows in the other, intended only war and mischief. But Judge Symmes suc-ceeded in convincing the chief he was wrong—by what persuasion or argument he does not say.[52]

The peaceful attitude of the Indians encouraged a large number of settlers to make their homes in North Bend. By the middle of May they had taken up twenty-four donation lots which extended for a mile and a half along the Ohio. Each of the donation lots had a comfortable log cabin covered with shingles or clapboards. Judge Symmes was so elated with his success that he soon laid off another settlement, South Bend, which was located several miles up the river. Later he established a third settlement, Sugar Camp, below North Bend.[53]

Of the first three settlements in the Miami Purchase the most important was Losantiville. Its accessibility assured it a growing trade. To the north spread the Miami Valley with its ancient trail leading to the Maumee; to the south the Licking flowed through the rich Blue Grass region of Kentucky. The ground on which Losantiville stood rose from the Ohio in two terraces covered with oak and hickory and black walnut. The upper terrace, being about ninety feet above the level of the Ohio and therefore beyond flood reach, afforded an admirable spot for a fort. General Harmar saw the necessity of building a stronghold to protect the settlements in the Miami Purchase and in August 1789 sent an expedition to choose a site for it. The leader of the expedition, Major John Doughty, who had laid out Fort Harmar in 1785-1786, followed seventy men under Captain Strong to the Miami where, after three days' reconnoitering, he settled on the upper terrace as the best place for the proposed fort. In the words of Harmar, it was designed to be "the most solid and substantial" stronghold on the frontier. A high stockade and a massive gate joined four blockhouses two stories tall, extensive barracks and other buildings—all of huge hewn logs perhaps twenty feet long. Later the fort was painted red, perhaps to impress its invincibility more firmly on the savage mind. "On account of its superior excellence," wrote Harmar to General Henry Knox, "I have thought proper to honor it with the name of Washington."[54]

Late in December the general made Fort Washington his new headquarters. Four days later Governor St. Clair arrived at Losantiville in a flatboat. Soldiers and citizens greeted him at the landing and escorted him to Fort Washington where he was saluted with fourteen guns.

Legend says that when the gouty governor arrived in the village he asked, "What in the hell is the name of this town, anyhow?"

"Losantiville, sir."

"Losantiville? What an awful name? God damn it, change it to Cincinnati!"[55]

A more widely accepted version of the incident is that reported by the pioneer writer, Judge Foster, who states that St. Clair learned the name of the village from Israel Ludlow, who greeted him at the landing.

The governor frowned at the fanciful name. "Give me," he exclaimed, "a name I can read and write!"

"Will you," asked the surveyor, "please to name it?"

"Let it be Cincinnati," replied St. Clair. This name was in honor of the Society of Cincinnati, which officers of the American Revolution had founded in 1783 and of which St. Clair was an honored and influential member. The Society took its name from Cincinnatus, the Roman patriot who left his plow to take up arms in defense of his country. At a banquet given in his honor two days after his arrival, St. Clair announced to the assembled citizens and officers that thenceforth Losantiville would be called Cincinnati.[56]

Judge Symmes, who took credit for suggesting the new name, confessed that he was confused over its gender. He wrote to his friend and agent, Jonathan Dayton:

Having mentioned Cincinnata, I beg, sir, you will enquire of the literati in Jersey whether Cincinnata or Cincinnati be most proper? The design I had in giving that name to the place was in honor of the order of the Cincinnati, & to denote the chief place of their residence—and as far as my little acquaintance with cases and genders extends, I think the name of a town should terminate in the feminine gender, where it is not perfectly neuter. Cincinnati is the title of the order of knighthood, and cannot, I think, be the place where the knights of the order dwell. I have frequent combats in this country on the subject, because most men spell the place with *ti* when I always do with *ta*. Please to set me right if I am wrong. You have your Witherspoons and Smiths, and indeed abound in characters in whose decision I shall fully acquiesce.[57]

Governor St. Clair stayed in Cincinnati only one week. Before departing on January 5, 1790, for Fort Vincennes he established a new county which at the suggestion of Judge Symmes he called Hamilton in honor of Alexander Hamilton, Secretary of the Treasury. Hamilton County extended between the Miami and the Scioto in present Ohio. At the same time the governor established courts and appointed the officers of the new county. William Goforth, William Wells and William McMillan were the judges; Israel Ludlow was the Clerk of Courts; and Cincinnati was the county seat. The town grew rapidly. The needs of the garrison at Fort Washington and the expeditions against the Indians gave the town an excellent commercial beginning. At the same time its merchants realized large profits from the heavy traffic on the Ohio and from the trade of the growing settlements in Kentucky and in the Miami Purchase. By the summer of 1792 the town counted three hundred fifty-four surveyed lots, over two hundred houses, a handsome church under construction and more than thirty warehouses.

At least one man frowned on all this prosperity. The Moravian missionary, John Heckewelder, saw nothing in it but the materialism of an essentially wicked society:

The city is overrun with merchants, and overstocked with goods. More than 30 magazines or warehouses can be counted, so that one injures the price of the other. It is a town teeming with idlers, and according to the report of respectable persons, they are a people resembling Sodom. Yet they hope that this place, as well as the others on the north bank of the Ohio, will perhaps in time, or soon, be purged of this wicked class, for experiences teach, that as soon as they are made subject to the law, they leave for Kentucky which lies just across the Ohio, and if they are stopped there, they push on the extreme boundary along the Clinch or Cumberland River, or even down as far as New Orleans. . . . Although according to that description this city consists principally of bad inhabitants yet a clergyman resides here. The present *one* belongs to the Presbyterian Church.[58]

3

The third area of settlement was in present Gallia County, and its first town was Gallipolis, the city of the French. Its origin may be traced to the Scioto Company, which was established at the same time as the Ohio Company. In the spring of 1788 its moving spirit, Colonel William Duer, sent Joel Barlow to Europe to sell six shares of the tract at a price high enough to meet the first installment due to Congress. Barlow was an impractical young poet who had fought in the Revolution and who had just published a bombastic poem, "The Vision of Columbus," which had won ephemeral fame. Because Barlow spoke French—or could say some French words and phrases—Duer regarded him as the right man for the job. The dreamy young man arrived in Paris in June. Instead of establishing a company which would dispose of the six shares at once, he tramped from house to house, from tavern to tavern, trying to sell a mere pre-emption in small lots to individuals while he ate up every farthing of the £500 sterling the Scioto Company had advanced him to defray his expenses. Then in the summer of 1789 when Barlow was reduced to despair and starvation, along came an English swindler with a satirical name, William Playfair, who saw in him a dupe by which he could fill his own pockets with French gold. He advised the worried and hungry young man that the French would buy nothing from an unknown foreigner but would buy anything from a seemingly reliable firm. Barlow saw in Playfair the solution to his problem. Here was a man whose long experience with French ways and customs and whose command of French would enable him to dispose of the Scioto lands. The two men enthusiastically formed a new corporation called the *Compagnie de Scioto* and Barlow sold to it three million acres of the Scioto lands, which were to be paid for in regular installments as the money poured in.[59]

Playfair wasted no time using his flamboyant salesmanship in an extensive advertising campaign. He allowed Barlow to contribute a few ideas to a pamphlet entitled *Prospectus pour l'éstablissement sur les rivières d'Ohio et de Scioto en Amérique* which pictured the Scioto tract as an earthly paradise. There, opposite the mouth of the Great Kanawha, would spring up a gleaming white city called Gallipolis, which the United States might consider as her new capital. Its ground was extremely fertile; its climate was delightful; you could live there in comfort without working, could even grow rich by investing a few dollars. If you were a little ambitious you could cover the ground with a sea of wheat. Tobacco and cotton would spring up with the profusion of grass. Hogs raised on uncultivated land would be an inexhaustible source of revenue. A start with three thousand sows would bring thirty thousand barrels of pork in a single season. Colonists from America, even from Europe, would flock to this land of milk and honey by the thousands, causing its price to rise sharply. This would enable the original settlers to sell a small portion of their property to meet their second payment.[60]

The *Compagnie de Scioto* offered extremely liberal terms. It would accept American securities at ninety per cent, though they could be bought for seventy per cent of their face value. Only half of the purchase price was needed as a down payment. The remainder could come as long as two years later from the sales of the livestock or crops.[61]

These extravagant promises caught the French people at the right psychological moment. The Bastille had fallen, the French Revolution had begun. Alarmed by these disturbances, which grew more violent with each passing day, Frenchmen thronged to the offices of the *Compagnie de Scioto* in the hope of retrieving in wild America the security and freedom they feared they had lost in civilized Paris. Business became so brisk that Barlow by early December reported to Duer sales totaling at least one million livres. These funds were deposited with a Paris banker named Monsieur Seline under an arrangement which placed them at Playfair's immediate disposal. Neither Playfair nor the funds remained in Paris long.[62]

In February 1790 the unsuspecting Barlow gathered the six hundred immigrants who had purchased and in the Ohio country and saw them off at Le Havre. Early in May they arrived in Alexandria, Virginia, only to learn that the Scioto Company had failed to meet its stipulated payments and that, therefore, their deeds were worthless. Moreover, the land its members thought they had bought really belonged to the Ohio Company. In these circumstances the French immigrants found themselves homeless in this country as well as in their own.[63]

Eventually word of their misfortune reached President Washington, who with other authorities took steps to compel the Scioto Company to reimburse them. The negotiations were so lengthy that some of the immigrants, either from need or impatience, settled in Philadelphia or New York or returned to France. At last the government persuaded Colonel Duer to transport the remaining immigrants to the Ohio country and allow them to settle on the Ohio River opposite the mouth of the Great Kanawha. They began to leave Alexandria in the last week of June 1790, crossing the mountains in wagons and then, at Buffalo Creek—now Wellsburg, West Virginia—embarking on the Ohio for their new homes. No gleaming white city gladdened their eyes when they arrived wearily at their destination. All they saw was an unbroken forest and a few rows of ugly huts, eighty in number, that Major John Burnham with thirty-six men had built for them at General Putnam's request.[64]

Though entirely ignorant of frontier life the immigrants determined to stay and make a success of their venture. Everything they did had to be learned with as many hard knocks as a schoolboy experiences with his Latin verbs, but their indomitable perseverance gave testimony that their lesson was thoroughly learned. Their number included men, women and children of every walk of life. Among them were Marquis D'Hebecourt, Count Marlatic, Count De Barth and Marquis Marnesia, all of whom belonged to the higher French nobility. The other immigrants were doctors, lawyers, shopkeepers, hairdressers, dancing masters, glassworkers, merchants, jewelers, goldsmiths, undertakers, cabinetmakers and mechanics. Many were wounded and some were killed in felling trees, but experience sharpened their wits. At last they discovered the expedient of tying a rope around a tree and placing two strong men at each end of it.[65]

Though they were willing to work they found the task of clearing the wilderness far more than they could perform. They solved this difficulty by enlisting Burnham's men. The Americans also gave or sold them meat and plowed their fields. The immigrants simply planted the seeds which they had brought from France together with a book on how to plant them.[66]

The few vegetables they raised that summer and autumn kept them from starving. The winter proved unusually severe; the Americans were gone; the Ohio was frozen; hunters had no meat to sell; no flatboats could come down the river with flour. When the immigrants had run through their money and their clothes had been reduced to tatters, they gave way to despair. The fear of Indians intensified their worries. Fortunately for them, the Indians mistook them for Canadians with whom they were on friendly terms, and let them alone.[67]

Such were conditions in Gallipolis when in 1792 General Putnam and John Heckewelder visited the town. They spent a whole day with goldsmiths and jewelers who showed them watches, compasses, and sun dials as fine as they had ever seen. But what especially intrigued them were two recently completed mantels. Putnam was so enchanted with the beautiful carvings of one of them that he paid twelve guineas for it. At the same time he bought a thermometer, a barometer, a glass tobacco pipe and a thimble-sized bottle with "a diminutive stopper" from a glassworker. In addition to these articles the glassworker manufactured medicine and nitric acid. Realizing that Putnam and Heckewelder were in daily need of light and fire, the glassworker presented them with a glassful of a substance which he had manufactured from bones and which burned steadily. Heckewelder seems to have been interested chiefly in the beautiful gardens and extensive rice fields. About a hundred yards from the Ohio River he found an ancient mound which the immigrants had converted into "a beautiful pleasure garden with a pretty summer house on top."[68]

Another visitor in early Gallipolis was H. M. Brackenridge, who left a vivid account of his travels on the Ohio frontier. In his tender years his father sent him with a guardian to the village of St. Genevieve in Louisiana to study the French language. After spending several years in St. Genevieve he made his way with his guardian northward in a flatboat toward his home in Pittsburgh. Exposed to inclement weather on the Ohio, he came down with ague and was taken to Doctor Saugrain's house in Gallipolis. The doctor was a sprightly gentleman who stood no more than six inches above four feet. The next day, says Brackenridge,

. . . the doctor tried his skill upon me, or rather upon my ague, and pretty much on the plan of another celebrated physician, whether on the principle of the *solviente universal*, I do not so well know, but certain it is, he repeated the very words recorded by Gil Blas: "*Bebe agua, hijo mio, bebe agua in abundancia*"—drink water, my son, drink plenty of water. But the ague was not to be broken off so easily; it still continued to visit me daily, as usual, all that winter and part of the next spring. I was but poorly clad, and was without hat or shoes, but gradually became accustomed to do without them; like the Indian, I might in time have become all face. My guardian left no money, perhaps he had none to leave; Mr. Saugrain had none to spare; besides as this was the period when the French Revolution was at its height, *sans culottism* was popular with those who favored the breaking up of social economy. Dr. Saugrain, however, and many others in Gallipolis were not of that party; they were royalists, who bitterly lamented the condition of their native country.[69]

Many Americans came to Dr. Saugrain's house to watch him use his chemical apparatus, which they were inclined to believe had a close resemblance to the black art. As soon as he broke the little glass tube, the phosphoric matches ignited spontaneously, an achievement which they thought beyond human power. His thermometers and barometers, with their scales neatly painted and their frames richly carved, were articles of wonder. But what astonished the Americans most of all was a large peach in a glass bottle whose neck was no wider than a common cork. Dr. Saugrain was too fond of his little trick to disclose that he had tied the bottle to a peach tree and inserted the peach when it was no bigger than a pebble.[70]

Dr. Saugrain's puny body carried a very stout heart. Once he descended the Ohio with two philosophizing friends who, being followers of Jean-Jacques Rousseau, believed in the pristine innocence of the children of the forest. Since they had no intention of harming the Indians they believed the Indians had no intention of harming them. But Dr. Saugrain, being a man of science, was naturally skeptical and kept his pistols loaded. Near the mouth of the Big Sandy they met a small band of Indians in a canoe and invited them to their boat. The Indians needed no second bid. No sooner did they board the boat than they greeted the would-be philosophers with their tomahawks. And they would have extended the same hospitality to Dr. Saugrain had he not anticipated them with his pistols, killing two of them. Leaping into the water at the flash of their guns, he succeeded in swimming to the shore, in spite of several wounds.[71]

Dr. Saugrain's adventure was symbolic of the pluck and common sense displayed by the French immigrants under adverse circumstances. More unkind was the fate that overtook the leading men of the shady Scioto Company. Playfair lost his ill-gotten gain; Barlow was recalled and sank with his poems into oblivion; Duer failed to pay his bills and was imprisoned; and Cutler, of course, died of gout. In 1796 the Ohio Company, which still claimed the site of Gallipolis, consented to sell it and the adjacent improved lots to the immigrants at the nominal price of a dollar and a quarter an acre. So they were privileged to buy their lands twice. But they had not done so badly. They still had the log huts built by Burnham and his men. They may have had some trouble and been out some money and certainly they had endured the hardships of pioneers, but they could own any amount of land they cared to claim.[72]

4

By this time a number of settlements had sprung up in various sections of the Ohio country. In the Seven Ranges groups of emigrants from western Pennsylvania and western Virginia squatted illegally in the shelter of Fort Steuben, named in honor of Baron von Steuben, the drillmaster of the American Revolution. The fort was eventually abandoned and burned down, but the squatters remained. Their titles were legalized and their cabins formed the nucleus of a number of towns, one of which was Steubenville.[73]

Several settlements appeared in the Virginia Military Tract between the Little Miami and the Scioto. The first of these was "Massie's Station," later Manchester, founded by the Virginia surveyor, Nathaniel Massie. From his station Massie conducted extensive surveys into the Virginia Military Tract in the face of Indian attacks, spring floods and winter storms. Early in March 1796 one of his surveying parties established "Station Prairie" on the Scioto, about three miles south of modern Chillicothe, while he himself with another party founded Chillicothe in the heart of the Shawnee country. Farther up the Scioto on its western bank another Virginian, Lucas Sullivant, laid out Franklinton, named in honor of his idol, Benjamin Franklin. Later Franklinton changed its name to Columbus.[74]

Up the Miami valley in present western Ohio lay a fertile region that had been a favorite hunting ground of the Shawnee. St. Clair, Dayton and Ludlow were quick to perceive that the center of this region, at the junction of the Miami and Mad rivers, was an ideal spot for a settlement. They bought the seventh and eighth ranges of townships, between the Mad River and the Little Miami, and in the fall of 1795 sent out a surveying party which traced a road through bramble and underbrush to the mouth of the Mad River, where Ludlow laid out the town of Dayton. Its citizens had to overcome the usual frontier difficulties before they felt secure in their new homes. The Indians stole nearly all of their horses, and transportation from Cincinnati was so slow that the prices of food-stuffs doubled and tripled and quadrupled. And that was not all. In time they discovered that Symmes had, with his usual optimism, sold them land he never owned by the patent that Congress had granted him several years before. They were obliged to choose between buying their properties from the government for $2 an acre or getting out. Some got out. Those who remained found a champion in Samuel C. Cooper, who secured legal titles to their properties by buying pre-emption rights.[75]

Another area of early settlement was the Western Reserve, a tract of land in present northeastern Ohio stretching about a hundred twenty miles from east to west and about fifty miles from north to south. This is the region the state of Connecticut "reserved" when she ceded her frontier lands to Congress. In 1795 the Connecticut Assembly authorized a committee of eight persons to sell the three million acres contained in the Western Reserve to a speculation company. Thirty-five men bought the tract for $1,200,000 and formed themselves into the Connecticut Land Company. It chose one of its members, Moses Cleaveland, to clear away the Indian claims to the region and to survey it into townships five miles square.[76]

Cleaveland was equal to his mission. Educated in law at Yale, experienced in discipline during the Revolution and devoted to the Company with a stake of $32,600, he combined the right equipment necessary for eventual success. This he confirmed with an advantageous physical appearance. One of his party, Amzi Atwater, who knew him well, pictured him as a dark-complexioned man with a broad face and very coarse features. His dress was "slovenly" and his conversation "very vulgar." But if he was no Beau Brummel and if he cursed or used four-letter words to punctuate his orders or arguments, he had the saving grace of looking like an Indian chief. Always capitalizing on his God-given gifts, Cleaveland donned Indian dress and in May 1796 left Dover, Connecticut, for the frontier.

Three days later he arrived in Albany, where he gathered fifty-one men, women and children and led them to Schenectady and up the Mohawk River. With five supply boats some of them crossed the Carrying Place to Oneida Lake and descended the Oswego River to Lake Ontario; others, including Cleaveland, continued overland to Buffalo. There Cleaveland, in the presence of all his followers, conferred with Joseph Brant and other chiefs for a settlement of their claims in the Western Reserve. The Indian-looking Yankee tactfully delayed his final conference with the chiefs until he could get them into a tractable mood by filling them with salt pork and firewater. This was unnecessary. Since the Treaty of Greenville had, two years earlier, driven the Indians from most of Ohio, including much of the Western Reserve, Brant and the other chiefs were delighted to accept all that Cleaveland had to offer. They agreed to an annuity of $500, or, that failing, to a present of $1,500 from the Connecticut Land Company. For this unexpected windfall of American dollars the chiefs promised to stay their tomahawks and let the white men help themselves to land already theirs by treaty.[77]

Again Cleaveland and his men set out, some by land, more by water, for New Connecticut, as they called the Western Reserve. At three o'clock in the afternoon of July 4 Seth Pease, astronomer and surveyor, stumbled on the northwest cornerstone of Pennsylvania and jubilantly shouted his discovery to his comrades. They gave three cheers and, crossing the line, advanced to Conneaut Creek where they pitched their tents. Weary but not dispirited, they marveled at the coincidence that had brought them to their destination on Independence Day. They gathered on a bank of the little stream and at their leader's command raised their guns for a federal salute of fifteen rounds and an additional one in honor of New Connecticut. Then they gave three cheers, supped merrily, "drank several pails of grog" to a number of toasts and went to sleep in "remarkable good order."[78]

The next day Cleaveland and his men began building a large log cabin which they named "Castle Stow" after their commissary, Joshua Stow. While the building was being completed, Cleaveland conferred with Chief Paqua and his son Cato of the small tribe of Massasagoes living on the banks of Conneaut Creek. Cringing like a whipped schoolboy, Paqua asked Cleaveland what he planned to do and, by way of allaying, his possible anger, presented him with a peace pipe. Assuming the haughty air with which a chief often awes his beaten foe, Cleaveland told Paqua he would not disturb his people as long as they worked and disdained firewater. "This," wrote Cleaveland, "not only closed the business, but checked their begging for more whiskey."[79]

The chief surveyor, Augustus Porter, with his assistant, Seth Pease, and five other men now began the survey. Beginning at Conneaut Creek, they ran the line to the forty-first parallel, then, turning westward, marked off the north and south ranges of townships. Meanwhile Cleaveland with another group had set out by boat to find a good location for a city in the center of the Reserve on Lake Erie. Coasting along the lake shore and scanning the forests and underbrush, they came to the Chagrin River which, since it was not shown on the map, they mistook for the Cuyahoga. Continuing for another twenty miles, he came to the mouth of the Cuyahoga, and there, on the precipitous and wooded bluffs that overhung the river, he found the spot he sought. He paced out a large public square, such as he had seen in his beloved New England, and requested his surveyors to build the beginnings of the town around it. They raised a cabin to shelter the surveyor, a log commissary for their supplies, and a cabin for Job Stiles and his wife, who were placed in charge of the supplies. Cleaveland proposed that the town be called Cuyahoga, but his men persuaded him to permit the use of his own name, and Cleaveland, later Cleveland, became the name of the most important settlement in the Western Reserve.[80]

Suddenly the surveying ceased. Not that the surveyors had completed their work; indeed, they had run only four ranges from the southern base of Pennsylvania. But Cleaveland faced grave difficulties. Sometimes some of the men became ill, and sometimes the rain was so heavy that they could not work. And as the season wore on, they lost their enthusiasm. They dawdled over their chopping; they complained about the meager meals; they damned the heat and cursed the mosquitoes. The surveyors and the chainmen often had to wait for the axmen to cut the thick underbrush and bramble for the compass sights and measuring. They had drunk the last drop of the New England rum that kept them going. Nobody could repair their worn shoes; nobody could mend their torn clothes.

Cleaveland tried to persuade them to remain for the rest of the year by drawing up a contract in which he promised to sell each of them an equal share, for $1 an acre, in a township east of Cleaveland named Euclid in honor of the ancient geometrician. But even this liberality failed to hold them. On September 21 Cleaveland and the other thirteen men remaining in Cleaveland sailed homeward in two small boats and a bark canoe. Subsisting on a "part of a barrel of flour, a bag of flour and two cheeses, and some chocolate," they sailed for eight miles in a fair wind before they learned that fresh supplies had arrived at Conneaut. They returned and continued their surveys for several weeks; but a cold snap in middle October disheartened them and again they took ship for the comforts of the East. Cleaveland never returned to the Western Reserve. Discarding his Indian dress, he devoted his time to his lucrative law practice.[81]

Only twelve persons now remained in the Western Reserve. In the cabin at Cleaveland dwelled the caretakers, Job Stiles and his wife and their friends Richard Landon and Edward Paine, founder of Painesville, who made his home with the Stiles when Landon fled with the first blast of winter. At Castle Stow in Conneaut wintered Elijah Gun and his wife. Here, too, lived the first independent settlers of the Western Reserve, James and Eunice Kingsbury, who had come out with their three little children and their nephew shortly after Cleaveland.[82]

In the spring of 1797 the Connecticut Land Company made another effort to colonize the Western Reserve. This time it encouraged fresh migration by voting to settlers one half of the lots still left in Cleaveland and all unsold lots in the five surveyed townships. The expedition, consisting of sixty-three persons under Reverend Seth Hart with Seth Pease as chief surveyor, started up the Mohawk from Schenectady on April 20 in six boats which carried ample provisions for each person: "One pound of chocolate, five pounds of pork, a small porringer of sugar, one bottle of rum, a half bottle of tea, and flour and bread not limited." Amply fed and in good spirits, the voyagers arrived on May 26 at Conneaut, where they learned that Elijah Gun and his wife had moved to Cleaveland.

The Kingsburys they found in "a low state of health." In the previous November Kingsbury made a journey to his native New Hampshire and caught pleurisy or pneumonia. Though wracked with pain and burning with fever, he started for Conneaut in bitter weather. With an Indian companion he toiled on horseback through snow sometimes five feet deep, covering only a few miles each day. When his horse died of exposure he made the rest of the journey on foot. On Christmas Eve he reached the cabin at Conneaut to find his wife ill with fever and their newly born son by her side. Finding no food in the cabin, Kingsbury dragged a sled to Erie, Pennsylvania, where he bought a bushel of wheat to keep his family alive.

But his wife was too sick and too weak to nurse her child, who died of starvation. The sick and sorrowing father put his dead child into a pine box and buried him deep in the woods. His wife, too, might have died had he not had the good fortune to shoot a pigeon. He made broth which helped restore her to health. But the Kingsburys had had enough of Conneaut; in the spring they accompanied Pease and his surveyors to Cleaveland, where Kingsbury built a cabin east of the public square. Later he built a more spacious dwelling on a bluff overlooking the town and lived in it with his family to a ripe old age.[83]

Reverend Hart established headquarters in Cleaveland, whence his surveyors scattered in all directions of the Western Reverse. In October Pease completed his work and returned home. At first few emigrants settled in Cleaveland, but once those who did obtained legal titles to their properties, the town made rapid progress. Scotch-Irish and German settlers from western Pennsylvania even thronged to neighboring Mahoning Valley, where one of them, John Young, established Youngstown. Soon all roads led to Cleaveland, the emporium of the region. Had Moses Cleaveland been privileged to live until today to view the magnificent city that bears his name, his dark, coarse face would have flushed with wonder, and with a volley of his favorite curses he would have demolished the inadequacy of a statement he made after his return home from the Western Reserve: "While I was in New Connecticut I laid out a town on the bank of Lake Erie, which was called by my name, and I believe the child is now born that may live to see that place as large as Old Windham."[84] The village of Old Windham in Connecticut has preferred to retain its ancient size.

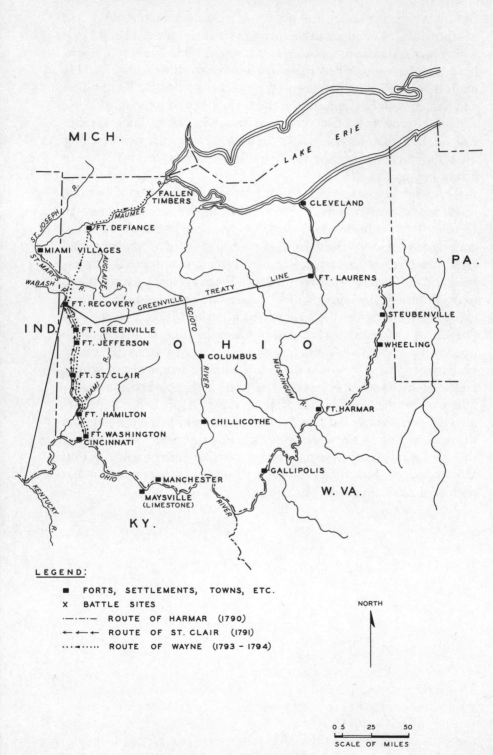

MICH.

LAKE ERIE

X FALLEN
TIMBERS

■ CLEVELAND

■ FT. DEFIANCE

MAUMEE R.

ST. JOSEPH R.

■ MIAMI VILLAGES

AUGLAIZE R.

ST. MARYS R.

WABASH R.

TREATY LINE

■ FT. LAURENS

PA.

■ FT. RECOVERY

GREENVILLE

SCIOTO R.

■ STEUBENVILLE

IND.

■ FT. GREENVILLE

O H I O

■ WHEELING

■ FT. JEFFERSON

MIAMI R.

■ COLUMBUS

MUSKINGUM R.

■ FT. ST. CLAIR

■ FT. HAMILTON

■ CHILLICOTHE

■ FT. HARMAR

■ FT. WASHINGTON
CINCINNATI

OHIO

■ MANCHESTER

■ GALLIPOLIS

KENTUCKY R.

MAYSVILLE
(LIMESTONE)

RIVER

W. VA.

KY.

LEGEND:

■ FORTS, SETTLEMENTS, TOWNS, ETC.
X BATTLE SITES
—·—·— ROUTE OF HARMAR (1790)
←—←—← ROUTE OF ST. CLAIR (1791)
····◄······ ROUTE OF WAYNE (1793 – 1794)

NORTH

0 5   25   50
SCALE OF MILES

FJM

Indian War

FINANCIALLY UNABLE TO WAGE WAR AGAINST THE INDIAN CONFEDeracy, Congress decided on the policy of conciliating the Ohio tribes. It instructed St. Clair to arrange a conference with their chiefs in the spring of 1788 and to spare no effort to reach an agreement with them regarding a boundary line. It suggested the Geographer's Line of the Ordinance of 1785 as a suitable boundary. St. Clair acted promptly. He invited the chiefs to a conference on the first day of May at the falls of the Muskingum.[1]

Joseph Brant, meanwhile, was facing grave difficulties in the confederacy. The tribes which composed it quarreled among themselves, preventing him from requesting and obtaining favorable terms with the Americans. The Wyandots and the Delawares refused to resist the Americans on the ground that they, as a border people, would in the event of war be the first to suffer invasion and the destruction of their towns.[2]

Even more dissentient were the tribes which composed the Iroquois. The Seneca, for example, refused to support Brant because they, too, were a border people and thus feared the same consequences as might befall the Wyandots and the Delawares. Their great chief, Cornplanter, had even made repeated efforts to persuade the United States to grant him certain guarantees in return for amicable relations with his people.[3]

These dissensions frustrated Brant's efforts to form an effective confederacy. The more he dwelled on his failure, the more he saw the wisdom of seeking a peaceful settlement with the United States. In this endeavor, however, he knew he would fail unless he could persuade the Miami and the Shawnee to surrender their claims to most of the Ohio country. To ascertain their attitude on this matter, he called a meeting of the confederacy at Sandusky in the Miami country. Here the Wyandots symbolized their desire for peace with the United States by presenting the Miami with a large string of wampum, one end of which they kept while they requested the Miami to hold fast to the other. The Miami refused. Then the Wyandots laid the string on the shoulder of the principal Miami chief, urging him to seek peace with the Americans in concert with the Iroquois. Without uttering a word the chief turned to let the string fall to the ground. Angered by this arrogant rejection of their request, the Wyandots rose, reproved the chief for spurning their good advice and left the council house. Like the Miami, the Shawnee stubbornly insisted on the Ohio River boundary as the basis for any treaty with the United States.[4]

Thus Brant failed also in his peace aims. Then occurred an incident that completed his disgust. At the falls of the Muskingum, where the conference with St. Clair was scheduled to take place, a few American traders had been killed in a scuffle with a group of Indians. Though no one could ascertain to what tribe the murderers belonged, St. Clair, mindful that Brant had been the guiding spirit of the confederacy, blamed the Mohawk for the crime. When word of this reached Brant, he became so angry that he abandoned all of his plans to attend the conference.[5]

The date for the conference had long passed. St. Clair, seeing in the late Indian dissensions an opportunity to accomplish his object with little expense and without bloodshed, sent messengers to Sandusky to remind the chiefs that the council fire had long been kindled. Mindful of the scuffle at the falls of the Muskingum, he changed the meeting place to safer Fort Harmar. The messengers took eleven days to reach Sandusky, where the Indians had been debating long and heatedly on whether they should attend the conference. At last, in December 1788, a few chiefs decided to meet the Americans and began to straggle into Fort Harmar. All the tribes except the Wyandots sent inadequate representation. Of the chiefs present, only four were formidable or influential: Shendeta and Duentete of the Wyandots, Cornplanter of the Seneca and Pipe of the Delawares.[6]

At the outset Duentete apologized for the scuffle at the falls of the Muskingum. He then bitterly denounced Brant, perhaps to forestall St. Clair's possible anger toward the Ohio tribes. "What he has done," said Duentete, "Is of no Effect, there is not truth in anything he has said, it was his fault that you and I could not meet

Sooner, to do the good work, we are at present about. . . . We think it is the Mohawk that is doing all this Contrary Work."[7]

For two more days Duentete continued his verbal warfare against Brant. He accused him of preventing the chiefs of other tribes from attending the conference and even of encouraging them to attack the Americans at Pittsburgh and Fort Harmar. St. Clair listened impatiently. What, he asked, would the Wyandots do if Brant attacked? The Wyandots turned to the Iroquois; since they had caused all the trouble, he said, let them answer the question. Thus indirectly accused of supporting Brant, Cornplanter was greatly angered. The Wyandots, he fumed, had given greater encouragement to Brant than had the Seneca; they and Brant were responsible for the refusal of the confederacy to meet the Americans at Fort Stanwix four years ago. Then he denounced the Indians for opposing that treaty. He drew himself up and, with great dignity, said, "I will tell you that I take Brant & set him down in his chair at home and he shall no more run About amongst the Nations disturbing them and causing trouble."[8]

Thus did Cornplanter disarm the Seneca as well as the other regional tribes. He had no choice now but to throw himself at St. Clair's feet and appeal to his sense of fair play. In a loud voice he said:

Father, listen to me. . . . You have now grown so big and so strong that none can injure you. Father, I hope you look up toward Heaven and return thanks to God for your greatness. Father, you told me that all this land is yours. I hope you will take pity on the Native inhabitants of this Country, as they took pity when you first arrived. . . . You have Charge of all this land, and I hope you will satisfy the Minds of all that are uneasy, let them know the Boundary line of your land and they will soon acquaint all the Nations with it, in order that they may be Satisfied.[9]

On December 29 whites and Indians assembled in great council. The main speaker was Shendeta. He had a dream, he said, which symobolically described how the Indians were cheated of their lands. In his dream he saw "that the Wyandot was the first man that the Great Spirit Placed upon the ground." Then came the Delawares, whom the Wyandots sent to the seashore to discover what beasts emerged from the water. The first beast was the French and the next one was the British, both of which asked for permission to remain on shore for only one night. This granted, the British begged for a little ground, as much as one cow hide could cover and just large enough to build a fire. This granted, the British gave the Delawares some firewater that made them "a little Giddy & foolish," while their hosts cut the cowhide into a string that covered miles around. When the Delawares became sober they said: "You have Cheated me for once; is this the way you are going to treat me always while you remain in this Country?" While the British said no, they bought another strip of land, as much as a man could walk in one day, and then hired their swiftest runners to deceive the red men again. Since that time, said Shendeta, the British and the Americans had continued to take land; but he could explain no more, for he had come to the end of his dream. "I am," he concluded, "but a foolish man that you see here standing."[10]

Shendeta's purpose in relating his dream was far from that of a foolish man. He sought as favorable terms as he could possibly obtain. While Cornplanter pleaded only for justice, Shendeta, showing the wampum belts which represented former treaties and the establishment of the Ohio River boundary, begged for pity, for compassion, for the old borders. "We are a poor helpless people," said Shendeta, pathetically.[11]

But Cornplanter desired only peace, and he induced the other chiefs to make some compromise. On January 4, 1789, they returned to the council and offered the land north of the Ohio and east of the Muskingum instead of insisting upon the Ohio River boundary. But through their spokesman they denounced with strong language the previous treaties with the Americans:

We don't understand . . . how you came to get this land from our Father [the British], as none of us Know any thing about. We cannot find out when it was that we should have given Our Lands to our Father. . . . We are desirous to Know how our Great Father came by the land for when the Great Spirit made the land it was for the Indians and not for the white people. We are very sorry that you did not make enquiry amongst us Indians before You entered into that business to Know whether we had given the right of the land to our Father, as you very well know that this Country did belong to us Indians. If you had done this at first all this trouble would have been saved, and to our Satisfaction. There was not two Nations appointed by us Chiefs, which were the Wyandots & Delawares, to go and hear what our Brothers had to say [at the Treaty of Fort McIntosh], as for other nations, that happened to fall in with those two nations, they were not sent, but were out hunting at the time.[12]

With these words they offered the Muskingum River boundary.

St. Clair flatly rejected their proposal. "Truly," he said, "If this is what we have been waiting for, our time has been spent to very little purpose." The fact that the British had cheated them, he continued, was no fault of the Americans; this was no ground for argument; they had forfeited their lands by fighting for the losing side. Thus the Indians had to swallow hard reality. Shendeta, however, begged for small concessions. Would the Americans remove a little from their side of the line? Would they agree to a trading system which would regulate prices, make license provisions for traders and provide smiths to repair their guns? Would they agree that two raccoons were fair exchange for one buck, a buckskin for a buck, and a bearskin for two bucks? Cornplanter, however, would have none of this; he was anxious to adopt the agricultural economy of the whites. "We shall see you," he said, "Upon our Lands and they will be planted with Corn & we shall be hunting Deer, we shall also plant corn, we Shall want our hoes & other Articles mended & for that purpose we would wish to have a Blacksmith Settled amongst us."[13] His wishes were granted.

On January 9 St. Clair dictated terms. The misunderstanding that existed between the Six Nations and the Wyandots and their allies made two separate treaties necessary. The first, signed by twenty-four of the sachems and warriors of the Six Nations, confirmed the boundary fixed by the Treaty of Fort Stanwix and in consideration of their lands promised them a quantity of goods valued at $3,000. The other treaties, signed by the Wyandots and their allies, confirmed the boundary line in the Treaty of Fort McIntosh. The posts at Michilimackinac and Detroit were reserved for the sole use of the United States. The Indians, however, were to be permitted to hunt within the ceded territory if they would "demean themselves peaceably" and molest no Americans. All horse thieves, Indian and white, were to be punished. All traders in the Indian country were obliged to get official licenses from the governor of the Northwest Territory. The United States and the Indians pledged that they would warn each other of any hostile movements.[14]

So ended the Treaty of Fort Harmar—a humiliating defeat for the Indians. St. Clair sent them back to the forests with words that will never lose their irony:

I fervently pray to the Great God that the peace we have Established may be perpetual, that he will be pleased to bless the Good

Works we have been about and to extend to your Nations the Glorious light of the Gospel of peace & the Blessings of civilization, that they may increase and prosper, that he will Grant us to live in Unity like Brothers, and that our Children may grow up and flourish like the Young tree and there be none to make them afraid.[15]

But in reporting the treaties to George Washington the governor spoke as if in another tongue:

The reason why the treaties were made separately with the Six Nations and the Wyandots, and more westerly tribes, was the jealousy that subsisted between them, which I was not willing to lessen, by appearing to consider them as one people. . . . I am persuaded their general confederacy is entirely broken: indeed, it would not be very difficult, if circumstances required it, to set them at deadly variance.[16]

2

Yes, the confederacy for the time being was broken. It doubtless would have disappeared entirely had not American policy provoked a division of it into war. This division was composed of the Miami and the Wea who dwelled on the banks of the Miami and in the valleys of the upper Wabash. Their supreme chief, Little Turtle, never trusted the Americans; he warmly supported confederation and urged the Ohio as the boundary between the Indians and the whites. His people had refused to participate in any treaty with the United States, had resented the squatters in and around Vincennes, had frowned on Clark's filibuster of 1786 even though it proved a failure and had refused to deal with Josiah Harmar when, in the following year, that general had occupied Vincennes for the United States.[17]

Joined by Mingo, Shawnee and the Cherokee, the Miami and the Wea began to move closer to the British stronghold at Detroit, though the Americans, anxious for peace, had offered to guarantee their lands. Inasmuch as the British had refused to give them assistance, Brant thought they should make some concession to the United States. But the Miami and the Shawnee disdained reality and continued to hope for British assistance. And they attacked several Kentucky settlements and seized boats descending the Ohio. The United States, protected only by a feeble garrison at Fort Knox, which was precariously provisioned from the remote base at the Falls of the Ohio, was powerless to stop these depredations. Disgusted with American incompetence and impotence, the Kentuckians took matters in their own hands and sent filibustering expeditions against the offending tribes.[18]

In the summer of 1788 a band of sixty Kentuckians under Patrick Brown advanced on Vincennes. Defying Hamtramck's orders to desist, Brown and his men attacked some inoffensive Piankashaw, killing nine of them. Enraged by this injustice, the tribes dwelling between the Wabash and the Maumee rivers increased their attacks. And the Kentuckians retaliated with larger and more frequent expeditions. In August 1789 Major John Hardin led a band of between two and three hundred Kentuckians against the Wea villages, destroyed them and killed twelve Indians. The mortified Hamtramck wrote to Harmar expressing suspicion that the Federal Government had permitted Kentuckians to cross the Ohio and attack the Wea villages. The general in turn wrote to Secretary Knox:

Will you be pleased to give me particulars and especial directions how to act with the inhabitants of Kentucky? Perhaps they may be secretly authorized to form these expeditions. It certainly places Major Hamtramck in a most disagreeable situation: and when Head Quarters are properly fixed opposite Licking River [Fort Washington], frequent applications will most assuredly be made to me, for at least hints for the few Federal troops to countenance and aid them in their operations; if we do not, numberless censures will be cast upon us.[19]

The problem of war against the Indian tribes rested, of course, with President Washington. He was still averse to the use of arms. Convinced that the chiefs desired peace and that the depredations were led by renegades, he requested Knox to exhaust every possible means to come to an understanding with the tribes. But the clamors of influential Kentuckians dissuaded Washington from this stand. Politically he could not afford to have a hostile Kentucky, which within two years was to be admitted into the Union. In the spring of 1790, therefore, he gave Kentuckians permission to conduct filibustering expeditions. On April 13 Secretary Knox informed Harmar that, in view of the continuing Indian attacks, Judge Henry Innes of Kentucky had been authorized to call out scouts. Harmar gave the command of the expedition to General Charles Scott, who on April 18 marched against a band of Indians stationed at the mouth of the Scioto. The discovery of four moccasin tracks prompted him to detach a small party of mounted men against the Indians, whom they scalped. This ended the expedition. Because he considered it a failure, Harmar made no official report of it to the War Department, though he later wrote that he had done everything in his power to make it a success.[20]

At this juncture Ensign Asa Hartshorne led a federal convoy of several small boats down the Ohio. One dark night a band of Indians attacked the boats as they lay offshore nine miles above Limestone and captured one of them. The hard-pressed Hartshorne hurried his boats to Limestone, which he reached in the following afternoon, and sent a few soldiers to pick up the dead and wounded at the place where the attack had been made. They found one man, one woman and three children killed and scalped. Hartshorne reported eight other persons missing.[21]

This event exasperated Knox so much that on June 7 he authorized Harmar to confer with St. Clair on the advisability of destroying the marauders "utterly, if possible," with the use of one hundred federal troops and three hundred Kentucky militia.[22]

3

Still President Washington hoped for peace. "A war with the Wabash Indians," he wrote to St. Clair, "ought to be avoided by all means consistently with the security of the frontier inhabitants, the security of the troops, and the national dignity." The president once more ordered St. Clair to summon the hostile Indians to a conference. If they declined, he was authorized "to call on the lieutenants of the nearest counties of Virginia and Pennsylvania, for such detachments of militia as you may judge proper." Though St. Clair believed the Indians "irreclaimable by gentle means," he obeyed the president's request because he doubted that the federal government was "prepared to chastise them."[23]

St. Clair addressed a long letter to the Miami tribes and sent it to Major Hamtramck in Vincennes with orders to have it translated into French, a language which most Indians understood. Hamtramck's interpreter soon reached the Indian village on Vermilion River, but, hearing of a plot to kill him, hastily returned to Fort Knox.[24]

Hamtramck then sent out Antoine Gamelin, a French trader who was living with the Wea and who had married the daughter of one their chiefs. In April 1790 Gamelin arrived at a Kickapoo village whose chief, Crooked Legs, welcomed him and returned a pleasant but equivocal reply to St. Clair's invitation. Gamelin then went to a village of the Piankashaw on the Vermilion. Though the chief and nearly all of his warriors favored the proposed conference, they added that they would not give their consent to it until they consulted the Miami, "their elder brothers." At the same time the chief warned him that the Shawnee, influenced by the British at Detroit, were sworn enemies of all Americans.[25]

Gamelin next came to a large Kickapoo village where, at a meeting of the chief and his warriors, he interpreted St. Clair's message, then presented them with two belts of white wampum as symbols of peace. But the chief was disappointed to learn that Gamelin had come with empty hands; he expected, he said, milk for himself and other chiefs to put them in a good mood, powder and ball to permit his young men to hunt and good broth for his women and children. Like the Piankashaw, they declared they could give no formal answer to St. Clair's summons without consulting the Wea, who owned the land that surrounded their village.[26]

Whereupon Gamelin held a meeting of the Kickapoo and the Wea in the village of his father-in-law. The chief said:

You, Gamelin, my friend and son-in-law, we are pleased to see in our village and to hear by your mouth the good works of the Great Chief. We thought to receive a few words from the French people; but I see the contrary; none but Big Knives is sending speeches to us. You know that we can determine nothing without the consent of our elder brothers, the Miami. I invite you to proceed to their village and to speak to them. There is one thing in your speech I do not like: I will not tell of it; even was I drunk I would perceive it; but our elder brethren will certainly take notice of it in your speech. You invite us to stop our young men. It is impossible to do it, being constantly encouraged by the British.[27]

Another chief then entered the circle and expressed strong distrust of all conferences with Americans, saying, "The Americans are very flattering in their speeches: many times our nation went to their rendezvous. I was once myself. Some of our chiefs died on the route, and we always came back all naked. And you, Gamelin, you come . . . with empty hands."[28]

Still another chief remarked sarcastically that St. Clair should not summon them to go to him but that they should summon him to come to them: "The chief of America invites us to go to him, if we are for peace; he has not his leg broke, having been able to go as far as the Illinois: he might come here himself, and we should be glad to see him at our village." He admitted that his people had taken up the hatchet, but only after the English had taunted them for being women. He added, "While they invite our young men to war, the old people wish for peace." Again the chiefs declined to attend the proposed conference without the consent of the Miami.[29]

In view of these sentiments Gamelin doubtless regarded his arrival on April 23 in the capital of the omnipotent Miami as the crucial point of his mission. Meeting with the Miami, Shawnee and Delawares in the presence of invited French and British traders, he presented two white belts of wampum to each of the nations. But when he recalled the Treaty of Fort Harmar, the Shawnee disavowed it, saying it had been signed only by a few irresponsible young men without the knowledge of the nation. This attitude, however, does not seem to have been shared by the other nations. In a private conference with Gamelin the leading chief of the Miami cleared their people of any responsibility for the attacks on the Ohio and blamed them on the Shawnee, whom he characterized as general disturbers of the peace.[30]

Gamelin then quite naturally visited the Shawnee village, whose chief, Blue Jacket, told Gamelin that he could not promise to attend the proposed conference until he heard from the English at Detroit.

"From all quarters," said Blue Jacket, "we receive speeches from the Americans and no two are alike. We suppose that they intend to deceive us—then take back your belts of wampum." And he advised Gamelin to speak to the English.[31]

Gamelin replied that his orders did not include a visit to Detroit, and that he would not go there unless he was forced. Whereupon Blue Jacket assumed a friendlier attitude:

"My friend," he said, "we are well pleased with what you say; our intention is not to force you to go to Detroit: it is only a proposal, thinking it for the best. Our answer is the same as the Miamis'." And he declined to go to the conference, though he promised to send messengers to Hamtramck with written answers within four moons.[32]

Thus ended Gamelin's mission. In May 1790 he returned to Vincennes convinced that the nations, encouraged by the English, would never swerve from their determination to keep the Ohio as their boundary. Hamtramck relayed the substance of Gamelin's report to St. Clair, who, seeing "not the smallest possibility of any accommodation with the Indians," made preparations for a military campaign.[33]

4

The governor was visiting in Kaskaskia. On June 11 he left that town and traveled by way of Kentucky to Fort Washington, where he spread word that he had decided on war. Kentuckians enthusiastically supported his plans. Encouraged by their clamor, he sent circular letters to nine Pennsylvania and Virginia counties, calling on each for its quota of the fifteen hundred men he estimated he needed for the forthcoming campaign. His plans were quite simple. On October 1 Harmar was to lead most of the federal and militia troops against the Miami villages, while Hamtramck was to march with three hundred militia against the less powerful Wea and Kickapoo.[34]

At the same time St. Clair, obeying Washington's wishes, reassured the British authorities at Detroit that he had no intention of attacking that town, though he pointedly hinted that they should give no assistance to the hostile Indians and that they should restrain the traders from instigating any more depredations against American settlers.[35]

St. Clair's plans, however, miscarried from the very start. The Pennsylvania militia were short two hundred men, and many of the Kentucky militia were unused to the woods and unarmed. Harmar was deeply chagrined with the low caliber of most of his men and officers. They were largely young boys and old men equipped with neither axes nor cooking utensils. Their arms were antiquated or needed repair. "Their whole object," wrote Major Ebenezer Denny, "seemed to be nothing more than to see the country, without rendering any services whatever." When they were asked what induced them to think that their guns could be repaired in such great numbers, they answered that "they were told in Kentucky that all repairs would be made at Fort Washington." The inspector observed sarcastically that all the firearms on the frontier had been brought in to be repaired by the gunsmiths of the regular army.[36]

No sooner did the officers rendezvous at Fort Washington than they began to bicker over the command. The senior officer was Colonel John Hardin, a man of experience, courage and genuine military ability; but most of the men preferred Colonel Trotter, probably because they felt he was as incompetent as themselves. To avoid possible mutiny or friction between the regulars and the militia, which his superior had advised him to prevent, Harmar had to yield to their wishes. Since he had no control over the militia, he saw the need of keeping them in a good mood.[37]

At the end of September the army moved out of Fort Washington. It consisted of 1,453 men, three hundred twenty of whom were regulars and the rest militia from Pennsylvania and Kentucky. Most of the soldiers were mounted. Three light brass fieldpieces comprised the artillery.

Faced with a number of difficulties, the regular officers made slow progress for several days. While they tried to instruct the militia how to fight and march, their pack horsemen allowed their charges to stray or be stolen by small groups of Indians. Two weeks of such dallying brought the army to a small branch of the Miami. There a horse patrol captured a Shawnee, who informed his captors that the Indians, aware of Harmar's approach, had deserted their towns. On this information Hardin with six hundred militia quickened his pace through flat country of beech and white oak only to find, on reaching the Miami towns, that the captured Shawnee had spoken truth.[38]

On October 17 the army arrived at a Miami village at the junction of two branches of the Miami, the St. Mary and the St. Joseph, about one hundred seventy miles from Fort Washington. The town consisted of a couple hundred wigwams and several good log huts which had been occupied by British traders. All around spread gardens, orchards and vast cornfields which the soldiers destroyed. The militia spent the day loading themselves with plunder.[39]

The next day Harmar ordered Colonel Trotter with three hundred men to explore the region for the Indians. This force soon met two Indians, whom they killed. Then, apparently satisfied, Trotter led his men back to camp.[40]

Much angered, Harmar gave the command of the detachment to Hardin, who in the morning marched out with two days' provisions. But the militia turned sulky and soon began to desert, until at last Hardin found himself with about half of his original force. Approximately ten miles from camp he suddenly stumbled upon a band of about a hundred Indians, who fired as they advanced. The thirty regulars in the detachment stood their ground, but all save a few of the militia fled without firing a shot and made for the Ohio River and home. Only six or seven regulars and their captain escaped; their hiding place was so close to the scene of the disaster that he could hear the Indians performing a victory dance over the bodies of their dead and mutilated foes. In the morning the captain and his men returned to camp.[41]

Thoroughly discouraged, the army left the Miami village and camped at a deserted Shawnee village nearby. That night two of the militia captains took a notion to trap some of the Indians who had carried off a few straggling horses. They hobbled a horse with a bell and hid in a hazel thicket. Soon an Indian stalked up and seized the horse. The captains rushed at him, cut off his head and brought it into camp, proclaiming that it should at least be worth a wolf's scalp.[42]

The army spent the next day destroying corn, beans, pumpkins, stacks of hay, fencing and cabins. A band of Indians attempted to harrass one of the burning parties, but some of the mounted troops got on their flank, killing two of them and driving off the others.[43]

In the morning, October 21, the army started back for Fort Washington. Harmar, wishing to avenge his losses and to forestall any attempt on the part of the Indians to harrass his already beaten troops, sent Major Wyllys with four hundred men, militia and regulars, to surprise those Indians who might have returned to their ruined villages and kill as many as they could. About midnight the major marched his men in three divisions, each of which was separated from the others by a few hundred yards for the purpose of coming upon the principal ruins at the same time but from different directions. As soon as they crossed the Miami, the two wings met a small group of Indians and put them to flight. Elated with their success, they disobeyed orders and pursued the Indians up the St. Joseph for several miles, leaving unsupported the center division, which was composed chiefly of regular troops. This was exactly what the Indians wanted, for a large group of them now attacked Major Wyllys, killing him and one hundred and eighty-three of his men and wounding thirty-one others. Those who escaped fled toward the two wings and met them returning from their pursuit of the Indians. The Indians pursued the militia up the St. Joseph for several miles and then, finding that a narrow creek separated them from their foes, withdrew. The militia collected their wounded and slowly returned to camp.[44]

Too proud, or too ashamed, to admit defeat, Harmar reported the expedition as a success. "Our loss," he wrote Knox, "was heavy, but the headquarters of iniquity were broken up." St. Clair, too, reported that Harmar had conducted a successful campaign. But nobody was fooled. Senator William Maclay of Pennsylvania stripped the affair of its coloring and exposed the naked tragedy.

The reports of the expedition, he said, "look finely on paper, but were we to view the green bones and scattered fragments of our defeat on the actual field, it would leave very different ideas on our minds. This is a vile business, and must be much viler."[45]

Such criticism, the number of dead and persistent stories of the insubordination of the militia eventually resulted in a court martial at Fort Washington to inquire into Harmar's personal conduct in the campaign. He was entirely exonerated.[46]

The campaign itself must be regarded as an utter fiasco. True, Harmar had destroyed the Miami villages and taken much plunder, but this was small gain compared to his losses. He had succeeded only in increasing Indian determination to oust the Americans from Ohio soil. The warriors had merely retreated, preventing Harmar from inflicting losses on their main force. They were much elated with their success. Rufus Putnam reported from Marietta that they vowed "not a Smoak should remain on the Ohio by the time the Leaves put out." The marauding parties and the massacres grew. Outlying squatters, women and children, lone travelers on road and river—all fell in increasing numbers to the tomahawk. Hiding on the banks of the river in groups of ten or twelve, the Indians killed over three hundred emigrants in a single year. Putnam predicted that, if effective measure were not quickly adopted, the public lands would lie unsettled and the government would face bankruptcy.[47]

5

On March 3, 1791, Congress, realizing that the situation demanded vigorous and immediate action, appropriated $312,686 for a new campaign. This time President Washington avoided the mistake of relying on militia alone; he planned to use a mixed force of militia and as many regulars as the government could afford. He authorized Henry Knox, at that time Secretary of War, to add a regiment of infantry to the regular army and to raise two thousand men to serve on the frontier for six months. The President commissioned St. Clair a major general and placed him in command of the campaign.

Knox assumed in his detailed instructions to St. Clair that by July 10 nearly three thousand men would gather at Fort Washington. He directed St. Clair to construct and garrison a number of forts along his route to the Miami villages. If the Indians continued their depredations

. . . you will use every possible exertion to make them feel the effects of your superiority; and after having arrived at the Miami village, and put your works in a defensible state, you will seek the enemy with the whole of your remaining force, and endeavor, by all possible means, to strike them with great severity.[48]

Knox instructed Samuel Hodgson, quartermaster general, to provide horses for the cavalry, pack horses to transport the baggage by land and boats to carry the troops down the Ohio from Fort Pitt.[49]

While St. Clair prepared for war, Washington made one more effort to conciliate the hostile tribes. He decided to summon the Indians to a council. For this mission he chose Colonel Thomas Proctor, a native of Ireland who enjoyed an excellent reputation in the late revolution and who was now a Philadelphia politician. Secretary Knox sent Proctor to Cornplanter, influential chief of the Seneca, with the request that he permit some Iroquois to accompany the commissioner to the Miami to help convince them of his sincerity. Inasmuch as Cornplanter had recently visited President Washington in Philadelphia and had pledged his support in maintaining peace, Knox felt confident that the chief would comply with the request. In April Proctor and Captain Michel Gabriel Houdin, a French officer who had shown gallantry and skill fighting in Massachusetts during the Revolution, arrived at Cornplanter's town on the Allegheny River in northwestern Pennsylvania. The chief welcomed the two men but refrained from committing himself until he could consult the rest of the nation. For this purpose he went with Proctor and Houdin to the Indian council house at Buffalo Creek on Lake Erie. After much debating the Indian squaws refused to let their men go by land to such bad people as the Miami, but they and the chiefs agreed to send a deputation of Indians with Proctor provided he could obtain a vessel to transport them to Sandusky. Whereupon Proctor applied for the vessel to Captain Andrew Gordon, British commander at Niagara, who politely replied that he was not authorized to grant such a request. Seizing on this obstacle to relinquish his mission, which he disliked, Procter pronounced it a failure and returned with Houdin to the comforts of Philadelphia.[50]

Even had he succeeded in obtaining the vessel, he still would have failed for more significant reasons. While Proctor was negotiating with the Indians at Buffalo Creek, Rufus Pickering arrived and asked the Iroquois to come to a separate treaty with the United States at Painted Post, at the present site of Newon, New York. The Iroquois interpreted this as an attempt to prevent them from conferring in unity and therefore as a blow aimed at the Indian confederacy. This was bad enough, but worse followed. The Iroquois received from St. Clair a message urging them to war against the Ohio tribes. The reaction of the Indians to this piece of double-dealing was best expressed by the Seneca chief, Cow Killer, when on May 24 he held council with the British:

These contradictory proceedings of the Americans greatly surprised us; Colonel Proctor at this time appearing very eager to hurry us off with him, whose intention we now thought was to involve us in a war with our Brethren that we immediately declined having anything more to do with him.[51]

By now the federal government feared that the Miami had received word of St. Clair's impending campaign against them, impelling them to strike the first blow against the Americans. To keep them confined to their own country Knox decided to send General Charles Scott on an expedition against the Wea villages on the Wabash. This was the first in a series of preliminary expeditions which were to continue until St. Clair was ready to march. On May 23, through unbroken forests and across the branches of White River, Scott with a force of seven hundred fifty Kentuckians began his advance against the Wea villages. Soon torrents of rain accompanied by lightning and wind storms slowed them down. As they inched along the high rivers, they found their route a succession of quagmires, some four to six miles wide, which bogged down their horses. But within eight days they succeeded in reaching the prairie south of present Lafayette, where they saw but could not overtake a mounted Indian scout from the villages. Pushing forward as fast as their worn horses could go, they arrived at two villages in early afternoon. Scott ordered a detachment to attack them while he led the bulk of his force to the main town, which lay in a grove a few miles away. When they arrived at the village, however, they found that the Indian scout had given warning and that many of the inhabitants had crossed the Wabash to safety. The soldiers leaped from their horses and dashed down to the riverbank, where they seized or killed Indians in five canoes. Scott then ordered Colonel James Wilkinson with a detachment of two hundred horsemen to cross the river a few miles above the town and pursue the fugitives. Wilkinson found the swollen river impassable; only a company crossed it by swimming or by boat and nabbed a few stragglers.[52]

Meanwhile, another officer, Colonel John Hardin, who was in charge of the guides, surprised what Indians remained in the main town, taking fifty-two prisoners and killing six warriors. The town had seventy substantial houses, some of which were well furnished. Several French families lived with the Wea and had introduced them to a semblence of culture. Books, papers and documents furnished evidence that the village had kept in touch with the British in Detroit. The Americans burned a large quantity of corn, household articles and peltries.[53]

Early next morning Scott ordered Wilkinson with five hundred men to attack Kethtipananunk, an important village at the mouth of the Eel River, but found, on examination, that many of his men and horses were too exhausted to traverse the eighteen miles of quagmires that separated them from the town. Three hundred sixty of the men, however, volunteered to venture the enterprise on foot. Wilkinson led them to the town, which they assaulted from all sides. But its inhabitants were vigilant and slipped across the river, scattering in the forest. The angry Wilkinson whereupon destroyed the town and returned with his men to camp.[54]

A few days later Scott sent sixteen of his prisoners, old squaws and children, to the Indians with a letter urging them "to come to a sense of your true interest" and resolve to make a lasting peace with the Americans. Scott assured them that the United States had

. . . no desire to destroy the red people, although they have the power; but, should you decline this invitation, and pursue your unprovoked hostilities, their strength will be exerted against you; your warriors will be slaughtered, your towns and villages ransacked and destroyed, your wives and children carried into captivity, and you may be assured that those who escape the fury of our mighty chiefs, shall find no resting place on this side of the great lakes.[55]

He waited for two days for a reply in vain; then he destroyed the town and return with his prisoners to the Falls of the Ohio.

Since St. Clair was still far from ready to begin his own campaign, he sent out another expedition. Its commander, James Wilkinson, set out with over five hundred Kentuckians from Fort Washington for the Miami town at the mouth of the Eel River. Like Scott, Wilkinson found that the most of the warriors had fled; like Scott, he captured women and children; like Scott, he burned cabins and cornfields. Next he started for a Kickapoo village sixty miles away, but the quagmires crippled half of his horses. Reduced at last to five days' rations, he wisely turned homeward. Like Scott, he had succeeded only in further infuriating the Indians by destroying their property. Once Wilkinson was gone, they returned to their villages and salvaged whatever property remained.[56]

6

Meanwhile St. Clair was making vain efforts to hasten his own formidable campaign. By early September his troops began to straggle into Fort Washington. He sent them to a camp at Ludlow's Station nearby, but since they arrived in desultory manner their officers were unable to train and organize them. St. Clair chafed at the delay; he wanted to reach the Miami towns before the autumn rain began and while the many pack horses could forage on the way. He was fat and gouty—a weak, suffering, elderly man, ill-tempered and somewhat old-maidish. Though he was zealous to do his duty, he knew he was totally unfit, physically and mentally, for the difficult task before him. His enormous vanity was shocked at the poor stuff he had to lead and made him angry with himself and with all the world. With Scotch fury he God-damned everybody and everything.

Impending disaster stalked his mind from the very beginning. First of all, Knox and Butler had fussed with him and had prevented him from moving forward for several weeks and perhaps longer—he couldn't remember. Then the government failed to supply boats to move troops and supplies down the river to Fort Washington. Then Harmar, sensing impending disaster, positively refused to take part in the campaign and resigned his command—God damn him! Then one of his best officers, Major Ebenezer Denny, wished to follow Harmar to Pittsburgh and to civil life. Then Harmar freely predicted defeat. Suspecting that Denny wished to resign, Harmar discouraged him. "You must go on the campaign;" he said, "some will escape, and you may be among the number."[57]

The militia grumbled from the very beginning: the pay was poor; the rations, inadequate; the Indian country, too far away. Privates received $3 a month minus ninety cents for laundary service; sergeants realized $3.60; lieutenants, $22; captains, $30; and colonels, $60. Soon the militia began to desert, claiming that their period of service had run out; a sergeant and nine of the militia disappeared one night; a sergeant and twenty-five men on the next. One hundred horses were stolen, some of which were cut from their fastenings under the very walls of Fort Washington. The force which had been promised St. Clair soon dwindled to 2,699 men, a part of whom were detached to garrison Fort Washington.[58]

But this was only the beginning of the tragedy. Before the army could move, autumn had set in with frosts that killed the forage for the cattle and horses. These animals, therefore, had to be turned loose for food in the forest. The morning roundup considerably slowed progress. And that was not all. The quartermaster general, Samuel Hodgson, surpassed every other department in bungling. Not a single horse did he supply for the campaign. The men entrusted with the animals knew nothing of their care, left them unbelled and fed them in such a way that they kicked one another. Hodgson supplied the army with only fifty axes; he furnished tents made of sheeting that let in the rain; and he provided regular cavalry saddles for large horses instead of small packsaddles for pack horses.[59]

Such were the circumstances under which St. Clair began his campaign. As the men came in he sent a considerable number of them to construct the first post in the proposed line of communication with the Maumee, and on the east bank of the Miami these troops built Fort Hamilton, a strongly fortified stockade which was destined to become the nucleus of the city of Hamilton.[60]

On October 4 St. Clair led his men out of Fort Washington. He moved so slowly that by October 13 he had gone forward only eighty-three miles. Here he constructed Fort Jefferson, the second post in the line to the Maumee, just south of present Greenville. The weather grew steadily worse, with heavy frost and heavy rain, while the supplies became increasingly irregular, causing much grumbling among the militia as well as among some of the regulars. St. Clair himself was so stiff with gout that he could neither mount or dismount his horse without assistance.[61]

The general's troubles increased as he advanced. Here are a few entries from Major Denny's vivid journal for the month of October:

17th—The new fort goes but slowly. Weather very bad; constant rain night and day. . . . Men desert; four of the first regiment went off since our arrival here.

18th—A continuation of wet, disagreeable weather. The army would have been without bread after to-day, had not a small supply of forty-eight horses arrived.

19th—All the horses of the army, quarter-master's as well as contractors, sent back for a supply of flour. Unpardonable mismanagement in the provision department. Troops put on half allowance of flour. Colonel Oldham, commanding officer of militia, directed to furnish an escort to go back with the horses. His men declare if they are sent on that duty they will not return. . . .

20th—The time for which the levies were enlisted begins to expire. Ten were discharged this morning; several a few days ago. The levies from Virginia claim their discharge. All of Captain Hanah's company from Alexandria, discharged. . . .

22nd—For want of sufficiency of flour, the General has been under the necessity of keeping the troops upon half a pound of that article daily, but the ration is made up of beef. . . .

23rd—Two artillery men attempted to desert to the enemy, were taken, tried, and sentenced to suffer death; were hanged along with one of the levies for shooting his comrade. . . .

31st—Militia show great impatience; their officers appear to have little influence. One-third turn out with a determination to go back, a few are prevailed on to stay; between sixty and seventy, however, march off in despite of everything, and swear they will stop the pack horses with provisions.[62]

St. Clair, concerned for the safety of his supplies and afraid that more of his army would desert, decided to smash the defection with an iron hand. He ordered Major Hamtramck and the First Regiment of regulars, the best regiment in the American army, to march twenty miles south or until they overtook the deserters and met the convoy. The wording of St. Clair's orders was faulty. He meant to say that if the provisions and deserters were not reached before Hamtramck had gone twenty miles, the latter was to turn back. The result was that on November 4, the day of the battle, the army lacked its most effective regiment.[63]

On November 3 St. Clair and his army camped upon the bank of a small branch of the Wabash, ninety-eight miles from Fort Washington. Here and there lay small patches of snow and pools skimmed with ice. On both flanks and along most of the rear the ground was low and wet. All around them the forest spread leafless and bleak. The men were so tired from marching on the swampy ground that, when they arrived, St. Clair made no effort to fortify the place. The regulars, occupying the high ground to set up their tents, found it so small that the militia had to camp about three hundred yards beyond the stream on either side.

That night the sentries were restless. Imagining that Indians were lurking around the camp, they fired frequently, alarming soldiers and officers alike. About ten o'clock General Richard Butler, second in command, sent out a captain with thirty men to reconnoiter. Within a few hours the officer reported an Indian army in the neighborhood; but Butler was not on speaking terms with his Goddamning superior and never relayed the information to him. The truth was that an Indian army under the great warrior, Little Turtle, had been following St. Clair for several days. The chief had refrained from attacking Hamtramck's crack troops, but when he learned that that officer had been sent to the rear, he disposed his braves for battle.[64]

At dawn the Americans paraded in the usual manner and were dismissed for breakfast. Suddenly the forest trembled with savage yells! The militia saw a sea of painted faces surging toward them! They fired a volley. Then, appalled by the whoops and yells, they ran like a herd of frightened sheep back to camp.

The Indians, painted black and red and wearing hawk or eagle feathers, spread to either flank and surrounding the regulars, forced them back on the high ground. To the furious *rat-a-tat-tat* of drums the regulars sprang forward, checking the Indians with volleys of musketry; but their artillery, impeded by huddling militiamen, boomed harmlessly, sending dense clouds of smoke to the treetops. Only now and then did the Americans catch glimpses of the deadly figures who, with rifle and tomahawk and knife, picked off their comrades with fearful rapidity.[65]

St. Clair and Butler passed and repassed one another as they walked up and down the lines from flank to flank. The commander was wearing a blanket coat with a hood. Eight bullets pierced his coat but did no other damage. Another bullet carried off a part of his queue. A bullet hit Butler in the arm and broke it; he had it put up in a sling and continued to walk up and down the lines, until another bullet struck him in the side. He had himself carried to the middle of the camp, where, propped up by knapsacks, he watched the issue of battle. Men and horses were falling all around him. St. Clair sent Major Denny to ask how Butler was: he felt well, he said. At that moment a young cadet from Virginia, who stood at the general's side, was hit on the kneecap by a spent ball that made him bellow with pain and shock. Butler laughed so hard that his wounded side shook. Denny, satisfied that the general's wound was not serious, took leave of him; but an hour later Butler died, either from his wound, or, as some pioneer writers said, from a tomahawk in his brain.[66]

The Indians, unimpressed by the artillery, swarmed on the gunners and killed all of them save one, whom they gravely wounded. As they seized the silent cannon they forced back the left flank of the army and stood on clear ground. St. Clair put himself at the head of a group of soldiers who rushed fiercely at the Indians with their bayonets and drove them from the ground. Again and again they returned. Again and again they fell back. In one of the charges a battalion under Colonel Darke drove the Indians across the river; but they closed in behind him, forcing him to fight his way back to camp. He was wounded and most of his men were killed. In another charge a company of infantry drove the Indians to a ravine filled with logs. There the Indians entrenched themselves and killed or drove off their attackers. Fighting with the Americans was Benjamin Van Cleve, a pack horseman who kept a journal of the battle. A skilled woodsman, he took to a tree and popped off a goodly number of Indians before he exhausted his ammunition. Then, finding himself alone, he ran back to camp as fast as his legs would go. He found that the Indians were again in possession of the artillery and that they had scalped the gunners they had killed. Another packer, Thomas Irwin, took a look at the slaughtered gunners and compared their bloody heads to pumpkins in a December cornfield.[67]

By now the officers, who during the battle had been the special target of the Indians, were nearly all killed or wounded. The leaderless soldiers, despairing of success, gave up the fight and crowded toward the center of the field. Whereupon the Indians contracted their lines and sent an avalanche of arrows and bullets on their victims from all directions. Major Denny wrote that the slaughter could hardly be imagined.[68]

Instant flight alone remained for the beaten survivors. St. Clair decided to fight his way by the broad road on which he had advanced. Mounting one of the few horses that survived, he gathered those fragments of the different battalions that contained the few men who still kept heart and head together and ordered them to charge and regain the road from which the Indians had cut them off. The men were in such a stupor that he had to repeat his orders; finally aroused, they moved only when they were told that they were in retreat.[69]

Colonel Darke and a few officers put themselves at the head of the column and, with the assistance of the coolest and boldest men, succeeded in forcing the Indians back from the road. This made an opening through which, wrote Van Cleve, the rest of the troops rushed like a drove of bullocks. Denny wrote:

The wounded who came off left their arms in the field, and one-half of the others threw theirs away on the retreat. The road for miles was covered with firelocks, cartridge boxes, and regimentals. How fortunate that the pursuit was discontinued; a single Indian might have followed with safety upon either flank.[70]

St. Clair himself was in danger of being captured or killed. He tried to stay behind and stem the torrent of fugitives; but, swept forward by the crowd, he failed. Then he attempted to ride to the front to rally his men. He failed again, for he could not spur his horse out of a walk.

Before reaching Fort Jefferson the fugitives encountered the regular regiment that had been so unfortunately detached a couple of days before the battle. The most severely wounded remained in the fort. The others fled to Fort Washington. Six hundred thirty men had been killed and over two hundred eighty wounded; less than five hundred remained unhurt. The army had taken a month to advance from Fort Hamilton to the scene of the battle. The survivors covered the same distance in just two days.[71]

St. Clair sent Denny to carry the news of the defeat to President Washington in Philadelphia. Bad roads and ice on the Ohio prevented him from reaching his destination for a month. The dispatches were brought in while Washington was eating his dinner. He read them but retained his calm demeanor until, at the end of the meal, his wife and all his guests, except his secretary, Colonel Tobias Lear, left the room. Then he began to pace back and forth in silent anger. Suddenly throwing himself on a sofa, he exclaimed:

"St. Clair defeated—routed; the officers nearly all killed, the men by wholesale, the rout complete! Too shocking to think of—a surprise in the bargain!"

With these words his anger mounted, causing him to rise suddenly from the sofa:

"Yes! Here on this very spot I took leave of him; I wished him success and honor. 'You have my instructions,' I said, 'from the Secretary of War. I had a strict eye on them, and will add but one word—beware of a surprise! You know how the Indians fight us!' He went off with that as my last solemn warning thrown into his ears. And yet, to suffer that army to be cut to pieces—hacked by a surprise—the very thing I guarded against! O God, O God, he's worse than a murderer!"

His fury wanted; he sat down again on the sofa; slowly, he collected himself.

"This must not go beyond this room," he said calmly to Lear. He reflected for a few minutes before he added: "General St. Clair shall have justice. I looked hastily through the dispatches—saw the whole disaster, but not all the particulars. I will hear him without prejudice; he shall have full justice."[72]

Later a committee of the House of Representatives investigated the cause of St. Clair's defeat. It found that he and his officers had shown marked courage during the expedition and that he had had to encounter stupendous obstacles. It therefore acquitted him with honor.[73]

7

The defeat they had inflicted on St. Clair filled the Indians with the zeal of crusaders. In the words of Rufus Putnam, they began to "believe them Selves invisible, and they truly had great cause of triumph." Alexander McKee, the Indian agent, prophesied that their success would unite them against the whites in numbers never "before known in this part of the Country." The triumphant Indians quickly revived the confederacy. Even the Delawares and the Wyandots, who had been willing to relinquish the Ohio River boundary, now joined the ranks of their more hostile brethren.

The British wasted neither time nor effort to encourage them with promises of support and with vivid pictures of future victories. They had practical reasons for their policy. They did not want to see their lucrative fur trade with the Indians fall into American hands. This was so important to them that they had insisted on retaining the forts in the Northwest Territory even though the region had gone to the United States by the Treaty of Paris. On their part, the Indians had their reasons for retaining British friendship. Regardless of defeat or victory, they needed British supplies, which McKee invariably furnished.[74]

In 1791 the Indians had apparent proof of British friendship. In the interest of the fur trade the British wanted a revision of the Treaty of Paris to permit the establishment of a neutral Indian barrier state north of the Ohio River. To this end the governor of Quebec, Lord Dorchester, instructed Sir John Johnson to sound the Indians in such a way that they would declare their grievances and suggest such terms as should be advanced in the diplomatic conferences then in progress between the United States and Great Britain. Johnson assigned this task to McKee, who in July 1791 assembled the Indians at the rapids of the Maumee and persuaded them to make a statement indicating the insecurity of their position and expressing a desire to obtain some kind of guarantee that the Ohio River would be regarded as the boundary between themselves and the whites. At the same time they expressed a willingness to allow the Marietta settlements to remain unmolested. These terms Dorchester sent to the British government, which approved them and used them as the basis of instructions to George Hammond, minister to the United States, to form a neutral Indian barrier state which British policy advocated in the interest of the fur trade. Such solicitude in their behalf impressed the Indians immeasurably.[75]

Small wonder that they assumed an attitude of invincibility. They began to talk of withdrawing every compromise they had offered the Americans; they vowed to kill every American who fell into their hands. And they soon translated their threats into action. In April 1792 President Washington, still anxious to establish a lasting peace, had, through Knox, sent Captain Alexander Trueman to the hostile tribes to invite them to a conference in Philadelphia. Trueman never reached his destination; his body was found in the wilderness north of Fort Washington. Knox then sent out Major John Hardin, who was murdered near Sandusky, his starting point. The next commissioner, Rufus Putnam, barely escaped death at Fort Jefferson. Nevertheless, he went to Vincennes to negotiate a treaty, but only a few Wea and Piankashaw appeared. There, on September 27, 1792, the Indians and Putnam signed a treaty that the confederacy quickly scorned and that the United States Senate therefore repudiated.[76]

The confederacy was interested neither in Putnam's treaty nor in any other treaty that failed to recognize the Ohio River boundary. To reassert this claim and to prepare an official and united reply to Washington's peace efforts, the confederacy in September 1792 assembled at the mouth of the Auglaize. The conference clearly showed British inspiration. The United States had rejected England's proposal that the two nations set up a neutral Indian barrier state. Whereupon England had adopted another diplomatic maneuver. John Graves Simcoe, governor of the new province of Upper Canada, had, through his agents, requested the Indians to ask for British mediation between themselves and the United States.

The purpose of this move was to show the power of Indian unity at a time when the Americans were still depressed over St. Clair's defeat. It inflated Indian confidence to the extent that it demanded the United States send delegates to a grand council at Sandusky in the following spring to "see justice done to us." With British protection the Indians anticipated success in their endeavor to obtain the Ohio River boundary.[77]

Still hopeful of a peaceful settlement while he prepared for possible war, President Washington sent Captain Hendrick Aupaumut, an Indian from the reservation at Stockbridge, Massachusetts, to the confederacy to ask it to adjourn and meet Putnam at Fort Jefferson. But the confederacy insisted that Americans get out of the Ohio country. They justified their attitude by recalling all the "deceit and cruelty and land robbery that they had suffered from the Americans." They reminded Captain Aupaumut of the Moravian massacre of 1782, of the heartless murder of Melanchy in 1786 and of the disdain with which the Americans had rewarded the Delawares for their services in the Revolutionary War. "And since that," they added, "every time the Big knives get ready to come against us, they would send [a] message to us for peace.—Then they come to fight us."[78]

No, the confederacy had no faith in American promises. Instead, it entrusted its reply to the American agent to the Iroquois, General Israel Chapin, who on November 13, 1792, aired it in a council held at Buffalo Creek. "We are and shall always look upon ourselves as the sole owners of this Country," said the Indians, "but as peace is good, we are willing to follow your advice and will listen to the Voice of Peace from the Americans, provided it is for our Interests, we have no objection to meet them at Sandusky."[79]

Encouraged by these words, President Washington undertook a final peace move. In March 1793 he appointed Benjamin Lincoln, Beverley Randolph and Timothy Pickering—all of whom were eminent Revolutionary War generals—to meet the hostile tribes at Sandusky. In his detailed instructions Secretary Knox authorized the commissioners to offer concessions that were almost humiliating. While they were to uphold the boundary line in the Treaty of Fort Harmar, they were to offer to relinquish the trading posts within the Indian country but were to retain the British-occupied posts which had been ceded to the United States by the Treaty of Paris. The United States was to offer to pay the tribes $50,000 in goods immediately and an additional $10,000 in goods to be delivered at whatever places were designated. Knox directed the commissioners to exclude all Americans from the conference save those mentioned in their instructions. They could permit Simcoe and the British agents, John Butler and Alexander McKee, "on the ground that, the intention of the United States being upright, they cannot have the least objection to the presence of any of the gentlemen of the British government."[80]

Arriving at Niagara on their way westward, the commissioners met Simcoe, who treated them with utmost courtesy, arranged for their passage through Lake Erie and detailed several army officers and Butler and McKee to accompany them. Inwardly, however, Simcoe suspected that their purpose was to "seduce" the Indians from the British alliance and to plan their "destruction and predetermined extirpation." The Americans, too, had their suspicions. Why did Simcoe plan to attend the conference? Their minds were somewhat eased when they learned that the United States would not accept open British mediation and that, therefore, Simcoe refused to attend the conference as a mere unofficial observer. Simcoe further allayed their suspicions by advising them to confer privately with the Indian chiefs and by assuring them that, whatever the outcome of the conference, he would see that they returned home safely.[81]

On July 21 the commissioners, after a long delay in Niagara occasioned by strong head winds, arrived in Detroit only to be told that they were not permitted to attend the conference. The reason was that serious dissensions had broken out among the Indian representatives. The Six Nations, under Brant's leadership, urged the Ohio tribes to accept the boundary formed by the Muskingum, Cuyahoga and Venango rivers; but they, angered by recent American settlements north of the river and by the government's warlike preparations, insisted on the Ohio River boundary. They placed their entire confidence in repeated assurances of British support.[82]

On July 20 they asked the commissioners whether they were willing to accept their terms. "If you seriously design to make a firm and lasting peace," they said, "you will immediately remove all your people from our side of the river." The commissioners replied coolly that they were instructed to negotiate only on the basis of the Treaty of Fort Harmar. They declared, however, that the United States was prepared to abandon that doctrine in the Treaty of Paris which stated that the king of England had ceded the Indian title to lands within certain boundaries. The commissioners admitted that their predecessors at Fort Stanwix, Fort McIntosh, Fort Finney and Fort Harmar had misconstrued that part of the Treaty. Since the King had not purchased the country from the Indians, said the commissioners, "of course he could not give it away; he only relinquished to the United States his claim to it."[83]

The confederacy deliberated for two weeks; then on August 16 two Wyandot runners brought the commissioners its reply. It rejected all compromise and insisted on the complete and immediate evacuation of all lands north of the Ohio. At the same time it expressed surprise that the United States could recognize the justice of Indian claims and yet expect the Indians to give up a part of their lands:

Brothers: Money, to us, is of no value, and to most of us unknown: and as no consideration whatever can induce us to sell the lands on which we get sustenance for our women and children, we hope we may be allowed to point out a mode by which your settlers may be easily removed, and peace thereby obtained.

Brothers: We know that these settlers are poor, or they would never have ventured to live in a country which has been in continual trouble ever since they crossed the Ohio. Divide, therefore, this large sum of money, which you have offered to us, among these people: give to each, also, a proportion of what you say you would give to us, annually, over and above this very large sum of money: and, we are persuaded, they would most readily accept of it, in lieu of the lands you sold them. If you add, also, the great sums you must expend in raising and paying armies, with a view to force us to yield you our country, you will certainly have more than sufficient for the purposes of repaying these settlers for all their labor and their improvements.

Brothers: You have talked to us about concessions. It appears strange that you should expect any from us, who have only been defending our just rights against your invasions. We want peace. Restore to us our country, and we shall be enemies no longer.[84]

And the conference ended. The commissioners prepared to return home. In their parting words to the confederacy they expressed regret at Indian unreasonableness: "The negotiation is . . . at an end. We sincerely regret that peace is not the result; but, knowing the upright and liberal views of the United States, which, as far as you gave us an opportunity, we have explained to you, we trust that impartial judges will not attribute the continuance of the war to them."[85]

8

As soon as President Washington received word of the failure of the negotiations he authorized hostilities against the Indians. After St. Clair's defeat Washington had sought a general whom he could trust. He chose General Anthony Wayne, who had earned an enviable reputation during the Revolution. In that conflict no other officer on either side showed Wayne's energy and blind courage. "He gloried in excitement and danger," says Roosevelt, "and shone at his best when the stress was sorest; and because of his magnificent courage his soldiers had affectionately christened him 'Mad Anthony.'" In September 1777 a British officer, Sir Charles Grey, surprised Wayne at night and severely bayonetted his brigade. This experience taught him to add caution to his military knowledge. Thereafter he insisted on the thorough drilling and ceaseless watchfulness that was to spell his success against the Indians in the Ohio wilderness.

His other engagements in the Revolution were nearly always successful, though the battles in which they were fought often ended in defeats. With the bayonet, which had become his favorite weapon, he drove the Hessians from Germantown and the British from Monmouth. But his greatest triumph came in 1779 at Stony Point, a British fort which stood on a hill near the Hudson River in the present state of New York. In the dead of night Wayne led twelve hundred chosen troops over mountains and through swamps and narrow paths straight to the fort, where, heedless of musketry and grape shot, he took at the point of the bayonet five hundred forty-three officers and privates prisoner in the most brilliant achievement of its kind of the Revolution. In the last year of the struggle Wayne campaigned against the Creek allies of the British in Georgia. One night these Indians under Guristersijo slashed down Wayne's sentinels and drove away some of his soldiers. Aroused from sleep, Mad Anthony snatched his sword and pistol and, mounting the first horse he saw, hurried his troops against Guristersijo's braves and drove them from the field. His bayonets thrust quicker and deeper than Guristersijo's tomahawks. The chief died in battle but not before he had shot down Wayne's horse. Mad Anthony half fell but recovered enough of his balance to kill the chief with one jab of his sword.[86]

Ten years had passed since those fabulous days. Wayne was now forty-eight years old and in continual pain from gout; but he retained all the alertness and vigor of his youth. In the spring of 1793 he floated with twenty-five hundred men down the Ohio to Cincinnati and established a base camp at Hobson's Course, near Fort Washington. His campaign was quite different from that of his unfortunate predecessor. He had almost twice as many men and over three times as large an appropriation as St. Clair. He planned to march against the Indians, not in fall or winter, but in summer when his men could subsist on the vegetables that the Indians raised and his horses could forage on the way. His troops were better paid and better fed and drilled with Spartan thoroughness. And they were flanked by Kentucky scouts who continually reported the numbers and whereabouts of the Indians. At no time were Wayne and his men in danger of being ambushed.[87]

The general spent five months at Hobson's Course, drilling his men in frontier tactics and organizing an effective network of spies and scouts. In October he advanced with his usual caution to a strong position about eighty miles north of Cincinnati and established Fort Greenville, named in honor of his deceased comrade-in-arms, Nathanael Greene. Two months later he rose from a sickbed to lead a small detachment twenty miles northward to the site of St. Clair's defeat, where he built a stockaded fort that he significantly called Fort Recovery.[88]

The British and Indians watched the advancing menace with trepidation. At this time Revolutionary France was at war with England. To strangle her enemy, England decreed the detention of all ships carrying products to and from any French colony. British naval commanders seized many American ships which had been provisioning the French West Indies since the beginning of hostilities. These confiscations and the imprisonment of American seamen, coming at the height of the Indian campaigns, produced an outcry for war against England.

On February 10, 1794, Lord Dorchester committed the indiscretion of assuring a delegation of Indians that they would soon have active allies, for war between his country and the United States was, in his opinion, inevitable. And he encouraged them with promises of immediate assistance, which they interpreted as formal pledges of support. Two months later Simcoe, at Dorchester's orders, had the effrontery to re-establish at the rapids of the Maumee, on American soil, the old English fort of the Miami to protect Detroit in case Wayne attacked that town. At the fort gathered the Wyandots and Ottawas from Lake Erie, the Chippewa from Lake Huron, and the Potawatomi from Lake Michigan. By the middle of June almost two thousand braves were ready to smash

Wayne's army in the same manner as they had destroyed St. Clair's two and a half years before.[89]

On June 30 the beguiled Indians struck hard at Fort Recovery, whose presence they regarded as intolerable mockery to their previous victory. Led by English and French rangers painted and dressed like Indians, they streamed down through the dense forest and rushed a camp of fifty dragoons and ninety riflemen just outside the walls of the fort. The Americans broke and ran for the fort, but nineteen of them were killed and nineteen more were wounded before they reached it. Confident in their superior numbers, the Indians rushed at the fort night and day, only to be driven back with heavy losses. At last they became discouraged and drew off to their villages.[90]

This failure was for them the beginning of the end. It foreshadowed the Battle of Fallen Timbers and the Treaty of Greenville. The confederacy fell in ruins. Not for nearly two decades did the Indians gather again in such formidable numbers. The English were negotiating a settlement with the United States and did not, therefore, take part in the attack on Fort Recovery. The disillusioned Chippewa, Wyandots and Potawatomi returned to their homes. Only thirteen hundred implacable Miami and their allies, provisioned and encouraged by McKee, remained in the field.[91]

Meanwhile Wayne, augmented by a force of sixteen hundred mounted Kentucky volunteers under General Charles Scott, began his inexorable advance toward the Miami towns. Reaching the junction of the Maumee and the Auglaize early in August, he spent a week building a strong stockade with four blockhouses which he called Fort Defiance. For weeks his soldiers had been cutting a wide road through the thick forest, toiling through thickets, defiles and beds of nettles more than waist-high, and building bridges across mosquito-infested streams. Now, at Fort Defiance, they rested their weary bodies while they feasted on roasted ears of corn and other fresh vegetables.

Their commander enjoyed none of this picnicking. A few days previously the low boughs of a large beech had inflicted deep cuts on his body. Yet neither old nor new pains hindered him from sending to the Indians a final appeal that they meet him and agree on a lasting peace. Referring to the British fort at the rapids of the Maumee, he warned them not to be misled by "bad white men who have neither the power nor the inclination to protect you." When the Indians, torn by dissension, failed to reply, Wayne resumed his advance, building another small fort, burning villages and destroying fields. The panicky Indians asked the British for immediate support but received from them only the usual vague and misleading promises. Wayne, knowing that the Indians fasted before a battle, managed to get word to them that on August 17 he would attack them at a place near the British fort called Fallen Timbers because a tornado had, some years before, overturned a large number of trees which now lay piled across one another in rows. On that day Wayne advanced, but, instead of attacking, camped ten miles away. There he stayed for three days, while his starving enemies impatiently awaited his arrival.

On August 20 five hundred warriors, able to stave off hunger no longer, wandered away to the British fort. In their absence Wayne arrived at Fallen Timbers. His arms and legs were swathed in flannel to assuage the great pain caused by gout and his bruises, and he was so impeded in his movements that he had to be lifted on his horse. When he had ridden a short distance, he heard sharp rifle fire from clumps of tall grass. The vanguard, composed of Kentucky volunteers, reeled before the barrage. Wayne, forgetting his pains, spurred his horse and yelled to the leader of his dragoons, who answered to the odd name of Robert Mis Campbell, to clear the enemy from the tall grass. On their horses they jumped over the fallen timbers and dashed with brandished broadswords into the ambuscade, where Little Turtle's sharpshooters picked off their leader and emptied a dozen saddles. The Indians, thinking that the battle was won, jumped with joyous yelps from their hiding places and ran into the woods.[92]

Wayne tore the bandages from his arms and yelled to his first line of infantry to charge with the bayonet. Discovering that Little Turtle and Blue Jacket had strung out their line in Indian fashion for about two miles, he bawled out to Scott to swing to the rear and assault their flank; but the fallen timbers made Scott's road impassable. The Indians, endeavoring to meet the bayonet charge and Scott's planned flank assault, had spread their line so thin that Wayne's men easily broke it. Unable to stop and load and seeing their comrades hacked down by the dozens, the tribesmen fled to the British fort nearby. To their dismay its commander, Major William Campbell, kept the gates closed. Little Turtle, Blue Jacket and Tecumseh, a young chief of the Shawnee, shouted for sanctuary in vain.[93]

The battle had lasted less than an hour. In so short a time Wayne had had no opportunity to use the bulk of his army. Scott's Kentuckians, impeded in their movements, hardly fired a shot. The rearguard came up when the battle was over. Only nine hundred of Wayne's soldiers saw action. He lost twenty-eight men dead and about one hundred wounded. The Indians left forty dead on the field, but they had perhaps carried off many more dead and wounded.[94]

Wayne's victory at Fallen Timbers enabled him to convince the Indians that they could expect nothing from the British. And he was careful to emphasize this point in all his messages to them. The first to accept his assurance of good will were the Wyandots, who replied that they hoped the Great Spirit would incline their hearts to his way of thinking. Next spring, they said, "you can depend upon us; we shall settle all matters to the satisfaction of all parties." Joseph Brant, who had worked for peace since the Treaty of Fort Harmar, blamed McKee for interfering in the Indian councils and misleading the tribes with sugared words. In a letter to a British official he expressed the hope that "if there is a treaty between Great Britain and the Yankees . . . our Father the King will not forget the Indians as he did in the year '83." All the other chiefs, having lost all confidence in the British, were psychologically ready to accept Wayne's terms. Their starving condition hastened their inclination. Resistance meant the prospect of losing all their cows and dogs and made them exasperated with the British. "They said they had been deceived by them, for they had not fulfilled one promise. It was concluded among them to send a Flag to Fort Defiance in order to make a treaty with the Americans."[95]

Gradually, in the early summer of 1795, the tribes began to assembled at Greenville. They hoped that Wayne would agree to establish the boundary line requested in the Treaty of Fort Harmar, whose validity they had accepted as a punishment of defeat. Wayne pledged to make the Treaty "a preliminary or foundation, upon which a permanent and lasting peace shall be established." He saw, too, the necessity of establishing trading posts among them as an inducement to win their allegiance from the British. To Secretary Knox he wrote:

The British agents have greatly the advantage in this business at present . . . which will always make the savages dependent upon them, until the United States establish trading-houses in their country, from which they can be supplied with equal facility, and at as reasonable rates. . . . Could I, with truth and propriety, pledge myself to the hostile tribes, that this measure would be adopted, and that they would, with certainty, be supplied in this way, in the course of the ensuing spring, as well as in the future, I am confident we should draw them over to our interest, notwithstanding every effort of the British to prevent it.[96]

On July 20 Wayne formally read and explained to all the tribes the terms of the Treaty of Fort Harmar. All accepted this as preliminary to peace save Little Turtle and his Miami. He pointed out that the lands of his people extended west to the Scioto and south to the Ohio. He said with chagrin:

I am much surprised to find that my other brothers differed so much from me on this subject; for their conduct would lead one to suppose that the Great Spirit, and their forefathers, had not given them the same charge that was given to me, but, on the contrary, had directed them to any white man who wore a hat, as soon as he should ask it of them . . . I expected in this council that our minds would have been made up, and that we should speak with one voice; I am sorry to observe that you are rather unsettled and hasty in your conduct.[97]

Wayne held his tongue until all the tribes, including the Shawnee and Ottawas, showed their willingness to agree to his terms. Then on July 24 he told them that further talk was useless. He read them the treaty which John Jay had concluded with the British government in the previous November. This secured for the United States the western posts which the British had promised to surrender in the Treaty of 1783. Then Wayne showed them that, by this treaty, "all the country, south of the great lakes, has been given up to America." Treaties, he said, should be sacredly fulfilled, but the British, on their part, did not find it convenient to relinquish the posts until now.[98]

Having exposed British perfidy, he sent them away for three days to consider his terms. Then on July 27 he reassembled them and read to them the treaty he hoped they would accept. He was generous in what he offered them. He promised them reservations for the protection of the tribes and to facilitate the establishment of trading posts at which they could "be furnished with goods in exchange for your skins and furs, at a reasonable rate." After a show of opposition on the part of Little Turtle, who protested that the treaty took the best part of their hunting grounds, the Indians on August 3, 1795, signed the Treaty of Greenville. It fixed a definite boundary running up the Cuyahoga from its mouth and following the line of the Treaty of Fort Harmar to the portage of the Tuscarawas, then to the forks above Fort Laurens, then westward to Laramie's store on a branch of the Miami, then to Fort Recovery, and thence southwestward in a direct line to the Ohio, opposite the mouth of the Kentucky. In addition the Indians gave up the right of way for several roads to Detroit, Chicago, Vincennes, Clarksville, Fort Massiac and other points, and ceded sixteen reservations at strategic sites for trading and other purposes. The Treaty promised $1,000 each to the Wyandots, Delawares, Shawnee, Miami, Ottawas, Chippewa and Potawatomi, and $500 each to the Kickapoo, Wea, Eel River Miami. Piankshaw and Kaskaskia. The tribes could take these annuities in the form of domestic animals, implements of farming and "other utensils convenient for them, and in compensation to useful artificers, who may reside with, or near them." The Indians granted to the United States the right to buy more land in Ohio, and the United States in turn promised to protect the Indians from aggressive frontiersmen. The tribesmen were given permission to drive squatters off their lands or punish them as they saw fit. The United States was entrusted with the fur trade in order to protect the Indians from rapacious traders.[99]

The Treaty of Greenville was Mad Anthony's sword of peace. It opened frontier Ohio to America.

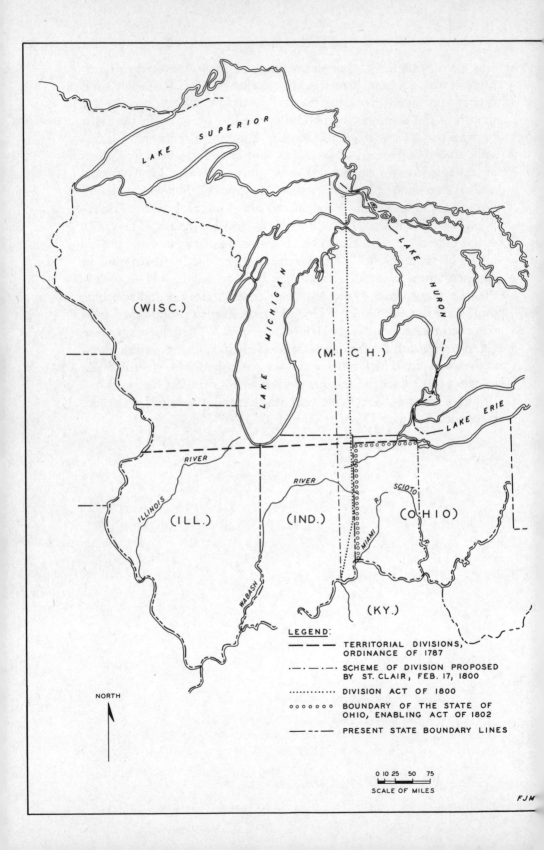

LAKE SUPERIOR

(WISC.)

LAKE MICHIGAN

(MICH.)

LAKE HURON

LAKE ERIE

RIVER

RIVER

SCIOTO

MIAMI R.

ILLINOIS RIVER

(ILL.)

(IND.)

(OHIO)

WABASH

(KY.)

LEGEND:

— — — TERRITORIAL DIVISIONS, ORDINANCE OF 1787

—·—·— SCHEME OF DIVISION PROPOSED BY ST. CLAIR, FEB. 17, 1800

·········· DIVISION ACT OF 1800

ooooooo BOUNDARY OF THE STATE OF OHIO, ENABLING ACT OF 1802

— —·— — PRESENT STATE BOUNDARY LINES

NORTH

0 10 25 50 75
SCALE OF MILES

FJM

Ohio: Pawn of Politics

FALLEN TIMBERS THREW OPEN THE FLOODGATES TO AN ENDLESS stream of emigrants. Revolutionary War veterans from Pennsylvania and Virginia, dissatisfied or disgruntled settlers from Kentucky and emigrants of all classes from New England poured into the region which Wayne's victory had made safe for settlement. They sought freedom and prosperity in their new homes. Instead they found arbitrary government and an autocratic governor quarreling with the territorial judges over their respective jurisdictions.

Governor St. Clair was now in the last stage of his dramatic career. He had spent thirty of his fifty-four years in America. In 1758 he left his native Scotland, where he took a degree in medicine, to serve under General Jeffrey Amherst in the French and Indian War. At the end of that conflict he purchased, with part of the considerable dowry his wife brought him, an estate in Legonier Valley, western Pennsylvania, where he built a fine house and gristmill. At the outbreak of the Revolution he joined the Americans, assuaging feelings of guilt by pledging his loyalty to George III while denouncing the "wicked ministry and corrupt Parliament." He led a battalion in the invasion of Canada but suffered defeat in several battles. Subsequently he served dutifully at Trenton, Princeton and Brandywine and assisted Nathanael Greene in the Carolinas. After the war he moved to Philadelphia, where he entered politics, which led him to Congress and eventually to the presidency of that body. The next year his influential connections and his friendship with George Washington, more than his political and military experience, brought him the governorship of the Northwest Territory.

Nothing in his life was more unfortunate. He persuaded himself that he was an aristocrat, though one of his supporters, Jacob Burnet, described him as "open and frank in his manners and accessible to persons of every rank." This dyed-in-the-wool Federalist, this Metternich of the frontier, had nothing but disdain for common people who, he believed, "wantonly perpetrate crimes that are a disgrace to humanity, and seem at the same time to be under a kind of religious enthusiasm, whilst they want the daring spirit that usually inspires." Secretly he despised democracy; he yearned for aristocracy, for monarchy, which he believed was the only form of government that God could support. While his boundless ego impelled him to accept the governorship of the Northwest Territory as a step to higher office, he hated the people over which he had been chosen to govern. He wrote Alexander Hamilton that on the frontier he felt like "a poor devil banished to another planet." From his boredom he escaped to the blandishments of the East so many times that Washington felt contrained to reprimand him. Had Washington been any kind of a psychologist he might have spared his friend much embarrassment. St. Clair's privations in Scotland— he was the youngest son and inherited nothing—and in America before his marriage had engendered feelings of inferiority which his inordinate pride compelled him to conceal under an aristocratic demeanor and a corresponding disdain for the common man. Gout, that disease of an age ignorant of balanced diets, failed to sweeten his disposition. He was unable to adjust his feelings to his position and to the spirit of the frontier. The flood of Jeffersonian democracy in Ohio swept him off his feet and eventually engulfed him.

No better fitted to his post was the territorial secretary, Major Winthrop Sargent, a New Englander who shared St. Clair's disdain for the common man. He scoffed at public opinion and wore his Harvard education on his sleeve. Like the Bourbons, he learned nothing and forgot nothing. Trained for a military life, he preached the supremacy of discipline; he saw no merit in the roaming and liberal-minded frontiersmen. An unyielding and unimaginative Puritan, he denounced as a vice every pleasure he felt he must not enjoy. Acting as governor during St. Clair's numerous absences, he won the stubborn hatred of the jovial, back-slapping, optimistic and story-telling frontiersmen by stretching his authority. They frowned on his firm and drastic attitude toward the squatters beyond the Miami settlements and on his connivance with prominent speculators; they laughed at his pompous manners and everlasting jeremiads. Had he made his residence in Marietta among the New

Englanders who understood his temperament, he might have ended his days as a successful speculator of his land company. Instead he made the grave error of living among the Kentuckians of Cincinnati. He failed to convert them to his views.

The three territorial judges were able men in wrong positions. Samuel Holden Parsons and James Mitchell Varnum were lawyers who understood almost nothing about the democratizing influences of the frontier. The only judge with any experience on the frontier, John Cleves Symmes, was more interested in speculation than in government. Of the later judges, Rufus Putnam had no legal training whatever and George Turner, an irascible Englishman, put money before speculation and speculation before government.

At the outset governor and judges quarreled over their legislative powers. Should they adopt laws from the original thirteen states, as the Ordinance provided, or frame their own to fit frontier needs? St. Clair felt that the territorial laws should be patterned after those of the original states; the judges, being a little more democratic, felt that the territorial laws should be "conformable to the Constitution" and consistent with "republican principles." To this practical policy St. Clair had eventually to yield, but he won a resounding victory over the question of whether his legislative powers were merely co-ordinate with their own. If the judges had had their way, they would have combined to enact their kind of territorial code despite his opposition. By his victory St. Clair clinched his own absolute power of veto.[1]

The mutual concessions enabled governor and judges to draw up a code of laws largely patterned after the Pennsylvania Code that St. Clair had brought with him. Needless to say, this struck most frontiersmen as autocratic. The New England settlers, being accustomed to a strong centralized government, accepted the new code with a measure of resignation; but the Virginians and the Kentuckians, who were crossing the Ohio in large numbers and who had known the freedom of the frontier, resented the code from the beginning. Before long the widespread dissatisfaction found expression in the columns of the region's first newspaper, the *Centinel of the North-Western Territory*, which first appeared in Cincinnati in the fall of 1793. Concealing their identities under pen names, the more literate frontiersmen sent in communications which were sometimes silly and often verbose. "Manlius" vigorously attacked the annual fee of $16 for licenses to merchants and traders, stating that it was graft for the great landowners, one of whom he said was a member of the territorial government. Another writer, "Vitruvius," accused St. Clair and the judges of "adopting" laws "culled from their own sprightly genious" for the purpose of robbing merchants and traders.[2]

The frontiersmen also stressed the need for speedier and more convenient justice in petty cases. Judge Turner, who for all his irascibility had some sense of popular rights, tried to persuade his colleagues and the governor to extend from $5 to $20 the limit for civil cases over which a local magistrate had jurisdiction. But the governor objected on the ground that the justices, being largely "illiterate and ignorant of the law," should not be entrusted with important matters. In vain did Turner remonstrate that in petty cases "plain good sense and integrity" dictated that, with the consent of the parties involved, a jury of six men should be substituted for the usual one of twelve. So frontiersmen involved in civil suits often had to bear the grievance of having to undertake an arduous and expensive journey to the distant county seat in order to collect a debt of more than $5. "Dorastus" showed the injustice of this law by pointing out that a recent session of the Hamilton County court had lasted fifteen days and had financially ruined many of the persons who had been obliged to attend it.[3]

The attacks against this law grew more acrimonious with each passing day. Finally "A Citizen and Friend of the Rights of Man" called upon "all good citizens of Hamilton County" to meet in Cincinnati on February 11, 1795, to draw up a petition to the "legislature" for the "redress of the many inconveniences resulting from some of the existing laws of the Territory." The settlers of the four most important settlements gathered on the specified day and signed the petition.

The frightened governor then hurriedly called the judges to revise the territorial code. Though they could not agree that the governor possessed an absolute right of veto, they pledged their support for the sake of the public good. They drew up Maxwell's Code, named for William Maxwell, owner of the *Centinel*, who first published the Code in book form. It included laws from the codes of several states. Twenty-five laws were from the Pennsylvania Code, one from the New Jersey Code, three from the Virginia Code, six from the Massachusetts Code and one was a composite from the New York Code and the Pennsylvania Code. Turner, supported by Symmes, revived his proposal to extend from $5 to $20 the limit for civil cases which could be decided by a single magistrate. Again St. Clair refused to change the law, this time averring that with justice "so cheap" many settlers "would merely bring suit to gratify their revengeful dispositions." The governor would do no better than to accept a compromise in the form of a law from the Pennsylvania Code which gave a justice of the peace final jurisdiction in a civil case involving less than $5 and original jurisdiction with the right to appeal in that involving between $5 and $12. Another reform permitted a justice of the peace to try cases of larceny under $1.50. A verdict of guilty carried a sentence of not more than fifteen lashes or a fine of not more than $3.[4]

Still another law required innkeepers and the "tippling houses" of Cincinnati, which St. Clair and Sargent denounced as "injurious to the public morals," to pay an annual license of $16. The popular reaction to this law was so strong that the fee of the annual license was reduced to $4 with the stipulation that licenses would be issued only on the recommendations of the magistrates.[5]

Maxwell's Code made important changes in the judiciary system of the territory. It more clearly defined the jurisdiction of the general court, required semiannual sessions at Marietta and Cincinnati and authorized the judges to try cases in other counties of the territory. At the same time it increased the jurisdiction of the county courts of quarter-sessions and kept the expenses of the litigants to a minimum by restricting any of their sessions to three legal days. The Code made a concession to the popular opposition of arbitrary taxation by providing for the election of assessors in each township. The frontiersmen were further protected from excessive taxation by restricting the county rate in any one year to not more than 75¢ on $200 of total assessment and not more than $1 per capita for single men owning visible property valued at $100.[6]

The legislative board contracted with William Maxwell to print one thousand copies of the new territorial code. St. Clair distributed two hundred copies among the territorial and the county officials. The remaining eight hundred copies Maxwell offered "in boards" to subscribers of his newspaper at 19¢ per fifty pages and to others at 30¢. Some of the laws in Maxwell's Code suited the needs of the frontiersmen; others were of dubious legal value. In any case, St. Clair and the judges had, by taking liberties with the original laws, ignored the restrictions laid down in the Ordinance. But Congress did not object, and the frontiersmen abided by Maxwell's Code, with a few other laws passed at irregular intervals, during the remainder of the necessarily arbitrary first stage of territorial government.[7]

2

Ohio began her movement for statehood soon after her first towns were founded. St. Clair had been governor of the Northwest Territory only a year when he learned that the settlers had "already got it into their heads to pass by the second stage of the temporary Government which was contemplated for that Country, and go forward at once to show that their numbers entitle [them] to become an integral part of the United States."[8] Though this desire declined during the Indian campaigns, when emigration temporarily ceased, it rose again after Fallen Timbers and grew in persistance until it eventually became a reality.

The great majority of the settlers, regardless of their political sympathies, favored statehood. Federalists and Republicans generally differed only in the manner of obtaining it. But the most ardent supporters of the movement were the Republicans, who, as admirers of Jefferson's ideals, decried servitude in any form and championed local autonomy and universal manhood suffrage. Their spokesmen, concealing their identities with impressive pen names, attacked St. Clair's arbitrary rule and the Ordinance in the few Republican newspapers of the region. One of these polemics, "Vitruvius," reminded his readers that the Ordinance anteceded settlement and that, therefore, the people had been prevented from forming a government of their own. To him the provision in the Ordinance which required five thousand male citizens of voting age in a division of the territory before it could elect a legislature was "impolitic, arbitrary, oppressive, and tyrannical." Emboldened by his own candor, he went on to attack St. Clair as a tyrant whose powers exceeded those which George III had imposed on the Americans just before the Revolution. He urged the settlers to end the "absolute, despotic, tyranical, and absurd system of jurisprudence," by calling for conventions in different parts of the territory for the purpose of drawing up remonstrances to Congress.[9]

The veteran polemic, "Dorastus," elaborated these arguments with unabated fury. The government of the territory, he averred, was "oppressive, impolitical, and altogether improper, and in its leading principles intirely [sic] opposite to those rights and privaledges [sic] belonging to freemen, & which no power on earth has any right to deprive them of." Arming himself with the ideas of Thomas Paine, the example of ancient Greece and the experience of the American colonies, he attacked as contrary to natural law the provision in the Ordinance which delayed statehood until the population of one division reached sixty thousand. No particular number of people, he continued, was needed to constitute a civil government; history provided many instances to the contrary; the settlers should, like all other free men, choose their own rulers and make their own laws. Would this not be better, he asked in conclusion, than to subject themselves to the present one?[10]

These arguments reflected St. Clair's unpopularity with the majority of the settlers. With incredible frankness he proclaimed to all comers that the average settler lived only for the service of his stomach, that he was purely emotional and that no reason could convince him and no judgment could direct him. He feared that, if the people were given a democratic government,

. . . our western Territory, instead of proving a Fund for paying the national debt, would be a Source of Mischief and encreasing Expense. . . . It had given such a Spring to the Spirit of Emigration, too high before, that tho' it is pregnant with the most serious consequences to the Atlantic States, it cannot now be held back.[11]

By these words he expressed the prevailing Federalist fear that the Atlantic States, by permitting their citizens to emigrate to the territory, were aiding in laying the foundations of a rival country, which eventually would either separate itself from the United States or hold political sway over the entire East. He was especially distrustful of Virginians, whom he considered "very licentious & too great a proportion, indolent and extremely debauched."[12]

His arbitrary rule and his prejudices, which he uttered with his usual indiscretion, accounted for his unpopularity. The Virginians and Kentuckians especially resented him and voiced their sentiments in toasts of Independence Day, 1795. One of them drank to "the old harlot of aristocracy—May she speedily be dunned out to the tune of *Ça Ira*." Another toasted "republican government . . . the most equal, just and happy." Still another drank to "the people and elective government of the Territory—May they possess virtue, wisdom and firmness to assert and maintain the indispensible rights of a free state."[13]

As a practical measure toward statehood they sought the second stage of territorial government, which provided a legislature. St. Clair, of course, discouraged this aim. Aside from psychological reasons, he opposed it because it meant the weakening of his own political career. We recall that he regarded the governorship of the territory only as a stepping stone to higher office: he had aspired to the vice presidency of the United States. But his defeat at the hands of the Indians had blasted his plans. He then had hoped to return to political life in his own state of Pennsylvania, but the rising tide of Republicanism there had precluded that possibility. Nothing now remained save for him to keep the governorship of the territory as long as possible.[14]

When the Republicans saw that St. Clair was making no effort to ascertain whether the territory contained the number of free males of voting age required for the second stage of government, they decided to find out for themselves. To this end they created in Cincinnati a Committee of Correspondence under the leadership of Judge William Goforth. The seven men who composed the Committee drew up a plan by which the constables of each township in Hamilton County should take the census at the time they made their annual list of taxable citizens. The plan authorized the Committee to appoint an agent with a good reputation to take the place of any constable who refused his services. The compensation stipulated for a constable or an agent was $9 from funds raised by popular subscription.[15]

The Cincinnatians adopted the plan and urged it upon the Republican leaders in other settlements of the Ohio country. At the same time the Committee issued a windy circular in which it urged the people to insist on their rights as free citizens. Then it moved to placate St. Clair with an invitation to dinner. The governor declined to accept it unless the Committee agreed to state "to [him] explicitly, the nature of their organization—the purposes they have in view, and how, and by whom they were appointed; together with the measures that they have pursued for accomplishing the objects that have been contemplated."[16]

The Committee replied by insisting on the census. St. Clair knew this was inevitable and reluctantly capitulated. Even so, he managed to save face. Without waiting for the magistrates of the various townships to submit their full returns, he issued a proclamation admitting that the required population for the second stage of government existed. In consequence, he appointed the third Monday in December 1798 for an election of the delegates of the territorial House. The qualified voters elected twenty-two men who, at their first meeting in Cincinnati on February 4, 1799 nominated ten men from which group the President of the United States selected five to compose the Legislative Council. The Republicans had won the first round in their fight for statehood.[17]

3

In the second stage of territorial government St. Clair lost none of his old prerogatives. He was still chief executive; he still possessed the power of absolute veto; his appointive power extended over the justices of the peace and the army officers; he licensed all lawyers and innkeepers; he could convene, prorogue and dissolve the assembly as he saw fit. To these advantages he could add the fact that the Federal Government paid his salary.[18]

While the assembly posed as a check to his extensive powers, it represented a limited constituency. Most of the incoming settlers had no voice in the government. It was a government of property. Only those owning fifty acres or their equivalent could vote for the delegates of the House, who, themselves, were subject to a property qualification of two hundred acres. Membership in the Legislative Council carried the more strigent requirement of five hundred acres.[19]

Yet in the second stage of government the people realized decided advantages over the first. The assembly had full power to enact laws within the framework of the Ordinance. The two Houses could now elect a delegate to Congress who could voice popular opinion in opposition to the policies of the governor. Nevertheless, these political gains failed to satisfy most of the more recent settlers who, embued with Jeffersonian ideals, clamored louder and louder for popular control of the government. In their fight for statehood they derived motivation from the fact that the second stage of territorial government strongly resembled the English colonial system over which the nation had just triumphed.[20]

The assembly showed itself a divided body from the very beginning. The Legislative Council, led by Jacob Burnet and supported by St. Clair, dedicated all its strength to a postponement of statehood. On the contrary, the House of Representatives gradually expressed more and more Republican sentiment and more and more hostility toward the governor as it armed itself in the cause of statehood. Its leaders were Dr. Edward Tiffin and his brother-in-law, Thomas Worthington, both Virginians who resented St. Clair's prejudices, hauteur and arbitrary rule. Tiffin, a native of England, practiced medicine; Worthington was a land speculator. Worthington was destined to become the father of Ohio statehood. In 1796 he had caught the Ohio fever and had made a trip west to the valley of the Scioto, where his fellow Virginian, Nathaniel Massie, was establishing Manchester. Entranced by the prospect of being a landowner, Worthington had bought several town lots from Massie and prowled around thickets and forests of bottoms and upland in search of good farming land. In 1797 he permanently settled in Chillicothe with his bride and began the Chillicothe party, which was dedicated to Jeffersonian ideals and statehood.[21]

Worthington was a tall young man of twenty-five with a florid complexion, an open face and a quiet and unassuming demeanor. This appearance concealed a passionate nature. Though brought up as a Quaker he was unconsciously a Calvinist who believed that he was one of the elect of God. At the least excitement his face would turn crimson with zeal or indignation. Then with a rude eloquence he would embrace a cause dear to his heart, or with deadly invective would slash an enemy like a rapier. His family motto, *Virtute Dignus Avorum*—worthy of one's ancestors—was to him a constant challenge to attain the highest ideals in his daily work.[22]

The undercurrent of hostility between the governor and the assembly soon came into the open. On October 3, 1799, the two House proceeded to elect a delegate to Congress by joint ballot. The two candidates were Arthur St. Clair, Jr., and William Henry Harrison, who had recently succeeded the hated Winthrop Sargent as secretary of the territory. The election of young St. Clair would of course assure his father's wishes in Congress. Harrison, on the other hand, was a Republican who counted Worthington and Massie among his best friends. Harrison won by a slight majority—a blow to St. Clair, though he concealed for the present whatever chagrin he might have felt and co-operated with the assembly in its legislative program.[23]

But peace was short-lived. On the last day of the session St. Clair showed his rabid Federalist hand. After praising the assembly for its industry in passing wise laws, he reminded it that he still enjoyed the power of veto and that he was determined "to follow the dictates of his own mind." In consequence, he had vetoed a number of the bills. One of these, passed through Massie's influence, proposed that the county seat of Adams County be changed from Washington to Manchester. Even more significant was St. Clair's veto of a bill authorizing a census of the eastern section of the territory. The census would have shown that the eastern section had the largest number of settlers and would, therefore, have sped the movement for statehood.[24]

The Republicans understood his motives only too well. They countered by sending Worthington to Philadelphia to help Harrison overthrow St. Clair, acquire local and territorial control and fight for statehood. With the assistance of able Republican congressmen the two men struck St. Clair a telling blow when on May 7, 1800, they pressed the Division Act through Congress. This act divided the territory by a line drawn from opposite the mouth of the Kentucky River to Fort Recovery and thence due north to Canada. The eastern section retained the title of Northwest Territory and its capital was transferred, rather arbitrarily, from Cincinnati to Chillicothe, the Republican stronghold. The western section was called Indiana Territory and had its capital at Vincennes with William Henry Harrison as its governor. The new territory was permitted to drop back to the first stage of territorial government but was to be permitted to advance to the second stage whenever a majority of its voters wished. Two months after the Division Act was passed, Connecticut surrendered the Western Reserve to Congress, which declared it a part of the Northwest Territory.[25]

St. Clair quickly fought back. To keep the original territory in its colonial stages as long as possible he proposed to Harrison that it be divided into three sections with the Scioto and a line northward from the mouth of the Kentucky as the two dividing lines. Warning Harrison that "almost any division into two parts must ruin Cincinnati," he repeated his belief that the settlers were incapable of governing themselves. At about the same time he wrote to his friend, James Ross of Pennsylvania, pouring venom on the people over which he had been chosen to govern:

A multitude of indigent and ignorant people are but ill qualified to form a constitution and government for themselves; but that is not the greatest evil to be feared from it. They are too far removed from the seat of government to be much impressed with the power of the United States. Their connection with any of them is very slender—many having left nothing but creditors behind them, whom they would very willingly forget entirely. Fixed political principles they have none, and though at present they seem attached to the General Government, it is in fact but a passing fancy, easily changed or even removed, and certainly not strong enough to be counted upon as a principle of action; and there are a good many who hold sentiments in direct opposition to its principles, and who, though quiet at present, would then take the lead. Their government would most probably be democratic in its form and oligarchic in its execution, and more troublesome and more opposed to the measures of the United States than even Kentucky.[26]

Such was his mood when on November 3 he convened the assembly at Chillicothe. Solemnly its members gathered in Abrams' big house, which stood on Second and Walnut streets and which furnished them with a billiard table for their recreation and with drink and food as they legislated. They hoped for peace but met only St. Clair's complaints and arrogance. He complained of a number of irregularities in Adams County; he reminded them of the need to establish exact boundaries for the existing counties. He told them that he might not meet with them again, for his term of office would expire on December 9. He closed his address in a most undignified manner. "The vilest calumnies," he thundered, "and the grossest falsehoods," had been circulated about him to prevent his reappointment, though he had worked assiduously for the welfare of the people in the territory.[27]

The assembly expressed regret for the "calumnies." The Legislative Council, moreover, assured him of its great confidence in his administration and hoped it would continue. Not so the members of the lower House. They merely said that they hoped his good intentions would prove an effective shield against wicked and malevolent attacks. And their local jealousies enabled him to win a majority of them to his side. The members from Hamilton County, for example, were incensed by the removal of the territorial capital to Chillicothe. They retaliated by forming a coalition with the members from Washington County to defeat the schemes of the Republicans from the Virginia Military Tract. This coalition supported St. Clair's pet scheme for three divisions of the original Northwest Territory, which would automatically make Marietta capital of the eastern and Cincinnati capital of the middle district. They also championed St. Clair for reappointment and elected William McMillan of Hamilton County to fill out Harrison's unfinished term and Paul Fearing of Marietta for the ensuing full term of two years. This choice assured in Congress a delegate who would look favorably upon St. Clair's scheme.[28]

These triumphs, however, failed to remove the friction existing between the governor and the territorial assembly. Most of its members insisted firmly upon their own powers in the creation of counties and in the location of county seats, and they requested him to return within ten days any bill that he vetoed so that they might give it adequate consideration. The governor replied angrily that neither the establishment of counties nor the location of county seats fell within their jurisdiction and that his veto power could be changed only by a change in the Ordinance.[29]

The assembly replied by asking McMillan to request a modified veto, such as that exercised by the President, and a change in the Ordinance that would grant the right to vote to all free citizens over twenty-one who paid a territorial or a county tax. This was a remarkable proposal from an assembly chosen by property holders, for it showed the strength of the Republican movement. The Legislative Council passed these instructions to McMillan only after heated debate.[30]

A week later St. Clair again told the assembly that on December 9 his commission would expire and that, therefore, legislative action would be suspended. This announcement came like a bolt from the blue, for the assembly had not completed its work. The governor, moreover, had delayed the announcement so that it could be made in the absence of the territorial secretary, Charles Willing Byrd, who had succeeded Harrison and who was an ardent Republican. Had Byrd been allowed to assume the governor's duties, as was his right, the assembly would doubtless have passed legislation damaging to St. Clair's plans. Even the governor's warmest supporter, Jacob Burnet, wrote disapprovingly that the announcement to prorogue the assembly had been withheld for the purpose "of preventing the interference of the secretary till it would be too late to accomplish the object."[31]

The immediate reaction to this apparently clever act on the part of the governor was to stimulate the clamor for statehood. The Republicans in the lower House now broke into open revolt. On the day before the session ended the members set up a committee which drew up an address to the people of the Northwest Territory. This called attention to the article in the Ordinance which required a population of sixty thousand to form a state and stated that this number would be shown in the census of 1800. Anticipating action for statehood in the new assembly in the fall of 1801, the address recommended that the people instruct their representatives "to govern themselves accordingly." Five hundred copies of the address were distributed throughout the territory. Privately St. Clair stormed and fumed and swore vengeance. But in a final address to the assembly he showed no indication of his feelings. Indeed, his words were strangely warm and kind.[32]

For he could still claim strong supporters. McMillan, for one, spared no effort to secure his reappointment. Moreover, his political position favored him. Under President Adams the Federalists were still in power, and the Senate had a Federalist majority. For the present Thomas Jefferson, depending on a Federalist House for his own election, could not help the Republicans in the territory. Eventually Adams nominated St. Clair for another term of three years, though he submitted recommendations for and against the appointment. A committee cleared him of the charges leveled against him by his political enemies, permitting the Senate to confirm him in office.[33]

The jubilant governor now redoubled his efforts to frustrate the Republicans in their aspirations for statehood. On November 25, 1801, the new assembly met in a new courthouse at the corners of Paint and Main streets in Chillicothe. It was a stone building of two stories with simple furniture and glass windows brought by water from the firm of Nicholson & Gallatin at New Geneva, Pennsylvania. A cupola, over which rose a gilt eagle standing on a ball, gave the building a judicial air. In each of the two rooms was a fireplace. The fireplaces, however, failed to clear the building of its mustiness and provide heat for the legislators. In the course of their duties they often left their chairs to warm their hands and backsides.[34]

At first both houses expressed willingness to co-operate with the governor. The Legislative Council congratulated him warmly and declared that his "numerous services" were "sacred pledges" of his "sincere desire . . . to promote the greatest happiness and prosperity of our infant country." Quite different was the mood of the representatives. The speech prepared by a committee under Massie expressed respect but failed to congratulate the governor on his reappointment. It stung him not by any bad it said but by the good it did not say.[35]

The governor had taken pains to organize his party for a real contest. On December 3 his supporters in the Legislative Council passed an act "declaring the assent of the Territory, northwest of the river Ohio, to an alteration of the ordinance for the government thereof." This proposed to divide the original Northwest Territory into three districts by running one line north from the mouth of the Scioto and another from the western boundary of George Rogers Clark's grant near the Falls of the Ohio. St. Clair knew that congressional approval of these divisions would mean the indefinite delay of statehood. On December 18 the lower House passed the bill. Massie immediately sprang to his feet and requested permission to present the Republican minority's protest. This was granted.

The protest was in the form of a petition and carried the names of seven members including Tiffin, Massie and Worthington. It claimed that any change in the boundaries of the territory was a violation of that part of the Ordinance which designated future divisions and which granted to each the right to become a state on attainment of the specified population. The proposed changes, moreover, would force the handful of property owners in the vast new territory of Indiana to meet the burden of taxation. The Republicans gave the protest wide circulation by having it printed in the *Scioto Gazette*. This led to numerous public meetings which culminated in petitions denouncing the proposed divisions. In a general meeting at Chillicothe the Republicans appointed Worthington and Michael Baldwin to lay the protest before Congress.[36]

Baldwin was cursing, whisky-drinking firebrand and a member of the lower House for Chillicothe. He hated the "Feds" from the governor down to his last scullion and prayed fervently for a speedy end to his rule. In the town's grogshops and taverns he gathered a gang of rowdies—he affectionately called them his "bloodhounds"—and incited them to raid St. Clair's boarding house and bring him out to see himself burned in effigy. But Worthington got word of the proposed demonstration and persuaded Baldwin to call it off. St. Clair wrote later that Worthington had to threaten to shoot Baldwin in order to stop him from persisting in his purpose.[37]

On Christmas Eve trouble broke out again. At Gregg House, as St. Clair's tavern was called, Rufus Putnam unhappily toasted his fellow Federalists as follows: "May the Scioto lave the borders of two great and flourishing states." Angered by this toast, Baldwin and his gang collected in a grogshop, fortified themselves with a few drinks and stamped down the street to Gregg House. Forcing their way into the tavern, some of them struck at William Schieffelin, Federalist representative from Wayne County, then collared him. The infuriated Schieffelin drew his dirk and would have plunged it into his attacker had he not been restrained. Breaking loose, he grabbed a pair of pistols off the mantel and ordered the rioters to get out. By now Gregg House roared with threats and insults. St. Clair was upstairs, writing. Hearing the commotion, he hurried down and, seeing upturned furniture and swinging fists and flying bottles, sent for Jeremiah McLene, the sheriff, and Samuel Finley, the justice of the peace. McLene was out of town, but Finley hastened to the tavern, hoping to find "uproar and confusion." Instead he found St. Clair expostulating with the rioters, both in the tavern and in the street, and warning them of the serious consequences of their actions. The governor then turned to prevent a fight between Dr. Samuel McAdow, a Republican, and Schieffelin, who had been insulting the memory of each other's ancestors. Finley sent the rioters home and went with Dr. McAdow, who was still shaking with anger, to another tavern.[38]

The furious governor furnished Finley with the names of the leading rioters and of persons who could testify as witnesses of the riot. The sheriff examined the accused persons but dismissed them when they swore they had neither planned nor done anything to incite trouble. At the same time McLene testified that Worthington on the night of the riot had wrested from Baldwin a promise that he would refrain from molesting any of the Federalists at Gregg House. The sheriff's testimony incensed the governor so much that he denounced him for malfeasance in office. The sheriff then resigned in disgust.[39]

On December 29 St. Clair laid the whole matter before the legislature, together with his correspondence with Finley, and asked that an investigating committee be set up to ascertain the culprits who had "maltreated certain members of the legislature." The committee took no action. Then, on January 18, 1802, it dismissed the matter as the irresponsible brawl of a few drunkards.[40]

4

Meanwhile on December 27 Worthington and Baldwin had departed for Washington, the new capital of the United States, to present the Republican protest over the new boundaries to Congress. Traveling by way of Lancaster, Zanesville, Wheeling, Cumberland, Shepherdstown and Fredericktown, they arrived at their destination early in January 1802 and put up at Mrs. Wilson's near the Capitol. A few days later Worthington received from Tiffin a packet of mail containing the names of a thousand persons protesting the high-handed measure of the Federalists. Massie later sent him copies of three petitions. Armed with these manifestations of popular support, Worthington and Baldwin sought out their friends in Congress. Among these were the strong Jeffersonians William Branch Giles, Baldwin's brother Abraham, Stevens Thomson Mason, John Breckenridge and John Brown, all of whom had corresponded with Worthington on the situation in the territory. Politically the times favored them. In the national elections of 1800 the "glorious victory" of Jefferson and Burr had re-established, in the words of an Ohio newspaper, "the pure spirit of Republicanism." Worthington told Abraham Baldwin that the Northwest Territory would rather become an "independent state" than remain "under the present arbitrary government, better fitted for an English or Spanish colony than for citizens of the United States.'" And Baldwin agreed, for statehood meant additional Republican votes in Congress.[41]

Michael Baldwin and Worthington also held conferences with President Jefferson, who expressed great interest in the political picture of the territory and, when informed that it was largely Republican in sentiment, intimated that he favored St. Clair's removal. At the end of January Michael Baldwin returned to Ohio, leaving Worthington to carry on the rest of the mission alone.[42]

Meanwhile, St. Clair had forwarded the division bill to Fearing. The territorial delegate to Congress in turn presented it to the House of Representatives, pointing out that it supported the boundaries of the states as planned by the American government under the Articles of Confederation. He then moved that the division bill be referred to a select committee for consideration. Arming himself with the petitions furnished by Worthington, Giles attacked the bill on the ground that it "would place the people of the Territory in a very disagreeable situation" by postponing statehood indefinitely and by perpetuating in office an unpopular governor and an unpopular legislature. Another of Worthington's friends, Thomas T. Davis of Kentucky, then moved that the bill be referred to the committee of the whole for immediate discussion. The bill provoked a series of fiery debates between Fearing and Giles and their respective supporters, but on January 27 Giles silenced his opponents and resolved that the bill "ought not to be assented to by Congress." Whereupon the committee of the whole passed the resolution, which the House immediately and overwhelmingly adopted.[43]

Having accomplished his immediate objective of defeating the division bill, Worthington moved with equal rapidity to his chief objective of achieving statehood for the Northwest Territory. To this end he asked his friends to write to Jefferson. On January 25 the president had received from Judge Symmes a letter which undoubtedly influenced him in favor of the Republicans. The judge had long resented St. Clair for refusing voting privileges to most of the settlers in the Symmes Tract because they had not yet paid for their grants in full. His feelings found expression in a complete indictment of the governor and of all his works:

By constitution a despot, as well as from his long imperious habits of commanding, he has become unsufferably arbitrary.

Like other tyrants, he places his confidence for advice and support, in the weak and the guileful of the citizens, who misguide and disgrace him.

The prosperity of the territory is, and always has been a secondary consideration with him. literally his will is law; and measures (however eligible, considered either as convenient, honorary, or pecuniary) which do not concentrate their good effect, in his family or among his favorites, are altogether inadmissible with him.

He is at war with those who do not approach him with adulation on their tongue.

He hesitates not, to sacrifice the best interest of the territory, when they come in competition whith his partial aims.

Though of courtly exterior; his heart, if judged of by the tongue, is illiberal beyond a sample.

Destitute of gratitude, he abhors the government that feeds him:— the public of private hand that relieves him in distress, confers no obligation.

Though a commentator of the sedition law,—is seditious himself. . . .

Wiser in his own conceit, then the other two branches of the Legislature, collective and unanimous; he withholds his assent to bills of the most salutary nature.

Under his long administration the people are not, nor have they ever been satisfied, and many detesting him, have fled the territory. . . .

Do these imputations need proof?—let fetters, prisons, flames, human-bones and tears bear testimony; while neglected french-rights, imbecility of Magistrates of his appointment, executive deception, unequal tenures in office, his Usurped prerogatives, and ill placed patronage, fill the North western territory with murmurs, deep—awful—dangerous; while his distracted government totters to its foundation. . . .[44]

This letter prepared the way for Worthington to denounce the governor when on February 1 he conferred with Jefferson. Later Worthington in a letter to the president summarized what he said. He felt no prejudice toward St. Clair as a man, he wrote, "but, on the other hand, viewing him rather with an eye of pity, it is not a pleasing task to me to be obliged, in defense of what I conceive the just and lawful rights of myself, in common with my fellow-citizens of the North-western Territory, to remonstrate against his conduct." He went on to substantiate Symmes' charges:

He had created prerequisites to his office which are unjust and illegal. For every tavern license granted before the last session of the Assembly he received four dollars; for every ferry license granted before the session of 1799, he received one guinea; he now receives one guinea for every marriage license by him granted. Fees are received on militia commissions, and are also charged on all the commissions of the civil officers in each newly-erected county, in proportion as the commission is lucrative.

He had attempted to make the judiciary dependent on his will; and when justices have acted with firmness and independence in giving such a construction to an existing statute law as appeared to them reasonable and right, their commissions have been revoked by his proclamation.

He is an open and avowed enemy to republican form of government, and an advocate for monarchy; is also an open and declared enemy to militia regulations, which declaration his practise hitherto has confirmed, as the militia in the Territory are without organization, although a good militia law has been enacted for two years past.

He has created, and endeavored to attach to himself a party, and in conjunction with them has made attempts, and in some measure succeeded, to destroy the harmony and divide the interests of the people. . . .[45]

Anticipating such charges, undoubtedly because he was guilty of them, St. Clair attempted to clear his name in a letter to Jefferson. He had spared no effort, he wrote, to promote the "general happiness" of the people. He had, moreover, encouraged industry and obedience to the laws, had encouraged the people to virtue in their lives and practices. He denied that he was greatly concerned for the loss of his office: he wished only to preserve his reputation from the permanent damage of a summary dismissal.[46]

Meanwhile, Worthington was working indefatigably for the enabling act which would permit the eastern part of the Northwest Territory to apply for admission as an independent state in the Union. Giles and Worthington enlisted the support of Albert Gallatin, Secretary of the Treasury, and during February drew up a long report in which they justified on political and economic grounds the admission of the eastern section of the original territory with boundaries about the same as those of the present state of Ohio. As chairman of the house committee on the Northwest Territory, Giles read the report and then pleaded for statehood on the ground that it would calm the disquietude which had resulted from the proposed division of the territory. The report aroused intense debates in which Fearing led the opposition. Completely disregarding the many petitions in favor of statehood, the congressional delegate argued that Congress had no right to form a state from only a portion of the original territory without the consent of the whole. To which Giles replied with equal emphasis that the territorial assembly was based on restricted franchise and did not, therefore, adequately represent the voice of the people, and that the only opponents of statehood were the governor, the congressional delegate, a few members of the assembly and a handful of citizens. The House accepted these arguments and adopted the report. Finally, on April 29 the bill passed both Houses. The votes showed that in general the representatives from the south favored and those of the New England States opposed the enabling act. On April 30 President Jefferson signed it. Two days later the jubilant Worthington started for home.[47]

But his task was by no means completed. The Federalists of Hamilton County were still determined to thwart his plans, though St. Clair himself was in Washington lobbying to keep his office. The Federalists wanted to summon the legislature in order to turn it into a convention which might reject the enabling act; but that stanch Republican, Secretary Charles Willing Byrd, refused to do so. The desperate Federalists then accepted a constitutional convention, for which Congress had provided in the enabling act, and attempted to enlist popular support to win a majority of delegates. St. Clair, who had returned gloomily from Washington early in July, joined McMillan and Burnet and other leading Federalists in deluging the newspapers with articles supporting their views. All their efforts proved vain. On October 12 the elections for delegates to the convention brought overwhelming victory to the Republicans. On the first day of the following month the delegates met at Chillicothe and organized for business by electing Edward Tiffin president and Thomas Scott secretary.

To try to persuade the delegates to reject the enabling act, St. Clair on the third asked for permission to address them. This was grudgingly granted, not to the man as Governor, but to "Arthur St. Clair, Esq."[48] His introductory remarks were gentle enough. So far as the laws had depended on him, he said, he had executed them faithfully and had endeavored to bring obedience and order to the assembly:

It was my duty to procure the good of the whole people, and it has been my only ambition to fulfill that duty. Errors, no doubt, I have fallen into. They were the errors of the head, not of the heart. They will be judged with candor, and viewed, I trust, with some indulgence. I could indeed have wished, gentlemen, that our political bark had been launched in gentler weather, and under better auspices, for I see a storm approaching in which, if she be not overset, she may at least suffer damage.[49]

With these words his mood changed drastically. Now he was again the rabid Federalist, the raging and despairing politician, the implacable enemy of Jeffersonian ideals. Now he was like a desperate gamester, bound to win or lose all at a single throw of the dice. "Party rage," he thundered, "is stalking with destructive strides over the whole continent. That baneful spirit destroyed all the ancient republics, and the United States seem to be running the same career that ruined them with a degree of rapidity truly alarming to every reflecting mind." And he vociferated on the tyrannies of the Federal Government. The people, he said, "needed no act of Congress" to "form a convention and a constitution. To pretend to authorize it was, on their part, an interference with the internal affairs of the country, which they have neither the power nor the right to make." Furthermore, the enabling act was "not binding on the people, and is in truth a nullity, and, could it be brought before that tribunal where acts of Congress can be tried, would be declared a nullity." Thus he denied Congress the right to legislate for the territories of the United States and repudiated its authority to change the provisions of the Ordinance, as that document specified. While his gesture was apparently for the good of the territory, it was actually designed to arrest the advance of Jeffersonian democracy.[50]

His speech had the opposite effect of that which he hoped to produce. Denying him the courtesy of a reply, the delegates passed a resolution declaring the expedience of forming a constitution and a state government.[51]

When St. Clair's speech was reported in Washington, it proved the last straw. Though his term would soon end with statehood, his numerous enemies, including Worthington and Gallatin, resolved to ask the President to remove him. The angry Gallatin enclosed a copy of the governor's speech in a letter he dashed off to the President:

The enclosed communication of Gov. St Clair to the convention is so indecent, & outrageous that it must be doubtful whether, notwithstanding his approaching political death, it is not incumbent on the Executive to notice it. He calls the Act of Congress a nullity— He misrepresents all its parts . . . He advises them to make a constitution for the *Whole* territory in defiance of the law . . .[52]

Jefferson had refrained from coming to a decision on St. Clair pending a thorough examination of the evidence against him. Now he hesitated no longer. At his request James Madison, Secretary of State, sent the odious Federalist a notice of dismissal:

The President observing, in an address lately delivered by you to the convention held at Chillicothe, an intemperance and indecorum of language toward the Legislature of the United States, and a disorganizing spirit and tendency of very evil example, and grossly violating the rules of conduct enjoined by your public station, determines that your commission of Governor of the Northwestern territory shall cease on the receipt of this notification.[53]

At the same time Madison sent Byrd a copy of this letter and informed him that in consequence of the action the function of governor devolved on him.[54]

St. Clair replied to Madison with a vitriolic essay on the cowardly manner in which he had been removed indirectly through his rebellious flunky, Byrd. And he poured his venom on Congress for passing the enabling act, which he regarded as "a violent, hasty, and unprecedented intrusion . . . into the internal concerns of the Northwestern Territory . . . indecorous and inconsistent with its public duty."[55]

He had already verbally hanged Worthington, Symmes and Tiffin as assassins of his political career. Tiffin pitied the "poor old Man" and asked his friends to refrain from pleading his case. On Christmas morning, 1802, "King Arthur," as Symmes called him, wrathfully hitched his horses to his coach, loaded it with books, papers and clothing, and, God-damning the day he had set foot on the Ohio country, departed for his home in Ligonier, Pennsylvania, where he was to spend the last sixteen years of his life in increasing poverty and bitter recollection of Worthington, the Judas of his painful career.[56]

Less than a month before St. Clair's departure from the Ohio country, the constitutional convention finished its work. The first constitution of Ohio embodied the principles of frontier Republicanism. Modeled on the constitution of Tennessee, the most recent frontier state, it provided for a full bill of rights, a powerful legislature, suffrage with certain qualifications to all white citizens and positive prohibition of slavery. The convention sent a copy of the constitution to Congress, and it was approved by February 12, 1803. A week later Jefferson signed the bill admitting Ohio into the Union as the seventeenth state. Its first governor was Edward Tiffin and its first senators Thomas Worthington and John Smith.[57]

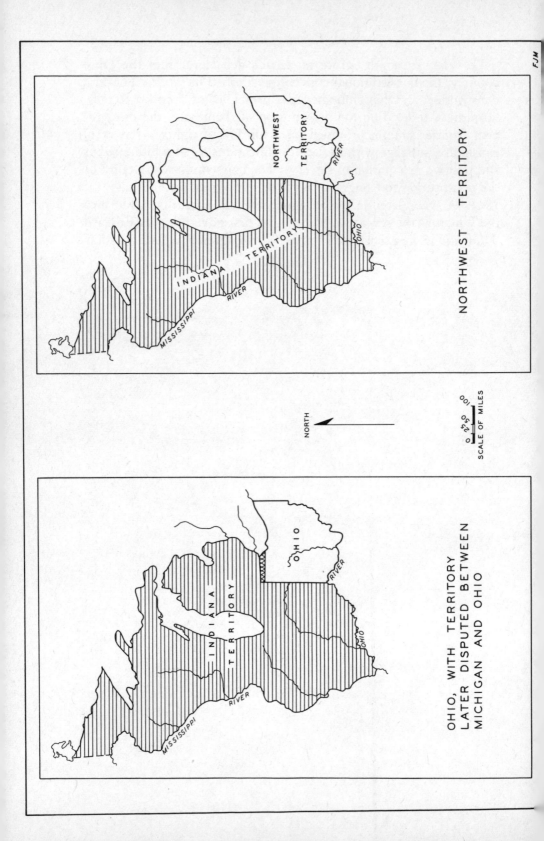

NORTHWEST TERRITORY

OHIO, WITH TERRITORY
LATER DISPUTED BETWEEN
MICHIGAN AND OHIO

NORTH

0 25 50 75 100
SCALE OF MILES

FJM

Indiana: Slave or Free Territory?

EARLY IN JANUARY 1801 YOUNG WILLIAM HENRY HARRISON PULLED up in his carriage at Colonel Vigo's spacious new house in Vincennes, alighted with George, his Negro servant, and, as prearranged, accepted lodging in the great parlor. Its rich panels and floor laid with alternating blocks of ash and walnut pleased him. The capital of the immense territory over which he had been chosen to govern delighted him from the start. Lying on the east bank of the Wabash and on the edge of a broad prairie bordered by uplands and a vast forest, it enjoyed a scenery which aroused the envy of all other settlements in the region. Its four hundred clapboard or plain log houses occupied neat rows between the river and the communal gardens of its French citizens. On the riverbank, by the stately old Church of St. Francis Xavier, Harrison examined the ruins of old Fort Sackville, which a fellow Virginian, George Rogers Clark, had captured during his memorable campaign twenty-two years before. Over the sunken buffalo trace that wound through the forest to the Falls of the Ohio, the lean and sharp-eyed governor once a week expected the postrider to bring him a letter from his wife, whom he had left with their children in Kentucky until he could build a home for them.

Harrison soon rejoined his wife and children. In May when the fruit trees were in bloom and the prairie was red with strawberries, he returned with his family to Vincennes, where eventually he bought a farm of three hundred acres and drew up plans to build on it his Georgian-style mansion, Grouseland, so called from the innumerable game birds he shot in his leisure hours.[1]

The governor was a soldier with medical training and a predilection for history. He was the youngest son of Benjamin Harrison, eminent member of the Continental Congress from Berkeley, Charles County, Virginia, and one of the signers of the Declaration of Independence. Because his boy showed some interest in natural history he sent him to Hampden Sidney College, recommended for the study of medicine by the family physician. Three years later young Harrison entered the office of Doctor Andrew Leiper in Richmond. His sympathy for the abolitionist "Humane Society" of the town, which was critical of his father's policies in the Virginia assembly, resulted in his removal to the medical school of the University of Pennsylvania in Philadelphia, where he found himself under the guardianship of Robert Morris, his father's boon companion. But the study of medicine soon proved insufferable to Harrison's adventurous temperament, and he expressed his dislike for it to Governor Richard Henry Lee, who suggested a military life. Contrary to his guardian's wishes, Harrison applied to Henry Knox, Secretary of War, for a position in the army. Knox appointed him an ensign in the Tenth Regiment of Infantry.[2]

Almost as soon as he donned his uniform he started toward a new life on the frontier. He walked from Philadelphia to Pittsburgh and from Pittsburgh to Fort Washington at Cincinnati, which he reached just as St. Clair was returning with his battered soldiers from his Indian campaign. Harrison's reception into the army was far from cordial. Jealous of his promotion, most of the officers and men hastened to assure him that a single march into Indian country would suffice to dampen his ardor for military life. This only raised his dander; he resolved to stick to his post come hell or high water; he deliberately underwent privation and undertook arduous tasks to harden his constitution. At the same time he beguiled his loneliness and eased his pains with endless quantities of military history, his first love: he devoured Herodotus, Thucydides, Caesar, Sallust and—inexcusably—Rollin. He became an expert of military tactics on paper; he led the Romans against Hannibal at Cannae and rewrote history by winning a resounding victory. Henceforth he adorned his letters with the names of Roman proconsuls and generals and battles. Years later Daniel Webster said that Harrison, in revising his inaugural address, had killed "seventeen Roman proconsuls as dead as smelts."[3]

In 1793 Harrison marched with Anthony Wayne as his aide-de-camp and a year later won his admiration at Fallen Timbers. On a journey to Kentucky he stopped at Lexington to obtain copies of the Treaty of Greenville and visited Major Peyton Short who introduced him to Judge Symmes's daughter, Anna, "a remarkably beautiful girl" with whom he fell desperately in love. But her father was too ambitious and too proud to give her hand to a mere army lieutenant; indeed, he forbade him to see her. That settled matters for Harrison. In Symmes's absence and with Wayne's blessings, the young lover took Anna to Doctor Stephen Wood, treasurer of the Northwest Territory and a justice of the peace, who married them hurriedly in the parlor of his log cabin and saw them safely off to Fort Washington.[4]

Three weeks later Judge Symmes encountered his son-in-law at a farewell dinner given by General James Wilkinson to his superior Wayne, who was about to depart for Philadelphia. "How do you expect to support my daughter?" asked the irate judge. "By my sword, sir!" replied the resolute young husband, fingering his scabbard. These militant words quickly calmed the judge; he warmed up to Lieutenant Harrison and eventually became his friend. And in the required time Harrison gratefully presented the judge with a grandson named in his honor.[5]

With a promotion to captain Harrison retired from the army and devoted much of his time to business in Cincinnati. In 1798, at the age of twenty-five, he entered the land office as register and a few months later succeeded Winthrop Sargent as secretary of the Northwest Territory with a munificent income of $1,200. The next year Worthington and his Republican friends at Chillicothe agreed to put up Harrison as their candidate for delegate to Congress, provided he promised to "obtain an amelioration of the laws for the sale of Public Land." Harrison promised, ran for the office, won the election, and, once in Washington, took steps to convert the plans of his Republican friends to reality.[6]

Harrison's Land Act of 1800 won numerous friends to Republican politics and sent thousands of emigrants streaming into the Old Northwest by lowering the purchasable amount from six hundred forty acres to three hundred twenty acres. Though it retained the minimum price of $2 an acre, as stipulated by the modified Land Act of 1796, it allowed the buyer to pay one fourth down and the balance in two, three and four years, with six percent interest or eight percent discount if the balance was paid before it was due. The Act established offices in four Ohio towns at which land could be bought at public sales during the first three weeks and at private sales thereafter. The Act virtually eliminated wealthy speculators. No longer could they gobble up the Ohio country, as poor settlers feared; no longer could they foreclose on farmers who had bought land in installments. No longer would Harrison's pockets be filled with petitions that he, as delegate to Congress, had presented at opportune times. Instead he had added a new phrase to the American vocabulary: "doing a land office business." His land law, printed in the *Western Spy,* became the favorite reading of pioneers at lonely firesides, at smoky camps. In his prolix manner—he never used one word where he could use two—he could boast that his Act had brought him the governorship of newly created Indiana Territory and that he had entered its capital in triumph—like Scipio Africanus returning to Rome from his conquest of Carthage![7]

Indiana Territory embraced what is now Indiana—save a triangular area in the southeast—the western half of Michigan, Illinois, Wisconsin and a part of Minnesota. Dropped back to the first stage of territorial government by the Division Act of May 7, 1800, its only officers were the governor, the secretary and three judges. It counted 5,641 civilized persons dwelling in villages scattered largely along its borders. Its capital, Vincennes, boasted a population of seven hundred fourteen; its most northernly settlement, Mackinaw, counted two hundred fifty-one persons. Of its entire population, one hundred sixty-three were reported as free Negroes and one hundred thirty-five slaves; about two thousand five hundred whites lived in what is now Indiana. Most of the people in the territory were Frenchmen who cared little or nothing for the blessings of democracy. Schooled in a monarchical form of government, they felt no terror for strong officials; they accepted them as naturally as night follows day. The only purely American settlement was Clark's Grant opposite the Falls of the Ohio, though a few Americans could be found in and around Vincennes. The population of the territory was largely Federalist.[8]

One of Governor Harrison's first problems was that of slavery. The sixth article of the Ordinance, which prohibited slavery in the Northwest Territory, had little weight with the population. Emigrants who objected to slavery usually stopped in Ohio; those who favored it continued westward to Indiana Territory, to Kentucky and to the Spanish possessions across the Mississippi. The French settlers and their American allies wanted the Ordinance changed, and, since the majority of the people in the early years of the territory were of the same mind, they had hopes that Congress would

relent. Indiana Territory was scarcely organized when its pre-
ponderant population of Frenchmen and southerners in the Illinois
region made its wishes known in a petition to Congress:

The mode your Petitioners wish and pray you to adopt is to
permit of the Introduction into the Territory of any of those who
are Slaves in any of the United States who, when admitted, shall
continue in a state of Servitude during their natural lives, but that
all their children born in the Territory shall serve the males untill
thirty-one and the females untill twenty-eight, at which time they
are to be absolutely free. To the adoption of such a modification
of Slavery your Petitioners can not conceive any well founded
objections will be made. It can not but meet with the support of
those who are friends to the gradual abolition of Slavery, and your
Petitioners can not entertain the Idea that any will be found to
oppose a measure which in the course of a very few years will, in
all human probability, rescue from the vilest state of Bondage a
number, and without doubt a considerable number, of Souls yet
unborn. Your Petitioners do not wish to increase the number of
Slaves in the United States by the introduction of any from foreign Dominions. Their wishes, on the contrary, tend considerably
to diminish the number of emancipating those who, whether born
in the United States where their parents reside or removed into the
Spanish Dominions, would otherwise be born Slaves.[9]

Anticipating the rapid settlement of Indiana Territory once slavery was permitted, the petitioners requested that Congress declare
null and void all Indian titles to the greater part of southern Illinois
and that the land be granted to emigrants who would open roads
through the wilderness and would establish taverns on them.[10]

Congress gave the petition small consideration. This, however,
failed to discourage the Illinois people. Determined to realize their
wishes, they petitioned Harrison to advance the territory to the
second stage of government, thereby providing them with a delegate to Congress. Since the Division Act of 1800 stated that no
specific population was required for the advance, Harrison could
easily have granted their request; but he refused from fear of weakening his position. Yet he remembered St. Clair's unpopularity and,
wishing to avoid it, hastened to justify his stand on the ground that
the second stage of government would mean taxes and expenses.[11]

The advocates of slavery remained adamant. In the fall of 1802,
while Harrison was visiting in the Illinois region, they urged him

to accede to their wishes. The governor then promised that on their written request he would call a convention to consider the expediency of admitting slavery in the territory. On receiving their request at his office in Vincennes he issued a proclamation calling for the election of delegates to the convention he had promised.[12]

The delegates, meeting in Vincennes on December 20, 1802, quickly drew up a memorial to Congress:

The Sixth article of Compact between the United States and the people of the Territory which declares that there shall be neither slavery nor involuntary servitude in it has prevented the Country from populating and been the reason of driving many valuable Citizens possessing Slaves to the Spanish side of the Mississippi, most of whom but for the prohibition contained in the ordinance would have settled in this Territory, and the consequences of keeping that prohibition in force will be that of obliging the numerous Class of Citizens disposed to emigrate, to seek an Asylum in that country where they can be permitted to enjoy their property.

Your memorialists however and the people they represent do not wish for a repeal of the article entirely, but that it may be suspended for the Term of Ten Years and then to be again in force, but that the slaves brought into the Territory during the Continuance of this Suspension and their progeny, may be considered and continued in the same state of Servitude, as if they had remained in those parts of the United States where Slavery is permitted and from whence they may have been removed.[13]

This memorial was sent to Washington, where it was laid before the House of Representatives on February 8, 1803, and referred to a committee of five. Less than a month of deliberation resulted in this adverse decision:

The rapidly increasing population of the State of Ohio sufficiently evinces, in the opinion of your committee, that the labor of slaves is not necessary to promote the growth and settlement of colonies in that region; that this labor, demonstrably the dearest of any, can only be employed to advantage in the cultivation of products more valuable than any known to that quarter of the United States; that the committee deems it highly dangerous and inexpedient to impair a provision wisely calculated to promote the happiness and prosperity of the Northwestern Country, and to give strength and security to that extensive frontier. In the salutary operation of this sagacious and benevolent restraint, it is believed that the inhabitants of Indiana will, at no very distant day, find ample remuneration for a temporary privation of labor and emigration.[14]

At the next session this report was referred to a new committee, which voted to suspend the sixth article of the Ordinance for ten years; but the committee of the whole failed to call up the report until after the period of consent fixed by the convention.[15]

The advocates of slavery then tried another scheme in their endeavor to escape from the Ordinance. Learning that the United States had purchased Louisiana, they petitioned Congress to join that territory to the Illinois country. Here again they met defeat. Late in March 1804 Congress divided Louisiana at 33° latitude, on the southern line of present Arkansas, and organized the southern part as the Territory of Orleans and the northern part as the District of Upper Louisiana. To provide government to sparsely settled Upper Louisiana, Congress attached it to Indiana Territory. This was merely a personal union in which the governor, the secretary and the three judges of Indiana Territory served also as the officers of Upper Louisiana. Otherwise, the two were distinct and separate political entities; none of the laws of one applied to the other, though Harrison in October 1804 met with his judges and passed six laws for Upper Louisiana. A little later Harrison visited St. Louis, the tiny capital of the territory under his jurisdiction, where he found the ladies "remarkably handsome, gentle, and well-bred, and the society . . . altogether a polished one." The wealthy landowner and trader, Auguste Chouteau, entertained him sumptuously and even made him the flattering offer of a partnership, which Harrison, of course, regretfully declined. The people, too, liked the governor for his affability and easy access, but as soon as he was gone they protested rigorously the union of their country to Indiana Territory on the ground that their officials were too distant from them and that Congress had joined them to the territory in which the Ordinance was the fundamental law as a preliminary to the abolition of slavery. Congress heeded their protest and on March 4, 1805, gave Upper Louisiana a separate government.[16]

Meanwhile Indiana Territory had passed to the second stage of territorial government. To bring this about Harrison reversed his stand of three years earlier. Realizing that the proslavery party was as yet in the majority, he decided to favor it to secure his official position. He was loathe to lose his office. The antislavery settlers were coming into the territory in ever-increasing numbers and would soon be influential enough to demand the second grade of territorial government in order to realize their wishes through a legislature. And they might even demand Harrison's removal. He resolved, therefore, to seize the opportunity and muster the pro-slavery majority to his side by removing the barriers to the admission of slaveholders. "Just as he had feared defeat from the Federalists in 1801 if they were given a change," wrote Homer Webster, "so now he feared defeat from the incoming and growing anti-slavery party if he did not act promptly and made himself secure while he could." But since he had opposed the second grade, he wisely kept in the background. Instead, he permitted his party to justify his change of mind on the ground that the population of the territory was now sufficiently large to lighten the added taxes and expenses necessitated by the advance in territorial status. On August 4, 1804, he issued a call for an election on September 11 to ascertain the will of the people. The election showed a desire for the second stage, and on December 5 Harrison issued a proclamation declaring that "Indiana Territory is and from henceforth shall be deemed to have passed into the second or representative grade of Government, and that the Good people of the Territory, from the date thereof, are entitled to the right and privilege belonging to that situation."[17]

The five weeks' notice which Harrison had granted for the election proved too little time to reach remote Wayne County in the northern part of the territory. This "unfairness" furnished its inhabitants with an excuse to petition Congress for separation from Indiana Territory. The senate committee to which the petition was referred reported favorably, stating that the county had a population of 3,972, that it was separated from Vincennes by three hundred miles of wilderness and that Detroit, being exposed to both Indians and English, needed local government to protect itself. The House of Representatives eventually concurred in this view and on January 11, 1805, Wayne County became Michigan Territory with boundaries stretching from the southern tip of Lake Michigan due east to Lake Erie and due north through the middle of the lake to Canada. Included in the new territory was a tiny part of the Upper Peninsula. Michigan Territory began life on July 1, 1805, with Detroit as its capital.[18]

2

The first assembly of the Indiana Territory met on July 30, 1805, and, after listening to Harrison's congratulatory address and his request for beneficent laws, got down to the business of slavery.

Less than a month later it passed "An Act concerning the introduction of Negroes and Mulattoes into the Territory." By this
act, which was known as the Indenture Law of 1805 and which
was revised and re-enacted in 1807, master and slave could make an
agreement before the clerk of the court as to the number of years
the slave wished to serve his master. The master could remove
from the territory within sixty days any slave who failed to reach
an agreement with him. No slave could be removed from the territory against his will. Slaves under fifteen years of age could be
brought into the territory and held—males until thirty-five and
females until thirty-two years of age—without any formality save
that of registry of their names and ages with the clerk of common
pleas. The children of a slave were to serve the master of their
mother—males until thirty and females until twenty-eight years of
age. A master was required to post bond in $500 that none of his
slaves should become public charge if he became free at the age of
forty and upward. A slave had the right to make complaint before
a justice of the peace, who could grant him his freedom.[19]

Most of the proslavery people east of the Wabash welcomed
the Indenture Law as a major victory; but those of the Illinois
country now clamored for complete separation from Indiana Territory. Believing that separation would improve their political fortunes and that it would secure complete and unrestricted slavery,
and fearing that the growing antislavery opposition of eastern Indiana would jeopardize the Indenture Law, they sent to Congress
a petition describing the disadvantages that had accrued to them
from their connection with the country east of the Wabash:

The road to Vincennes is one hundred and eighty miles through
a dreary and inhospitable wilderness, uninhabited, and which, during one part of the year, can scarcely afford water sufficient to sustain nature, and that of the most indifferent quality, besides presenting other hardships equally severe, while in another it is in part
under water, and in places to the extent of some miles, by which
the road is rendered almost impassable, and the traveller is not only
subjected to the greatest difficulties, but his life placed in the most
imminent danger.[20]

But this transportation difficulty paled into insignificance compared
to the obstacles imposed by a merciless nature:

From the obstacles already but very partially described, and
from the peculiar nature of the face of the country lying between
these settlements and the Wabash, a communication between them

and the settlements wast of that river cannot, in the common course of things, for centuries yet to come, be supported with the least benefit, or be of the least moment to either of them. This tract of country consists chiefly of extensive prairies, which scarcely afford wood or water, which utterly precludes the possibility of settlement to any extent worthy of notice. From the existence of this serious fact, a bar to the interchange of mutual good offices, and of private interests and concerns, is raised upon a foundation too firm to be shaken or surmounted.[21]

From these premises the petitioners, who numbered three hundred and fifty, showed the impossibility of harmony between the two sections of the territory. Hatred and discord, they predicted, would destroy its peace and prosperity. But what they particularly deprecated was the dastardly manner in which they had been "precipitated into the second grade." They accused Harrison of calling for the vote of the people on petitions from only one county, asserted that a mere handful of the Illinois people had voted, and most of them against the second grade, and, referring to the fact that Wayne County had not voted at all, sneered at the governor in italics for being *"satisfied that there was a majority of the freeholders in the territory* in favor of entering into the second grade of government."[22]

The committee to which this petition was referred reported on it unfavorably:

A Territory when once erected into a State, cannot be divided or dismembered without its own consent; the formation, therefore, of two States out of this Territory, originally intended by the Ordinance of 1787, could not constitutionally be effected, if the two sections were once permitted to form one State, without the consent of that State, however necessary the extent and population of that Territory might render such division.[23]

The committee also declared that a division of the territory so soon after it had passed into the second grade would be impolitic and unjust, and that it should be made only when either section had sufficient population to enable it to form a state government.[24]

Their defeat fired the Illinois people to greater determination. They bombarded Congress with petitions. Typical among these was one insisting that the Illinois country had a population of 5,000, reiterating the burdens they had endured from their connection with the region east of the Wabash, and even deriving substance for argument from Napoleon's victories at Austerlitz and Jena. The French tyrant would now dictate peace and would turn his conquering army against the United States. "We cannot but shutter," said the petition, "at the horrors which might arise from a *disaffection in the West:*—and can it be much to the American people to grant to their brethren in this distant region a government to which, in an evil hour, they can speedily fly for direction and support?"[25]

To their supplications and arguments Congress paid no heed. But time was working in their behalf. In the fall elections of 1808 the antislavery party east of the Wabash and the anti-Harrison and proslavery party from Illinois combined to form a House of Representatives that favored division. A little later they drew nearer to the realization of their hopes when the territorial assembly elected Jesse B. Thomas as delegate to Congress to succeed Benjamin Parke, a pro-Harrison man who had resigned. Thomas had migrated from his native Maryland to Kentucky and from Kentucky to Indiana Territory where, at Lawrenceburg, he practiced law with his brother. Drifting into politics, he worked assiduously but not always honorably at confirming his pet maxim, "You cannot talk a man down, but you can whisper him to death." He won several small posts. As soon as he was elected he declared openly for division, assuring his constituents that "if they would take his word, he would give his bond." Meeting no opposition he kept his pledge. As a member of the committee of five which Congress set up to study the possibility of separation, Thomas on December 31, 1808 reported that most of his people were in favor of it. Their only objection, he said, was the increased expense that the national government would incur by establishing a new territory; but he pointed out that the value of its public lands would increase to exceed its cost. Congress accepted his arguments and on February 3, 1809 President Jefferson signed the act establishing Illinois Territory. It included that part of Indiana lying west of the Wabash River by a line due north from Vincennes to the border of Canada. The Harrison party, which stood for slavery and union of the territory, had been forced to accept the division act. Indiana Territory was now reduced to about the present dimensions of the state.[26]

3

By this time Indiana Territory had a population which was largely against slavery. In the past eight years waves of emigrants

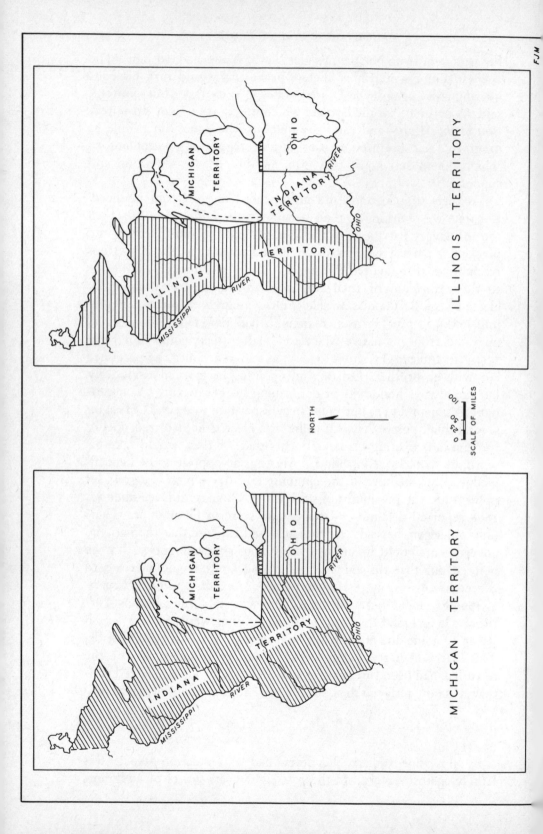

ILLINOIS TERRITORY

MICHIGAN TERRITORY

SCALE OF MILES

NORTH

from Kentucky and the Carolinas had been pouring into the beautiful Whitewater Valley, on which stand Richmond and Brookville. Many of them were Quakers of Scotch-Irish, Huguenot, and German stock—the Coxes, McCoys, Rues, Blunts, Holmans, and Hoovers—founders of prominent Indiana families who sought healthier climate or economic betterment or a region free of the institution of slavery, which they heartily disliked. On learning that Governor Harrison was proslavery, they joined his political enemies and abided their time to elect a legislature that opposed slavery and a delegate to Congress who would work for the admission of Indiana as a free state.[27]

They found a champion in young Jonathan Jennings. His father, from whom he derived a fierce hatred of slavery, was a physician and a minister of the Dutch Reformed Church. Soon after Jonathan's birth in 1784, he migrated with his large family from his native Hunterdon County, New Jersey, to Fayette County, Pennsylvania, where he accepted the ministry of Dunlap's Creek Church. Here Jonathan grew up and attended the Presbyterian School at Canonsburg in adjoining Washington County. With some knowledge of Latin, Greek, and higher mathematics, Jonathan went to Washington, the county seat, to study law in the office of John Simonson. Then, early in 1806, he studied more law with his brother Obadiah in Steubenville, Ohio, and took a trip down the Ohio to Indiana Territory. So far he had been a migratory bird, going and coming with the seasons; now he resolved to settle down and amount to something. Where should he go? For a time he thought of joining another brother in Virginia; but the west promised a greater future, and he finally chose Vincennes, where he was admitted to the bar. In 1807, while he waited for clients, his excellent penmanship landed him a clerkship in the land office and an assistant clerkship to the territorial legislature. Despite his successes, he was unhappy in Vincennes: the town was "full of rascals." He wrote to David G. Mitchell, who had married his beloved sister Ann, that

I was very near being Clerk to the House of Representatives of the Territory, and I believe I might have been elected, had I played a double part, but being under promise on certain conditions not to offer; I could not reconcile it to myself to offer, and thereby wound my promise.[28]

But perhaps the cause of his unhappiness was not so much the rascals of Vincennes as discontentment with his lot in life. His adventurous mind was continually conceiving plans for gaining wealth: he talked of opening a wholesale store to sell cotton and whisky to the merchants of Brownsville, Pennsylvania; in case of war with England, he planned to buy a boat and run a contraband cargo to the West Indies; he persuaded members of his family to lend him money to speculate in public land, promising them a certain percentage of his profits. He purchased the land at public sales, but illness prevented him from working for so many months that he was forced to sell the land at a great discount. At the same time his bitter denunciations of slavery earned him the displeasure of Governor Harrison, who had him discharged from the post of Clerk of the Board of Trustees of Vincennes University, which had been organized in 1806. This increased his dislike for Harrison and made him all the more determined to work for his removal and for the admission of Indiana as a free state.[29]

Realizing that he could not combat slavery as long as he remained in Vincennes, he decided to move to Clark County, in southeastern Indiana, where, at Charlestown, dwelled a group of Quakers who would agree with his sentiments. When he had packed his belongings and about to mount his horse, Nathanael Ewing, for whom he had worked at the land office, came out to bid him farewell.

"Look us up a good candidate for Congress," said Ewing.

"Wouldn't I do?" inquired Jennings.

The thought struck Ewing favorably; they believed he would succeed should the people in the eastern counties accept him as a candidate. Determined to ascertain how he stood with them, Jennings rode to Charlestown, where he talked to its founders, the Begg brothers, and to their numerous friends, who agreed that he should be the candidate for the antislavery people in Clark County. Jennings then sped to Lawrenceburg, sixty miles to the northeast in Dearborn County; but there the Harrison party was strong and gave him no encouragement. Its leaders, General James Dill and Captain Samuel Vance, were close friends of Harrison, who had given them official jobs. Dill, an Irish lawyer who had married Eliza Lawrence, General St. Clair's oldest daughter, and who charmed everybody with his white flannel summer suits, his elegant manners and his perpetual boutonnière, looked with withering condescension on the young whippersnapper who dared to dream of disturbing the natural order of things.[30]

Among the Quakers in the northern part of the county, however, Jennings met with success. As soon as they had received a call for an election for delegate to Congress they made preparations for a public meeting to decide on a candidate. At log-rollings and other social gatherings they notified their friends and assembled with them at Elkhorn Creek, about a mile above its mouth, where a number of logs had been cut to build a house. This "Log Convention," as it is known in Indiana history, required only a few minutes to decide that it wanted no part of slavery, no part of the Indenture Law, and no part of Thomas Randolph or any other person identified with Harrison's proslavery government. As a temporary candidate the Quakers accepted George Hunt, a surveyor of ability, who agreed to withdraw should Clark County accept a candidate who concurred in their ideas.[31]

To obtain this information they delegated Joseph Holman, a youth of twenty, to confer with the people of Clark County. In Charlestown he learned that its inhabitants concurred in the ideas of their neighbors and that they had chosen Jennings as their candidate. But Jennings' boyish appearance disappointed the people of the upper Whitewater Valley. Some called him "a beardless boy," others dismissed him as "a cold potato." His political chances darkened when Dill and Vance arrived from Lawrenceburg and circulated falsehoods about him in the interest of their own candidate, Randolph. But when they discovered that Randolph was disliked they proposed Vance as a candidate and induced the pliable Hunt to withdraw.[32]

At this juncture Holman returned from Charlestown to find his people holding a meeting in one of the log cabins. Seeing him come in, Jennings asked:

"What news from Clark's Grant?"

Unwilling to convey the result of his mission to a perfect stranger, Holman ignored the question. Instead he went outside with a friend and informed him of what had happened. Then he joined his neighbors and whispered the information to each person save Jennings. Not a word did they disclose to him; what was the meaning of their coolness? Presently Holman and his father approached and showed him a number of handbills in which Dill and Vance charged that, when he worked at the land office, "he had bid up land against actual settlers and forfeited his bids in the interest of speculators, who afterwards bought it in at a reduced price." Jennings easily cleared himself of the charge: he and the other bidders had accepted $150 from Governor Harrison to enable him to buy the land for the noble purpose—so the governor's supporters hastened to explain—of protecting some poor men who claimed title to it. The Holmans and their friends gave Jennings their wholehearted support. Joseph even followed him like an affectionate pup around the countryside and assisted him in overcoming the political doubts of suspicious settlers.[33]

The campaign was now in full swing. While Jennings spent most of his time in Dearborn, Clark and Harrison counties, his friend Ewing worked hard for him in proslavery Knox. In his personal approach to his potential voters Jennings proved himself a master of frontier psychology. He knew how to bend far enough to gain friendship without losing respect.

His opponents had none of his charm. One day Randolph, who was again a candidate, came on horseback to the farm of David Reese in Dearborn County. The farmer extended the customary welcome:

"Light you down." And when Randolph dismounted: "Shall I see you to the house?"

Randolph accepted the invitation, remained in the house for a few minutes, and rode away.

Next day Reese gave Jennings a similar reception.

"Send a boy up with my horse," replied Jennings, "and I'll help roll."

And he rolled with the other men until sundown. Then, while he talked politics, he joined them in throwing the maul and pitching quoits. Though he was strong enough to "carry up a corner" of a log cabin with his axe and keep ahead of a dozen mowers in the field, he permitted them to win every game. These denials of his own athletic prowess earned him large political dividends. Even Dill had to admit that Jennings, wherever he went, drew all men to him.[34]

His victory in the election, which was held on May 22, 1809, greatly angered Harrison and his political puppets. One of them, Waller Taylor, planned to pick a quarrel with Jennings, then kill him. But the successful young candidate disarmed him with an avowal of esteem and much silence. On June 3 Taylor wrote to his friend Randolph as follows:

I expected the fellow would have been so much elated with his success that he would have been insolent and overbearing, but he says very little on the subject, and is silently preparing to go on to the city. Our meeting was not cordial on my part; I refused to speak to him until he threw himself in my way and made the first overtures, and then I would not shake hands with him. He has

heard, I am told, of everything I said against him, which, by the
way, was rather on the abusive side, but he revenges himself on me
by saying that he never did anything to injure me, and professes
esteem. He is a pitiful coward, and certainly not of consequence
enough to excite resentment, nor any other sentiment than contempt. He may rest in peace for me. I will no longer continue to
bother myself about him. I expect before you have received this
you will have passed through the list of your enemies in asking
them over the Wabash to partake of your company and the amusement you wish to afford them. I make no doubt they will decline
your invitation, although it may be couched in the most polite and
ceremonious style: if they do, you will have acquitted yourself
agreeably to the rules of modern etiquette, and can then be at liberty to act afterward to them in whatever way may best suit
your humor.[35]

For the present his humor was ill. He was so incensed over his
defeat that he challenged Dr. Elias McNamee, a Quaker who had
published derogatory articles about him in a newspaper, to a duel.
Whereupon the doctor went to a judge, informed him that his religion forbade him to fight and requested that he order Randolph
to post a bond to keep peace. Randolph called McNamee "a base
slanderer, an infamous liar and a contemptible coward"—and kept
peace.[36]

The defeated party overlooked no opportunity to demolish Jennings with contempt and ridicule. Even in gatherings on Independence Day, when political differences were thrown aside, their
denunciations of Jennings were proportionate to the quantity of
whiskey and the capacity of its imbibers. Near Vincennes Governor Harrison presided at a public celebration during which Jennings was toasted as "the semblance of a delegate—his want of
abilities the only safety of the people—three groans." On the same
day and in the same county another of the governor's supporters
proposed: "Jonathan Jennings—may his want of talents be the sure
means to defeat the anti-republican schemes of his party." Most
of the newspapers echoed similar sentiments.[37]

Meanwhile Governor Harrison faced new difficulties. On learning of the establishment of Illinois Territory he redistricted Indiana
Territory and called for a new legislature of the usual eight representatives, who were elected on the same day as the delegate to
Congress. At that time he was ignorant of the fact that in the
previous February Congress had passed a Suffrage Act which gave
the territorial assembly the right to apportion the representatives

and which required the minimum number of nine. Nevertheless, the governor convened the legislature of eight members and declared that he regarded them a valid body. The majority concurred in his opinion, but some disputed it and, after wresting with the matter for five days, they agreed to dissolve. They memorialized Congress for its decision. At the same time they apportioned the representatives as Harrison had done, though they gave one more to Dearborn County to make nine in all, as the Suffrage Act prescribed. Though most of them opposed slavery they surprised friends and enemies alike by passing a resolution to recommend to Congress that it reappoint Harrison governor. His third term had expired on July 4, 1809, but President Madison had not yet reappointed him.[38]

They delegated Randolph to present the memorial to Congress. He undertook this mission for a more personal reason. With the aim or reviving his political career and of discrediting Jennings he had drawn up a memorial of his own. In this he charged irregularity in regard to part of the returns from Dearborn, where Jennings had a majority, and attempted to prove that no election had been held in three precincts of that county. The committee on elections, to which the memorial was referred, reported back to the House that Jennings' election was illegal and that his seat should, therefore, be vacated. But Jennings rejected this decision. Jumping to his feet he was so eloquent in showing himself as Harrison's opponent and Randolph as the governor's stanchest supporter that he quickly retrieved what ground he had lost. On January 12, 1810, when the yeas and nays were counted, the House stood squarely against adoption of the committee's report. Even those who considered Jennings' election invalid were loath to voice that opinion. "I shall vote against the sitting delegate," said one of them, "because I am clearly of the opinion that the election was illegal; but I am sorry for it, for I understand that the sitting delegate is the people's man, and the other is the Governor's man, his Secretary of State, or Attorney General, or something or other."[39]

Harrison's legislature aroused no such sympathy. On November 28 its memorial was referred to a committee which held that the election of the representatives was illegal. Congress therefore authorized Harrison to reapportion the territory and then to hold an election for a new assembly. All this he speedily did. The duly elected assembly, convening on November 12, 1810, created new counties and passed a number of salutary laws. But its most noteworthy legislation was the repeal of the Indenture Law of 1805.

Thanks to James Beggs, President of the Council, whose vote broke the deadlock between the members of the two parties in the legislature, Indiana returned to the fold of free territories and did her share in the progressive democratization of the United States. And the weathercock governor approved the repeal, for he realized that most of the inhabitants opposed his proslavery policy. Moreover, the War of 1812 had not yet begun to furnish him with a new field of activity. Yet the Indenture Law had offended western democracy more by principle than by accomplishment. In its five years of existence it had increased the number of slaves in Indiana from twenty-eight to two hundred thirty-seven.[40]

4

Jennings spent so much time ascertaining the legality of his office that his first time expired before he could take steps toward the realization of his plans. In 1811 he ran against Randolph again and gave him a sound drubbing—thanks to his defense of Quaker pacifism in the war with Tecumseh and to the excellent penmanship of his handbills, which adroitly reiterated his hatred for slavery and which appeared in the sashes of every schoolhouse in the territory.[41]

At about the same time he increased his popularity at home by marrying Ann Gilmore Hay, the daughter of an influential settler who had migrated from Rockbridge County, Virginia, to Harrodsburg, Kentucky, and from Harrodsburg to Charlestown. A typical frontier woman, Ann imparted to her husband her constancy during his days of adversity and her quiet approval in his hour of triumph. To Jonathan she was "indeed a good girl, and if she does not render me happy, no other woman could," for, he admitted, "I am not so very easily pleased."[42]

In a letter to his sister Ann, who lived in Washington, Pennsylvania, he rejoiced in his good fortune of having found a wife whose disposition was similar to hers:

What think you, is the news? It is important and such as you never knew before. Yes! I am married and have a wife, a little black eyed wife, and you another sister and a namesake, I wish you were acquainted with her. I am sure you would love her, not only for herself, but likewise for my sake. Her disposition is very simular to yours & what can I say more. In the course of another year I expect to take her with me to see you, and in the mean time I will

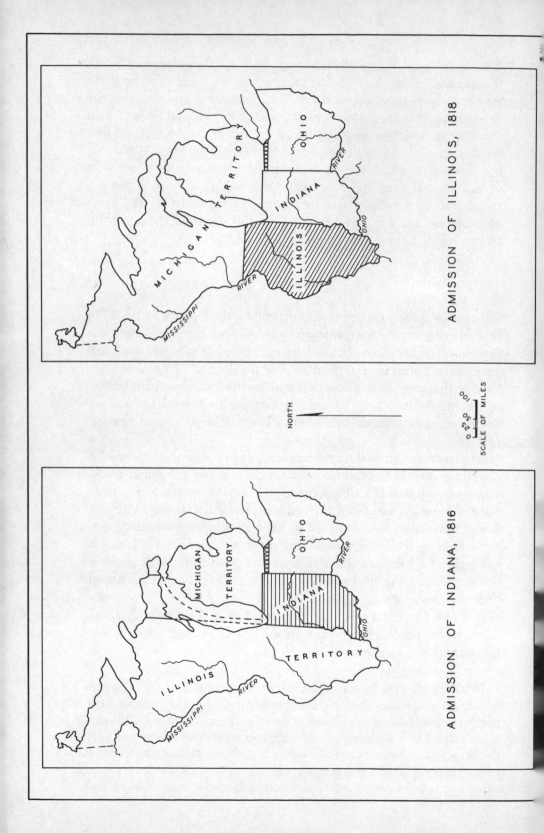

ADMISSION OF ILLINOIS, 1818

ADMISSION OF INDIANA, 1816

NORTH

SCALE OF MILES
0 25 50 100

bring you a lock of her hair, which will serve you as a memento of her who is near the bosom of your Brother, and will of course, be near to yours. She is anxious to see you and have your friendship, and I am sure you have hers.[43]

Ann, who "says very little of what passes," accompanied her husband to Washington on horseback and assisted him in his political duties. When malaria broke out in Washington she nursed some of the sick, sometimes as long as twenty hours a day.

Jennings wasted no time in pressing for statehood. Now that his party controlled the territorial legislature, he could count on its wholehearted support. In December, 1811 it sent him two memorials, one favoring statehood and the other praying that "the inhabitants of the Territory may be authorized and empowered to elect the sheriffs of their respective counties." The memorial asking for statehood was referred to select committees including Thomas Worthington, chairman of the Senate, and Jennings, chairman of the House. In reply the governor's friends, James Dill and Peter Jones, members of the territorial legislature, on January 13, 1812 presented to Congress a petition protesting against the memorial that requested statehood. This was referred to Jennings' committee, which deliberated for three months before it recommended that Indiana should be admitted into the Union as soon as this action agreed with the interest of the United States. Then the Territory introduced a resolution recommending statehood for Indiana when it reached a population of thirty-five thousand. Congress, however decided to delay an enabling act until the territory could show a population of sixty thousand, as stipulated by the Ordinance of 1787.[44]

The territorial legislature did not meet in 1812 because of hostilities between the United States and England. In the early fall Harrison was appointed to the command of the Army of the Northwest and on December 28 resigned his governorship. His successor, Thomas Posey, was, like Harrison, a Virginian and a soldier. He had served in Dunmore's War, in the Revolutionary War as a captain and in Wayne's campaigns against the Indians in Georgia and in Ohio. Later he settled in Kentucky, where he was elected to the state senate and chosen speaker of that body. In 1809 when hostilities were anticipated with England, he was commissioned major general of the state militia. When war failed to come and his forces were disbanded, he migrated to Louisiana, where in 1812 Governor Claiborne appointed him to fill a vacancy in the United States senate.

The new governor's military career and political experience made him a kind of rallying point for those who opposed statehood. But in the past three years Jennings' party had controlled the legislature and, through it, the political life of the territory. In 1812 Jennings had defeated Waller Taylor for the office of delegate to Congress. Two years later he ran against Judge Elijah Sparks. "He was a good citizen," wrote Dunn, "and a man of respectable attainments, but it was child's play for Jennings to beat him, for the immigration to the Territory was constantly adding strength to his party."[45]

Early in 1815 Jennings presented to Congress a memorial asking for statehood. It was laid on the table. At Jennings' request the Indiana legislature then took a census of the territory; it showed a population of 63,897. Armed with a figure above that which the Ordinance stipulated for statehood, the legislature drew up another memorial and sent it to Jennings, who presented it to Congress at the close of the year:

. . . Whereas the inhabitants of this territory are principally composed of emigrants from every part of the Union, and as various in their customs and sentiments as in their persons, we think it prudent, at this time, to express to the general government our attachment to the fundamental principles of the legislation prescribed by congress in their ordinance for the government of this territory, particularly as respects personal freedom and involuntary servitude, and hope they may be continued as the basis of the constitution.[46]

The memorial was referred to the committee headed by Jennings, who on January 5, 1816, reported an enabling act. Then followed a delay of three months, which was due not to any objection to the admission of Indiana but to opposition to the admission of Mississippi. On April 13 the enabling act of the two states finally passed the House of Representatives, which two days later concurred in the Senate amendments. President Madison then signed the bill.[47]

During all this time Jennings' political foes had done everything in their power to discourage statehood. Late in January they began in the *Western Sun* a series of articles signed "Farmers & Patriots" in which they criticized President Madison for issuing in the previous month a proclamation asking squatters to remove themselves from public lands that had been sold. The President, they wrote, had no such authority. Three weeks later "A Settler" repeated the charge but blamed it on the President's designing advisers. They added:

Might not Mr. Jennings (As I have no doubt his cunning lead him) say to himself, my friends make the representations to the President, get the proclamation issued—and then I can move Congress to pass a special act or resolution excepting the settlers on the public lands in the Indiana Territory. Then, forsooth, I can, with more assurance & prospect of success, offer as a candidate for Governor of the State. And this deep laid scheme I am informed is going fast into operation. The proclamation issued—The motion made and Jonathan Jennings declared by his friends in this quarter of the territory as a candidate for the Gubernatorial chair!!! Let my fellow citizens judge these men—they want offices.[48]

Four days later "A Settler" demanded information of what Jennings had been doing from month to month since his first term as delegate to Congress and sarcastically commented on his "duties" to his friends:

Mr. Jennings and his friends should no longer be confided in—they must no longer force themselves upon the people—if they have only studied their own selfish and contracted views, their ascendency will be more injurious hereafter than it has been heretofore—our approaching change into a state points to the necessity of changing men also, and for that change I pray.[49]

Jennings' opponents prayed in vain. The glaring inconsistence of holding him up as the man who controlled the President's decisions and at the same time portraying him as a loafer and an insignificant character resulted in their political undoing. The election for delegates to the constitutional convention, for which the enabling act provided, proved an overwhelming victory for Jennings' party. On June 10 they met in a new courthouse in Corydon, which since 1813 had been the new capital of the territory. But the weather was so hot that the delegates sought the shade of a great elm about a furlong away on one of the banks of Indian Creek and there, no doubt, several committees met. Jennings was elected president of the convention. Two centuries of experience in colonial self-government, in state making during Revolutionary War days, in framing two constitutions for the union, and in the making of new states, had created such confidence that one of the easiest tasks of the American frontiersmen was to form a constitution. In eighteen working days the convention produced an instrument of government that granted generous manhood suffrage, frequent elections and ample provisions for education, a penal code, libraries and asylums. The strong influence of Jennings and his Quaker friends was seen in the article that solved the slavery question:

There shall be neither slavery nor involuntary servitude in this state, otherwise than for the punishment of crimes, whereof the party shall have been duly convicted. Nor shall any indenture of any Negro or mulatto hereafter made and executed out of the bounds of this state be of any validity within the state.[50]

In early December Congress and the President approved the constitution and Indiana took her place among the states of the Union. Her grateful people elected as their first governor the father of Indiana statehood, Jonathan Jennings.

Tecumseh

THE TREATY OF GREENVILLE PROVED ONLY A RESPITE IN THE struggle between the whites and the Indians. By it the latter surrendered only southern Ohio, southeastern Indiana, and a few small and scattered areas elsewhere. Save for military posts and some isolated settlements their country stretched unbroken to the Great Lakes and to the Mississippi and beyond. To this vast country the whites had solemnly guaranteed them title. We have seen that, at the turn of the nineteenth century, the American population was confined to Clark's Grant opposite the Falls of the Ohio and to and around Vincennes. But in the succeeding decade this had changed. Thousands of new immigrants settled wherever they pleased and gave Indian rights scant consideration. Hardy and well-armed Virginians and Kentuckians broke across treaty boundaries and took fertile lands to which they could claim no valid title. White hunters trespassed far and wide in Indian territory until, by 1810, great regions which a quarter of a century before abounded in deer, bear, and buffalo were as useless for Indian life as desert land. Moreover, the Indians were cheated despite laws which guaranteed them safety for their persons and property. Indeed, they might be murdered with impunity. To Abraham Lincoln's uncle shooting an Indian on sight was a virtue, an act which any true-blooded pioneer should applaud. Governor Harrison's opinion of the local tribes was shared by most frontiersmen:

I can tell at once upon looking at an Indian whom I may chance to meet whether he belongs to a neighboring or a more distant tribe. The latter is generally well-clothed, healthy, and vigorous;

the former half-naked, filthy, and enfeebled by intoxication, and many of them without arms excepting a knife, which they carry for the most villainous purposes.[1]

On their part the tribes detested the whites. They especially wanted to stop them from carrying firewater, which sapped the vitality and lowered the morality of their young warriors. Though congressional laws forbade the sale of spiritous liquors to the Indians, the courts construed them to be operative only outside the bounds of states and organized territories. Governor Harrison reported that the six hundred warriors who lived on the Wabash drank six thousand gallons of whiskey and killed one another in drunken brawls.[2]

This growing wretchedness produced the champion of their rights. The young Shawnee chief, Tecumseh, had refused to sign the Treaty of Greenville and had thereby expressed his defiance of white arms. His father was Puckeshinwa, a Kiskopoke, one of the four of the twelve Shawnee clans that had survived, and his mother was Methoataske, a Muskogee Creek. With their people they had migrated from the Tallapoosa to the Scioto and later settled at Old Piqua, near present Springfield, Ohio, where Methoataske gave birth to a son.

She named him Tecumseh, meaning Shooting Star, because at his birth a meteor had streaked across the sky. And a historic meteor he was, lighting up the dark annals of Indian life for a moment with his vision of glory. In his boyhood he showed himself a mixture of Christian tenderness and Indian ferocity. He hunted and fought sham battles with cruelty, but he shook at the sight of human sacrifice and urged his friends to abandon the practise of human torture.[3]

In Old Chillicothe, which he often visited, he met James Galloway, a scholarly Pennsylvanian who had served with George Rogers Clark in the Illinois country. Galloway's daughter, Rebecca, a golden-haired and blue-eyed beauty, taught Tecumseh a little English, read the Bible and Shakespeare to him, and introduced him to Alexander the Great and other classic heroes, whom he learned to admire almost as much as did his great adversary, William Henry Harrison. Before long Tecumseh fell in love with Rebecca, called her Star of the Lake, brought her gifts of meat and furs, and eventually asked her father for her hand. Galloway, whose wide reading and open intelligence had perhaps dissipated what prejudice he may have felt toward Indians, raised no objection; he merely left the decision to Rebecca. By now the girl had grown quite fond of her Indian suitor. His handsome face, his noble bearing and his quick intelligence—assets which had elevated him to the rank of chief—were, in her strong, independent mind, rare enough on the frontier to merit serious consideration. She would become his wife, she told him, if he would adopt her family's ways and dress. Tecumseh replied that he would give his answer within another moon. When he returned, he told her quietly that he had decided to retain the respect and confidence of his people by remaining an Indian. He never saw Rebecca again. And he never loved another woman.[4]

He began to express hatred for the whites. One of them had treacherously killed his father, and his mother, while he sucked, had taught him to hate all white men. When he grew old enough to be ranked as a warrior she would take him every year to his father's grave and make him swear to destroy all Americans.[5]

His hatred stimulated his mind to thoughts of a glorious mission. He dreamed of reviving the confederacy of Pontiac, of Joseph Brant; he began to urge the tribes to unite to protect themselves against the whites; and his reflections led him to the belief that all the Indians owned the land in common and that, therefore, no Indian or Indians could sell any of it without the consent of all. He began to visit tribe after tribe, exhorting them to unite to resist the encroachment of their white enemies. The oratorical gifts of Cornstalk, to whom he had listened in his boyhood, and the crusading zeal of Joseph Brant, whom he knew well, combined in Tecumseh to make him the idol of his people. When he spoke on the glorious theme of Indian confederation his handsome face "lighted up, his firm and erect frame swelled with deep emotion, which his own stern dignity could scarcely repress; every feature and gesture had its meaning, and language flowed tumultuously and swiftly, from the fountains of his soul."[6]

Tecumseh had a brother, Loud Mouth, a one-eyed mystic who later became known as The Prophet. Abandoned by his mother when he was four years old, he developed a sense of insecurity which he attempted to relieve with the aid of firewater. An impractical dreamer who found manual labor distasteful, he was regarded as a loafer and an aimless wanderer of the forest. He had neither the character nor the genius of his brother. "The very sense of loneliness and rejection that impelled Tecumseh to leadership over the young warriors," wrote Glenn Tucker, "sent his brother to the comforts of the bottle."[7]

Loud Mouth's excessive zeal, which often transported him to the paroxyms so common in primitive religions, gave the whites, and especially the religious group known as the Shakers, the erroneous impression that he was an epileptic. Actually he belonged to that countless number of miracle workers who have appeared from time to time since the dawn of civilization and whose connection between psychological and organic processes modern science has not yet adequately explained. Loud Mouth was not entirely a charlatan. As soon as he became the religious leader of his people he was a changed man, abjuring war and abstaining undeviatingly from firewater. The Master of Life, he said, appeared to him in each of his numerous trances, directed him to warn his people of their terrible danger and endowed him with the power of curing diseases, of evading death, and of destroying secret heresies. With overpowering fervor and often with much weeping he disclosed to his followers that the Master of Life commanded him to bid them spurn the white man's dress, drink, food and customs. With forbidding frown and warning finger he preached on the deadly sin of marriage between white men and Indian women.[8]

When the venerable Shawnee prophet, Change of Feathers, died in 1805, Loud Mouth found inspiration in the words of Jesus, "I am the Open Door," to change his name to the last two words. Open Door or The Prophet, as the settlers called him, formed a religion by combining his brother's antiwhite doctrine with Indian ritualism and legends and the preachings of noted prophets of the past.[9]

Early in 1806 he went to the village of Woapikamakunk, where he summoned the Indians of the surrounding country to hear his revelations. Among those present was the old Delaware chief Teteboxti, who had embraced the Moravian faith. As a Christian he had refused to recognize the Prophet's religious leadership and had signed a treaty with Harrison. The Prophet accused him of being one of the governor's secret agents and of poisoning Indians. Though Teteboxti hotly denied the charge, he was seized and suspended between two poles over a slow fire. This made him cry out that Brother Joshua, another Christian Delaware, had the poison in a bag at his house. Some of the Prophet's followers had Joshua brought in with the bag but they found no poison in it. Deprived of his power to do harm by having his bag confiscated, Teteboxti was relieved of his ordeal, while Brother Joshua was released pending the Prophet's arrival.

When the religious leader appeared in the village he commanded all of the Indians to sit in a circle and hear him pronounce judgment on Teteboxti, Brother Joshua and others accused of poisoning Indians and signing treaties with Harrison. After performing the customary ceremonies for such occasions the Prophet condemned the accused persons to death. Ten Indians with blackened faces took Teteboxti to nearby Anderson, knocked him on the head with a tomahawk, and threw him alive into a fire. The other accused persons suffered similar fates.[10]

Word of these atrocities prompted Harrison to send to the Delawares a message in which he expressed his intention of exposing the Prophet as a fraud:

Who is this pretended prophet who dares to speak in the name of the Great Creator? . . . Demand of him some proofs . . . some miracles. . . . If he is really a prophet, ask him to cause the sun to stand still, the moon to alter its course, the rivers to cease to flow, or the dead to rise from their graves. If he does these things, you may then believe he has been sent from God.[11]

The Prophet was ready to oblige. Some months earlier a British agent had, by forecasting a total eclipse for June 16, 1806, told him that he could cause the sun to darken. He proclaimed his readiness to perform the miracle. The day of the eclipse dawned bright and clear. At the designated hour the Prophet, wearing a dark robe, a crest of raven's wings in his hair and a black scarf over his sightless eye, appeared among his followers and, pointing his finger at the sun, commanded it to disappear. The sun did his bidding. Frenzy seized his followers, terror struck his doubters. And the Prophet cried out with all his strength to the Master of Life, beseeching him to lift his shadow from the face of the sun. And the sun shone with its usual brilliance.[12]

The tribesmen flocked to the Prophet to witness further miracles, and word sped through the region that he never failed them. He caused pumpkins to grow as large as wigwams and ears of corn that sufficed to feed twelve men. And the Master of Life was pleased and promised to destroy his enemies with hailstones of crushing weight.[13]

Enchanted by countless tales of miracles, the Indians in 1807 abandoned their spring plowing to make war clubs. To combat possible trouble Governor Harrison organized three companies of Indian rangers, while he ordered the Indian agent, Captain William Wells, to send two trustworthy Indians to ascertain the Prophet's intentions. Wells reported no progress: "They appear deff to ev-

everything I say. . . . The Prophet tells them . . . the great spirit will in a few years distroy every white man in America. It is my opinion that the British are at the bottom of this business."[14]

He spoke the truth. During the latter half of 1807 the threat of war between the United States and Great Britain swept through the prairies and aroused settlers and Indians alike to military activity. In June the British man-of-war *Leopard* fired on the American frigate *Chesapeake*, killing three and wounding eighteen of her crew and, when she was boarded, forcing others to accept British service. Governor Harrison, convinced that this affair and the Prophet's activities stemmed from the same hostility, urged the territorial legislature to adopt measures of defense.[15]

Tecumseh, too, expected war. Fearing that his brother's Greenville mission was too close to the white settlements for comfort, he directed him to move his headquarters to the junction of the Wabash and Tippecanoe rivers. Accordingly, in May 1808 the Prophet led eighty warriors and their families to the designated place, where they began to build the new mission that became known as Prophetstown.[16]

2

In the ensuing months Tecumseh with a few friends ranged among the tribes, trying to persuade them to form a solid front against the white man's greed for land. At one of the Potawatomi villages on the upper Illinois River he met the young warrior Shabbona, who immediately joined him. Journeying up the Fox River and then across the Rock River, Tecumseh and his friends arrived at a village of the Sauk and Foxes, where he added Black Hawk to his roster of dedicated disciples. Next they visited the Winnebagos and Menominee on Green Bay. Though their cautious chief, Tomah, declared for peace, he put no obstacles in the way of those of his young men who clamored to follow Tecumseh.

From Green Bay Tecumseh led his friends down the Mississippi to Rock Island and from Rock Island across central Illinois to present Attica, Indiana, on the east bank of the Wabash, where, under an ancient oak—Tecumseh's Council Oak—he assembled the Kickapoo who pledged their wholehearted support in his endeavor to stop the Americans, their ancient enemies, from encroaching on their hunting grounds. But in the country of the Wyandots Tecumseh encountered difficulties. Their chief, Crane—a conciliatory old man—expressed doubt that Tecumseh would succeed in his aims and therefore cautioned his young men to remain neutral. Nonetheless, half of the tribe joined Tecumseh, though it refused to follow the example of the Ottawas and migrate to the Tippecanoe River. By now Tecumseh could count several thousand supporters. Encouraged by his success, he traveled with the formidabe Shawnee, Jim Blue Jacket, and some Winnebagos to the deep south and then into present Florida, where the Seminole expressed their readiness to join the confederacy he planned. In the summer of 1809 Tecumseh returned to the Wabash.[17]

Meanwhile the Prophet had fulfilled his brother's request to remain in Prophetstown and try, during the crucial months ahead, to gain Harrison's good will. Moreover, his followers needed food and clothing and the governor was the only man who could provide them. On August 1, 1808, he sent Harrison a letter in which he protested that his only aim was "to introduce among the Indians, those good principles of religion which the white people profess." At the same time he expressed a desire to visit Vincennes and clear up the bad impression the governor had recived about him:

Father, I was told that you intended to hang me. When I heard this, I intended to remember it, and tell my father, when I went to see him and relate to him the truth. . . . I also heard that you wanted to know, my father, whether I was God or man; and that you said, if I was the former, I should not steal horses. I heard this from Mr. Wells, but I believe it originated with himself. The Great Spirit told me to tell the Indians, that he had made them and the world— that he had placed them on it to do good, and not evil. . . .

My father, I have informed you what we mean to do, and I call the Great Spirit to witness the truth of my declaration. The religion which I have established for the last three years has been attended to by the different tribes of Indians in this part of the world. Those Indians were once different people; they are now but one; they are all determined to practice what I have communicated to them, that has come immediately from the Great Spirit through me.

Brother, I speak to you as a warrior. You are one. But let us lay aside this character, and attend to the care of our children, that they may live in comfort and peace. We desire that you will join us for the preservation of both red and white people. Formerly, when we lived in ignorance, we were foolish; but now, since we listen to the voice of the Great Spirit, we are happy.

. . . You have promised to assist us. I now request you, in behalf of all the red people, to use your exertions to prevent the sale of liquor to us. We are all well pleased to hear you say that you will endeavor to promote our happiness. We give you every assurance that we will follow the dictates of the Great Spirit.

We are all well pleased with the attention that you have showed us; also with the good intentions of our father, the president. If you give us a few articles, such as needles, flints, hoes, powder, etc. etc. we will take the animals that afford us meat with powder and ball.[18]

He followed this pious letter to Vincennes, where he persuaded the governor that he was more of an asset than a liability to the United States. Harrison wrote to Henry Dearborn, Secretary of War, that the Prophet "is rather possessed of considerable talents and the art and address with which he manages the Indians is really astonishing." The governor added that he could not judge how successful the Prophet would be in persuading his people to outlaw war but that he was sure his hatred for firewater "proceeded from principle" rather than from "empty profession." On the whole Harrison was "inclined to think that the influence which the Prophet has acquired will prove rather advantageous than otherwise to the United States."[19]

Confident of the Prophet's good intentions, Harrison sent his followers supplies amounting to $102, which sum he carefully deducted from the annuity due to the Shawnee by the Treaty of Greenville. On the advice of President Jefferson the governor asked the Indiana legislature to adopt laws prohibiting the sale of liquor to the Indians. He added that "the progress of intemperance" was "so destructive" that "whole villages had been swept away."[20]

But the governor's hunger for more land combined with political circumstances to make a conflict between the Indians and the whites inevitable. The diminished boundaries of Indiana which had resulted from the establishment of Illinois Territory in 1809 caused the rising tide of emigration to demand another land cession. Though President Jefferson professed to be a beneficent father to the Indians, his greed for land equaled that of any settler on the frontier. "His humanity to the Indians," wrote Adams, "suffered the suspicion of having among its motives the purpose of gaining the Indian lands for the whites."[21]

This attitude was intensified when, early in 1809, James Madison succeeded Jefferson and chose a Massachusetts physician, Dr. William Eustis, Secretary of War. Eustis, says Tucker, "viewed his duty toward the Indians in terms of a military campaign rather than

humanitarian responsibility and a task for intelligent diplomacy."
He went along with the governor's desire to obtain the rich Wabash
and White rivers bottoms, "which were fertile and productive beyond the imagination of the residents of some of the seaboard
states."[22]

In the extreme south the Indian boundary line was now at the
Wabash, thanks to the treaties which Harrison had signed in 1804
and 1805 with the Miami, Eel River Indians, Wea, Piankashaw,
and Delawares, who had surrendered a strip of country fifty miles
between the Ohio and the White rivers. The treaties, however, had
proved very unpopular with most chiefs and had aroused them to
long debates on how to prevent the white men from occupying the
ceded areas. Tecumseh's determination to unite the Indians undoubtedly received some impetus from these treaties.[23]

To justify his intended aggression Harrison pointed out to Eustis that Vincennes lacked adequate protection and that the Prophet
and his followers could, at high water, easily come down the river
in canoes faster than a man could ride on horseback. The Secretary
relayed the letter to President Madison, who eventually decided to
authorize the cession. Whereupon Eustis advised Harrison "to take
advantage of the most favorable moment for extinguishing the
Indian titles to the lands lying east of the Wabash." Harrison wasted
no time instructing John Johnston, Indian agent and successor of
William Wells at Piqua, to send out runners to summon the tribesmen to a conference at Fort Wayne. Harrison thought the time
very opportune. Tecumseh had gone from the Wabash to enlist
the support of the Iroquois in his plans for Indian union and could
not possibly return until long after the treaty had been consum-
mated.[24]

Supplied for an absence of six weeks, on September 1 the mounted
governor left Vincennes with his secretary, Peter Jones; his interpreter, Joseph Barron; George, his Negro servant; a French guide;
and two Indian orderlies. Journeying on a recently opened road,
he crossed southern Indiana to North Bend, Ohio, where one morning he "agreeably surprised" his father-in-law, Judge Symmes, at
his farm work. Then he continued to Cincinnati, now a metropolis
boasting a population of 2000, where he was amazed to find hundreds of new emigrants seeking titles at the land office. The last
leg of his journey brought him to his destination through Dearborn
County in eastern Indiana.[25]

The chiefs were coming in as he arrived, but he observed that
none of them belonged to the group responsive to Tecumseh. De-

termined to secure the attendance of every chief in the region, he sent out runners to bring in the laggards. The runners failed to interest any of the Shawnee save Chief Blackhoof who, as a signer of the Treaty of Greenville and a beneficiary of the annuity allotted to his tribe, had spurned Tecumseh's leadership and had agreed to lend his influence—as little as it was—in favor of the cession. The Potawatomi chief, Five Medals, was in Fort Amhertsburg receiving British bounty. The Delawares and what few Potawatomi were present asked Harrison for firewater. He refused to give it to them, perhaps because he felt that it should be served as a reward for the right conclusion rather than as a goad to a right start. When the venerable chief of the Miami, Little Turtle, arrived on September 19, the governor visited each chief and informed him that his purpose in calling the meeting was to buy land. As soon as the interpreters had been sworn in, Harrison made a long speech in which he pointed out the advantages of their agreeing to his proposition. With the annuities they were to receive they could clothe their women and children. And he added that he saw no end to the European wars, which had resulted in the "advance" in the price of goods and the depression of their peltries." The little game left in the tract he proposed to purchase would not sustain them. They required, therefore, "some other plan of support"; he suggested that they raise hogs and cattle, an occupation which he said was not difficult.[26]

At the end of his speech he showed them a rough sketch of the country he wanted. Though few understood it, their spokesman, Chief Owl of the Miami, replied that they would "take what you said into consideration & will return you an answer."[27]

The Potawatomi and the Delawares, who insisted on firewater, favored the sale; but the Miami remained silent. The governor then had a private interview with Little Turtle. The chief was undecided about the sale, not because he saw no merit in it but because he was afraid that the dismissal of his son-in-law, William Wells, for holding out on some of the annuities might affect his standing with the government. Harrison assured him that he would be treated as he had been before. So the chief agreed to "exert himself to the utmost of his power to effect the proposed treaty," though he foresaw difficulties in the division of the annuities. To discuss this matter the Miami in the evening went to see the governor in his tent and asked him for firewater for their young men. This time the governor saw the advantage of befuddling them; he gave each tribe two gallons. His generosity was quickly rewarded. Before

he went to bed he received Winamac, who told him that he came
to make him sleep well by informing him that the Indians had accepted his proposition.[28]

Firewater had made Winamac unduly optimistic. For several
more days the tribes could not make up their minds, and Harrison
was constrained to bring them to some agreement by making another speech in which he asked: "My children, what disconcerts you?
Have you not always received justice from the hands of your father?
What is it he asks of you? Nothing but what you can spare."[29]

These words moved Little Turtle to the extent that he asked his
fellow chiefs to give the governor a favorable reply. To hasten
such a decision Harrison made still another speech, which this time
lasted two hours, and in which he denounced the British for involving the Indians in ruinous wars. This stroke of psychology convinced the chiefs that Harrison was their unalterable friend and
brought him a speedy agreement. On September 30 the Indians,
numbering nearly fourteen hundred, signed the Treaty of Fort
Wayne, by which Harrison bought for $10,550 in annuities and
cash a tract of about three million acres on the Wabash and White
rivers. Less than a month later he signed another treaty with the
Wea who for an additional annuity of $300, the promise of another
annuity of $100 and a present of $1,500, recognized the Treaty of
Fort Wayne. Lastly, on December 9, the Kickapoo followed suit
for an annuity of $400 and goods amounting to $800. The Treaty
of Fort Wayne was the last Harrison signed with the Indians while
he was governor of Indiana Territory. All told he had signed with
them twelve treaties by which he acquired seventy-five thousand
square miles. Most of this expanse of land lay west of the Wabash
and in 1809 became a part of Illinois Territory. The ceded lands
that remained in Indiana formed in the southern end of the territory
a wide belt resembling a crescent.[30]

3

Failing to enlist the Iroquois of the Mohawk Valley to his Indian
confederacy, Tecumseh, bitterly disappointed, began his journey
back to the Wabash. And his disappointment changed to anger
when his runners met him on the way with word of the Treaty of
Fort Wayne. Harrison had shown contempt for him and his tribe
by negotiating a treaty during his absence. The beloved Shawnee
country on which his proud and invincible people dwelled and

hunted for centuries had been surrendered for a few jugs of whiskey and a handful of silver! And surrendered by irresponsible chiefs whose only claim to the lands rested, ironically enough, on his principle of common ownership!

Great was his fury—but greater still was Harrison's fear of Shawnee vengeance. The governor sent the French trader, Michel Brouillette, to Prophetstown to ascertain what the Prophet contemplated. Brouillette stayed in the village for over six weeks and then returned to Vincennes, deposing "on the Holy Evangelist of Almighty God" that the Prophet "was not friendly to the United States and particularly that he was much exasperated at the cession of Lands made last [autumn]." The Prophet moreover referred to Harrison as "that bad man at Vincennes" and threatened to challenge him to a duel or to go to Washington and ask the Great White Father to remove him.[31]

Whatever his intentions, the Prophet soon showed his hostility. In June 1810 Harrison sent up the Wabash to the Indian villages a pirogue loaded with the salt which was part of the annuity due them by the Treaty of Fort Wayne. At Prophetstown the young French boatmen rolled off the few barrels alotted to that village, but the Prophet forbade his people to touch them. When the boatmen started to take the unwanted barrels back to the pirogue, Tecumseh, who had recently returned from New York, "grabbed the head boatman by his hair, shook him violently, and called him an 'American dog.'" Then he ordered a few of his men to return the barrels to the pirogue, which sailed for Vincennes. Brouillette, too, suffered from Tecumseh's indignation. A swarm of angry Indians stripped his cabin of food and tobacco and sent him scurrying to the safety of Vincennes, where he spread tales of approaching war. Harrison replaced him with Toussaint Dubois.[32]

The town and the surrounding countryside were so alarmed that Harrison was constrained to call a public meeting to discuss prompt measures of defense. Two companies of militia were alerted for possible trouble. At the same time Harrison sent Colonel Vigo to ascertain the sentiments of the Miami, whom some Wyandots were trying to induce to join the Prophet. Vigo soon returned with word that the Prophet had seduced only one Miami chief and that no trouble seemed imminent.[33]

Swayed by confusing reports of Indian military strength, Harrison sent Joseph Barron to the Prophet with a conciliatory letter in French, a language which most Indians understood. Though the governor knew that Tecumseh was "really the efficient man—the Moses of the family," he regarded the Prophet as the principal troublemaker:

Notwithstanding the improper language you have used toward me I will again endeavor to open your eyes to your true interests. Notwithstanding what bad white men have told you I am not your personal enemy you ought to know this from the manner I received and treated you on your . . . visit to this place. . . .

There is yet but very little harm done but what may easily be repaired. The chain of friendship which unites the Whites with the Indians may be received and be as strong as ever—a great deal of that work depends upon you—the destiny of those who are under your direction depends upon the choice which you will make of the two roads which are before you. One is large, open and pleasant, and leads to peace, security and happiness—the other on the contrary is narrow and crooked, and leads to misery, to ruin. Do not deceive yourself, do not believe that all the Indians united are able to resist the force of the 17 fires even for a Moon.

I know your Warriors are brave, ours are not less so, but what can a few brave Warriors do against the innumerable Warriors of the 17 fires. Our blue coats are more numerous than you can count, and our hunting shirts are like the leaves of the forests or the grains of sands on the Wabash. Do you think that the red coats can protect you, they are not able to protect themselves, they do not think of going to war with us, if they did in a few moons you would see our flags wave on all the Forts of Canada.[34]

He concluded the letter by requesting the Prophet to state his reasons for accusing the United States of purchasing "land from those who had no right to sell," and by promising him that he would restore the lands he had purchased at Fort Wayne if the Shawnee could prove ownership to them.[35]

At Prophetstown Barron and his escort found the Prophet seated on a dais that served as his throne. He looked at the messenger for a few minutes as if he did not know him, though he knew him well. Then he said angrily:

"For what purpose do you come here? Brouillette was here; he was a spy. Dubois was here; he was a spy. Now *you* have come. You, too, are a spy. There is your grave; look at it!" So saying, he pointed to the ground near where Barron stood.

Tecumseh, hearing his brother's angry words, rushed out of a nearby hut, assured Barron that his life was in no danger, and asked him to state his business. Whereupon Barron translated Harrison's letter. Tecumseh replied that he would himself go to Vincennes and see the governor.

He took Barron to his tent and talked with him in the dark until long after midnight. He had no intention of making war on the whites, he said, but how could he keep on good terms with them if they refused to remain within their present bounds? He added:

The Great Spirit gave this great island to his red children. He placed the whites on the other side of the big Water, they were not contented with their own, but came to take ours from us. They have driven us from the sea to the lakes, we can go no farther. . . . Our father tells us we have no business on the Wabash; the land belongs to other tribes. But the Great Spirit ordered us to come here and we shall stay.[36]

In the afternoon of August 12, 1810, Tecumseh, accompanied by his brother and about three hundred warriors, arrived in the outskirts of Vincennes, where he spent several days polishing the speech he had prepared to deliver to the governor. Then he went with thirty of his warriors to meet Harrison at Grouseland. In front of the porch was an arbor over which the governor had placed a canopy. Beneath this in the shade he had arranged chairs on which sat the officers of Indiana Territory, the Supreme Court justices, a group of ladies, and the town's leading citizens—all of whom he had invited to witness his meeting with the colorful Shawnee. Behind his friends he posted his guard, a platoon armed with pistols in their belts.

All this display annoyed Tecumseh. He declined to approach the porch. "Houses are made for white men to hold councils in," he said to Barron; "Indians hold theirs in the open air."

"Your father," said Barron, "requests you to sit by his side."

In a flash Tecumseh lifted his arm skyward.

"*My* father?" he queried. "My father? The Great Spirit is my father! The earth is my mother—and on her bosom I will recline." With these words he sat on the ground and crossed his legs. His warriors, painted brilliantly and dressed in neat deerskins, squatted around him.

Thus the chief faced Harrison and said, simply:

"I am Tecumseh."

Harrison saw a handsome man with an aquiline nose and cheerful hazel eyes. On his head he wore a handkerchief into which he had thrust an eagle's feather. In his belt was a tomahawk mounted in silver and a hunting knife in a neat leather case—presents from the British. Tecumseh looked earnestly at the governor. He remembered having seen him at Fallen Timbers sixteen years before— "a very young man sitting by the side of General Wayne."[37]

Speaking in the Shawnee tongue, which Barron interpreted, Tecumseh expanded his theory that the Indian lands belonged to all the tribes and that, therefore, none could be sold without the consent of all. He vowed that the chiefs who had signed the Treaty of Fort Wayne would be punished; his warriors would reduce them to the status of common men. He began a discussion of the relation between the whites and the Indians in America. The French, he said, had discovered them, had adopted them as children, and had given them presents without asking for land. Then came the English, who had quarreled with and conquered the French and who had taken the Indians into war against the Americans. After many of their young men had been killed, both sides agreed to bury the hatchet at Greenville, where the Americans promised that they would treat them well, "not like the British, who gave us but a small piece of pork every day." But the Americans proved no better than the British. And he recalled Gnadenhutten, where men, women and children were innocently slaughtered. The Americans also made false promises to the Shawnee. They gave them flags and called them their children. "These flags will be a security to you; if the white people intend to do you harm, hold up your flags and no harm will be done you." The Shawnee followed this course in good faith. What happened? The person bearing the flag was murdered with others in their village. "Now, my brother," said Tecumseh, "after this conduct can you blame me for placing little confidence in the promises of our fathers, the Americans?"

The Americans, continued Tecumseh, had forced the Indians to commit aggressive acts. "You try to force the red people to do some injury. It is you that is pushing them on to do mischief." He charged that Americans tried to prevent the Indians from uniting and that they dealt with the tribes individually. He refused to consider an invitation to visit the President until he had completed his confederacy.[38]

He reiterated that the Treaty of Fort Wayne had been signed by only a few irresponsible chiefs. Its prime mover, he said, was Harrison's friend, Winamac, "the black dog that makes lies and tells them, to cause white men and red men to hate each other!" But in the future, he continued, he was prepared to punish "those chiefs who may come forward to propose to sell their land. If you continue to purchase from them it will produce war among the different tribes and . . . I do not know what will be the consequence to the white people."

Tecumseh emphasized that he alone was the leader of his people. "I am a Warrior and all the Warriors will meet together in two or three moons from this. Then I will call for those chiefs that sold you the land and shall know what to do with them. If you do not restore the land you will have a hand in killing them." Again he warned Harrison to rescind the Treaty of Fort Wayne:

If you . . . cross the boundary of your present settlement it will be very hard and produce great troubles among us. How can we have confidence in the white people? When Jesus Christ came upon the earth, you killed and nailed him on a cross. You thought he was dead, but you were mistaken. You have Shakers among you, and you laugh and make light of their worship.[39]

When Tecumseh had finished speaking Harrison rose from his chair on the porch and began his reply. For several minutes he dwelled on the many instances of justice which the white men had accorded the Indians. Tecumseh's face gradually tightened with anger. Suddenly springing to his feet and pointing at Barron, he shouted:

"Tell him he lies!"

A hubbub of voices pervaded the council. Tecumseh's braves leaped to their feet and drew their tomahawks from their belts. John Gibson, Secretary of Indiana Territory, who also understood Shawnee, drew his pistol. "Those fellows mean mischief," he bawled out to Lieutenant Jennings, "you'd better bring up the guard." Twelve riflemen appeared. As soon as Barron translated Tecumseh's words, Harrison drew his sword. Winamac, who lay in the grass, cocked his pistol. William Winans, a Methodist preacher who lived with Harrison, ran into the house, got his shotgun and stood guard at the door. The governor's wife shooed their children into the house. The riflemen were ready to shoot, but Harrison ordered them to put down their guns. Then he rebuked Tecumseh. He would listen to no more insults, he said, as he adjourned the council and strode into the house with his guests. Tecumseh led his braves back to camp.[40]

His anger subsided as quickly as it had risen. He was sorry he had lost his temper. The next morning he called Barron to apologize to Harrison for his conduct. The governor had prepared for trouble. He had collected two more companies of militia from the neighboring settlements, had joined them with those of the town, and had paraded his entire force with great clatter through the streets. Nevertheless, he gladly granted Tecumseh another council.[41]

The chief was all the more friendly for having found an outlet for his pent-up resentment against the whites. He sat on a bench with Harrison and moved closer and closer as they talked. Harrison shifted his position. Tecumseh moved closer still. Harrison objected. Tecumseh laughed and asked how he liked being pushed clear off, just as he was pushing the Indians off their land.[42]

On August 21 the council reconvened. Tecumseh told Harrison that some white people were "not true Americans" because they were endeavoring to fill the minds of the Indians with evil toward the United States. One of such persons had told him that he had heard the governor call the Prophet a bad man who would forbid traders from selling their articles in Prophetstown. This man also told Tecumseh that Harrison was to remain in office for two more years, that then he would be succeeded by "a good man who was a true friend of the Indians," and that in the meantime his purpose was to cheat the Indians of their lands. Tecumseh added that another American told him that Harrison was about to assemble the Indians to buy more land, though the government had instructed him to do so only when it was offered to him. This American advised Tecumseh to go to Vincennes and object strongly to the purchase of more land and characterized Harrison as being "very smooth with the Indians" when he wanted land but becoming "boisterous" if his wishes were denied. And Tecumseh advised the governor to desist from fomenting trouble with the tribes: "I alone am the acknowledged head of all the Indians."[43]

Here the governor asked Tecumseh to state explicitly whether he intended to prevent surveyors from marking the land recently purchased and whether the Kickapoo would receive their annuities.

Tecumseh replied:

Brother. When you speak to me of annuities I look at the land and pity the women and children. I am authorized to say that they will not receive them.

Brother. We want to save that piece of land. We do not wish you to take it. It is small enough for our purposes. If you do take it you must blame yourself as the cause of trouble between us and the tribes who sold it to you. I want the present boundary line to continue. Should you cross it, I assure you it will be productive of bad consequences.[44]

Neither man would yield an inch. Since the government had acquired the land by fair purchase, answered Harrison, it would support its right by the sword. As he adjourned the council he promised to take Tecumseh's claims to the President. Next morning Harrison called on his guest to bid him farewell. During the night Tecumseh had weighed the governor's last words, for he inquired why the President should seriously consider his claims. "The Great Chief is so far off he will not be injured by the war. He may still sit in his town and drink his wine while you and I fight it out." With these words Tecumseh with three chiefs departed on a recruiting tour of Illinois and Michigan territories. Then he crossed the Detroit River to confer with British officials in Canada.[45]

4

Harrison had long before planned an invasion of Prophetstown. As the military and religious center of the Indians the village posed as a threat to his own capital and to the surrounding settlements. Only fear of Tecumseh as a military genius had prevented the governor from realizing his aim. Before he could strike he must await a pair of favorable circumstances: Tecumseh must be absent and the Indians must furnish him with overt acts which would justify his aggression. President Madison opposed war with England and wanted no trouble with the Indians on the frontier. Furthermore, Prophetstown lay seventy miles beyond the boundary in Indian territory. A march against the village would be tantamount to an invasion of another nation without presidential or congressional sanction. Harrison knew that Madison was, like Jefferson, a strict observer of the constitution and would reject his intentions.

The chief irritated Harrison by remaining for the time being at Tippecanoe. Yet the governor as a student of history and as an aspirant to the heroic life could not help admire the qualities that had made Tecumseh the leader of his people. He assumed something of the tone of his favorite Roman historian, Tacitus, when later he passed on his opinion of Tecumseh to Secretary Eustis:

The implicit obedience and respect which the followers of Tecumseh pay to him is really astonishing and more than any other circumstances bespeaks him one of those uncommon geniuses, which spring up occasionally to produce revolutions and overturn the established order of things. If it were not for the vicinity of the United States, he would perhaps be the founder of an Empire that would rival in glory that of Mexico or Peru. No difficulties deter him. His activity and industry supply the want of letters. for Four years he has been in constant motion. You see him today on the Wabash and in a short time you hear of him on the shores of Lake Erie or Michigan, or on the banks of the Mississippi and wherever he goes he makes an impression favorable to his purposes.[46]

The overt acts he sought were more obliging. Two Potawatomi killed four soldiers on the Missouri River. Harrison, hearing that the murderers were hidden in the village of Chief Main Poc, sent Wells to ascertain whether they were there. When Wells reported that he found no trace of them Harrison contended that they had fled to Prophetstown and asked the Prophet to surrender them. The reply came from Tecumseh, who denied that he was shielding the murderers but added that, even if they were present, he would not give them up.[47]

In the next few months overt acts became plentiful. In May 1811 the Wea seized two of the surveyors on the recently purchased land, took their only food and rifle, and then scared them off. In the following month, when a cargo of salt passed the Tippecanoe, the Prophet seized it and directed the boatmen to tell Harrison "not to be angry . . . as he had got no salt the last year and had more than two thousand men to feed." In reporting this incident to Secretary Eustis the governor complained that he was "very much at a loss how to proceed. To sit still and suffer this scoundrel to come into this town with six or eight hundred men without having an adequate force to oppose him does not appear to me proper and yet I am certain he will come and equally of his bad intentions."[48]

Deeming the time not yet ripe to permit him to march against Prophetstown, he did the next best thing of sending one of his officers to the village with a threatening letter:

Brothers, what can be the inducement for you to undertake an enterprise where there is no little probability of success; do you really think that the handful of men that you have about you are able to contend with the power of the Seventeen Fires, or even that the whole of the tribes united could contend against the Kentucky Fire alone?

Brothers, I am myself of the long knife fire; as soon as they hear my voice, you will see them pouring forth their swarms of hunting-shirt men, as numerous as the musquitoes on the shore of the Wabash. Brothers, take care of their stings.[49]

Since he had not yet completed his confederacy, Tecumseh for the present had no desire to risk an encounter with Harrison. In his reply, therefore, he expressed his intention of visiting Vincennes within eighteen days to straighten out his differences with the governor. But his distrust of Harrison's intentions made him equivocate about the exact time of his arrival. "Brothers," he wrote, "we cannot say what will become of us, as the Great Spirit has the management of us at his will. I may be there before that time, and may not be there until the day."[50]

Ten days before Tecumseh arrived Harrison received from Secretary Eustis a letter whose contents he was to regard as authority to move against the Prophet:

The fourth regiment, with a company of riflemen, making in the whole 500 men, is ordered to descend the Ohio from Pittsburgh, with all possible expedition. . . .

The authority of the executive to call out the militia in a case like this . . . is considered entirely competent: and in case circumstances shall occur which may render it necessary or expedient to attack the prophet and his followers, the force should be such as to ensure the most complete success. This force will consist of the militia and regular troops. . . .

If the prophet should commence, or seriously threaten, hostilities he ought to be attacked; provided the force under your command is sufficient to ensure success.[51]

But though Eustis the Indian hater spoke out clear and bold he had failed to take into account Madison's love of peace. Three days later, therefore, he was obliged to write to Harrison again, retracting his militant words:

Since my letter of the 17th instant, I have been particularly instructed by the President, to communicate to your excellency his earnest desire that peace may, if possible, be preserved with the Indians, and that to this end every proper means may be adopted. . . . Circumstances conspire at this particular juncture to render it peculiarly desirable that hostilities . . . should be avoided. . . . I am instructed to inform you, that the President indulges the hope and expectation that your exertions and measures with the Indians, will be such as may render [a] march to the Indian territory unnecessary, and that [the soldiers under your command] may remain liable to another disposition.[52]

To this letter Harrison paid no heed. Instead he bent all his efforts to raising a strong force, for the frontiersmen had, since the depredations by the Potawatomi, demanded action against Prophetstown. The Kentuckians knew that Harrison meant to attack the Indians at Tippecanoe and were eager to take part in the campaign. Among them was Joseph H. Daveiss, an able lawyer who had prosecuted Aaron Burr in 1807 and who now offered Harrison his services as a volunteer: "Under all the privacy of a letter I make free to tell you that I have imagined there were two men in the West who had military talents; and you, Sir, were the first of the two. It is thus an opportunity of service valued by me." Harrison accepted Daveiss' service and gave him the command of the dragoons, a mounted force of about one hundred thirty men from Indiana and Kentucky.[53]

Meanwhile Tecumseh on July 27 had appeared in Vincennes with 175 warriors armed with tomahawks and knives and some with bows and arrows. Again he placed no trust in Harrison's intentions. And the alarmed governor immediately summoned three companies of local militia and tried to make them appear as a much larger force by marching them and changing their quarters. He also had parties of foot and horse alerted day and night and had the Indian encampment watched carefully.[54]

When the council opened, Harrison refused to discuss the recent purchases. These now rested with President Madison and Tecumseh might, if he wished, go to him and hear his decision. Harrison then asked Tecumseh to explain his brother's seizure of the salt. Instead of replying, the chief chided Harrison for never being pleased—last year he complained because the salt was refused, this year because it was taken.[55]

A violent rain halted the council until the next morning, when Harrison asked Tecumseh to prove his sincerity by surrendering the two Potawatomi who had murdered the four soldiers on the Missouri. Tecumseh again evaded a direct reply. Instead he began a lengthy speech in which he disclosed his plans. With great difficulty, he said, he had united the northern tribes; soon he would journey to the southern tribes and ask them to join the confederacy. As the Indians had not complained when the Seventeen Fires formed a union, so the Seventeen Fires should not complain when the Indians were doing the same thing. He reiterated his desire for peace; he would send messengers in every direction to warn the tribes to refrain from hostile acts during his absence. He atoned for the murders his people had committed by presenting Harrison with ceremonial wampum.[56]

As the governor accepted it he asked a final question: would Tecumseh prevent the whites from settling on the land which the Wea had ceded? Tecumseh replied that he hoped nothing would be done in his absence. He explained that Indian hunting parties might resent any new settlement and might cause trouble.[57]

The council continued into nightfall. Harrison made a short reply. Pointing to the moon, which shone brightly, he said that it "would sooner fall to the earth than that the President would suffer his people to be murdered with impunity—and that he would put his warriors in petticoats sooner than give up a country which he had fairly acquired from its rightful owners."[58]

With these words he closed the council. On August 5 Tecumseh departed with twenty-four warriors for his mission in the south. The other Indians soon returned to Tippecanoe. At last Harrison's cherished "circumstance" had arrived! No sooner was Tecumseh gone than Harrison made preparations to march against Prophetstown. As rapidly as he could he collected his forces and sent them up the eastern bank of the Wabash sixty-five miles to Battelle des Illinois, on the present site of Terre Haute, Indiana. On October 6 he joined them and put them to work to build on a bluff near the camping ground a stockaded fort with blockhouses at three of its angles. Four days later, while soldiers worked on the fort, Indians fired on the sentries, one of whom they wounded. Henceforth Harrison acted as though war had actually begun.[59]

On October 28 the soldiers completed the fort, which they christened with a bottle of whiskey in honor of their commander. The next day Harrison sent the army up the river, while he remained at Fort Harrison to send Miami messengers to request the Prophet to permit such friendly tribes as the Winnebago, Potawatomi and Kickapoo to return to their tribes. He also requested him to surrender what horses his followers had stolen and the murderers of the whites.[60]

The next day he joined his army, which crossed to the west bank of the Wabash in order to avoid the woods. Reaching the mouth of the Vermilion on November 2, he built a blockhouse, which he called Fort Boyd in honor of one of his officers, Colonel John P. Boyd. Then he crossed the Vermilion and continued up the Wabash. Though he was now in Indian country and therefore looked for resistance, no native barred his way, and he moved on, keeping in open country until on the evening of November 5 he arrived to within eleven miles of Prophetstown. Henceforth small groups of Indians appeared in front and on the flanks. Nevertheless, Harrison continued to advance against the village, while he sent his interpreter and leader of the scouts, Captain Toussaint Dubois, to try to arrange an interview with the Prophet. When the Indians replied with insults and threatening gestures, Dubois returned and reported the failure of his mission.[61]

While Harrison prepared to encamp, Major Daveiss reconnoitered at the head of a detachment of dragoons. In a cornfield he met three Indians, one of whom, Chief White Horse, arranged a parley with Harrison. The chief expressed surprise and alarm that the governor should allow his army to advance after he had sent messengers to Prophetstown with assurances of peace. To which Harrison replied that he had no intention of attacking the village if the Prophet met his demands.[62]

The next day Harrison led his army to within a hundred and fifty yards of Prophetstown. Chief White Horse again protested the invasion. Harrison, sitting on his grey mare, assured the chief that no harm would befall the village and that he sought only suitable camping ground for the night. White Horse obligingly pointed in the direction of Burnet's Creek, nearly three miles from the mouth of the Tippecanoe. And there the Americans camped on a ten-acre piece of dry ground that rose in the shape of a blunt flatiron several feet above the wet prairie. Harrison, availing himself of the terrain, arranged his force of about 1,000 men in the form of a truncated pyramid. Three hundred of his best men faced Prophetstown and three hundred more guarded the opposite side along the creek.[63]

Learning of these military preparations, the Prophet decided to strike first. Tecumseh had strictly enjoined him to refrain from fighting. For the British, whom he solicited for assistance, had advised him that they possessed neither men nor supplies to fight a war on the American frontier and that, in addition, they had their hands full for the present fighting Napoleon in Europe. But Tecumseh was now many miles away, and Harrison was at hand; and the Prophet felt that religious duty demanded that he defend his followers. His plan called for a hundred warriors to kill Harrison— the man on the gray mare—while he was asleep and to surprise his men in their camp.[64]

That night the Prophet donned his dark robe, mixed a sacred potion in a kettle and, muttering an appropriate incantation, assured his followers that the power of their enemies would be rendered as harmless as sand and their bullets as soft as rain. As for the Americans themselves, half of them would be rendered as motionless as posts and the other half would startle and run like sheep at the first noise.[65]

At four o'clock in the morning a few soldiers rose and rekindled the campfire to warm themselves before reveille. A gentle rain fell intermittantly. One of the sentinels suddenly stopped and stared toward a thicket of willows. He was sure he had not imagined the rustling. He ran a few steps toward his comrade and whispered: "Let's fire and run in; Indians in the bushes." A moment later the whiz and thud of an arrow sent them scurrying to the safety of the camp. One of them saw an Indian emerge from the bushes and fire his rifle without aiming. Whereupon one of a small group of Indians killed him, while the others attempted to frighten the Americans away with horrifying yells. At the same time their bullets ripped into tents and campfires, sending live coals skyward in all directions. The violence of their attack enabled them to enter the tents, where they tomahawked and scalped two men and an officer and wounded another in the arm.[66]

Aroused from sleep, Harrison put on his boots while he called to his Negro servant, George, to fetch his grey mare. In a few minutes George returned "confoundedly frightened" to announce that the mare had broken loose from her picket during the night. Whereupon another orderly brought up a black horse, which Harrison mounted and led away. The incident proved for him a stroke of good fortune. A few minutes later Harrison's aide, Colonel Abraham Owen, found the mare and mounted her. Mistaking him for Harrison, the Indians in ambush instantly shot him dead.[67]

In the dim grey light of early morning the Indians made a series of attacks on the American line. Harrison shifted his men often to ward off attack after attack and took personal command at every point of danger. He approached a badly battered company to find Ensign John Tipton sighting down a barrel.

"Where's your captain?" he asked.

"Dead, sir."

"Your first lieutenant?"

"Dead, sir."

"Your second lieutenant?"

"Dead, sir."

"Your ensign?"

"Here, sir!"

Harrison promised him immediate assistance and turned to rally a militia company which was on the point of melting away.[68]

Soon he returned to the line facing Prophetstown, where he reluctantly permitted Major Daveiss to try to dislodge a group of troublesome Indians in a nearby thicket. Wearing a white surtout, Daveiss proved an easy target for the ambuscaded enemy, which ended his terrestial hopes with three bullets.[69]

In the growing daylight the Indians, having everywhere met stiff resistance, shrank from another attack. Harrison, seeing that they had spent their fury, decided to charge them simultaneously from both flanks. He shifted three companies of regulars to the left and two to the right and supported them with militia and dragoons. Then the sound of a bugle sent a charging and yelling mass of soldiery against their half-concealed enemies. Amid the deafening roar of musketry, the agonizing screams of the wounded and dying, and the huzzas of the victors, the redskins, yelling in despair, fled to the safety of a marsh which was impassable for horses. The battle was over.

It cost Harrison sixty-one men killed and one hundred twenty-seven wounded. The Americans took what supplies they needed and burned Prophetstown to the ground. The Indians left thirty-eight dead on the battlefield. Their wounded can never be ascertained, for they carried off many of them. Some of those who sought the protection of the marsh eventually went to Amherstburg, where the British fed and clothed them. Others appeared at Fort Wayne to receive their annuity. The rest starved to death during the rigorous winter months that ensued. The Prophet fled to the mouth of Wildcat Creek, whence he returned with others to the Tippecanoe to await Tecumseh's return.[70]

Late in February or early in March 1812 the chief arrived on the Tippecanoe. The charred ruins of his beloved home was his first information of what had occurred. Later he poignantly set down his feelings:

I stood upon the ashes of my own home, where my own wigwam had sent up its fire to the Great Spirit, and there I summoned the spirits of the braves who had fallen in their vain attempt to protect their homes from the grasping invader, and as I snuffed up the smell of their blood from the ground I swore once more eternal hatred—the hatred of an avenger.[71]

In an effort to escape his brother's wrath, the Prophet blamed Winamac and the Winnebagos for the attack. Tecumseh was undeceived. He upbraided the Prophet, pulled his hair, and threatened to kill him. As for Harrison, he hastened back to Vincennes to escape Tecumseh's possible retaliatory measures, "With every mile he covered and with every hour he reflected on the battle," wrote Glenn Tucker, "Harrison's victory grew more impressive to him, and the process of ballooning it continued after he got home." He wrote Eustis that the Indians had sustained the severest defeat in the history of their relations with the whites. And the whole country believed him and made Tippecanoe—a mere border skirmish that settled nothing—one of the great victories in American history. In twenty-nine years it grew so big that it won Harrison the presidency of the United States.[72]

The Frontier War of 1812

O<small>DDLY</small> <small>ENOUGH,</small> <small>AMERICA'S</small> <small>MOST</small> <small>UNSUCCESSFUL</small> <small>MILITARY</small> <small>VEN-</small>ture—the War of 1812—has aroused one of the bitterest controversies among American historians. With a closer look at the background and the chronology, they have discarded as unsubstantiable President Madison's arguments—arguments accepted by several generations of Americans—that the war was the result of British practices of violating the American flag on the sea, of harassing the Atlantic coast, of impressing American seamen, and of plundering neutral commerce with paper blockades.

Historians now generally agree that the War of 1812 was largely a frontier war—that frontier demands forced it on a peaceful East, that frontier arms won most of its victories, and that frontier ambitions dictated peace. But they disagree vehemently as to the underlying motives involved.

The first historian to blast the old theories was Howard T. Lewis, who in 1911 declared emphatically that the War of 1812 was the direct result of greed on the part of the frontiersmen for the rich and ample reserves of land in Canada. A decade later Louis Morton Hacker supported this view and gave it elucidation. He averred that the frontiersmen cared little or nothing whether Great Britain impressed American seamen and that she and Napoleon confiscated American cargoes. The primary cause of the war, said Hacker, was frontier need of Canadian lands. Ignorant of crop rotation and unskilled in progressive methods of farming, the frontiersman felt constrained to keep on the move to avert hunger. He felt he needed virgin soil in order to survive. But why did he especially covet

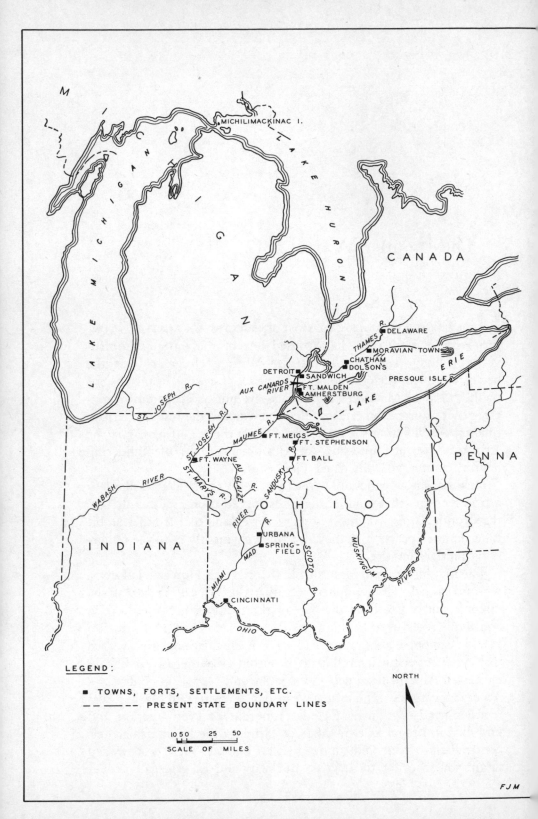

M

. MICHILIMACKINAC I.

LAKE MICHIGAN

LAKE HURON

CANADA

MICHIGAN

THAMES R.
DELAWARE

MORAVIAN TOWNS
CHATHAM
DOLSON'S

DETROIT
SANDWICH

AUX CANARDS RIVER

FT. MALDEN
AMHERSTBURG

PRESQUE ISLE

LAKE ERIE

PENNA

ST. JOSEPH R.

ST. JOSEPH R.

MAUMEE R.

FT. MEIGS
FT. STEPHENSON

FT. WAYNE

FT. BALL

AU GLAIZE R.

ST. MARY'S R.

SANDUSKY R.

OHIO

WABASH RIVER

MAD R.

MIAMI R.

URBANA
SPRING-
FIELD

MUSKINGUM RIVER

SCIOTO R.

INDIANA

CINCINNATI

OHIO

LEGEND:

■ TOWNS, FORTS, SETTLEMENTS, ETC.
----- PRESENT STATE BOUNDARY LINES

NORTH

10 5 0   25   50
SCALE OF MILES

FJM

Canadian lands? Why not the limitless prairies to the west? Hacker explained that the frontiersman considered them unfit for settlement because he thought them remote from centers of communication and because they lacked timber and rivers with adequate water supply for drinking and running mills. The frontiersman, said Hacker, regarded timber as the most important element of his existence:

Without standing timber the pioneer could not erect his rude log cabin and his barn; without timber neither the pioneer nor the farmer had fuel to make life supportable in the cruel winter months. In this primitive agricultural economy the presence of abundant wood was as important as the very soil itself. The railroads had first to make their appearance; coal had to be discovered in the Ohio valley; and wire had to be turned out for fencing, before the prairies could beckon to the settler.[1]

To Julius W. Pratt this view was insupportable because it assumed that only treeless plains remained unoccupied. In truth the unsettled area included such timbered land as a third of the state of Ohio, nearly all of Indiana, sections of Illinois, all of Michigan and Wisconsin, much of Minnesota, and stretches of hardwood in southern Missouri.[2]

Another historian, D. R. Anderson, writing about the same time as Lewis, believed that the War of 1812 resulted primarily from fear on the part of the frontiersmen of a general Indian uprising encouraged by British officials in Canada. They believed that its conquest was the only practicable solution to their problem. To which Hacker countered that the frontiersmen could not have felt much terror for the Indians, who they knew were inferior in numbers as well as in intelligence.[3]

A few years later Edward Channing introduced still another factor into this growing controversy. He theorized that the South wanted the Floridas in order to increase slave territory and that it obviated possible opposition to such an acquisition in the North by suggesting the conquest of Canada. Pratt, who gave this interpretation its most complete presentation, averred that the South was almost unanimous in demanding the Floridas for agricultural, commercial, and strategic reasons and that before the war southern and northern Republicans agreed to balance the acquisition of Canada in the north with the annexation of the Floridas in the south. Pratt also supported Anderson's thesis by asserting that the frontiersmen were convinced that they would be in danger as long as the British remained in Canada to encourage Indian attacks.[4]

Most historians regard Pratt's views as those best supported by documentary evidence. Tippecanoe was no decisive victory. It led to no permanent peace between the Indians and the whites. In the minds of the frontiersmen the red menace remained as real as before. A series of incidents before 1812 tended to confirm their suspicion that as long as the British controlled Canada they would encourage the Indians to attack the white settlements. Before Fallen Timbers the Indians counted the British as their allies. The tribes often returned home from Malden, across the river from Detroit, carrying the firearms and other articles they had bartered for furs, and they hunted and warred with British-made guns. Harrison's soldiers found British rifles and tomahawks at Prophetstown. To the frontiersmen all this was incontestable proof that the Indians intended eventually to wipe them out. In vain did British officials protest that they had never encouraged Indian attacks. As justification for their suspicion of Indian intentions the frontiersmen could recall an endless chain of depredations. The young War Hawk, Felix Grundy, expressed their feelings in a speech before the senate:

. . . I can remember when death was in almost every bush, and every thicket concealed an ambuscade. If I am asked to trace my memory back, and name the first indelible impression it received, it would be the sight of my oldest brother bleeding and dying under the wounds inflicted by the tomahawk and the scalping knife. Another, and another, went in the same way! I have seen a widowed mother plundered of her whole property in a single night: from affluence and ease reduced to labor with her own hands to support and educate her last and favorite son—him who now addresses you. Sir, the ancient sufferings of the West were great.[5]

No matter that the Indians may have suffered even more severely at the hands of the white men. The Americans thought only of holding the land on which they had settled and of grabbing as much more as they could. Christopher B. Colman expressed their attitude with admirable accuracy:

Their own advance seemed to them to be the natural order and the law of their life; the stealthy, deadly warfare of the Indians was a shadow across their path, creating a combination of fear and ferocity unintelligible to those whose lives and households are not in constant peril. Their only way out was to secure title to additional tracts of land by some form of purchase, make resistance hopeless for the Indians, and shove them on farther west and north.[6]

Had he won a great victory instead of a mere skirmish at Tippecanoe, Harrison might have allayed frontier fears; but he had neither the supplies nor the men to drive the Indians from their own lands. When hostilities broke out between the United States and Great Britain, the Indians resumed their raids, which greatly distressed the Indiana frontiersmen "We were in fine spirits," wrote a settler of the Whitewater Valley, "until the battle was fought at Tippecanoe. . . . After that, we lived in continual fear; . . . we were then few in numbers and completely in the power of the enemy."[7]

Though fear of a general Indian uprising is doubtless a leading cause of the frontier war of 1812, other factors must be considered. One of the leading authorities of the American frontier, Ray Allen Billington, pointed out that for four years previous to the war an economic depression engulfed the pioneers. The lack of roads in the Ohio valley forced the farmers to sell such bulky products as corn, wheat, and cattle only in the port of New Orleans. And they had to sell at prices a month old, had to spend another month and considerable sums in reaching the port, and had to compete there with many other merchants. And that was not all. On the journey they often had to brave the attacks of pirates and Indians, endure privation and fatigue, only to encounter at their destination a bustling strangeness that overawed them and a threat of tropical fevers that constrained them to sell their wares at whatever prices they could obtain and hurry homeward. Only a fortunate few sold their products at a profit.[8]

At first the waves of immigration that poured into the Great Lakes Frontier absorbed all its farmers could produce; they enjoyed prosperity as long as their wares reached European markets. But in 1806 the British blockade of European ports began to bring depression to the American frontier. Its farmers then reasoned, and reasoned correctly, that they could retrieve the markets they had lost only when the United States forced Great Britain to lift her blockade. Naturally they applauded when the Embargo Act of 1807 kept American ships at home and objected vociferously when eastern influence forced Congress to adopt the less stringent Non-Intercourse Act of 1809. And when, by the end of 1811, the depression grew acute, they became convinced that nothing save war with Great Britain would restore prosperity.[9]

The bloodshed at Tippecanoe clearly increased frontier resentment for the British and gave incalculable support to the war party in the Twelfth Congress, which met for the first time early in November, 1811—a month earlier than usual. The war party, composed of western men whom John Randolph dubbed the War Hawks, found itself in full control. Its most prominent members were Henry Clay, speaker of the House of Representatives, John C. Calhoun of South Carolina, Peter B. Porter of the frontier region of New York, Felix Grundy of Tennessee, and George M. Troup of Georgia—aggressive young men who had personal reasons for promoting a war of expansion. The War Hawks demanded war with the conquest of Canada as its major objective. A select committee under Clay reported a set of six resolutions recommending an increase of 10,000 men for the regular army, a levy on all vessels of war not in active service, and the arming of merchant ships.[10]

During their debates on the resolutions the War Hawks in the House disclosed their designs on Canada. The United States was to deprive Great Britain

. . . of her extensive provinces lying along our borders to the north. These provinces were not only immensely valuable in themselves, but almost indispensable to the existence of Great Britain, cut off as she now in a great measure is from the north of Europe.[11]

Felix Grundy dwelled on the benefits that should accrue to the frontiersmen from the invasion:

We shall drive the British from our Continent—they will no longer have an opportunity of intriguing with our Indian neighbors, and setting on the ruthless savages to tomahawk our women and children. That nation will lose her Canadian trade, and, by having no resting place in this country, her means of annoying us will be diminished.[12]

While the War Hawks debated they received reports of British intrigue among the Indians. These fired them to greater fury. The British had sent the Indians substantial presents of ammunition, had passed Fort Wayne on a mission to the Prophet, and had invited the tribes to meet at Fort Malden early in the spring. Worse still, the War Hawks heard that the hostile Potawatomi chief, Marpot, had been seen in the neighborhood of Fort Malden with a hundred and twenty of his best warriors and that he would strike at the white settlements as soon as the British gave him the signal![13]

These reports, together with the skirmish at Tippecanoe, the bellicose speeches of the War Hawks, and the delusion that the British were inciting the Indians to destroy the whites, engendered in the frontiersmen a fierce determination to conquer Canada. Their paranoid tendencies found expression in their newspapers. The *Fredonian* of Circleville, Ohio, declared that the Americans had suffered indignities and that these could be appeased only "by the restoration of our rights, or the conquest of Canada."

In ensuing months the same newspaper clamored for war. It conjured up another Wayne who would force the Indians to become friends of the Americans and another Washington who would destroy "the base remains of royal perfidy" in Canada. The Ohio *Muskingum Messenger* demanded "WAR! WAR! WAR!" as "the last appeal of nations." The *Reporter* of Lexington, Kentucky, predicted an early victory: "Let every arm be nerved for the glorious contest; every voice prepared to bid it welcome!—England we can punish." Toasts received numerous huzzas all over the frontier: "May the starry flag of 1812 float triumphantly over the ramparts of Quebec."—"May the Twelfth Congress no longer tamely submit to British outrages, but wrest from her every foot of possession she holds in North America." Toasts at Fourth of July dinners glowed with convivial optimism: "Canada—may it soon be counted as another star adorning our political hemisphere."[14]

Thus by the spring of 1812 the American frontier from the Ohio to the Mississippi clamored for an invasion of Canada. The frontiersmen felt that they must drive the British from North America in order to be free to continue their policy of "justice and benevolence" toward the Indians—a policy consisting of pushing the boundaries of the settlements ever farther into the country which the whites themselves had guaranteed to the Indians by treaty. The Great Lakes frontiersmen were ready to take steps to satisfy their ambition to develop their region without peril from the Indian conspiracies which they believed orginated in Canada.[15]

In December 1811 Congress adopted the resolutions of the War Hawks and in the following June, after some hesitation on the part of President Madison and a few others, it gave way to western demands and declared war on Great Britain. Thomas Jefferson expressed confidence that it would be short. "Upon the whole," he wrote Thaddeus Koskiusko, "I have known no war entered into under more favorable auspices." His confidence increased with time. He assured Colonel William Duane that "the acquisition of Canada this year as far as the neighborhood of Quebec, will be a mere matter of marching, and will give us experience for the attack on Halifax next, and the final expulsion of England from the American continent."[16]

Nathaniel Macon, however, had no such roseate views. He wrote to a friend:

Whatever we do, we do it rashly, and scarcely do anything in the second best way, and generally find out weeks after, that we have not acted in the manner we ought to have done; in this manner we shall, I apprehend, get to war, not half fixed for it, under the belief that then we shall do things as we ought to do; this will I fear on experience be discovered a mistake."[17]

These were words of wisdom. Macon was one of very few Americans who maintained a realistic view in the face of national hysteria. Never was the United States so woefully unprepared for war. Her standing army counted less than seven thousand men. True, she had in addition seven hundred thousand militiamen, but these were scattered far and wide, seldom responded to the requisitions of the Federal Government; indeed, they often positively refused them. And at critical times the militia contingents refused to leave their respective states or, of course, the country at the command of their officers. In wartime these circumstances limited the American army—including regulars, volunteers and militia—to barely fifty-six thousand men. Most of the regulars had insufficient training and the militia hardly any at all. The molding of this raw material into a trained army required efficient officers, but even those of the regular army were largely incompetent and inexperienced in commanding large bodies of men.[18]

The general officers were no better. The ranking senior officer, Major General Henry Dearborn, had acted as a deputy commissary during the Revolutionary War. Like most mediocre men in high office, he was overcautious, hedged on matters that demanded immediate solution, and talked from both sides of his mouth at the same time. His superior, Dr. William Eustis, should never have left symptoms and medicines. He could give large orders, but these more often than not miscarried because they had no brains behind them. President Madison was a master of arguments but a minion of crafty men. The fortifications were old and inadequate and many of them had been designed for defense against the Indians.[19]

The plan of campaign called for a three-pronged invasion of Canada from points four hundred miles apart: Detroit, Niagara, and

Lake Champlain. Dearborn was to lead an expedition against Montreal by way of Lake Champlain, while generals Stephen Van Rensselaer and Alexander Smyth on the Canadian center struck across the Niagara River. The main thrust was to be the invasion of Upper Canada from Detroit. This was entrusted to the Governor of Michigan Territory, Brigadier General William Hull.

2

The war produced no more pathetic figure than Hull. Sixty years old, he felt he was past the age when men win military glory; he wanted only to remain in his civil post. Yet in his youth he fought bravely for the independence of his country, was promoted from captain to lieutenant-colonel, and retired with honor to practice law in his native New England. Later he served as a judge of the court of common pleas, as a state senator, and as commander of a militia division. In 1805 he was chosen governor of the newly-established Michigan Territory.

On July 9, 1812, Hull received from Secretary Eustis orders to invade Canada. "Should the force under your Command be equal to the Enterprise," wrote Eustis, "consistent with the Safety of your post you will take possession of Malden and extend your conquests as circumstances may justify." Hull replied that he would cross the river within a few days.[20]

At dawn on July 12 he was as good as his word. He crossed unopposed and occupied Sandwich, now the city of Windsor, Ontario. But he had no desire for battle; he hoped to win Canada by his mere presence; he hastened to address a conciliatory proclamation to the Canadians:

You will be emancipated from tyranny and oppression, and restored to the dignified station of freemen. . . . I have a force which will break down all opposition, and that force is but the vanguard of a much greater. . . . The United States offer you peace, liberty, and security—your choice lies between these and war, slavery, or destruction. Choose then; but choose wisely.[21]

This verbal flatulence temporarily relieved his own fears as well as those of the inhabitants of Sandwich. Strongly pro-American, three hundred sixty-seven of its inhabitants, together with some from the Malden garrison, sought protection in the American lines.[22]

Hull quaked at the thought of bloodshed, but this did not prevent him from writing Eustis that he was preparing to attack Fort Malden perhaps within a week. He reported that a large Indian council was assembling at Brownstown and that he felt sure it would decide on neutrality. He addressed to the regional tribes a proclamation in which he told them that the United States would respect their lands and rights in return for neutrality. Many of the tribes assented and agreed to attend the general council that he planned for August at Piqua; but Tecumseh and his followers, having already scorned Hull's announcement that the war was the white man's war, joined the British at Fort Malden.[23]

On July 16 Hull, learning that a British force had crossed the north side of the Aux Canards River, sent Colonel Lewis Cass with a strong force to reconnoitre in the region. Exceeding his instrutions, Cass advanced to the Aux Canards bridge, met a small force consisting of militia from Amherstburg and some Indians under Tecumseh, and forced it to withdraw. Determined to hold the bridge, he sent Hull a messenger asking him to advance with his army; but the commander replied that his army would be too exposed and ordered Cass to return to the main force. When Cass withdrew the British advanced, tore up the planks of the bridge, and anchored the *Queen Charlotte*—a brigantine of one hundred eighty tons with ten twenty-four pounders, three long guns and a crew of two officers and twenty-seven men—at the mouth of the river to provide flank protection from the Detroit River. Tecumseh crossed it with his followers in single file on the stringers of the bridge and attacked a few of Colonel Duncan McArthur's one hundred fifty men whom Cass had sent to ascertain the position of the brigantine. Whereupon McArthur brought up his entire force and pushed Tecumseh back across the bridge, only to retreat to Sandwich when the *Queen Charlotte* fired on him with her large guns.[24]

Meanwhile Hull continued to toy with the idea of attacking Fort Malden. He needed no coaxing to conclude that his six-pounders were no match for the twenty-four pounders that guarded the fort. His own twenty-four pounders were far from ready, and even if they had been he could not have transported them over the marshy sections of the road that led to the fort. So he gingerly set to work to build rafts on which he planned to float his guns on the river past the impassable parts of the road—despite the danger of attack by naval units.[25]

Misfortune was his destiny. At the end of July two Chippewa runners brought him word that Fort Michilimackinac had fallen to a combined force of Indians and British. He realized too well the significance of this setback. Now the northern tribes would flock to Mackinac Island and obtain the captured supplies by pledging their allegiance to the British cause. But even more distressing—the British now controlled Lake Michigan and could send Indians by water routes to attack him on the rear.[26]

The ensuing days brought him greater misfortunes. He soon learned that the Wyandots had pledged him their loyalty only to join the British. At about the same time he discovered that his provisions had dwindled to seventy thousand rations of flour and twenty-one thousand rations of salted meat—enough to last just twenty days! He was greatly alarmed, for his supply route with Ohio had to pass the west shore of Lake Erie and follow the Detroit River, where hostile Indians had maintained a blockade since the end of July, had killed several American soldiers, and had captured their dispatches.

Hull had sent to Governor Return J. Meigs of Ohio an urgent call for provisions, and now this friend responded by assembling a generous convoy of three hundred cattle and seventy pack horses, each carrying two hundred pounds of flour. At its head he placed Captain Henry Brush with sixty-nine militiamen whose number was to increase with regulars who had been ill or wounded and left in several places.

On August 4 Brush led the convoy up to the Raisin River, thirty miles south of Detroit, where he learned that Tecumseh awaited him at Brownstown on the Huron River. Unwilling to expose his convoy to this danger, Brush sent a messenger to request Hull for an escort to Detroit. After elaborately arguing this simple matter with his officers Hull consented to send Major Thomas B. Van Horne with his battalion of one hundred fifty men to Brush's assistance. Carrying Hull's dispatches and the soldiers' letters home, Van Horne crossed the river, picked up a few mounted men and some Ohio militia, and camped for the night at the Ecorse River. In the morning he advanced along the river road because he had failed to find a back trail in his endeavor to avoid an encounter with Tecumseh. Near the village of Monguagon his leader of scouts, Captain William McCullough, and a Negro servant were ambushed, killed and scalped. At about the same time Van Horne learned from a Frenchman that a large force of Indians and British were preparing an ambush at Brownstown; but, having heard so many false reports, he paid no heed to the warning.[27]

The Americans soon approached Brownstown. When the vanguard of twenty-five men came within fifty yards of his concealed warriors, Tecumseh signaled to them to fire. At such close range the effect was deadly. What men of the vanguard were not killed or wounded ran away in panic, while the other troops, as they came up, were too confused to shoot straight. Erroneously believing that the Indians were in large numbers and fearing that his force would be surrounded, Van Horne sounded a retreat. This soon became disorderly. In their effort to get away the Americans abandoned Hull's dispatches and the soldiers' letters. Tecumseh chased them for about seven miles up the road toward Detroit and then called back his warriors. By this time Van Horne had run with most of his men all the way to the Ecorse River, where he loaded his wounded in a canoe and then continued posthaste to Detroit, which he reached by nightfall.[28]

Meanwhile Tecumseh had again turned his attention to Brush and had kept him from advancing with the convoy. At the same time he sent to the British officers at Fort Malden the dispatches and letters the Americans had abandoned during their retreat.[29]

Van Horne's ignominious adventure should have shown Hull the wisdom of postponing an attack on Fort Malden until his heavy artillery became available. Instead he put on a bold front and began to talk of making an immediate assault on Fort Malden. On August 7, while he simulated preparations for the attack, he told his officers that he had received word that British regulars from the Niagara region were marching to reinforce Fort Malden and that no attempt was made to stop them. Now more than ever was Hull frozen to his post. He told his officers that an attack on the fort was too great a gamble. Should they not retreat instead to the Raisin River or the Miami, reform their supply lines, and await reinforcements? The Ohio officers replied that their men would desert if he made an attempt to retreat, and he knew they meant what they said. In the face of this threat Hull decided to recross the river. On August 8 he returned to American soil without any interference from the enemy.[30]

At Detroit his position was hardly better than it had been at Sandwich. Wasting no time in his plan to try to reopen his supply line, he ordered Lieutenant Colonel James Miller to force open a passage down the river to Brush's convoy. Miller obeyed immediately; at the head of six hundred men he began to march toward Brownstown. Concealed in a ravine near Monguagon lay over four hundred British and Indians, waiting to arrest his advance. When in the afternoon the Americans came in view the British and Indians began firing. This time the American vanguard, led by the intrepid Captain Josiah Snelling, formed into a square and held its ground, while the main force removed their knapsacks and rushed into battle formation.

For a quarter of an hour the battle ranged along the riverbank and through the adjacent oak forest. Observing a movement in the forest and thinking it signified an attempt on the part of the Americans to flank them, the British poured a galling fire in its direction, and brought down a number of Tecumseh's Indians who, hard pressed by the Americans, had unexpectedly shifted their position. Enraged by the error, the Indians fired on their allies, momentarily disconcerting them.

At this juncture the British commander, Major Adam Muir, ordered his bugler to sound a bayonet charge for his grenadiers, who had just arrived on the field. But the grenadiers mistook the signal for an order to retreat, and retreat they did, demoralizing their comrades. They ran to a position a quarter of a mile in the rear, where Muir, though wounded, rallied them. But not for long. Tecumseh's warriors, howling like a pack of hungry wolves as they fought hard, alarmed their allies to the extent that they took to their boats and made for the Canadian shore. When the Indians, feeling themselves deserted, followed suit, Miller pursued them for a mile or so until the American cavalry leader, Captain Sloan, became so unnerved that he lost his voice.

Snelling pulled him off his horse and mounted it in his stead. His long red hair streaming all over his face, he continued the chase, riding in his anger so far away from his troops that, when he regained his composure, he feared Tecumseh would entrap him. He wheeled his horse, returned to his troops, and led them toward Monguagon almost as swiftly as he had pursued the enemy. The contest cost Muir four men killed and fifteen wounded. Tecumseh made no report of his losses, which were undoubtedly heavy. Miller found the bodies of forty warriors on the field.[31]

Hull's failure to force a passage to the Raisin River convinced him that his position was extremely perilous. He resolved now to risk no more engagements until he had obtained supplies and reinforcements. He was relieved to learn that reinforcements were on the way; but the supplies still remained with Brush, who refused to budge from the Raisin without an escort. The British, reasoning that Hull would continue to send detachments to Brush and thereby weaken his own garrison, were content to let the convoy stay where it was. Even Hull advised Brush to remain at the Raisin, though he authorized him to advance by a back trail and cross the Huron River at Godfroy's trading post if he felt he could get by safely.

When Brush replied that he would try, Hull ordered Colonels McArthur and Cass to assemble four hundred picked men to go to meet him. The two officers were reluctant to leave Detroit, for at that time they were hatching a plot with their Ohio men to remove their useless commander, but they obeyed him when he ordered them to march immediately. They were to take the back trail to the Huron River and, if the convoy was not there, to find it and escort it to Detroit.[32]

On the same day, August 14, the British moved against Detroit. Their commander, Major General Sir Isaac Brock, was in every respect Hull's opposite. Six feet three inches tall, he was a man of commanding stature. In his admirable biography of Tecumseh, Glenn Tucker described Brock as "strong as a bull from his native island of Guernsey, but considerate and gentle in his administrative work on a rough frontier." With these lovable personal traits he combined a long record of military experience. He had fought in Sir Ralph Abercromby's campaign in the Netherlands in 1799 and had served under Sir John Moore. Four years later he arrived in Canada, where he put down a regiment that had mutinied and then won its complete loyalty.[33]

While Hull vacillated in his purported endeavor to attack Fort Malden, Brock, with invincible resolution, prepared to storm Detroit. Availing himself of Hull's withdrawal from Canada he praised his soldiers and the members of his staff on their unexpected success. He reinstated all those who as deserters had been regarded as traitors, and promoted all of his officers. At the same time he gained the loyalty of the Indians by appealing to their pride as warriors and by requesting their approval of his plans to attack Detroit. The Indian commissioner of Upper Canada, Colonel Matthew Elliott, introduced him to Tecumseh. The two men shook hands and immediately became fast friends, for each saw in the other the qualities that made him the leader of his race. Here was one white man that Tecumseh could trust. *"This* is a *man!"* he said to Shabbona, and his followers approved his words with a chorus of guttural "Ho! Ho!"[34]

At dusk on August 14 Tecumseh with six hundred warriors crossed the river south of Sandwich and ranged the woods that surrounded Detroit. The next day Brock sent Hull a summons of surrender:

The force at my disposal authorises me to require the immediate surrender of fort Detroit. It is far from my intention to join in a war of extermination, but you must be aware, that the numerous body of Indians who have attached themselves to my troops, will be beyond controul [sic] the moment the contest commences. You will find me disposed to enter into such conditions as will satisfy the most scrupulous sense of honour.[35]

The threat of an Indian massacre or captivity preyed cruelly on Hull's misery, but he feared his officers' wrath too much to surrender. Furthermore, he hoped to hear from McArthur and Cass and to complete last-minute defenses. Several hours later he replied to Brock that he "was prepared to meet any force which may be at your disposal, and any consequences which may result from any exertion of it you may think proper to make."[36]

Brock's answer removed all doubt of equivocation. At four o'clock that afternoon the shore batteries of the *Queen Charlotte* and of another brig, the *General Hunter,* opened up with a terrifying cannonade, smashing the fort in several places and setting it on fire. The cannonade also killed several men, including Lieutenant Porter Hanks, the unfortunate officer who had surrendered Fort Michilimackinac and who was just then undergoing a military hearing to clear himself of his conduct at that post. The American cannoneers stood at their guns with lighted matches, ready to attempt to repel any invasion from across the river; but Hull, shifting between defiance and despair, seemed too stupefied to give the order to fire. Did he expect reinforcements? Did he expect Brush to come to his assistance? He was destined to realize neither. At Godfroy's trading post McArthur and Cass found no trace of Brush, who had doggedly remained at the Raisin River. So McArthur and Cass began to retrace their steps to Detroit.[37]

On the morning of August 16 Brock crossed the river with seven hundred thirty men. His original intention was to take up a strong position and force Hull to attack it; but, learning that Colonels McArthur and Cass were approaching Detroit, he decided to storm the fort while Tecumseh attacked the town.[38]

Black despair seized General Hull. He sat on the ground in an old tent, unconsciously putting into his mouth quid after quid of tobacco and spitting juice that landed on his neckcloth, his whiskers, his cravat and his vest. He seemed oblivious to the shots from British cannon that boomed all around him. Only once did he shake off his stupor. "My God!" he bawled to one of his officers, "What shall I do with these women and children?" His voice trembled; his nerves jangled; his heavy features were drawn with intolerable fear. He feared the massacre of women and children; he feared for his life; he feared the undisguised contempt and sneers of his officers and men. At last he could tolerate himself no longer. Hearing that Tecumseh had surrounded the town and that two companies of the Michigan militia had deserted to the enemy, he ordered his son, who held the commission of captain, to hoist a white flag. Within an hour Tecumseh and Brock occupied the town and fort.[39]

On the same day McArthur and Cass arrived in Detroit and laid down their arms. Brock sent two of his officers to arrange the terms of surrender, which Hull signed in the face of sneers on the part of some of his officers. Because Hull had rejected his original offer, Brock refused to grant the customary honors to the defeated garrison. Yet his terms were extremely liberal. He sent home the officers and men of the Ohio and Michigan militia on their promise not to serve in the war until they were exchanged, and granted the Ohio militia transportation behind the Indian lines. He had Hull and most of his regulars placed on boats and taken to Montreal until they could be regularly exchanged. He retained only those whom he regarded as deserters from the British service.[40]

The convoy under Brush was included in the terms of surrender. At Brock's command, the Indian commissioner, Colonel Matthew Elliott, sent his son to request Brush to give up the convoy. The doughty captain, however, declared that Hull had no right to surrender and threw young Elliott into the guard house. Then he harnessed his horses and yoked his oxen and returned with the convoy to Ohio, leaving a request that the authorities release Elliott on the following day.[41]

On the day before Hull surrendered, the garrison at Fort Dearborn, on the present site of Chicago, met disaster in battle with four hundred Potawatomi under Main Poc. Hull had warned the commander of the garrison, Captain Nathan Heald, of the impending attack and had ordered him to retire to Fort Wayne. Heald obeyed, but he had advanced less than two miles with his men and the members of his and their families when, on a sand dune, he saw the enemy and attacked it. Of the ninety-one persons who left the fort that morning only twenty-seven, including Heald and his wife, survived to describe their horrible experiences. The next morning the Indians entered the fort and burned it to the ground.[42]

In the early fall of 1812 Hull was paroled. Returning to his home in Newton, Massachusetts, he immediately requested a review of his conduct at Detroit. In the following February the court-martial met in Philadelphia with General Wade Hampton presiding; but President Madison, suspecting that it was a prejudiced body, dissolved it without explanation. In January 1814 another court-martial met in Albany with General Dearborn presiding and with the future president of the United States, Martin Van Buren, serving as judge advocate.

Since his own papers had been destroyed and since the court refused him access to official government documents, Hull was unable to defend himself successfully. Several of the regular officers who had been called as witnesses were impartial; but Hull's former Ohio militia officers, including McArthur and Cass, condemned him forthwith. In its need of finding a scapegoat for its failure in the opening campaign of the war, the administration accepted the most incriminating testimony. The court-martial found Hull guilty on all charges of cowardice and on most charges of neglect of duty and conduct unbecoming an officer. Though it was unable to find him guilty of treason, it sentenced him to be hanged. President Madison, however, commuted the sentence in consideration of Hull's services during the Revolution.[43]

Broken in spirit, Hull returned home to write his memoirs. In recalling his ignominious surrender he perhaps found some solace in the knowledge that, though he had accomplished nothing, he had accomplished no less than had the generals on the other two Canadian fronts. Early in October 1812 Van Rensselaer, who commanded at Niagara, sent Captain John E. Wood with a force of regulars to take Queenston Heights. Wood succeeded in securing a lodgment until Brock brought up reinforcements and defeated him with a loss of more than a thousand killed, wounded, and captured. The New York militia refused to cross the river, arguing that their officers had no authority to lead them out of the country, and looked on while their comrades were mauled on the other side. Brock lost his life in this fight. Van Rensselaer resigned his command. His successor, General Alexander Smyth, ordered an attack above the falls of the Niagara but accomplished even less than Van Rensselaer. He too resigned.[44]

Henry Dearborn, leading the largest army ever to fight under the Stars and Stripes up to that time, wasted precious time at Plattsburg on Lake Champlain awaiting negotiations toward peace. When this prospect faded, he marched across the river, but his militia men refused to fight on foreign soil. This and his own morbid fear of British might have induced him to return to Plattsburg, and there he remained.[45]

3

In reply to Hull's request for reinforcements, Secretary Eustis had appointed a Tennessee planter, James Winchester, to the rank of brigadier general and had requested him to gather a force and lead it to Detroit. Winchester was as old and as incompetent as Hull. Such leading Kentuckians as Isaac Shelby, who was again governor, General Charles Scott, and Henry Clay, scoffed at Winchester's appointment and made William Henry Harrison, whom they considered a much more competent officer, a major general in the state militia by brevet. Whereupon Harrison proceeded from Frankfort to Cincinnati, where he persuaded Winchester to allow him to assume active command of the entire force, including the regulars under Colonel Samuel Wells, and to take up instead the less honored task of recruiting. Receiving word that hostile Indians had surrounded Fort Wayne, Harrison resolved to march to its relief. On his way, at Piqua, he recieved from Eustis a letter informing him of his appointment to the rank of brigadier general and assigning him to the defense of the areas of Indiana and Illinois. Harrison was unwilling to accept the federal commission, for, in the absence of any further instructions from Eustis, it would make him inferior in rank to Winchester and therefore under his command.

At Harrison's approach the Indians retired from Fort Wayne, which they had been besieging. Though they had done little damage to the fort itself, they had destroyed its outlying Indian factory, crops, and livestock. Vowing vengeance for this destruction, Harrison pursued the Indians to the Miami villages, which, however, he found deserted. He burned them and the crops, and returned to Fort Wayne, where he found Winchester. Still unwilling to accept the federal commission, he turned over his command to Winchester and proceeded to St. Mary's. There he found a letter in which Eustis requested him to co-operate with Winchester in regaining Michigan Territory.

Obeying orders, he planned to march to the St. Joseph in Michigan, cross the country of the Raisin River, and attempt to surprise Detroit; but he had no intention of serving under Winchester. He wrote him that he had decided to decline the federal commission and that he regarded his own commission as major general of Kentucky militia as superior to that held by his correspondent. This question of rank had caused much confusion and inspired an exchange of letters among Eustis, Harrison and Winchester. The problem was solved when President Madison on the recommendations of Henry Clay and other Kentuckians appointed Harrison to command the extensive forces—about ten thousand men in all—to be known as the North Western Army, which was to protect the frontier, capture Detroit, and move against Upper Canada.[46]

Harrison wasted no time announcing to Eustis his plans for an autumn campaign. To this end he planned to move with three columns to the rapids of the Maumee River and thence push against Detroit. At about the same time he sent Brigadier General Samuel Hopkins with two thousand Kentucky militia to clear the way to the rapids by destroying the Indian villages between the Wabash and the Illinois rivers. These were encouraging beginnings, but they became nothing more. Harrison's doubts about the success of his plans increased as the fair weather lessened. "If the fall should be very dry," he wrote Eustis, "I will take Detroit before the winter sets in; but if we should have much rain it will be necessary to wait at the rapids until the Miami of the Lakes is sufficiently frozen to bear the army and its baggage."[47]

Even the pessimistic part of this sentence proved optimistic. Constant rains forced Harrison to halt before he reached the Maumee. Only one division of five Kentucky regiments under Winchester succeeded in inching toward the rapids. November brought a series of hard frosts and thaws that stalled Winchester's sleds, wagons, and pack horses. When he arrived at the neighborhood of Fort Defiance, he could go no farther. And there he remained for the rest of the year, his men suffering from lack of food and clothing and threatening to mutiny.[48]

Harrison, too, was facing difficulties. In his endeavor to advance he alternated his headquarters between Franklinton, at the present site of Columbus, and the village of Delaware, only to find one place as bad as the other. The supplies he needed for ten thousand men never arrived on regular schedule, perhaps, as he suspected, because the contractors were more interested in profit than in patriotism. He gleaned no encouragement from either the condition or the position of his army. One column was stalled and starving near Fort Defiance. Another, under Brigadier General Edward Tupper, was unable to advance beyond Urbana, a hundred miles from the Maumee. Hopkins, in his expedition up the Wabash, had

burned Prophetstown only to follow his deserting soldiers homeward. And Harrison was riding through the mud, making speeches
everywhere in his endeavor to keep his force intact for the great
push which, however, seemed remote from realization. From
Franklinton he wrote Eustis that

. . . I am not able to fix any period for the advance of the troops to
Detroit. It is pretty evident that it cannot be done upon proper
principles until the frost shall become so severe as to enable us to
use the rivers and the margins of the Lake for transportation of the
baggage and artillery upon the ice. To get them forward through
a swampy wilderness of near two hundred miles in wagons or on
pack-horses which are to carry their own provisions, is absolutely
impossible.[49]

He stayed in Franklinton for another month with no prospect of
advancing. Some of his wagons had been abandoned in the mud,
his pack horses shivered from cold and exhaustion, and his boats
capsized in low water. Then, in December, he ran out of flour—
his soldiers subsisted on half-spoiled beef and hickory roots.
Typhus, that disease of unscrubbed bodies and dirty cots, deci-
mated his ranks quicker than could a stealthy enemy. By the end
of December their number shrank to about a thousand. Yet Harrison still planned a winter campaign. A few days before Christmas he sent word to Winchester to march to the rapids to prepare sleds for the expedition against Detroit. Receiving long-sought
provisions, he rushed them over the hardened ground to the Maumee along with his artillery. At the same time he obtained several
brigades of reinforcements which he sent to fortify the Sandusky
River.[50]

By this time Eustis had resigned. The Secretary of State, James
Monroe, acted as Secretary of War until January 13, 1813, when
John Armstrong assumed that post. While directing the War Department Monroe sent Harrison a letter expressing concern over
the delay of the campaign. Harrison replied that the weather had
not permitted him to realize his plans and that he hoped to move
with four thousand men to the rapids by January 20.[51]

But Winchester arrived there first. Obeying Harrison's orders,
he began to build a fortified camp. The men were still working
on it when, ten days later, Winchester received two Frenchmen
from the village of River Raisin, which was also known as Frenchtown because of the single nationality of its population. The

Frenchmen informed Winchester that the British were unaware of his presence and assured him that he could easily defeat the small British and Indian force in the vicinity and capture an estimated three thousand barrels of flour and a quantity of corn and wheat waiting to be transported to Fort Malden. Later came other Frenchmen informing him that their friendship for the Americans had been discovered and begging him to save their village from expected destruction and them from the possibility of imprisonment or death.[52]

In view of these circumstances Winchester disobeyed Harrison's orders to remain where he was. On January 17 he sent Colonels William Lewis and John Allen with nearly seven hundred men toward River Raisin. Marching around the icy border of Maumee Bay for forty miles, these troops on the following afternoon arrived on the south side of the mouth of the Raisin River. The British and Indians saw them approach and opened fire. Undaunted, Lewis led his men across the frozen stream, drove the enemy into headlong flight, and pursued it for several miles. His losses were twelve dead and fifty-five wounded. Though he found only twelve Indians dead on the field he knew that in their retreat during the night they had carried off many more. The villagers welcomed the Americans with joyous shouts and feasted them with apples, cider, butter, sugar-loaf, and whiskey.[53]

Lewis sent Winchester word of his victory and, wishing to hold his position, requested reinforcements. The general sent his best troops—three hundred regulars under Colonel William Wells—and followed them in a cariole to celebrate the victory in person. He passed Wells and his men and arrived that night at the village, where he conferred with Lewis. Then he crossed the river and made his headquarters at the comfortable home of Colonel Pierre Navarre, over a mile away from his men.

Though they were in hostile country he had neglected to warn them of a possible attack or to order them to seek the protection of a nearby orchard and hollow. They stood in a semi-circle on an open field, without artillery, without engineers, and with little ammunition. The watchful and experienced Wells pointed out to Winchester the exposed position of his men and urged him to send scouts to Brownstown to ascertain a report that the British were rallying for an attack. But Winchester was comfortable and comfortable he wanted to remain. He replied that tomorrow would be time enough.[54]

At that very hour the British commander, Colonel Henry Procter, was marching against the Americans with nearly six hundred white soldiers and an equal number of Indians under the Wyandot chief, Roundhead, who had assumed command in the absence of Tecumseh. Procter was Brock's successor at Fort Malden. He was a fat man with a turned-up nose that accentuated his disdainful attitude. One of his own officers described him as "one of the meanest-looking men I ever saw." Underneath his disdain he concealed an ineptitude that impelled him to run away from problems that he could not solve. His hauteur infected everybody save British regulars—a disastrous attitude for one who had to rely for success largely on militia and Indians. Unconsciously, he courted Braddock's fate.

Ahead of Procter, sailors from the vessels tied up at Amherstburg marched with five small field pieces. Early in the morning of January 22 these rudely aroused the Americans from sleep. The deep rumbling of the guns, "prolonging their reverberations like the roar of distant thunder" and mingling with the terrifying yells of the Indians, must have seemed to the Americans like a sudden convulsion of nature. The British, concentrating on Wells's unprotected regulars in the open field, mowed them down like young clover before a scythe. Aroused from sleep by his host, Winchester threw on his uniform over his nightshirt and called loudly for his horses; but when these arrived he disregarded them and instead began pacing up and down in front of the house for fully fifteen minutes, seemingly loathe to surrender his comfort. Finally he mounted one of the horses, placed his son on another and crossed the frozen river.[55]

This dallying cost him dearly. He ordered the regulars to withdraw across the river; but they, being pursued by mounted Indians, could not re-form, and many of them were struck down and scalped. Allen was killed and Lewis and Winchester, in trying to get away on their horses, fell into Roundhead's hands. Stripping them of their uniforms and thus leaving Winchester in his undershirt, Roundhead took them to Procter, who induced Winchester to sign an order to the rest of the Americans, under Major George Madison, to surrender or face the alternative of being massacred by Indians. Short of ammunition and surrounded by bleeding men, Madison reluctantly accepted terms. The Kentuckians cursed or shouted or cried as they dashed their rifles to the ground.[56]

They looked like a mass of scarecrows. Their bodies were covered with the filth of several seasons and few of them wore winter garments. Some of them still retained their summer dress, which consisted of cotton frocks of various colors that fell to their knees. Their hats were slouched and worn bare, and their long hair fell matted and uncombed over their cheeks. They had slept in dirty blankets which they fastened around their bodies with leather belts. Their axes and enormously long knives gave them the air of brigands. The only distinction between the uniform of an officer and that of a soldier was the officer's short rifle and sword instead of the soldier's long rifle and knife.[57]

Fearing that Harrison might arrive with reinforcements, Procter left for Fort Malden with his troops and what American soldiers could walk. He left sixty-four wounded officers and men in two houses at River Raisin with the intention of sending sleds for them on the following morning. The Indians accompanied Procter to Stony Creek, where they surrendered their prisoners for a liberal supply of whiskey.

Half-crazed with drink, two hundred of them smeared their faces with red and black paint and returned that night to River Raisin, where they awoke the wounded men with terrifying yells. Then they lunged at them with tomahawks, knives, and clubs. Some of them died horribly in pools of blood; some cried out for mercy; some crawled to safety; some arose and walked out, though they had been unable to move themselves on their beds for four days. Some of them were spared and marched on the road to Fort Malden, only to be massacred when they proved too slow. The road was strewn with bodies mutilated by buzzards and wolves.

Some of the Indians went to Amherstburg, where each proudly displayed a half dozen or more scalps fastened to sticks. Other Indians took the heads of slain soldiers to Detroit and stuck them on the picket fence of the fort for the American residents to gaze upon. The British feared to remove the heads. And there they remained for weeks, the matted hair deeply stained with frozen blood and the skulls turning blue. Some of the eyes stared, some of the mouths gaped or smiled, depending on what had crossed the soldiers' minds—joy or sorrow or sweethearts or wives and children or friends and pleasant homes—when the winter frost fixed their features as they died.[58]

Harrison was unable to help the wounded men. He sent an army physician with a soldier under a flag of truce to assist them as soon as Procter should permit. The two men never reached their destination. Near the rapids of the Maumee a group of Indians killed the soldier and wounded the physician, who was taken to Procter at Fort Malden. The haughty British commander asserted that the flag of truce and Harrison's authorization were pretexts to gain military information, and sent the physician to jail in Montreal.[59]

4

The battle and massacre at River Raisin cooled Harrison's ardor for an immediate invasion of Canada. He was as afraid of Procter as Procter was afraid of him. Instead of continuing northward to meet Winchester, as he had intended, he paid heed to Augustus Caesar's advice to place caution before boldness and decided to retire to the rapids of the Maumee. In so doing he aroused the displeasure of his Kentucky militia who wanted him to advance on Detroit and who now talked of going home. To keep them with him he had to promise to advance on Fort Malden at the earliest opportunity. But a long period of thawing weather made the passage of the river perilous and the roads impassable. By the end of February he had no choice but to release the Kentuckians and call off the winter offensive.[60]

He now took the defensive. On elevated ground which had a ravine in its rear and a small stream on one of its sides he began to construct a fortified camp that would control the river and that could easily be defended from land attack. While Fort Meigs, named in honor of the governor of Ohio, was being built, Harrison sent two hundred fifty men under Captain Angus Langham to try to set fire to the *Queen Charlotte* and other ships anchored at Fort Malden; but the Americans abandoned the mission when they discovered open water at Middle Base Island. Thinking that the weather would prevent any serious British moves and that, therefore, the fort could hold its own without his presence, Harrison went to Cincinnati to arrange for reinforcements and to visit his family.[61]

Late in March he learned that Procter was preparing to attack the fort and he hurried back with three hundred men, leaving a brigade of Kentucky militia under Brigadier General Green Clay to follow. About two weeks later Procter appeared at the Maumee with nine hundred eighty-four regulars and militia and twelve hundred Indians under Tecumseh and other chiefs. After allowing the fort to be built, the British commander had resolved to besiege it as though he could take it by battering its earthen ramparts. He brought all his artillery from Detroit, including two twenty-four pounders. He could count, too, on two gunboats, the *Eliza* and the *Myers*, to shell the fort from upstream.

While Procter's men placed the guns in position on the north bank of the river, Tecumseh's warriors crossed to the south side to attack the fort in that direction. On May 1 Procter's big guns began to boom and kept up the murderous fire for several days.[62]

On May 3 Clay with his Kentucky brigade of twelve hundred men arrived at Fort Defiance, where he learned of the siege of Fort Meigs. He immediately put his men into eighteen boats and hurried to the rescue. Procter was so neglectful of his advantages that he allowed Clay to advance and even to communicate with the besieged fort. He was able to arrange with Harrison a general attack on the investing column. Harrison's messenger, Captain John Hamilton, brought Clay orders to land eight hundred of his men a little distance above the fort on the opposite bank and to storm and seize the enemy's batteries, spike them, and destroy the carriages. Then they were "instantly to return to their boats and recross the river." At the same time Harrison was to lead a sortie from the fort and take the British guns in the rear.[63]

Clay sent a detachment of seven hundred ninety-six men in twelve boats. Their leader, Lieutenant Colonel William Dudley, landed with them on the north side of the river and moved through a forest for a mile and a half to the British batteries, which were briskly firing on the fort. With thunderous yells of "Remember River Raisin!" Dudley's men, at his command, charged the enemy and captured and spiked eleven of the heavy guns without losing a man. Wild huzzas rose from the fort as the British flag came down.[64]

With his field glass Harrison had been watching Dudley and his men with intense interest. When he saw the British flag lowered he signaled to Dudley to fall back to his boats and cross the river. But his men, having tasted victory, became so sure of themselves that they dallied, resolving to avenge the massacre of their fellow Kentuckians at River Raisin and gratifying their curiosity by inspecting every detail of the enemy's position.

Harrison grew nervous. "Can I never get men to obey my orders?" he asked with mingled anger and alarm. Meanwhile Indians attacked the riflemen, who defeated and pursued them almost to the British camp. At this juncture the British artillerymen were reinforced. Returning to the batteries, they recaptured them, took some of the Kentuckians prisoner, and drove the others toward their boats.

The Indians, too, had been reinforced and had turned fiercely on Dudley and his men, scattering them through the forest. There the

skulking Indians trapped those who were still alive and forced them
to lay down their arms. Of the nearly eight hundred men who had
followed Dudley from the boats four hundred eighty were killed
and one hundred fifty were captured. Dudley himself was tomahawked and scalped. The survivors escaped to Fort Meigs.[65]

Meanwhile the remainder of Clay's brigade had, after battling a
swift and swollen current, and round shot from British batteries,
succeeded in reaching the fort without losing a man. The Indians
and a few British militia escorted the prisoners to old Fort Miami,
where Procter had his headquarters and where they were to be
loaded on gunboats and taken to Montreal. As they neared the
fort the Indians stripped the Kentuckians of their clothes and then
forced them to run the gauntlet. With guns, tomahawks, clubs,
and knives they killed between twenty and thirty of them before
they reached the fort and threw their bodies into a ditch. The
survivors they took to the fort, where they attacked them again,
shooting or beating out the brains of four of them.

A British officer who tried to stop the Indians was shot down.
Procter, who was nearby, must have heard the commotion and
understood its significance, but he made no attempt to stop the
massacre, even when a British officer reported it to him. Every
prisoner might have fallen to one weapon or another had not
Tecumseh heard the uproar and dashed down to the fort on his
horse.

When he saw what was happening his eyes flamed with anger.
"Are there no men here?" he shouted, as he grabbed an offending
Indian by the throat and hurled him to the ground. "Every Indian," wrote Glenn Tucker, "slunk away, cowed by one resolute
man. None could bear to be seen by the frenzied chief whose face
was more threatening than his tomahawk." But in that very incident—in the blind cruelty of his people and in their inability to
restrain their feelings in time of war—he saw the hopelessness of
his plans to form an effective confederacy. His anger gradually
gave way to anguish. "My poor Indians!" he moaned. "My poor
Indians! Oh, what will become of my poor Indians!"

Then, as if he were ashamed of his moment of weakness, he recaptured his anger. Dashing up to Procter he demanded to know
why the Indians had not been restrained. "Your Indians," replied
the British commander with his usual hauteur, "cannot be controlled; they cannot be commanded." At this Tecumseh, who had
just proved the contrary, shot back: "Begone! You are unfit to
command!" Then he hurled at him the grossest of Indian insults:
"Go and put on petticoats!"[66]

Back at Fort Meigs the battle was still raging. Harrison ordered a sortie to attack the British battery near the ravine in the rear of the fort. Colonel John Miller with three hundred fifty regulars held their fire until they were within easy range and then volleyed in unison and charged with bayonets, driving the British artillerymen away. The Americans spiked the guns and then, finding themselves facing a superior number of Indians, withdrew to the fort with their wounded and forty-one prisoners, including two officers.[67]

After this action Procter abandoned the siege. Discouraged by Indian desertions, by his failure to reduce the fort, and by word that Fort Meigs was about to receive reinforcements, he ordered his guns unplugged and made preparations to withdraw. To conceal his intention and thus obtain the best possible terms, he sent an officer to request Harrison to surrender the fort. Harrison regarded the request as an insult and sent back word that it should not be repeated. That ended the matter. On May 9 Procter with his regulars and Tecumseh with what few Indians remained under his command loaded the artillery on their gunboats and departed to board their larger ships for Amherstburg. The Americans bade them farewell with a few salvos and the gunboats replied with a few shots that killed several men and an officer.[68]

5

Two days later Harrison turned Fort Meigs over to General Clay and started for the Lower Sandusky to take steps to fortify that region against possible attack. Once he accomplished his purpose he planned to advance against Fort Malden. After alerting Cleveland and the Western Reserve he went to Franklinton, where he called for reinforcements and urged on Governor Meigs the need of building forts to protect the American shore of Lake Erie.[69]

Meanwhile Procter, at Tecumseh's urging, returned to invest Fort Meigs. But Clay, who was still in command, forbade his men to leave the fort. To draw the Americans out, Tecumseh resorted to the ruse of dressing up some of his warriors as frontiersmen moving in to reinforce the fort and fighting the Indians as they advanced. The ruse failed when a rainstorm forced Tecumseh to stop the firing and shouting of the sham battle. The pretended siege ended as quickly as it had begun.[70]

Several days later Harrison learned that Procter had appeared near Fort Stephenson, a stockaded post near the Lower Sandusky. Its commander was Major George Croghan, a Kentuckian of twenty-one years who had served as a volunteer at Tippecanoe and who was one of Harrison's favorite officers. Since Croghan's garrison was small and his artillery consisted of a single six-pounder, Harrison advised him that the fort would be untenable against heavy artillery and that, in case of attack, he should immediately destroy his supplies and retreat.[71]

On August 1 Procter appeared near Fort Stephenson and sent three officers, Colonel Elliott and Captains Chambers and Dixon, to demand that Croghan surrender "to spare the effusion of blood, which we can not do should we be under the necessity of reducing it by our powerful force of regulars, Indians, and artillery." Croghan replied: "My commandant and the garrison are determined to defend the post to the last extremity, and bury ourselves in its ruins, rather than surrender to any force whatever."

"Look at our immense body of Indians," interposed Dixon. "They can not be restrained from massacring the whole garrison, in the event of our undoubted success."

Chambers eagerly added that British success was certain.

Dixon tried to persuade him to surrender. "It is a great pity," he said in a beseeching tone, "that so fine a young man as you, and as your commander is represented to be, should fall into the hands of the savages. Sir, for God's sake, surrender, and prevent the dreadful massacre that will be caused by your resistance."

At this Ensign Edmund Shipp, who had gone out to meet the British officers, coolly replied: "When the fort shall be taken, there will be none to massacre. It will not be given up while a man is able to resist."

As Shipp was returning to the fort he bumped into an Indian who, springing from a bushy ravine, tried to take his sword. Dixon stopped Shipp from killing the Indian. Croghan, who had been watching the conference from the ramparts, shouted: "Shipp, come in and we will blow them to hell!"

The ensign ran into the fort, while the British officers returned to Procter. Presently the British opened fire from their gunboats and from a howitzer on shore. Croghan answered with his six-pounder, which his men nicknamed Good Bess or Old Bess, until he found his ammunition running low. Then he had Old Bess moved from place to place to give the impression that the fort was strongly armed and finally concealed the cannon behind a masked embrasure at the weakest point, which the British would undoubtedly assault. Meanwhile the British kept firing at the fort in vain. Seeing his Indians becoming uneasy, Procter grew impatient and resolved to try to take the fort by storm. Late in the afternoon he emplaced three mobile six-pounders within easy range of the fort and tried to breach the stockade by concentrating on the weakest point, where Old Bess was hidden. Croghan strengthened the position by piling against the pickets bags of sand and sacks of flour that materially broke the force of the cannonade.[72]

When his light guns proved ineffective Procter, at the urging of his officers and the Indians sent a strong force to assault the fort. Protected by dense billows of smoke and flame, the British regulars advanced in three columns of about one hundred twenty men each nearly to the edge of the protecting ditch that surrounded the stockade. Croghan let them come to within thirty paces of the fort and then opened up Old Bess with scrap iron and grapeshot that raked the British for the full length of the ditch, while rifle shots poured on them from the merlons in the corner blockhouses. The survivors raced back to the boats and the Indians shot back into the woods. During the night the British and Indians carried away the wounded but left their dead, which counted fifty soldiers and two officers, in the ditch. Croghan lost one man killed and seven wounded.[73]

At nearby Camp Seneca, which he had fortified, Harrison had heard the intermittent cannonading and had sent reconnaissance scouts to ascertain its meaning. They brought back word that large bodies of British and Indians had encircled Fort Stephenson for some distance. Whereupon Harrison, thinking that Procter had numbers superior to his own, decided to stay where he was. "The blood be on his own head;" he said, "I wash my hands of it." Each commander was afraid of the other. While Procter was actually running away from his supposed pursuer, Harrison impatiently awaited Croghan's arrival at Camp Seneca so that he could set fire to it and retreat to the Upper Sandusky.[74]

The honors of victory went to Croghan. He basked in a sea of congratulations pouring in from every nook and post of the country. Harrison, in his official report, spoke of him with the highest praise. The women of Chillicothe bought and presented him with an elegant sword, while Congress voted him profuse thanks. President Madison promoted him to the rank of lieutenant colonel by brevet.[75]

By this time the Federal Government was convinced it could never invade Canada successfully until it built a fleet that would challenge the supremacy of the Great Lakes with the British. Hull as early as 1811 had advised Eustis to build a fleet, but he was ignored until Harrison's army began to suffer a series of setbacks which culminated in his failure to march to Croghan's rescue. Now every section of the land clamored for Harrison's removal; but Secretary Armstrong, while he deplored the general's shortcomings, thought the time unsuited for a change of command. So he ordered Harrison to organize a force of seven thousand men to cross Lake Erie in boats under cover of a fleet.[76]

The Federal Government, indeed, had already begun the construction of a fleet at Presque Island, at the present site of Erie, Pennsylvania; but the men in charge of it had made slow progress until, at the end of March, 1813, Captain Oliver Hazard Perry, then only twenty-eight years old, arrived and took command. He found timber no problem. He quickly completed two brigs and three schooners out of planks sawed from trees that were felled in the neighboring forest; but he met difficulties in his attempts to secure ordnance and crewmen because his immediate superior, Captain Isaac Chauncey, wanted to build up his strength on Lake Ontario and therefore saw fit to release only a few men for service on Lake Erie. Fortunately, American victories along the Niagara permitted Perry to conduct five vessels from Buffalo to Erie to join his potential fleet. By July 10 his fleet was completed; but he found himself with only enough men to officer and man only one of the brigs. Moreover, he had yet to get his ships clear of the shallow sandbar at the entrance of the harbor.[77]

The British, too, were active in their naval base at Amherstburg. One-armed Commodore Robert H. Barclay, commander of the warships on Lake Erie, had served with Nelson at Trafalgar and could count on experienced officers and men. He was having built a brig named the *Detroit;* but he too had no crew to sail her and he felt that without her his fleet would be weaker than that of his enemy. And even if he surmounted this obstacle he still could not get at Perry's ships on the other side of the sandbar. So he hovered off shore until July 31, when he sailed back to Amherstburg to replenish his supplies and, perhaps, to ascertain what Procter was doing.[78]

Perry now saw his opportunity to reach the open lake. On the following day he had his ships towed down to the sandbar, where he lightened them by removing their guns. To each side of his largest ship, the *Lawrence*, named in honor of that gallant captain of the *Chesapeake*, he had attached a large flat-bottomed boat called a scow or "camel," had it filled with water, and had strong timbers thrust across it through open gunports. Then he had the water pumped out of the scows which, as they became lighter, rose under the timbers, lifting the *Lawrence* higher in the water. As she cleared the sandbar her crew hastily remounted her cannon. The other brig, the *Niagara,* cleared the sandbar in the same manner.[79]

As soon as he had crews for all his vessels he cruised between Erie and Canada for two or three days, looking for Barclay. Failing to find him, Perry put into Sandusky Bay. He was still there when, on August 19, one of his officers came on board the *Lawrence* to inform him that General Harrison, accompanied by Colonels McArthur and Cass and twenty-six chiefs of the friendly Ohio tribes, had arrived from Camp Seneca to confer with him.

As soon as Harrison and his party came on board he and Perry arranged plans for a campaign and for transporting their troops across Lake Erie to Fort Malden. The Indian chiefs regaled Perry and his men with a breathless war dance. Harrison then returned to headquarters with his companions and sent Perry one hundred recruits to act as marines and to supply some of the places of the men who were ill. Some of the recruits were strapping Kentucky hillbillies who carried long rifles on their shoulders and who had never seen a ship. They wore blue linsey-woolsey hunting shirts, red belts and blue pantaloons fringed in red. They rambled through the ship, slapping the big guns with their calloused palms and uttering rude approval and praise of everything they saw.[80]

In the western end of Lake Erie, close to the Ohio shore, lay a small archipelago called Put-in Bay, which afforded Perry an excellent harbor and a convenient starting point for an attack on Amherstburg. With the intention of drawing Barclay out to fight, Perry sailed for the British base. There he found the enemy ships moored under the guns of the fort. Learning that Barclay was unwilling to meet him in the open lake and realizing that he could not attack him without subjecting his own ships to the disadvantage of fire from the British fleet and from the fort, Perry returned to Put-in Bay to wait impatiently for a chance to fight.

From the craggy eminence of Gibraltar Island, Perry day after day pointed his spyglass anxiously in the direction of Fort Malden. On the evening of September 9 his chance came. Barclay, finding himself short of provisions, sailed for Long Point, the chief deposit of supplies for the British on the banks of the Detroit River. His fleet, bright with new paint, consisted of the *Detroit,* nineteen guns; the *Queen Charlotte,* seventeen guns; the *Lady Prevost,* thirteen guns; the *Hunter,* eight guns; the *Little Belt,* two guns; and the *Chippeway,* one gun. This imposing number of guns, both short- and long-range, gave Barclay a slight advantage; but Perry had larger caliber guns and could, therefore, discharge twice the weight of shot in a general broadside. In addition, Perry's eight ships weighed more than Barclay's six ships. To use his long-range guns effectively, Barclay would elect to fight from a distance; Perry, on the contrary, hoped to bring on a close action as soon as possible to take advantage of his short cannonades.[81]

At a conference of his officers Perry assigned to each ship the task of engaging a British ship of like size. Thus the *Lawrence* was assigned to the *Detroit*, the *Niagara* to the *Queen Charlotte*, and so on. As the conference closed Perry brought out a square blue flag which bore in large letters of white muslin the alleged dying words of Captain Lawrence: "Don't Give Up the Ship!"

"When this flag shall be hoisted to the main-royal mast-head," said Perry, "it shall be your signal for going into action." As his officers were leaving he added: "Gentlemen, remember your instructions. Nelson has expressed my idea in the words, 'If you lay your enemy close alongside, you can not be out of your place.' Goodnight."

At sunrise Perry pointed his spyglass in the direction of Fort Malden and saw lengthening sails on the horizon. Cries of "Sail ho!" rose from the American fleet as it passed out from the labyrinth of islands into the open lake. To Perry sight of the enemy proved the best tonic for his recent attack of bilious fever. Ordering the *Lawrence* to be steered close to the *Detroit*, he displayed the battle flag.

"My brave lads," he said, "this flag contains the last words of Captain Lawrence. Shall I hoist it?"

"Ay, ay, sir!" they all shouted, as if with one voice, and they cheered wildly as the flag went up the main royal masthead of the flagship. The battle was on.

At eleven-thirty A.M. the band of the British squadron struck up "Rule, Britannia." As the last notes faded on the blast of a bugle, a twenty-four pounder boomed over the water toward the *Lawrence*, now only a mile and a half away. It missed its target, sending a geyser of spray skyward. Five minutes later another shot crashed through the side of the ship, killing one of her crew. Then the *Detroit*, the *Hunter*, the *Queen Charlotte*, and the *Lady Prevost* poured shot after shot—thirty-four in all—at the *Lawrence* as Barclay endeavored to destroy her and her commander and then smash the other ships in detail. And Perry was still too far away from the *Detroit* to retaliate effectively. His shots fell short, while

Barclay continued to pour upon Perry a heavy storm of round shot from long-range guns.[82]

Perry noticed that Lieutenant Jesse D. Elliott kept his *Niagara* at a respectable distance from the *Queen Charlotte*, which the battle plan called for him to attack. And he was firing only his two long-range guns! Why was he keeping aloof? By now the *Lawrence* was badly crippled; her rigging was nearly shot to pieces; her sails were torn to shreds; her spars were battered into splinters; her guns were dismounted; she lay on the lake, like a helpless wreck. But the *Niagara*—swift, staunch, unhurt—she stood off from battle! What was the meaning of her captain's strange conduct? His behavior became even more puzzling.

The *Niagara* spread her sails before a lively wind, but instead of going to the relief of the *Lawrence*, she bore off toward the head of the British fleet, passed Perry's ship to the windward and left her exposed to the still galling fire of the enemy. When the *Niagara* was within half mile of the shattered vessel Perry made a daring decision. He removed his blue nankeen sailor's jacket, which he had worn all day, and put on the uniform of his rank. Then he summoned Lieutenant John Yarnell and said to him:

"I leave the *Lawrence* in your charge, with discretionary powers. You may hold out or surrender, as your judgment and the circumstances dictate."

With these words he got into a rowboat, holding his personal pennant and his "Don't Give Up the Ship!" flag half folded around his body. Barclay, who was badly wounded, detected him. Knowing what to expect should Perry succeed in reaching the *Niagara*, he hurled all his ammunition—cannon balls, grape, canister, and musket shot—on the rowboat making for the *Niagara*. The oars were splintered; bullets peppered the sides; the crew was soaked with spray. Heedless of danger, Perry stood up in the rowboat until his oarsmen persuaded him to sit down. The crew of the *Niagara*, which had been watching the battered rowboat with breathless anxiety, cheered loudly as its unharmed occupants reached the ship. Lieutenant Elliott, who had received no signal from Perry and who, therefore, presumed him dead, gaped in amazement as the commodore appeared at the gangway.

"How goes the day?" He could think of nothing else to say.

"Bad enough," replied Perry, dryly; "why are the gunboats so far astern?"

"I'll bring them up."

"Do so."

Elliott pushed off in the rowboat in which Perry had come to hustle the lagging gunboats, while Perry, running up his pennant as well as his battle flag, bore down on the enemy amid the cheers of his men. Accompanied by his schooners, the *Ariel*, the *Scorpion*, and the *Caledonia*—which the Americans had captured in an earlier battle—Perry steered between the *Lady Prevost*, the *Little Belt*, and the *Chippeway* on his larboard and the *Detroit*, the *Queen Charlotte*, and the *Hunter* on his starboard and let go with broadsides of solid shot and canister until the combatants were enveloped in smoke. When this cleared, the *Queen Charlotte* struck her colors, while the *Little Belt* and the *Chippeway* attempted to escape to leeward. The *Scorpion* and the *Trippe* chased, overtook, and forced them to surrender. At three P.M. Barclay lowered the flag of the *Detroit*, which was now a complete wreck. When the wind blew away the smoke of battle, Perry and his men found that the two squadrons were interlocked.[83]

Meanwhile Yarnell, after consulting his men, had struck the flag of the helpless *Lawrence*. When her crew heard the triumphant shouts of the British they cried, "Sink the ship! Sink the ship! Let's all sink together!" But though she had surrendered she was still free. As soon as Barclay surrendered, her exhausted crew flung out the Stars and Stripes from her masthead. This time the cheering voices were few and feeble, like a melancholy variation of the boisterous outpouring that preceded the battle.[84]

Reboarding the *Lawrence*, Perry received the vanquished officers, who offered their swords to him in token of surrender. He courteously refused them. At that moment he was genuinely concerned with Barclay's severe wounds and with making his imprisonment as comfortable as possible.

On the back of an old letter Perry wrote to Harrison a message known to every American schoolboy: "We have met the enemy and they are ours: Two Ships, two Brigs one Schooner & one Sloop."

The same admirable directness characterized his message to William Jones, Secretary of the Navy: "It has pleased the Almighty to give to the Arms of the United States a signal Victory over their enemies on this Lake. The British Squadron, consisting of two ships, two brigs, one schooner and one sloop, have this moment surrendered to the force under my command, after a sharp conflict."[85]

The battle cost the British forty-one killed and ninety-one wounded and the Americans twenty-seven killed and ninety-six wounded, of whom twenty-one were killed and sixty-one wounded on board the *Lawrence*. The victory dispelled the gloom that had settled over the Great Lakes Frontier since the beginning of the war. Bonfires, illuminations, salvos of artillery, and public dinners attested to the popular satisfaction in every town and village of the Great Lakes Frontier. The heavy metal of Perry's ships no less than his own stubborn courage had won a victory that restored American confidence and that destroyed British hopes of military success. The victory gave an entirely new complexion to the war. It won for the United States complete control of Lake Erie. Procter now found himself in a predicament similar to that of Hull at Detroit. The British commander could no longer hope to retain Detroit and Fort Malden; indeed, he was forced to give up his campaign on the Sandusky to avoid starvation and entrapment. At last the road to Canada was wide open to Harrison's army.

6

By this time the general had completed his plans for an invasion of Canada. He had written to Governor Shelby, calling for fifteen hundred mounted men and inviting him to take part in the forthcoming campaign. He hoped that the governor would not object to a nominal command. Remembering his Roman history, he added: "Scipio, the conqueror of Carthage, did not disdain to act as lieutenant of his younger and less experienced brother, Lucius."[86]

The aging governor overlooked this thoughtless allusion and accepted the invitation. He called for mounted volunteers to assemble at Newport, opposite Cincinnati, at the close of July. The response greatly exceeded his expectations. Soon he found himself at the head of thirty-five hundred men, whom he led toward Lake Erie. At Urbana he organized his forces into eleven regiments, then grouped them into two divisions under Joseph Desha and William Henry. From Urbana he pushed on to the Upper Sandusky, then to Fort Ball, on the present site of Tiffin, Ohio, and finally to the Portage River, now Port Clinton, Ohio, where he joined his forces with those of Clay's Kentuckians under McArthur. Harrison ordered Colonel Richard Mentor Johnson, a young War Hawk, to remain at Fort Meigs with his cavalry until the expedition should sail and then to march to Detroit.[87]

On September 20 Perry ferried the regulars to Put-in Bay on South Bass Island. The militia followed two days later. There they all remained for three days, until, with the advent of fair weather, they ferried to Middle Sister Island. Thence Harrison and Perry on the *Ariel* reconnoitred the Canadian shore and selected a suitable place for debarkation. At Bar Point they found the naval buildings and storehouses burned and the place deserted. Harrison ordered his adjutant general to issue directions for the invasion of Canada the next morning.[88]

Harrison's plans called for an invasion in two wings, one consisting of three militia brigades under Shelby, who was expected to strike at Tecumseh's warriors, and the other consisting of the regulars under Harrison. The invasion was to be protected by the guns of Perry's fleet and by three light fieldpieces accompanying the vanguard.

The next morning the invading army in eighty small boats left Middle Sister Island and advanced to Hartley's Point, about four miles below Amherstburg, which Harrison and Perry had chosen as the landing place. Every fife and drum played "Yankee Doodle" as the Americans landed that afternoon and, finding the place deserted, marched rapidly to Amherstburg and camped there for the night.

At the approach of the Americans Major General Procter, in obedience to the orders of Major General Francis De Rottenburg, commander of Upper Canada, retreated along the Thames. Harrison, learning that the British commander had left town only an hour before, sent a cavalry force of twenty men after him to prevent him from destroying the bridge across the Aux Canards River. They found British soldiers trying to set fire to it and scattered them with a few volleys. Harrison then advanced toward Sandwich eighteen miles away; but destroyed bridges over unfordable creeks prevented him from reaching the town for two days. On the same day, September 29, Colonel Johnson with his cavalry entered Detroit to find that McArthur had occupied the town with seven hundred men after defeating a body of Indians. The inhabitants shouted or wept with joy as McArthur ended Procter's martial law and reestablished the civil government of Michigan Territory.[89]

At Harrison's orders, Johnson with his cavalry crossed the river, where he joined other leading officers in a council of war. They decided to pursue Procter up the Thames—a hard march, Harrison told his soldiers, "but no man must grumble or complain or even *think* of his wife or sweetheart until Procter and his army are overtaken and defeated." At the head of nearly three thousand men including two hundred Indians and one hundred fifty regulars, he pushed ahead over roads and woodpaths strewn with the golden and russet leaves of oak trees. Arriving at the farm of Matthew Dolsen on the evening of October 3, he camped on the high wooded banks of the Thames, where they found Perry's boats, the *Scorpion*, the *Tigress*, and the *Porcupine*, ready to cover their advance along the river or its tributaries.[90]

Accelerating his retreat as Harrison advanced, Procter reached Chatham, a village consisting of a blockhouse and a cluster of cabins on McGregor's Creek, which flowed into the Thames between steep banks. With him was Tecumseh, who strongly disapproved of the retreat and who followed him reluctantly. The chief had advised Procter to allow Harrison to debark with his army on the Canadian shore and to move toward Amherstburg and Fort Malden. Tecumseh then would fall on Harrison's flank and rear while Procter would attack him in front with his regulars and militia. Should Harrison take Fort Malden, Tecumseh would make a stand on the Aux Canards River and would, if necessary, retire gradually to a more favorable position. But Procter, thinking only of saving himself and his sick wife and children, rejected this plan. Seeing the British commander "tying up everything and preparing to run away," Tecumseh lost his composure and called him "a miserable old squaw." Procter needed Tecumseh's warriors too badly to pay any mind to his insult.[91]

The British commander had promised Tecumseh that he would make a stand at Chatham. But now Procter wanted only to get away before the Americans arrived. Leaving Lieutenant Colonel Augustus Warburton in charge of the army, he went to Moravian Town, twenty-three miles away, to look after his personal baggage and to see his family safely on the way to Delaware, near the present city of London, Ontario.[92]

Tecumseh refused to retreat a step farther. He thought Chatham ideal for defense. "This is a good place," he told Warburton. "Here we either defeat Harrison or leave our bones." The sight of McGregor's Creek flowing into the Thames filled him with homesickness: "When I look on these two streams," he said to Warburton, "I think of the Tippecanoe and the Wabash."[93]

On the morning of October 4 Warburton detected Harrison's approach and, being in no position to offer battle, ordered a retreat to Moravian Town. Six miles up the Thames he and his men met Procter, who was returning to take charge after depositing his personal belongings and sending his wife and children to Burlington Heights at the western end of Lake Ontario. Resolved to fight the Americans alone, Tecumseh stationed his warriors at two bridges and waited. The first to appear was Colonel Johnson's cavalry, who forded McGregor's Creek, charged on the defenders of the ruined bridge and drove them away. Tecumseh, too, was beaten. Deserted by Chief Walk-in-the-Water and sixty of his Wyandots and raked by murderous fire from two six-pounders which Major E. D. Wood had planted at the edge of the town, Tecumseh and his warriors retreated up the south side of the Thames to Arnold's Mill, at the Thames Rapids, twelve miles above Chatham. In the skirmish Tecumseh had been wounded in the arm by a rifle shot, but he bandaged his wound and fought on until he was forced to retreat.[94]

Johnson pursued him to the Thames Rapids while Harrison brought his infantry troops and formed them in battle order preparatory to crossing the river. Here they captured a Canadian wagoner who informed them that Procter's army had halted just three hundred yards farther on. Tecumseh had joined him and had badgered him into making a stand.

The chief surveyed the ground and found it provided advantages against the enemy. On one side the Thames flowed between high and precipitous banks and on the other side a marsh ran parallel with the river for several miles. Close to the river was a short and narrow swamp with a strip of ground between it and the marsh. Along the river the road to Detroit ran through a forest of beech, sugar maple and oak interspersed with underbrush. The British regulars were posted between the swamp and the river and their artillery was planted on the road near the riverbank. The Indian right wing under the Chippewa leader Oshawahnah extended from thicker underbrush between the swamp and the marsh to some distance along and just within the borders of the marsh. It was so disposed that it could easily flank Harrison's left. The Indian left wing, commanded by Tecumseh, occupied the narrowest point between the swamp and the marsh.[95]

Colonel Richard Mentor Johnson advanced cautiously and found the enemy ready to fight. Harrison had planned that his infantry should make the initial attack, but Major Wood, who had been reconnoitering the enemy's position, informed him that the British were drawn up in open order. This information persuaded Harrison to incur the danger of changing the prescribed mode of attack. Instead of ordering Henry's division to fall upon the British front, as he had planned, he ordered Johnson to charge it with his cavalry. The colonel ordered his brother, Lieutenant Colonel

James Johnson, to attack the British regulars with one battalion while he with the other fell on the Indian wings. Harrison with Perry, Cass and a few others sat on their horses near the riverbank, where the commander could observe and direct all movements.[96]

At the sound of a bugle the American battalions advanced cautiously among trees and underbrush and over fallen timber toward the huddled British regulars, who fired on them. Most of the horses recoiled with fright, dumping their riders and forcing them to run for cover. The imperious voice of their commander soon hurried them back. Remounting and yelling "Remember River Raisin!" they knifed through the British lines, cutting them to pieces. Then, wheeling right and left as they poured a murderous fire into the rear of the broken lines, they rounded up redcoats by the scores. In less than an hour most of Procter's force of more than eight hundred men were in their hands.

The British general himself was no where to be seen. At the outset of battle he had jumped into his carriage, which he held in readiness, and whipped away with his personal staff, a few dragoons, and some mounted Indians. Johnson sent a small force to pursue Procter. The Americans soon caught up with his carriage but found it empty. The poltroon had reached his primary objective—the security of Burlington Heights.[97]

Meanwhile the battalion under Colonel Richard Mentor Johnson had encountered trouble. Tecumseh's warriors held their fire until the Americans were close and then mowed them down. Johnson's vanguard was composed of twenty men who called themselves the Forlorn Hope—tough Indian fighters under Colonel William Whiteley, who, nearly twenty years before, had helped James Robertson clean up the Chickamauga in Tennessee. Fifteen of his men were killed and four wounded. The crimson of the sumac, the gold of the maple, and the copper of the oak merged with the red and black war paint on the Indians, camouflaging them from their enemies. Several times the Americans had to fall back on their infantry.

Tecumseh's stentorian voice rose above the din of battle, urging redcoats to fight and braves to stand firm. Simply dressed in buckskin, he was undistinguishable to the Americans from any of his warriors. A white silk handkerchief bound a single eagle's feather to his hair, a silver medal given him by George III hung from his neck, and a bandage on his arm covered the wound he had received at Chatham bridge. Suddenly he staggered over a fallen tree, resting on his rifle and then, as he grew weaker, letting it fall to the ground. His fierce spirit soon succumbed to a piece of lead. The white hope of an Indian confederacy died with him. No man knows who fired the bullet, though Colonel Johnson, among many others, claimed that distinction; it eventually won him the vice-presidency.[98]

As soon as the Indians discovered that their leader was dead they became convinced that the Great Spirit was angry. They fought no longer, and fled to the safety of the marsh. That night they returned to bury their dead and to search for Tecumseh's body. They found their dead leader where he had fallen—his heart pierced by a bullet and his skull battered by the butt end of a gun. Otherwise he was untouched. Lying near him was a handsome Potawatomi chief bedecked in plumes and ornaments. One of Johnson's men, David King, nineteen years old, had shot him, shouted triumphantly, "Whoop, by God! I have killed one damned yellow bugger!" and flayed every inch of skin from his body. The Potawatomi had been mistaken for Tecumseh. But no Indian could have mistaken another man for Tecumseh; nature fashioned him and then broke the mold. That night they buried him with the other dead so close to the Americans that they could see their campfires. Yet no man has ever found Tecumseh's grave.[99]

The Battle of the Thames was a clearcut American victory. Procter lost twenty-eight officers and six hundred six men killed or captured; Harrison reported seven killed and twenty-two wounded —a figure obviously short of the truth. The Indians left thirty-three of their comrades dead on the field, but they had carried off many more—how many, no man knows. Some were lost in the marsh. So ended the last important engagement of the war in the Great Lakes Frontier. The other actions were of a minor nature and of little consequence. Harrison returned with his victorious army to Detroit, where he planned another campaign; but the approach of winter weather kept him inactive for the present. The Kentucky militia save Johnson's cavalry left for home. The regional tribes accepted an armistice by which they agreed to surrender all prisoners and furnish hostages in return for the right to occupy their normal hunting grounds until a formal treaty could be signed. Harrison and Perry were idolized from Maine to Georgia; bonfires and illuminations filled the frontier; towns vied with one another in paying tribute to the heroes of Lake Erie and the Thames; babies were named in their honor; and Congress voted Harrison the thanks of his countrymen and a gold medal.[100]

The war dragged on for another year. Then, on Christmas Eve

1814 the representatives of the United States and Great Britain met at Ghent, Belgium, and signed a treaty of peace without victory but with honor. Neither nation gained or lost a foot of soil. Nevertheless, the United States profited widely. She increased her prestige, gained rapid and permanent independence from Great Britain for her fur trade and for her raw and finished products, ended the Indian menace in the Great Lakes Frontier, making possible its settlement with little bloodshed, and obtained new heroes for her political arena. The war, too, had its element of irony. Two weeks after the peace was signed, and before word of it could reach the United States, Andrew Jackson trounced the British at New Orleans in the greatest land victory of the war.

Statehood for Illinois

Nινιαν edwards was thirty-four years old when, on june 11, 1809, he assumed his duties as governor of Illinois Territory. His ceaseless industry and admirable flexibility of mind were expressive of his prime. He was a man with immense knowledge of frontier needs patiently garnered from wide and practical experience. Possessed of an ample fortune, he could afford independent and impartial political beliefs in his official duties. He was no man's pawn. In the nine years that he served as its governor Illinois Territory enjoyed a growth and a degree of democracy unknown in any other territory of the time.

He seems to have taken all knowledge for his province. From his home in Montgomery County, Maryland, he went to Dickinson College at Carlyle, Pennsylvania, where he began the study of law. In those days half of the curriculum was devoted to the reading of history; but young Edwards had received such a thorough grounding of this subject from his father that he could afford to give its time to medicine. He became almost as eminent in his knowledge of medicine as in his knowledge of law. But before he finished his law course at Dickinson he migrated to Kentucky, where his father planned to buy a farm and to locate lands for his older brothers and sisters.[1]

There gay companions introduced him to sensual pleasures which for a time threatened to shatter his aspirations to rise to distinction, though he luckily was elected to the Kentucky legislature as a representative for Nelson County before he attained his majority. In this position he showed such legalistic acumen that he was reelected almost unanimously in the following year.

In 1798 he was admitted to the bar and subsequently to the courts of Tennessee.[2]

About the same time he broke away from his pleasure-seeking friends by moving to Russelville in Logan County. By dint of almost monastic study he rose rapidly in his profession, until he became known as one of the best lawyers in Kentucky. He amassed what was then considered a fortune. In the courts of Kentucky and Tennessee his forensic skill surpassed that of such notable lawyers as Henry Clay, Felix Grundy, and J. H. Davis; but unfortunately his dissipations had so impaired his health that he was forced to give up his practice for an appointment in the judiciary. He became presiding judge of the general court and soon after circuit judge, an office he held until in 1802 he received a commission as major to command a battalion of Kentucky militia. The following year he was appointed judge of the circuit in which he resided. At about the same time he returned to Maryland, where he fell in love with and married Elvira Lane, who came from a respectable family in the vicinity of his father's old home. In 1806 he was appointed judge of the Kentucky court of appeals and two years later Chief Justice of the state.[3]

The territorial secretary and three judges were as admirably suited to their positions as was Governor Edwards. With his knowledge of French, which he spoke fluently, and his experience as a lawyer, Nathaniel Pope, a native of Kentucky, exerted a powerful influence over the unprogressive and rather unruly French inhabitants of the older towns. The most outstanding of the three judges, Jesse B. Thomas, was a seasoned politician who, as we have seen, had served as a delegate to Congress. The other two judges, Alexander Stuart and Obediah Jones, were educated men of polished manners and unbiased judgments. As though in keeping with the proslavery agitation responsible for the establishment of the territory, all of its early officers were either natives or residents of slave states; but they were men of wide experiences and balanced opinions who avoided the snares of party politics and who worked indefatigably to provide the territory with the laws it needed to establish order and encourage prosperity.[4]

At their first session the governor and the judges obviated political incertitude by adopting the laws of Indiana Territory. Then, by gradually broadening the interpretation of their powers, they passed additional laws as circumstances required. In the next two years they adopted thirty-four laws, of which only twelve adhered to the limitations which the Ordinance imposed on their jurisdictions. The rest either repealed sections of the Indiana Code or were modified to suit local needs. Six of the twelve laws they had adopted outright came from the Kentucky Code, with which they were, of course, familiar. Though they realized that this clearly violated the spirit of the Ordinance, which specified that territorial laws should be taken only from codes of the original states, they felt that the six Kentucky laws suited frontier needs and would be familiar to the numerous settlers who had migrated from that state.[5]

To secure more effective enforcement of the territorial laws, the governor and judges revised and simplified the judicial system. Unable to secure men who could qualify as judges of the courts of common pleas, they abolished such courts and invested their judicial functions, both criminal and civil, to the circuit courts, which sat twice annually in each of the two county seats, Kaskaskia and Cahokia, with one of the judges of the general court presiding. The governor and judges assigned the administrative functions of the court of common pleas, such as the levying of local taxes, to the county court, which met six times annually and over which presided three or more justices of the peace. The general court they left undisturbed. When they found that even this system was too complicated for the widely scattered settlements of the territory, they abolished the circuit courts, leaving only the general court to try the more important cases twice annually at each of the county seats. Eventually the increase of population forced the governor and judges to restore the court of common pleas to cope with the business formerly assigned to the abolished courts.[6]

The unrestricted environment of the frontier engendered a lawlessness and immorality that necessitated a stringent criminal code. Conviction for a crime or even a misdemeanor meant cruel punishment. The burglar or robber was sentenced to Moses' Law—that is, forty stripes save one—was imprisoned for three years, and was fined in triple value of the article or articles he had stolen. Rape or arson brought a sentence of death by hanging. The bigamist was lashed three hundred times on his bare back and was fined $100 in addition. The perjuror or suborner had to pay a fine of $60, had to bare his back to Moses' Law and had to surrender his right to hold office, give testimony or serve as a juror. Assault and battery carried a fine of $100. The horse thief had to pay the full price of the stolen animal to its owner and received from fifty to two hundred lashes; if he repeated the offense he was sentenced to be hanged. The stealing of a hog, a shoat or a pig brought a fine of not less than $100 and a whipping. Any person who broke the Sabbath by drinking or gambling or quarreling or doing or performing "any worldly employment or business whatever (with some exception in favor of ferrymen)" or by taking part in any sport "shall forfeit for every such offense a sum not exceeding two dollars nor less than fifty cents, to be levied by distress; and in case the fine can not be collected in that way, he is required to work on the highways for two days." Any person of sixteen and upwards found guilty of swearing by God, Jesus Christ or the Holy Ghost was punished in the same manner as Sabbath breakers. Cockfighting, gambling or horse racing brought a stiff fine and a sentence to work on the roads for two days. Vagrants and persons suspected of supporting themselves by gambling were required to find work for nine months; if they failed, they were sentenced to Moses' Law. Lotteries were prohibited by requiring a forfeiture of the whole sum won at them.[7]

Despite their southern background the governor and judges early showed they were no advocates of slavery. To Edwards it was "a great evil that should never have been admitted into any state or territory." Unwilling to arouse the animosity of the slaveowners, however, they left the Indenture Law of 1807 undisturbed. Immigrants from the border states and the free states were outnumbering those from the slave states and eventually would exert their influence to abolish what little slavery remained in the territory. Even now the labor supply from the free states precluded any need for additional slaves.[8]

Edwards followed the same wise policy in dealing with the Indians. In his endeavor to promote their good will, he issued a proclamation forbidding the sale of intoxicating liquors to them within twenty miles of Peoria. At the same time he instructed Thomas Forsythe, the Indian agent at Peoria, to enforce the law.[9]

Within a short time Edwards and the judges had brought order out of chaos and had started the territory toward the second stage of government, which permitted it to have its own legislature and to send a delegate to Congress. Following the precedent established in Indiana Territory, Congress empowered Edwards to organize a territorial assembly as soon as the people expressed a desire for it. On October 1, 1810, the inhabitants of Kaskaskia held a meeting at which they drew up a memorial favoring the second stage of government. This received unanimous support, for all the political factions looked forward to a movement which would provide them with a greater degree of self-government and a delegate to Congress. At first Edwards favored a postponement of the change.

Most of the settlers were squatters who patiently awaited the year 1814, when they could buy land. Because they owned no land, they had no voting privileges. The number of voters constituted scarcely a tenth of the permanent residents. The region south of Kaskaskia, for example, had three or four voters in fully a third of the population of the territory. This meant that a very limited minority would control the territorial assembly—unless voting privileges were given to more people.

In fact, the Great Lakes frontiersmen in recent years favored greater participation in local government. By an act of 1809 Congress had democratized the government of Indiana Territory to the extent of permitting the people to elect a delegate and the councilors, though the voting qualifications remained unchanged. Why not grant the same privileges to the people in Illinois? Edwards, finding the people persistent in their requests for the second stage of government, wrote to his friend, Colonel Richard Mentor Johnson, then a member of Congress from Kentucky, explaining the situation and asking his assistance in securing an act removing the property qualifications for settlers whose titles to their land had not been confirmed. At the same time the governor dispatched to the speaker in the House of Representatives two petitions in which the people of Illinois prayed for the privilege to vote.

Johnson acted promptly. On May 20, 1812, Congress approved a law enabling the settlers of Illinois to establish "the most democratic form of territorial government to be found in the United States at that time." It granted voting privileges to every white male twenty-one years old who had paid a county or territorial tax, no matter how small, and who had resided in the territory for one year. The act further stipulated that the people instead of the legislature should elect the delegates to Congress as well as the five councilors for the five districts designated by the governor.[10]

Presently Governor Edwards issued two proclamations in one of which he added three counties to the original two to serve as the districts of the five councilors, and in the other called for an election for the delegate to Congress, the five councilors, and the representatives. The delegate, elected on October 10, was Shadrach Bond, a pro-Harrison man who had served as a representative and councilor in the legislature of Indiana before that territory was divided.[11]

The first territorial assembly, which met on November 25, devoted much of its time to making the adjustments necessitated by the establishment of the three new counties and to restoring to the courts of common pleas the jurisdiction they exercised under the laws of Indiana Territory. Thus the judges of the general court found much time on their hands—a situation pleasing only to themselves. In August 1813 Bond wrote to Edwards, who had left the territory for a short time, that the grand jury of each of two counties had reprimanded the territorial judges for absenting themselves from the territory and for failing to attend to their duties. Judge Stuart resigned before the reprimand took place. His successor, William Sprigg, by no means improved matters by refusing to recognize the right of the legislature to regulate the court. Bond wrote to Edwards that he was "trying to get a law passed to compel our judges to perform such duties as our Legislature have required of them."[12]

The courts of common pleas with their untrained judges committed so many errors in law that the legislature, in December, 1814, heeded widespread indignation and again abolished them. It assigned their administrative duties and their judicial functions to a county court of three men. At the same time it organized the three territorial or United States judges into a supreme court, which was directed to hold two courts annually in each county and a court of appeals in the capital. Judges Thomas and Sprigg were unwilling to assume the additional duties and responsibilities that these changes imposed on them. They angrily dashed off a letter to the legislature protesting the changes and denying that it had any jurisdiction over the supreme court which, they argued, was an entirely new organization and therefore responsible neither to the Ordinance nor to the legislature.

Confounded by this argument, the legislature forwarded the judges' letter to Edwards and requested his opinion of the matter. The astute governor pointed out that the Ordinance provided for a court of three judges "who shall have a common law jurisdiction" but that it said nothing about when or where that jurisdiction should be exercised; it therefore was subject to whatever changes and direction the territorial legislature proposed. The judges refused to acknowledge the validity of the governor's interpretation. Whereupon the legislature forwarded to Congress all the letters and documents bearing on the controversy and requested it to return a solution. In reply Congress in 1815 passed an act regulating and defining the duties of the United States judges for the territory of Illinois. This conceded victory to Edwards and the legislature; it required the United States judges to hold circuit courts in each county.[13]

Even so, the new law proved unsatisfactory in some of its details. The legislature then asked Congress to make such changes as would be required in the future. On April 29, 1816, Congress obliged with a new law; but unfortunately its phraseology was so obscure that it permitted the irate judges to claim that its validity would not extend beyond the following session of the legislature. This interpretation, if accepted, would have resulted in the situation that existed before the congressional law was passed.[14]

At the next session of the legislature the House committee in charge of the judiciary reported a bill designed to establish two independent circuit judges, who were to receive $800 each and who were to hold three courts annually in each county. By relieving the United States judges of circuit work, this bill, if enacted, would have restored harmony in the government of the territory; but the legislature felt that the people should not have to pay the judges for services which were a part of their duty to perform. It therefore passed another bill which continued the system in force under the congressional law. Judge Thomas and a new judge, Thomas Towles, a native of Kentucky, held their circuits in accordance with the law, though they questioned its validity. But Judge Sprigg persisted in his belief that the congressional law had expired and that the territorial law violated the spirit of the Ordinance. Instead of making his rounds he went to Maryland; and when he returned he refused to obey the law. As a result the people of his circuit lacked the facilities to determine lawsuits, and criminals remained untried.[15]

These circumstances prompted the legislature to settle the matter without delay. At its second meeting in December 1817 Representatives Bradsby and Matheny of St. Clair County strongly opposed any concession to the judges; but they proposed a bill which the majority of their colleagues persuaded themselves to accept as an expediency rather than as a compromise. This provided for the appointment by the governor of two circuit judges, who were to receive a salary of $1,000 each and who were to be relieved of all circuit duties but were to hold instead four general courts a year, two at Kaskaskia and two at Shawneetown. At the same time the legislature passed a resolution requesting the territorial delegate to Congress to lay before the House of Representatives charges against Judge Sprigg for ignoring the territorial law to hold courts and for absenting himself from Illinois "for an unreasonable time." Sprigg saved himself by resigning. His successor, Richard Graham, proved very malleable to the wishes of the legislature and corrected what Sprigg had undone. Harmony at last had returned to the progressive government of Illinois Territory.[16]

2

The appetite for democracy grows with the first taste. The people of Illinois, having savored the most democratic form of government in the Great Lakes Frontier, clamored for more of it. In 1814 the territorial legislature drew up a memorial to Congress, praying for the repeal of the clause in the Ordinance which gave the governor an absolute veto:

To freemen this clause wears the aspect of slavery—vesting our Executive with a Despotism that can frustrate the most deliberate and well digested measures of our Council and House of Representatives. . . . The good people of this Territory have the privilege, the trouble and the vast expense of electing and sending Representatives in a Legislative Capacity to convene and to consult together for the public good but by their mutual and most elaborate exertions they become not law-makers but only recommenders of laws.[17]

This memorial unconsciously began the movement for statehood. Henceforth it found increasingly persistent expression in the columns of the territorial newspaper, the *Western Intelligencer*, which in 1818 was to change its name to the *Illinois Intelligencer*. On the eve of an election for a new delegate to Congress to succeed Shadrach Bond, a correspondent who signed himself "Aristides" in an eloquent article deplored the "colonial and degraded state of this country, under the government of the Ordinance, that accursed badge of despotism, which withholds from the people, the only true source of all power, a Participation in those rights guaranteed by the constitutions of every state in the union." And he warned the voters of the territory to take care to elect a delegate who would "advocate a redress of colonial grievances, and honestly exert his influence to obtain that change (so long withholden) which will place us on that proud eminence of freemen." The people heeded his advice and elected Nathaniel Pope, who in his capacity as secretary had shown unquestioned zeal for the betterment of the territory.[18]

But the man directly responsible for the statehood movement was a mere stripling twenty-four years old. Daniel Pope Cook was to Illinois what Thomas Worthington had been to Ohio and Jonathan Jennings to Indiana. He was not a native of Illinois. In this respect, however, he was not unique; most of the early statesmen of Illinois migrated from the older states—notably Kentucky, mother of the Great Lakes Frontier. Frail because of tuberculosis, he was unable to take full advantage of even the meagre educational opportunities of his time and place. Because of his illness his attendance at school was irregular; but his mind was uncommonly supple, wiry and active.

When Cook was eighteen, his father sent him to St. Genevieve, where he found employment in William Shannon's general store. But he was a clerk only in body; his mind wandered across the Mississippi to Kaskaskia, where his uncle, Nathaniel Pope, was secretary of Illinois Territory. He soon joined him and began with him the study of law. At the end of two years he was admitted to the bar in Kaskaskia, where he soon established a good practice, though in those days few men supported themselves by their professions alone. He practiced law in the courts of all the organized counties of the territory save those along the Wabash. At the same time he served Governor Edwards as his auditor of public accounts. But even this added activity failed to fill his time, and he purchased from Matthew Duncan the only newspaper in the territory, the *Western Intelligencer*, which at that time published little but foreign news and advertisements of land sales.[19]

These assiduities ruined his health, and his physician recommended a sea voyage to restore it. Even then he chained vacation to business. In Washington his uncle's recommendation landed him an appointment as bearer of dispatches to John Quincy Adams, minister to the Court of St. James. The austere New Englander admired the boy and asked him to accompany him back to the United States. Arriving in Washington early in September 1817 he began looking for a political job. At the end of the month he was still looking. He wrote Governor Edwards that he was uncertain just what he would do:

I can get a clerkship in the State department with a good salary, but I won't go into it; it is too confining. I shall know in a few days whether I go as Secretary of Alabama Territory or not. The President, it is feared, has made up his mind; if so, I shall fail; there is no situation vacant at present for me but that; I have Adams' assurance to befriend me at any time.

In a postscript he added: "I am not yet well. May it not be better for me to return to Kaskaskia and wait for prospects in that country if I don't go to Alabama?"[20]

Destiny guided his steps back to Kaskaskia. There he did not wait for prospects; he proceeded to make them. Two days after his return he published in his newspaper an editorial that electrified its readers. It said in part:

While we are laboring under so many of the grievances of a territorial, or semi-monarchical government, might not our claims to a state government be justly urged? That part of our territory which must ultimately form a state, will no doubt be willing to take the burthen of a state government upon themselves at this time, rather than submit any longer to those degredations [*sic*], which they have so long been compelled to put up with. We hope in our next to present to our readers, such a view of the subject as will induce our fellow citizens, as well as the legislature, to take such measures as will bring it before the national legislature, at their approaching season. We invite a discussion of the measure by such gentlemen as have, or will reflect on the subject.[21]

The promised review on the subject of statehood duly appeared. Cook first dwelled on the objections. The main objection would be the added expense to the people, but he hoped that the state officers could at first be persuaded to accept smaller salaries than those paid to the territorial officers. Another objection would be the ignorance of the people. This, he explained, was based on the assumption that the majority of them were French. Actually, nine tenths of the voters were Americans who, before migrating to Illinois, had participated in state government.[22]

More significant were the advantages. The legislature would be free of the restraint of the governor's absolute veto and would, therefore, become the supreme voice in the internal affairs of the state. Referring to the difficulties which the legislature had encountered in attempting to enforce the judiciary law, he wrote: "Crimes of the blackest dye, (even murder itself,) have defied its feeble powers and laughed in guilty triumph at their suffering victims. Honest labor has had its bread taken out of its mouth, and injuries of all kinds have implored relief in vain."[23]

He adverted to the practicability of obtaining the blessing of Congress for admission with a population less than the sixty thousand required by the Ordinance. Such an admission, he argued, could not possibly harm the country; on the contrary, it would prove a positive advantage, inasmuch as it would relieve Congress of the burden of having to legislate for the affairs of the territory and would, moreover, encourage immigration. He averred that slavery would never be tolerated when a state government was formed: "Many on both sides of the question are remaining in the anxiety of suspense, to know how it will be settled. It is therefore desirable to settle the question at as early a period as possible, for the purpose of giving relief to those who are wanting to emigrate to the territory."[24]

The public reaction to the review was so favorable that Governor Edwards felt obliged to approve it in a meeting of the legislature. He congratulated the members and the people "upon the flattering prospects which our astonishingly rapid increase of population affords that our present temporary government must soon give place to one more congenial to the principles of natural liberty." He urged the members to pass a law to take a census of the territory without delay.[25]

To the adherents of statehood, however, this ordinary procedure seemed too leisurely. By this time Cook had been elected clerk of the House of Representatives, a position which afforded him ample opportunity to exert considerable influence on its members. Through his tireless efforts the House, on the very day on which the governor delivered his message, passed a resolution to appoint a committee to draft a memorial to Congress "praying for the territory to be admitted into the Union, with all the rights and privileges of a state government." The rapidity with which the memorial was passed attested to the unanimity of opinion on the matter. Within a week the memorial was written, adopted, approved by the Council, and laid before the governor.[26]

In style and expression it strongly resembled Cook's review. It characterized the territorial government as "a species of despotism in direct hostility with the principles of a republican government" which "ought to exist no longer than *absolute necessity* requires it." The memorial estimated the population at "not less than forty thousand souls" and described those fit to meet the responsibilities of state government as largely immigrants from the Atlantic and western states.[27]

Why were the antislavery people so anxious to achieve statehood without delay? Aside from the fact that by now most of the settlers, and especially those in the northwestern counties, had migrated from states where slavery was held in abhorrence, they had learned that the people of Missouri Territory also had petitioned Congress for admission. If Missouri came in as a slave state—and few men doubted that she would—the adherents of slavery in Illinois could present strong arguments to permit it there also. The passage of slaveholding immigrants across the territory to settle in Missouri incensed those who dreamed of rapid development. They would be in a position to prove their claim that exclusion of slavery would not retard Illinois if she could achieve statehood before her rival across the Mississippi. They therefore bent all their efforts to bring Illinois to statehood with a free constitution before any possible constitution of Missouri could become a subject of discussion.[28]

But in this endeavor they met difficulties, not from Congress but from circumstances at home. The Indenture Law of Indiana continued in operation when Governor Edwards and the judges had decided in their first session to adopt the laws of that territory. Embarrassed by this situation, the legislature now hastened to draw up an act to repeal the Indenture Law; but after much heated debate between the members on the new act, the governor on December 17, 1817 vetoed it as invalid.[29]

The legislature next took steps to remove doubt of the willingness of Congress to grant statehood without evidence of the population required by the Ordinance. It enacted a law establishing commissioners to take a census of the territory between April 1 and June 1, 1818. Fearing that its estimate of the population might prove optimistic, the legislature passed a supplementary act in which it predicted a great increase of immigration between June 1 and December 1, 1818. In anticipation of this event the act directed the commissioners to continue to take the census in their respective counties of all persons who moved to them between June 1 and December 1, and to submit their additional returns to the territorial secretary's office as soon as possible. The act obviated unnecessary expenditure by providing for curtailment of the additional service should Congress authorize the people of the territory to form a state government.[30]

By this time the memorial praying for statehood had reached Washington. Its success of course depended on the territorial delegate, Nathaniel Pope, who on January 16, 1818, duly laid it before the House of Representatives. It was immediately referred to a select committee of which Pope was chairman. In a report of his progress to the editors of the territorial newspaper he said that his only difficulty would be that of ascertaining whether the territory really had the population mentioned in the memorial. He hoped to evade this difficulty by having removed from the possible Enabling Act the proviso which called for a census before a Constitutional Convention could be authorized. At that time thirty-five thousand people was the ratio of congressional apportionment. Pope was confident that the committee would raise no objection if the territory could show this number.[31]

On January 23 the committee reported an Enabling Act. It authorized the voters of Illinois Territory to choose delegates for a convention which would determine the expediency of forming a state constitution. The proviso which Pope wanted to eliminate directed the United States marshal of the territory to take a census and submit his returns to the convention. The Act was read twice and transmitted to the committee of the whole in the House of Representatives.

When the Act came up, Pope introduced an amendment fixing the boundary of the proposed state about forty-one miles north of the line proposed in the Act and fifty-one miles north of the dividing line proposed in the Ordinance. His purpose was to gain a part of Lake Michigan for the state and thereby a connection with Indiana, Ohio, Pennsylvania, and New York through the Great Lakes. The House could not object to the amendment, inasmuch as the dividing line proposed in the Ordinance had been ignored in the case of Indiana. Thus Illinois received a region of over eight thousand square miles in which lie the greater parts of fourteen counties and which includes the present city of Chicago with nearly half of the population of the state. Pope failed, however, in his endeavor to eliminate the census proviso from the Act. Yet he lost nothing, for the committee agreed to modify the Act to direct the convention to permit the territorial legislature instead of the United States marshal to settle the matter of the population.[32]

On April 6 the Act passed the House without opposition. In the Senate, however, Tait of Georgia objected to the Act. Congress, he said, had no proof that the territory had a population of forty thousand or even enough to entitle it to a representative in Congress. He therefore urged postponement of further consideration on the matter; but he was opposed by Morrow of Ohio, Talbot of Kentucky, and Barbour of Virginia, who accepted the population given in the memorial as nearly accurate. Fiery debates, of course, ensued, but they soon cooled down and died; and the Enabling Act was read for the third time and passed. It was then sent to President Monroe, who approved it on April 18. The champions of the statehood movement in Illinois had succeeded in their endeavor to obtain an Enabling Act before Missouri.[33]

3

Church bells ling-longed and bands played marches and people embraced one another with happy exclamations when, on April 29, Kaskaskians learned in their newspaper that Pope had succeeded in his mission. The neighboring states joined in congratulating Illinois on her good fortune. The *Kentucky Argus* prophetically envisioned for the new state a glorious future: "The agricultural and mercantile advantages of this state will render it a star of the first magnitude in our constellation of free states. . . . *We hail thee, sister Illinois, and are ready to welcome thee in our happy Union.*" The editors of the territorial newspaper celebrated the occasion by changing its name from *Western Intelligencer* to *Illinois Intelligencer*. They explained that they believed the new name more appropriate, "in as much as it is the same establishment from which the first paper emanated in the territory, and more particularly as we shall soon go into a state under the name of Illinois."[34]

The small proslavery element was of course disappointed, though they still hoped that Congress could be induced to overlook the restriction on slavery in the Ordinance. But they realized that they would never succeed in this aim if they deprecated their numerically superior opponents during the campaign for delegates to the constitutional convention. Their quest for delegates was therefore quiet. The delegates were to be elected in July for the convention which was to meet in August. Daniel Pope Cook spent most of his time writing for his newspaper articles designed to hinder the proslavery people from gaining voters. He charged them with promoting the election of men who were in favor of postponing the framing of a constitution. At the same time he left no doubt about how he stood. He wrote:

If we should have it in our power to elect a convention, we should certainly know beforehand what the *elected* will do on this subject. If the advantages of a state government are worth struggling for, I should certainly recommend the election of men who will favor such a decision when in the convention.[35]

By the middle of June all census returns were in save those of the remote parts of the territory. The recorded population temporarily gladdened the proslavery group which wished to delay statehood. It showed 34,620, more than five thousand short of the number Congress agreed to accept in the Enabling Act. But they lapsed into gloom when Nathaniel Pope, who had returned from Washington at the completion of his mission as delegate, announced that the required number would be realized before the convention met and that, therefore, the campaign to elect its delegates would continue.[36]

The candidates adopted typically frontier methods of campaigning. By now a new newspaper had appeared in Shawneetown, making two in the territory; but these of course could reach only a small portion of the voters. So politicians circulated handbills in which the merits of their respective candidates were colorfully and adroitly depicted. Still another method of campaigning was house to house canvassing. Its general nature was admirably described in a poem entitled "Candidates," which appeared in the *Illinois Intelligencer* just five days before the election:

> In dreary woods, remote from social walks
> I dwell. From year to year, no friendly steps
> Approach my cot, save near election days,
> When throngs of busy, bustling candidates
> Cheer me with their conversation so soft and sweet—
> I list' with patience to their charming tales,
> Whilst gingerbread and whisky they disperse,
> To me, my wife and all the children round.
> Some bring a store of little penny books
> And trinkets rare for all my infants young.—
> My health and crops appear their utmost care,
> Fraternal squeezes from their hands I get—
> As tho' they lov'd me from their very souls:—
> Then—"Will you vote for me my dearest friend?
> Your laws I'll alter, and lop off taxes;—
> 'Tis for the public weal I stand the test,
> And leave my home, sorely against my will:
> But knowing that the people's good require
> An old substantial hand—I quit my farm
> For patriotism's sake, and public good;"
> Then fresh embraces close the friendly scene,
> With protestations firm, of how they love.

But what most rarely does my good wife pleate,
Is that the snot nos'd baby gets a buss!!
O that conventions ev'ry day were call'd,
That social converse might forever reign.[37]

The elections took place in the first week of July and on the first Monday of the following month the successful candidates took their seats in the constitutional convention under the presidency of Jesse B. Thomas. Kaskaskia knew no such excitement since George Rogers Clark led his trudging men down its narrow and crooked streets forty years ago! Men and women and children from all parts of the far-flung territory thronged Bennett's tavern and every house and store and overflowed into the streets and surrounding fields to learn the deliberations of the thirty-three men—all the soul of august solemnity—who composed the constitutional convention.

In their first deliberations they necessarily got down to the business of ascertaining whether the population of the territory sufficed for them to proceed with the framing of a constitution. The committee assigned to this duty happily reported a population of 40,258, an increase of fifty-six hundred thirty-eight over the first reports of June and sufficient to permit the convention to continue with its work. Jubilantly the antislavery delegates, who were greatly in the majority, directed all their efforts toward framing a constitution. In just two weeks they completed their task.

The constitution of the new state was typically American in that it contained a bill of rights and provision for a bicameral legislature. The only article that deviated from those of the usual state constitutions was that regarding slavery. In this the antislavery delegates showed that liberality initiated by Edwards at the beginning of the territory. The goodly number of slaveowners were permitted to keep their slaves and indentured servants. But thereafter neither indenture nor slavery was to be permitted "except within the tract reserved for the salt works near Shawneetown, nor even at that place for a longer period than one year at one time; nor shall it be allowed there, after the year . . . any violation of this article, shall effect the emancipation of such person from his obligation to service."

The children born of Negro and mulatto slaves were to be declared free, the males at the age of twenty-one years and the females at the age of eighteen years. "Each and every child of indentured servants shall be entered with the clerk of the court in which they reside, by their owners within six months after the birth of said child." Thus without interfering in any way with existing property rights in slaves or indentured servants, the constitutional convention of Illinois wiped out the territorial indenture system for the future and paved the way for Illinois to join the roster of free states.[38]

In the middle of September occurred the first election for state officers. Shadrach Bond, who had lived in Illinois for twenty-four years and who, therefore, was better known than the other leaders of the territory, was elected governor. In the fall the state legislature elected the two senators to Congress. One of the successful men was Ninian Edwards, who had led the territory from chaos to law and order and prepared it for its march toward statehood. Daniel Pope Cook also ran, but the legislature felt he was too young and too sick to assume the heavy responsibilities of that office and turned him down. Instead it showed its gratitude for his achievements in behalf of statehood by electing him attorney-general. In that capacity he made such a brilliant record that he dissipated all fears about his age and illness. At the next election to Congress he defeated his opponent by a wide majority. Unfortunately, tuberculosis had already reduced him to skin and bones. In vain he traveled to Cuba and to New Orleans for his health. He returned to Kentucky, his adopted home, to die at the age of thirty-six.

11

Pioneer Days and Ways

THE YOUNG PIONEER ALIGHTS WITH HIS WIFE AND SMALL CHILDREN from his ox-drawn and canvas-covered wagon. He has traveled from one of the eastern states in search of land, which means economic security, even possible wealth. Before him spreads the quarter section of land he bought at the government price of $1.25 an acre. It brightens his eyes with hope for himself and his family. The river that runs through his property will provide him and his family with drinking water and, in the absence of roads, with access to other frontiersmen. The surrounding forest will furnish mast for his hogs and wood for shelter and warmth. He no longer needs to fear Indian attacks. Tecumseh is dead and the War of 1812 is over and the red menace is passed. Here, in the Great Lakes Frontier, the average pioneer, such as himself, can safely settle down in his new home.

His first home is temporary. He saws down several buckeye trees, pegs them to a cross timber, plants them and covers three of their sides with logs, brush and clay mud. In the open side, which usually faces south or is protected from the winds, he builds a log fire to keep him and his family warm in winter and to protect them from wood varmints at night. This cabin is his palace. He throws bearskins or wolf or cat pelts or buffalo hides on the ground inside as a kind of housewarming for his family. The skins serve them as a floor as well as mattresses and covers.

Soon his neighbors visit him and offer to help him raise a better cabin. On the appointed day they meet and level the ground. An axman at each corner fits the notches and, as the walls of the cabin rise, his friends skid up the logs with forks and hand spikes. The strength of the corner joints depends on the skill of the notcher. And the straighter and more uniform the logs the narrower the chinks between them.

The door and window involve no more work than that of cutting or chopping, and then framing, spaces in one or more of the walls. Filling in the chinks with tough clay or mortar is usually the chore of the wife or older children just before the cold spell sets in. The rafters are long and slender young oaks that support shakes or clapboards split from bolts of oak or ash three or four feet long. Pegged to the rafters and weighted down with blocks, the clapboard roof becomes an unyielding stockade against the cruelest elemental assault.

Another cheerful ally in the surrounding bleakness, the fireplace, merits dexterous handling. It is usually cut in one of the end walls. Around it the pioneer and his friends build a pen of small split and notched logs, then an inner pen and fill the foot or more of space between them with clay. By burning or removing the inner pen the pioneer realizes for the fireplace a protecting back and jambs four or five feet high. Above this rises his chimney, a diminishing square of rived sticks heavily plastered with clay.

To exclude the weather and admit the light he covers the window with greased paper until he can afford to buy glass. The door he fashions ingeniously. He pegs broad slabs to heavy cross battens that are longer than the width of the door. The holes in one side of the projecting ends he asserts to a heavy wooden pin at the door frame and fits the wooden drop latch on the other side into a notch. The latch, controlled by a latchstring that passes through a hole and hangs outside, assures him and his family of undisturbed sleep after a day of heavy labor.

He may dream of an even better home—one of hewn logs with glass windows, hinged doors, smooth walls and floor and frames and finishing of yellow poplar, all of which he usually realizes as he prospers. The house would have two or as many as three rooms and would suffice for his large family and, perhaps, for his friends and kinfolk.[1]

2

The furniture of the Great Lakes frontiersman depended on his ability and taste. If he possessed the necessary tools—and he often did—he could easily make his own furniture. He built his beds at the cabin corners by driving stakes or poles into the ground or through holes in the floor and then running rails to the walls. Across this framework he stretched thongs of deerskin or twisted elm bark that served as springs for bearskin mattresses or grass ticks. As his children grew up, he secured privacy for himself and his wife by making the outer supporting stakes high enough to be furnished with a concealing curtain. From forked or crooked branches of trees he made hooks on which to hang clothes and other articles. His tables were thin splits of poplar several feet wide pegged to crosspieces into which he fitted legs of oak or buckeye. He made his chairs, which were usually rude puncheon benches with three legs, to conform with the wavy floor or the bumpy ground. Slabs of large logs with wooden pins served as tables.[2]

The "cooking irons" were the most important of the household utensils. Among them were a rotund, bulbous pot with a flare at the top to hold the lid; a long-handled frying pan with three legs, known as the "spider"; and a deep iron oven with legs and edges turned up to hold the hot coals on top. The well-to-do housewife boasted a thin, smooth board and wooden paddle essential in making hoecakes. She owned, too, an enclosed frame of tin two or three feet long known as a "reflector," in which she roasted her meat, or baked her pies, cakes and bread. It stood on short legs near live coals at the hearth and reflected heat on the food inside. It had a flaring top which could be thrown back on its hinges whenever the cooking needed attention.[3]

The Great Lakes frontierswoman hailed a cook stove with delight. It afforded great relief to her face, hands, and arms so often blistered by large open fires. The prosperous lady usually owned a "Dutch oven," a dome rounded like a beehive and made of small boulders or bricks and mortar or tough clay wrought and beaten into shape. It retained enough heat to cook the food after the fire built in it had been raked out. Another product of pioneer versatility was the hominy pestle, a piece of beech or maple stump burned into the shape of a bowl. A familiar relic of those fabulous days was the rude trough that caught the sap of maple trees. It was hollowed out of a short split log.[4]

The common utensil for drinking or dipping vessels was the gourd, which a writer of pioneer life called "one of the most adaptable and convenient gifts of nature to man." In the absence of manufactured articles it proved a boon: it played a conspicuous part in a variety of purposes. Attached to a long string it hung as a dipper beside the spring or well; it was a companion to the cider barrel and whiskey jug; it complemented the wash pan and the milk pail; it served as a repository for countless small articles including needles, pins, buttons and fish hooks; it was indispensable for soup, soap and sap. As a rattler to sooth crying babies it deserves to be immortalized in song.[5]

The interior of a pioneer home told an eloquent tale of pioneer life. The rifle, powder horn and bullet pouch usually hung on a pair of deer antlers over the fireplace. Hanging from the rafters were often dried herbs, little bags of dried fruit, pumpkins, sacks of nuts, slabs of bacon, jerked venison, smoked hams and bunches of candles made by dipping wicks in a bucket of hot tallow. The hickory broom was a sapling several inches in diameter with slivers fluffed out and bound to the lower part of the handle by a string, rope or the stalk of a durable dried weed. On the walls were knives and bows carved in Indian fashion with scenes depicting war or the hunt. Crude shelves contained wooden spoons, plates, bowls and noggins.

The loom, a ponderous and formidable machine, was assembled without nails and could be taken apart and stored when not in use. In the homes of well-to-do pioneers the loom had a room all its own or occupied the abandoned temporary first cabin. It required a pair of strong arms and much mechanical flexibility to thread it, trip the treadles to raise or lower the heddles for alternative threads, jerk or throw a fast shuttle and pound the cross thread evenly with the batten. The inseparable companion of the loom was the spinning wheel. The large ones for wool weaving were made of hardwood, were rotated by hand, and necessitated walking to and fro as the horizontal spindle drew and twisted the rove. Flax weaving required a smaller spinning wheel run by foot pedal.[6]

The strong influence of the Indian was apparent in frontier clothing. The pantaloons, hunting shirts and moccasins were made of deerskin with or without the hair. A buckskin hunting shirt gave its wearer the jaunty air and elegance of an Indian. It fitted closely, could be worn as an outer garment and was usually fastened at the waist with a belt. The foppish pioneer would have Indian women fringe it heavily along the edges and ornament it and his moccasins with beads and brightly colored porcupine quills. With ordinary care a deerskin suit lasted many years. It was very warm until it became wet. Then it grew as cold and heavy as armor. And the pantaloons shrank to the knees and the shirt contracted at the waist. One school teacher seated himself in his deerskin suit behind his desk and did not rise until his suit was dry. He found himself encased as in a suit of tin—without any allowance for joints. The washing of such a suit was, needless to say, difficult; pounding and stretching it while it was drying only ruined its shape and enlarged it by several sizes. In dry, cold weather deerskin moccasins worn with woolen socks made excellent footwear for hunting, but in soft snow or rain they were worse than useless.[7]

The pioneer women usually wore linsey-woolsey, a warm and durable cloth woven from looser homespun yarns. Its cotton counterpart, "jean," was men's most useful apparel. Some of these yarns or cloths remained in their natural colors; others were dyed for variety and ornamentation. A region's predominant tree determined its favorite color. Black, for example, predominated in sections of Indiana that obtained their dyes from the hull of the black and white walnut, while brown predominated in sections that used the darker browns of the black walnut or the tawny tints of the white walnut or the butternut. The king of colors was indigo blue, which could be produced only by the most skillful blend of dye and urine that had been aged at the hearth or chimney corner. Ironically enough, this evil-smelling decoction produced what the pioneers were pleased to call the "aristocratic color" so much prized for Sunday or holiday wear. Linseys were checked or striped brown or blue by alternating madder with copperas, or copperas with maple bark.[8]

This rough and coarse apparel had no earthly purpose save that of keeping its wearers warm in winter and cool in summer. Remote was any consideration of taste. From early spring to late autumn pioneer boys and girls and many men and women went barefooted. In summer small children, male and female, wore nothing save a tow shirt that hung loosely from the shoulders down to the knees. A boy's first pair of pantaloons was as long as his father's and large enough to expect him to grow up to them and even outgrow them rather than wear them out.

Nothing on the frontier was funnier than the sight of a boy wearing his first Sunday-go-to-meetin' suit. It was usually made of brown or blue jean and roomy enough for two boys his size. His trousers bagged at the knees and in the seat and dragged and folded over his cowhide shoes; the front of his vest swung from hip to hip; his coat bulged and sagged at the shoulders and at the elbows and hid half of his hands. His round-crowned, stiff-rimmed hat emphasized his greenness and completed his discomfort and disgust. His only ambition just then was to regain his identity by pulling off his scarecrowish outfit and putting on his rumpled and well-worn roundabout or tailless coat.[9]

The "warmus" or "waumus," as it was generally called, was a kind of red flannel or striped linsey shirt that frontiersmen wore over their vests and pantaloons. This venerable descendant of the hunting shirt and ancestor of the sweater could be worn with or without a belt.[10]

At home women wore plain cotton or linen or wool dresses which they slipped over their heads and fastened behind with a drawstring. Those natural allies, babies and old women, wore caps made of calico, muslin, cambric and bobinet. Younger women protected their heads, faces, and necks from the summer heat with straw bonnets or sunbonnets of colored calico stretched over stiff cardboard and puckered behind. The Quaker women preferred plain gray or brown shawls or sunbonnets supplemented by neatly folded cambric handkerchiefs around their necks. They eschewed as worldly any ruffles and flounces on dresses and all jewelry save a modest throat pin or cameo. Their bonnets in public were of silk woven on buckram frames in the manner of the women of their sect in England. The younger women wore soft gray; the middle-aged women, darker grays and browns; and the old women, shiny black. Inasmuch as Quaker fashions never changed, two or three bonnets lasted a lifetime.[11]

The pioneers advanced westward on their hunting skill. They brought little food with them; the lack of roads and poor communications with other settlements forced them to rely on themselves. Their hunting prowess rewarded them with fabulous quantities of bears, deer, wild turkeys, geese, ducks, partridges and pigeons. In Indiana wild turkeys gathered in flocks of five hundred or more; bears, deer and squirrels often destroyed grain fields; and deer, curiously enough, relished the green leaves of the young tobacco. Pigeons flew in flocks so numerous that they darkened the sky like a passing rain cloud. They traveled as far as two hundred miles to feed on ripe beechnuts and then roosted in the forest, piling on one another from the lowest to the topmost branches and screaming so penetratingly that they could be heard as far as six miles away. At night men with lanterns and poles killed hundreds of pigeons at their roosting place without risking much personal danger. But the grand manner of killing them was by setting fires simulta-neously to different parts of the high grass, leaves and shrubs around their roosting place. Then down they swooped in immense numbers and indescribable confusion to be roasted alive. The next day they were gathered up in heaps two feet deep.[12]

The fish were even more numerous than the pigeons. Shoals of fish in the Driftwood River covered half an acre. A pioneer writer, Judge Finch, stood on a bank of the White River and saw, six inches below the surface, monster muskellunge and gar in such large numbers that the two varieties mingled like a happy family as they sunned themselves. Disdaining the slow process of fishing with hooks, frontiersmen along the Wabash used gig and seine which brought as many as fifty barrels of bass or wall-eyed pike in a single haul. We hasten to authenticate these fish stories.[13]

Pioneer food made up in substance and quantity what it lacked in taste and variety. One of the standard dishes was "hog an' hominy," that is, pork served with Indian corn cooked soft after its hulls had been boiled away in lye. Poor families supped on corn-meal mush and milk—when the taste of leeks and wild garlic was absent from the milk. Otherwise mush was served with sweetened water, molasses, the gravy of fried meat or even bear's oil.

The Great Lakes frontiersmen usually favored the dishes of their native regions. Thus Yankees were fond of beans and pie, and Southerners of hot biscuits, salt pork, ham, eggs, mush, grits, molasses, potatoes and gravy for breakfast. The aroma of sauer-kraut more often than not could be traced to the cabin of German immigrants or of a family of German ancestry. "Pone"—a corn-bread enriched with milk and yeast—and "johnny cake" or "hoe-cake"—a cornbread flattened on a board and containing bear grease, lard or butter—were the hardy forbears of our pancakes and waffles.

The prairie of Illinois with its great variety of flowers had the reputation on the frontier of producing more honey than any other part of the world. Many families relieved their heavy diets of meat with pumpkins, squashes, potatoes, beans and roasting ears that they grew in their "truck patch." The forests blessed them with a superabundance of berries and nuts. At first coffee and tea were unknown and later, when they proved expensive or unobtainable, were disdained as "slops" fit only for women and children.[14]

Three weapons conquered the Great Lakes Frontier: the ax, the rifle and the plow. With his ax the frontiersman cleared the forest and built his log cabin; with his rifle he protected himself and overcame his enemies; with his plow he cultivated his land and, in the first half of the nineteenth century, made the Great Lakes Frontier the breadbasket of America. No Dodge or Cassady fash-ioned his plow; no factory in Albion or South Bend produced its moldboard, landside and share. The moldboard had been a thriv-ing white oak with redoubtable qualities of length and strength, and the landside and share were products of the blacksmith's art.

To hold down this breaker with seven yokes of oxen was no sinecure. Beneath the surface a mass of interwoven and interlaced roots and grub conspired to thwart the plowman's triumphant march up and down the field. He had to exercise quick judgment and suppleness of motion to avoid the big roots of an oak or a walnut. With proper determination and purpose the share could easily cut through four or five inches of solid oak; but failure meant the uselessness of a second attempt. Then hands tugged furiously at the handles of the ensnared plow to the accompaniment of language less congenial than the usual "gee!" "haw!" and "giddap!" After this maddening experience harrowing was holiday fare. Drawn by two oxen the harrow with its inch-square teeth yanked out the loose grub and partially leveled the ground.[15]

Before the invention of McCormick's reaper the use of the crude and heavy cradle at harvest time required stamina and experience. In the hands of an immature boy it was an instrument of torture. A writer of pioneer life, A. C. Glidden, charmingly describes his escape from the odious task of cutting sandy clover:

The edge of the scythe and my strength both reached the vanishing point long before we reached the corner, and every stroke was a turn of the wheel to rack me with pain. I was positively gritty, but the grass had that quality in both the comparative and superlative degrees. I became an astronomer during that harvest season. The angle of the sun's rays was critically observed. The growing acuteness of the angles as the sun climbed toward the zenith interested me exceedingly. I could tell almost to a minute when the eleven o'clock angle was reached. There is no palliative for an aching side and an empty stomach like the study of astronomy on such an occasion. The eye may grovel toward the gritty grass, but the thoughts are busy with the calculus, to determine the position of the sun. One may hear some indistinct orders behind him about "pointing out," but the point above all others in which he is most interested is the one in the zenith. I have been interested in the study of conchology—have held shells to my ear and listened to the sounds of the sea murmuring within, but the sound of a conch shell calling to dinner in haying time, has been more captivating than those. I sometimes use a scythe now to mow mulleins, and through the influence of household importunity I occasionally mow the front yard, but I view the hanging of the scythe in the carriage house with a good deal more complacency than when I was swinging it through sandy clover.[16]

In the rich soil vegetables grew to unbelievable sizes. Farmers vied with one another in growing the largest vegetables and towns and states waged bitter vegetable wars which often degenerated into liars' clubs. Detroit proclaimed a twelve-inch turnip that weighed twenty-three pounds; Cleveland countered with a one hundred thirty-one-pound pumpkin and two cucumbers four and one-half feet long; and Vandalia, Illinois, seeing an opportunity to outshine the larger towns, boasted a beet nineteen and three-quarter inches in circumference, thirty-one inches long, and weighing nine and three-quarters pounds. Then Alton, Illinois, crushed all competition with a one hundred forty-three-pound pumpkin, a forty-pound muskmelon, and a patch of Rohan potatoes that averaged five hundred twelve bushels an acre.[17]

3

Every part of the sprawling Great Lakes Frontier had a number of ruffians who hung on the rim of civilization to trap and hunt and occasionally to fight Indians and make rude clearings in the forests. They came largely from the mountain regions of Tennessee, Kentucky and Virginia—warmhearted and generous fellows who when inflamed with drink became abusive, profane and obscene. Then they entertained a number of peculiar notions that impelled them to throw up their fists. To refuse an offered drink of whiskey or to offer to pay for food and lodging was to invite a fight. They demanded an apology or a fight with any reflection on their strength, physical courage, prowess or truthfulness; "and when the bottle was circulating freely among them the cause for offense multiplied in a sort of geometrical ratio."[18]

But they had a code of honor that governed their fights. Every man must "fit fa'rly," must forswear "unfa'r holts," and must cease fighting as soon as his antagonist cried " 'nuff." Then the fighters must shake hands, drink together and be friends. He who transgressed this code by disregarding the " 'nuff" or by using a knife during the fight fell into disgrace. Nevertheless, the code was far from unjust; it permitted the fighter such generous latitude as striking, gouging, biting, hair-pulling, scratching, kicking and even stamping on his fallen victim. These passages at arms usually occurred at militia musters, elections, public sales, shooting matches and, on Saturday afternoons, at grocery stores and coffee houses. The reward for pugilistic renown was often face lacerations, a bloody nose and black eyes swollen shut.[19]

The disposition to fight requires no difference of opinion. To a bully such effeminacies as neat clothing, correct speech and gentlemanly bearing were distasteful enough to give offense. With a stick he would draw a circle around himself and dare anybody to enter it; or he would load himself with whiskey and terrorize the town, profanely boasting that he could "whup" the best or all of the men in it, until somebody challenged him. Theoretically amenable to the law, these "disturbers of the peace and dignity of the State" paid heavy fines which went to the seminary fund of their respective counties. One bully boasted that he had paid enough in fines to support at least one corner of the seminary at Franklin in Johnson County, Indiana. Many of these rowdies would sell their land and move on as soon as their part of the state became settled enough to restrict their freedom. Sometimes, however, they stayed on to prove that under favorable circumstances their aggressive qualities were sources of strength to responsible citizenship.[20]

To the frontiersman the most popular of all sports were the shooting match, "goose pullings" and horse racing. The shooting match gave him an opportunity to demonstrate his skill with his long rifle—his inseparable companion that had provided him with meat, defended his home and protected him and his family. An added incentive to the shooting match was the possibility of winning such prizes as venison, beef, cornmeal or other provisions. The contestant would cock his gun, put his left foot forward, lower his head, throw back his shoulders, bend his knees and fire seventy-five to a hundred yards at a target which usually consisted of a board or the smooth surface of a tree marked with two or three circles around a bull's eye. His marksmanship served him well in military service.

Once a volunteer from Henry County, Indiana, applied for a place in a squad of sharpshooters that was being organized in camp. He claimed some experience with the old fashioned squirrel rifle. The officer asked: "Where did you have the experience, what did you shoot at and about what was your average success?" "Well," replied the volunteer innocently, "I hunted turkeys on Blue River in Henry County, Indiana. I can't tell how it averaged, but my wife always used to be about two weeks behind with her pickin.' "[21]

The requirements for a prize winner at a goose pulling were a dexterous hand and an insensate heart. A goose or gander with its neck well greased or soaped was nailed by its webbed feet to the top of a post or the stump of a small tree. The game required a horseman to grasp the fowl's head and tear it from its live and struggling body as he raced past.[22]

Horse racing was little more than reckless galloping on bumpy roads or in partially cleared fields. The prospects were better for broken limbs than for speed. A few gamblers exchanged some money for the skins of raccoons and other fur-bearing varmints. Some men settled their quarrels in accordance with the stringent code of the frontier.[23]

The majority of the frontiersmen preferred sports that offered relief from loneliness. Corn huskings attracted men and women of all ages to the designated barn, where they divided the corn in two equal piles and chose sides and leaders. Then, at a signal, flying hands attacked the ears of corn amid loud chatter and merriment. As a diversion they played a game known as "Brogue it about!" Sitting close together in a circle on the ground or floor, they drew up their knees to form a tunnel through which they passed a thimble or some other small object amid cries of "Brogue it about! Brogue it about!" One of them pounced on the person suspected of having the object, whereupon another from the opposite side pummeled him with it and then sent it "brogueing" on.[24]

In the newer villages of Indiana and Illinois young people held parties at which they danced quadrilles and jigs and, later, waltzes, schottishes, polkas and mazurkas. In places dominated by such religious groups as the Quakers and Disciples of Christ, who frowned on dances as activities that encouraged drinking and immorality, young couples entertained themselves with play parties or frolics in which they marched around as they sang in unison:

> We are marching down towards Old Quebec
>   Where the drums are loudly beating,
> The Americans have gained the day
>   And the British are retreating.
>
> The wars are o'er and we'll turn back
>   No more forever to be parted:
> We'll open the ring and choose a couple in
>   Because they are true-hearted.[25]

As they sang they marched around the room until they came to the line:
> We'll open the ring and choose a couple in

when they formed a circle around the entire room by joining hands. Then they bade one of the girls enter the circle and choose her partner from among those forming it. They chorused:

> Green grow the rushes, O!
> Kiss her quick and let her go!
> But don't you miss her ruffle, O!

The young man kissed her and left the circle. The play continued until the girls one by one were kissed out of the circle.

Then began a new play:

Oh I don't want none o' your weev'ly wheat,
 An' I don't want none o' your barley,
But I want some flour in half an hour
 To bake a cake for Charley.

Th' higher up th' cherry tree
 Th' sweeter grows th' cherry,
Th' more you hug and kiss a gal
 Th' more she wants t'marry!

Yes, Charley he's a fine young man,
 Oh Charley he's a dandy,
An' Charley is the very lad
 That et th' striped candy.

Grab her by th' lily-white hand
 An' lead her like a pigeon,
Make her dance th' Weevily Wheat
 An' lose all her religion!

Over th' river t' feed them sheep
 On buckwheat cakes an' barley,
We don't kear whut th' ol' folks says—
 Over th' river t' Charley.

Again each young man kissed his partner while his friends chorused:

Green grow the rushes, O!
Kiss her quick and let her go!
But don't you miss her ruffle, O!

At the next play the frolickers promenaded two by two around the room while one of the young men stood in the center of the floor. They sang:

The miller he lived close by the mill,
And the wheel went round without his will;
With a hand on the hopper and one in the bag
As the wheel goes round he cries out "grab!"

At the word "grab" the young man in the circle took one of the girls by the arm while her partner caught the arm of the girl ahead of him, and so on, until all of them made amusing confusion by taking one another's girl as they tramped around the room. The odd man entered the circle and continued the play or started a new one, as his friends wished.[26]

These frolics often started courtships that led to marriages. The girl would invite her young man to "beau her home" which, serving at once as parlor, living room, bedroom and kitchen for her family, was hardly conducive to ardent courtship; but love always found a way. In winters the lovers would sit by the fireplace where, says a frontier chronicler, "a tallow candle or greasy lamp would cast a faint sickly ray on the nervous swain as he shifted first one leg, then the other, over his knees and tried to keep up a conversation with the family group." When the girl was older than her brothers and sisters, she and her lover had to tolerate their winking, blinking and tittering until she sent them to bed. The quietude permitted the young man to ascertain how he stood with the girl's parents. If they approved of him, they would retire to permit him to make love and propose. If, on the contrary, they disapproved of him, they stayed up and sulked until midnight. If the girl wanted no more of him or was interested in another beau, she would persuade "pap" and "ma" to "sit him out" until a late hour. By this manner they politely informed him that "his room was better than his company."[27]

The young couples of those days enjoyed considerably less freedom of companionship and, in consequence, "less prolonged playing at love for amusement or experience" than those of a later period. The couple easily solved the economic problem of marriage and set the wedding day. The "invite" or "give-out" was usually composed by the local schoolmaster and was carried by the groomsman from house to house. Here is an invitation to a wedding in a backwoods community of southern Indiana:

Rev. Mr. Hilsbury asqr.,—you are pertikurly invited to atend the house of mr. Abrim Ashford asq. to injine upon [it] the yoke of konjegal mattrimunny with his dater miss Susan Ashford as was— thersday mornin next 10 aklok before dinner a.m.

        mr. Joseph Redden
        your humbell sarv't
        mr. William Welden, groomsman

p.s. don't say nuthin about this 'ere weddin that's to be—as its to be sekrit—and to morrer Billy Welden's goin to ride round and give the invites—and all your settlemint's to be axed.[28]

The "sekrit" soon became the common knowledge of the community, which gleefully anticipated several days of feasting and frolicking.

On the day of the wedding the bridegroom and his friends gathered at his father's house and journeyed on horseback toward the bride's house. When they approached it, two of them were chosen to "run for the bottle." The winner shared his trophy, usually corn whisky, with his friends as they completed their journey. The well-to-do bridegroom usually wore a tailor-made suit of English broadcloth with velvet collar and brass buttons. The average bridegroom appeared in homespun and new cowhide boots. The bride wore her mother's or aunt's wedding dress or one of calico or muslin and a bobinet cap, cotton stockings and kid slippers.[29]

In certain sections of the Great Lakes Frontier the bride-to-be rode to church on a pillion behind her father's saddle. After the marriage ceremony the pillion was removed and strapped behind the bridegroom's saddle. The couple then rode off on their honeymoon, which they enjoyed in the company of their friends. The wedding party, gathering in the cabin where the couple was to spend the night, prepared a feast that made the table reel "under the weight of roast beef, pork, and turkey, stacks of cakes, pies, and crullers, with corn and wheat bread, butter and home-made molasses—all plentifully interspersed with cabbage, beans, potatoes, baked custard, pickles, catsup and pepper-sauce."[30]

Sometimes the main dish was a gargantuan pot-pie which overwhelmed with its aroma of several kinds of meat. A frontier writer who attended one of these weddings described the pie as a "doughy sepulchre of at least six hens, two chanticleers, and four pullets" cooked with a half peck of onions in a large caldron. Around the pie were wild turkeys which had been so overcooked that the juices were evaporated and the flesh as dry as cork; "but by way of amends quarts of gravy," which moistened the "stuff'nin," were "judiciously emptied on our plates from the washbasin bowls." Our delighted chronicler continues:

But who can tell of the "sasses"? for we had "biled petaturs"!— and "smashed petaturs"! i.e. potatoes rolled into balls as big as marbles, and baked brown. And there were "bil'd ingins"!—"fried ingins"!—and "injins out of this here pie!" Yes, and beets of all known colours and unknown tastes!—all pickled in salt and vinegar and something else! And there were pickled cucumbers, as far as salt and water could go; and "punkun-butter"!—and "punkun-jelle"!—and corn bread in all its glory! . . .

In addition to all these matters tea and coffee were severally handed, while the girls in attendance asked each guest—"Do you take sweet'nin'?"[31]

After the meal the couple and the guests danced to the music of a fiddle or two. In the small hours of the morning the girls followed the bride to the loft of her cabin and put her to bed. When the girls descended the young men performed the same office for the bridegroom while they regaled him with jokes concerning the pleasures of procreation. At intervals the celebrants sent up food for the couple until the party broke up.[32]

The wedding provided a stranger with excellent opportunity to enjoy the charm of frontier speech. It was a blend of the English of the Elizabethan Age, which had survived among the Appalachian frontiersmen, and Scotch-Irish, German and Indian usages. The Great Lakes Frontiersman "heered" that his neighbor's "dater" was "acoming fursh in th' spring." He sometimes confused nouns and verbs: "That 'ar shoat'll meat th' hull fambly a month, easy." He boasted of his hunting prowess by claiming that at "bar hunts" he was "numerous." His "pap" was "as cross as a bar with two cubs and a sore tail." He was "pretty much in dainger" because his father "was down on him like the whole Missouri on a sandbar." He never "seed" his sister so "afeared" and "comfluttered" as when she saw a "copper sneck a-curlin' up" at her feet. He shot at a bear that went "lickety splittin' " down "th' holler." One of the girls in town was "high-ern a kite" with a "woodscolt" to an "ornery" and "pid-dlin' " schoolmaster. He didn't want to remain single too long. Even now he was "spunkin' up to an all-fired, tarnation, slick gal, clean grit, I tell yeou neow." He admitted he cared nothing for "tom-cattin' around;" he wanted to settle down and raise "a passel" of children.[33]

4

Of the numerous problems that beset the pioneer, that of maintaining his health was doubtless the most important. Doctors were few and far between, and the science of medicine was still in its infancy. The standard equipment of the average pioneer doctor consisted of a lancet, which was usually a kind of pocketknife with a small cleaver on the end of the blade, leeches, a few pills and tinctures which he himself compounded and some crude splints and bandages. More progressive doctors like Daniel Drake, who practiced in Cincinnati, used stethoscopes, tooth forceps and a few obstetrical instruments. The average doctor diagnosed diseases with his eyes, ears and nose. He saw scarlet fever and ague, heard pneumonia and tuberculosis and smelled typhoid fever and measles. Blood-letting was his usual method of treatment. His life was, needless to say, one of danger and privation. Sometimes he rode on his horse for four or five hours over a wide stretch of wilderness or a swamp or a swollen river before he arrived at the house of his patient. And he stayed for several hours, treating and consoling his patient and earning his admiration and gratitude. His fees were small and more often than not were paid in vegetables rather than in money.[34]

The most prevalent diseases of the frontier were the ague and its many varieties. The ague was so common on the frontier that it was regarded not as an illness but as an unpleasant concomitant of life: "He ain't sick, he's only got the ager." The better educated people used quinine to cure the hot spells and chills and unbearable aches and pains that symptomized the illness. The ignorant resorted to the superstition of wearing live spiders around their necks and drinking their own urine. Home remedies for ague included wine mixed with two teaspoonsful of a strong tea made from the bark of a fir and a yellow birch, a strong decoction of white ash bark and a brew of mullein and sassafras roots. One eminent physician prescribed three large pills made of cobwebs. Another popular specific for ague, especially if it seemed to be developing into pneumonia, was calomel, that panacea of a hundred frontier ills:

> Then Calomel, you great deliverer! come;
> Purge from my eye this ochre hue,
> And clear my head again;
> Make me benevolent and true
> And just to other men;
> And the first worthy deed I do
> I'll own, O Calomel! my virtue is from you.[35]

Another prominent physician, Anthony Hunn of Kentucky, frowned on calomel as causing teeth to rot and fall out and the bones of the upper jaw to fall out in the form of horse shoes. One of his numerous followers condemned the drug in skipping quatrains:

Physicians of my former choice
Receive my counsel and advice
Be not offended though I tell
The dire effects of Calomel.

And when I must Resign my breath
Pray let me die a natural death
And bid you all a long farewell
Without one dose of Calomel.[36]

During the summer months many people contracted diarrhea, cholera morbus, flux and bilious fevers supposedly caused by thundering and lightning and heavy rainfalls. Doctors confused typhoid fever with typhus or regarded them as one disease and blamed them on putrid vegetable and animal matter in the night air, green apples and grapes, worry, fear and lack of sleep. Dr. Drake thought that typhoid fever and typhus were two diseases but that the first led to the other if the patient was not bled in its early stages. On the contrary, averred Dr. Benezet—the use of the lancet was certain to result in instant death.[37]

A disease that attacked humans as well as animals was what the pioneers called "milk sick," "sick stomach," "the trembles," "the slows" or "the puking fever." None of the standard specifics, not even the miraculous calomel, could deliver the victim from the clutches of death. What caused it? Some doctors blamed the polluted streams and marshes; others pointed to vegetable poisons conveyed through milk or flesh of domestic animals. At times the disease depopulated whole villages and towns and drove the citizens of neighboring settlements to regions which they believed enjoyed more salubrious climate.[38]

Among other prevalent diseases were measles, pneumonia or "lung fever," erysipelas or "St. Anthony's Fire" and the croup or "the bold hives." If your child had the measles you gave him "nanny tea," a decoction of sheep dung dissolved in hot water. The prescription for pneumonia was the same as that of any cough: large quantities of a syrup consisting principally of spikenard and elecompane. If this failed to cure the victim, his or her kinfolk had recourse to choruses and incantations. The superstitious cured erysipelas by drinking the blood of a black cat. The scarcity of black cats with whole ears and tails attested to the wide practice of this superstition. If your child had the croup, you gave him the juice of roasted onions or garlic. If that failed to break his fever, you sweated him with a dose of Virginia snake oil. If you had faith in the efficacy of the Pennsylvania German theory, you added the physic of a half pint of white walnut bark which had been peeled downward. If your child needed to vomit, you gave him the same amount of white walnut bark which had been peeled upward.[39]

Constipation and worms were eternal frontier complaints. Dr. Tissot's prescription for constipation depended on the degree of its obduracy. For cases liable to persuasion he recommended the rather mild specific of twenty ivy leaves and three sprigs of hysop boiled in one pint of skim milk and a half pint of beer. More stubborn cases, however, needed more drastic cures: a cow heel, two quarts of milk, nine ounces of hartshorn shavings, two ounces of isinglass, one-fourth pound of sugar candy and a trace of ginger that had been left to cool in a pot. For desperate cases Dr. Tissot prescribed milk from the breast of healthy women, apples, apple juice sharpened with lemon juice, cider whey, barley water and water gruel mixed with fine flour.[40]

Needless to say, lack of sanitation was responsible for many frontier diseases. Swarms of houseflies descended on outhouses and manure piles and then invaded kitchens and milk houses, falling into pails of milk and cream, covering dried fruit, molasses, bread, butter and cheese, and congregating noisily on the mouths of sleeping children. Cockroaches and red ants marched impudently across tables, beds and chairs and over meat plates, proving "tarnation spry" to merciless blows from knives and spoons and switches of branches and leaves or dusters of paper strips. Chickens, ducks, geese, cats and dogs fraternized in yards and on porches and sometimes wandered into cabins, leaving malodorous evidence of their visits on floors, chairs and tables. Rats and mice invaded cabins and barns in unconquerable numbers, biting men, women and children as well as domestic animals and filling women with dread or anger.[41] The Pied Piper cheated destiny by confining his activities to Hamlin Town.

Frontier superstitions seemed as numerous as varmits. Their hold on frontier society started at the cradle and ended at the grave. A baby whose face was washed in his baptismal water was certain to grow handsome, but his mother doomed him to the life of a thief if she cut his nails before he was nine months old. A child was immune to snake bite until he was seven years old; if he were bitten after that age he could draw out the poison by tying a toad around his neck—provided he disdained strong drink and gunpowder. One warded off the croup by wearing around his neck the front right foot of a mole tied to a black thread. To safeguard against epilepsy you ate a rattlesnake's heart or slept over a cow barn or passed three times through a split shellbark hickory. If the tree healed and grew you were certain to recover. You cured earache by inserting into your ear the kinkiest hair you could find from a Negro's head or oil from a weasel's ears—providing the animal was of the same sex as yourself. You cured a cold by wearing a wool stocking around your neck; mumps, by rubbing the swelling against a pig trough; wounds and injuries, by carrying a wolf's right eye inside the right sleeve of your coat. Cobwebs and horse manure usually stopped excessive bleeding; if it continued, shift your pocketknife from one pocket to the other while you chanted: "Christ's wounds were never bound." Did you suffer from rheumatism? Relieve it by carrying buckeyes or potatoes in your pocket. Did you want to relieve a chronic cough? Eat from a blue dish, catch a live fish, thrust it down your throat and then throw it back into the water. Or you could wear around your neck a spider sewed in a thimble. Asafetida or catnip or calomel or a bag of camphor around your neck protected you against contageous diseases.[42]

5

The Ordinance of 1787 encouraged education as well as religion. But the building of public schools was left to the state legislatures, which for half a century were too poor to appropriate the necessary funds. Many pioneers, too, regarded education or learning with suspicion. Their attitude toward public instruction in particular and learning in general depended on the degree of their understanding. Some of them looked on learned men as crafty, unpatriotic, irreligious or immoral; some thought them snobbish, pretentious or unsociable; some were jealous of them. The Pennsylvania Germans and the Quakers frowned on public schools for financial and religious reasons, while the "frontier aristocracy," which often pressured state legislatures, regarded any "booklarnin'" beyond the three R's as engendering a social equality that would eventually deprive them of their influence. But the great majority of the Great Lakes frontiersmen wanted their children to enjoy the educational advantages of which they themselves had been deprived. They eventually established a free school system long before their fellow countrymen in Massachusetts and New York. A then little-known lawyer from Illinois who signed his papers and letters "A. Lincoln" expressed their aspirations with these words:

. . . I can only say that I view it as the most important subject that we as a people can be engaged in. That every man may receive at least a moderate education and thereby be enabled to read the histories of his own and other countries, by which he may duly appreciate the value of our free institutions, appears to be an object of vital importance.[43]

The great poverty of the Great Lakes frontiersmen is the principal explanation for their failure to provide public schools. But they provided what schools they could afford. The first school in the Great Lakes Frontier was the blockhouse of the garrison at Marietta, in the present state of Ohio, and the first teacher was Major Austin Tupper, General Benjamin Tupper's oldest son. In those days few houses were built to serve exclusively as schools; often a cabin, a barn, a porch or a blacksmith shop sufficed for the purpose. The earliest schoolhouses were the cheapest and plainest log cabins. One of such schools in Jackson County, Indiana, had neither floor nor chimney nor window. Much later schoolhouses enjoyed the luxury of the paper covering that served as a windowpane and that owed its translucence to a generous supply of hog's lard or bear's oil. On cold days a fire blazed on a raised clay platform or hearth, sending sparks and smoke up through a large opening in the roof. This opening also provided light by which the children studied their lessons as they sat next to the walls and faced the center on benches made of split logs. No plane had ever touched those benches. The bad boys lined the seats of their pantaloons with large pieces of buckskin for protection, more from their splintery benches than from their teacher's ferule. The girls doubtless resigned themselves to the vulnerable features of the dress—a costume designed by thoughtless tradition.[44]

Some of the early schools in Ohio and Indiana were equipped with portholes from which the schoolmaster and the older boys could shoot at possible hostile Indians. We have no record that any school was beleaguered while it was in session nor that any schoolmaster brought his rifle to defend his charges in case of attack; but then posterity wisely records few of the specific acts of man.[45]

Children often had to walk to school three or four miles or more through forest and cleared fields. During the early autumn months this excursion afforded endless delight. The path on which the children walked was covered with rustling leaves and serpentined over hill and through hollow past a wonderland of color and fragrance and innocent wild life. But the autumnal rains soon converted forest and cleared fields into quagmires that often swallowed up many of the children's only shoes. Boots for boys and booties for girls were as yet unknown. When winter blanketed the countryside with snow, many boys and girls drew stockings or pieces of cloth over their ankles to keep it out of their shoes. From the hard frosts of November to the ice storms of February boys and girls attended school with their feet encased in socks or stockings badly worn at the heel or toe. In 1825 a pioneer writer, Sanford Cox, often saw the boys and girls of Lafayette, Indiana, skating on ice, some with shoes, some barefooted. This should occasion no surprise. Some pioneer youngsters had gone barefooted so long that their feet had become hardened and calloused enough to resist any degree of cold. They could walk for a considerable distance over the snow and ice without suffering more than they bore with reasonable fortitude. If a boy's duties demanded prolonged exposure, however, he would stand for a few minutes on a heated block of wood, which he called his "stove," and then make a dash for the schoolhouse. Sometimes he substituted a flat, light piece of rock which retained the heat much longer than did wood.[46]

The general incompetence of frontier teachers was a problem that remained unsolved for many years. The average teacher of the Great Lakes Frontier was an adventurer from the East or from England, Scotland or Ireland who sought temporary employment during winter while he waited an opening in business. The pioneers held him in slight esteem, not because he was a teacher, but because he did not labor with his hands. He was often a homeless fellow who did much hunting while he roamed from place to place in search of work. Whenever he heard of a good teaching prospect, he would write an article of agreement in which he promised to teach for a quarter of a school year at so much per scholar. Thus many incompetent men taught school. The ability to teach reading, writing and arithmetic was all that was required of them. The teacher who could "cipher" all the sums in the most popular text of the time, Pike's Arithmetic, up to and including the rule of three, was considered a mathematician of no mean ability.[47]

The wages paid to the average pioneer teacher were so low that they brought little respect to his profession. One of the shortsighted aspects of American life has been the low salaries paid for all manner of intellectual pursuit. John M. Harney, who subsequently became famous as the editor of the *Louisville Democrat*, walked all the way from Oxford, Ohio, to the State Seminary—now Indiana University—at Bloomington to accept the chair of mathematics at $250 a year. Early in the nineteenth century schoolmasters in Ohio, Indiana and Michigan taught school at $1 per scholar. Sometimes they realized as much as $6, out of which sum they paid $1 for their board. Some of the teachers were young women. Lois Ann Gear received 75¢ per scholar and later $1 per scholar for teaching in one of the best schools of the Western Reserve.[48]

The school terms were usually called "quarters" and were of two kinds: the long quarter of thirteen weeks and the short quarter of twelve weeks. Many of the teachers were physically handicapped. Over a period of five years one school in Jackson County, Indiana, employed a one-eyed teacher, a lame teacher, an epileptic teacher, a teacher who educated himself for the ministry only to abandon it for alcohol and a teacher who "got drunk on Saturday and whipped the entire school on Monday." Uneducated pioneers could easily find justification for their notion that a man turned to teaching only when he found he could do nothing else. One man, a liquor salesman, became a teacher when he grew too fat to conduct his business successfully. Another was described as "a rude, eccentric individual who lived alone and gained a subsistence by hunting, trapping, and trading." Still another was an alcoholic who drank during school hours. He carried the bottle with him but he had enough respect for his profession to refrain from taking it into the schoolhouse. He hid it outside. One day two of his pupils stole it and drank its contents—a feat that made them sick and earned them a severe thrashing to boot. One Thomas Ayres, who taught in Switzerland County, Indiana, regularly took an afternoon nap during school hours "while his pupils were supposed to be preparing their lessons, but in reality were amusing themselves by catching flies and tossing them into his open mouth." One early schoolmaster of Detroit had been a sailor who loved to take his charges into the woods to roast potatoes. Another eternally hungry teacher cracked hickory nuts between recitations on one of the puncheon benches of the school. A fiddler named Owen Davis conducted one of the so-called "loud" schools. While his pupils spelled and read at the top of their voices he found comfort by fiddling zestfully such popular airs of the day as "Old Zip Coon" and "The Devil's Dream." One pupil repeated the word "heptorpy" from morning until noon and from noon until evening to impress his teacher with his diligence.[49]

The prevailing sentiment favored frequent use of the rod. Parents regarded the schoolmaster who neglected to whip his charges as a failure. One morning the father of a pupil named Sam bluntly told the schoolmaster he was making a grave mistake:

"You're not whipping anybody."

"Why, who'll I whip?"

"Whip Sam."

"What for? He's lazy, but I can't whip him for laziness, can I?"

"Yes, give it to him. Sam's my boy and I know he needs it every day."[50]

Conscientious teachers were dedicated to discipline—especially during the devotions that opened the school day. One morning an old teacher who had been married and widowed by turns was occupied in writing a love letter. When his pupils came in he carelessly left the half-written letter on his desk and proceeded to open school with a prayer. Kneeling down he prayed with his whip in his right hand and his right eye open. One of the boys stole up to the desk and began to read the letter. The old man broke off in the middle of a sentence and gave the culprit a sound thrashing. Then with grave equanimity he resumed his devotions.[51]

School books were as scarce as money. In his illuminating essays on school life in frontier Indiana, Judge D. D. Banta wrote that all the books of his neighborhood could be packed in a bushel basket. The contents, however, far outweighed the paper. The titles included the Bible, *Robinson Crusoe, Gulliver's Travels, The Pilgrim's Progress*, and Josephus' *Antiquities of the Jews* and *Wars of the Jews*. Schoolmasters emphasized spelling and reading above all other subjects. Noah Webster's spelling book, which every school child was expected to own, also contained reading matter consisting of moral lessons: correct spelling and reading enhanced correct living. When the school child had learned to spell sufficiently well, he was required to pronounce the words in the book at first sight. After he had read the elementary speller several times, he passed to another book—if he could find one. In 1836 William Holmes McGuffey published in Cincinnati his *First Reader*, which took and held the field against all other competitors for several generations. This unique reader proved of incalculable benefit to the Great Lakes frontiersmen. More than any other book it was responsible for acquainting them with such authors as Bryan, Whittier, Longfellow, Hawthorne, Irving and many others.[52]

The pupil's next task was to learn to write. His mother usually made his copy-book by sewing a few sheets of foolscap together, his pen from a goose quill, his ink from maple bark, sumac or acorns and vinegar and his inkstand from a cow's horn sawed off and fitted with a wooden watertight bottom. His first exercises were "pot hooks and hangers"; but eventually he evolved a neat, round-hand copy resounding with patriotic or moral precepts, such as: "Commandments ten God gave to men"; "Eternal vigilance is the price of liberty"; "George Washington was the father of his country"; and "Evil communications corrupt good manners."[53]

In arithmetic class you never recited—you merely "ciphered." And you found the rules in your arithmetic book as clear as mud: "Take for the first dividend as few of the left hand figures of the dividend as will contain the divisor, try how often they will contain it, and set the number of times on the right of the dividend, etc." Eventually Alexander Ray came to the rescue of American school children by publishing an arithmetic text that was both graphic and clear. It quickly supplanted all other arithmetic texts.[54]

Such were frontier schools. Some of the students went from them to the numerous regional academies, where they were exposed to such subjects as Greek, Latin, Spanish, French, Italian, logic, philosophy, English literature, geography and astronomy. History, alas, was not as yet an academic study. The academies in turn served as preparatory schools for the few local universities, which were then in the toddling stages of their careers toward the renown they later achieved as among the finest institutions in the country.[55]

6

The Ohio River was the great natural highway of the Great Lakes Frontier. As the only important navigable river flowing westward in eastern North America, its usefulness to the development of the American frontier was incalculable: to the early hunters, traders and explorers it was what the Wilderness Trail had been to Daniel Boone and his followers; to George Rogers Clark and Anthony Wayne it was the military road on which they advanced with their men to conquer the frontier for white settlement; to the frontiersmen who came after the Indian wars it was a broad and smooth avenue to the promised land. It carried their meager belongings to their new homes and started at least three of the states in the Great Lakes Frontier on their march to statehood.

The explorers came in canoes, the soldiers on rafts or flatboats known as "broadhorns" and the settlers in keelboats made in boating yards along the Monongahela river towns of Morgantown, in present West Virginia, and of Brownsville, Elizabeth and Pittsburgh, Pennsylvania. For the first two decades of the nineteenth century the keelboat, which derived its name from the longitudinal timber that gave it rigidity as well as protection against accidents, ruled the western rivers, carrying numerous passengers and as much as fifty tons of freight including flour, salt, pork, barrel staves made in the oak forests of Indiana, pottery, bricks, wheels, cider, peach brandy, molasses, sugar, coffee and hides up and down the Ohio from Pittsburgh to the Mississippi. Manned by rough, ribald and tanned men who had served in the slackening fur trade or in Indian wars, the keelboat floated rapidly downstream; but its struggle against the current was almost Homeric. Then all hands lined either side of it with poles thrust against their shoulders and set or lifted them with grueling toil as it inched upstream. Sometimes, when the river was too deep for poling, the crew would swim ashore with a cordelle and apply all their strength to coax the reluctant vessel forward.[56]

The keelboat succumbed to progress. In 1811, four years after Robert Fulton launched his *Clermont* on the Hudson, Nicholas J. Roosevelt and his associates built at Pittsburgh a steamboat named *New Orleans* in honor of its destination three thousand miles away. Painted sky blue and equipped with a jutting bowsprit, it presented an awesome spectacle as its magnificent length of one hundred thirty-eight feet with a beam of twenty-six and one-half feet dwarfed the motley sails and keelboats along the Ohio and trailed woodsmoke down the river at eight miles per hour. At Cincinnati and again at Louisville it stopped to replenish its wood supply, while men, women and children trooped aboard to gaze in amazement at its mysterious machinery and to visit Roosevelt and his wife, baby and Newfoundland dog. The steamer waited for high water and then successfully ran the falls as farmers gathered along the river-banks and confidently expected it to blow up at any moment. It passed on to Cairo and the Mississippi and eventually arrived at New Orleans, where it remained based for two years and engaged in carrying rich cargoes to Natchez in water free from the perils of the snag-infested Ohio.[57]

Other steamers soon appeared on the Ohio. Among them was the *Enterprise* under Henry M. Shreve. It reached New Orleans just in time to help Andrew Jackson win the greatest American victory in the War of 1812 and then returned to Louisville, silencing scoffers by braving the currents of the Mississippi in twenty-five days. Then Shreve built the *Washington*, a palatial double-decker with a shallow draft made possible by the use of a high pressure engine with horizontal cylinders. After some difficulty with Fulton and his associates, who claimed a monopoly of navigation on the Mississippi, Shreve returned upstream to make another trip from Louisville to New Orleans in forty-one days. In the next twenty years two hundred steamers plied rivers of the Great Lakes Frontier, opening up a number of river ports and bringing prosperity to industrious farmers. The technical improvements that expedited traffic and the highly competitive system that resulted from private ownership of the steamers caused a drastic reduction in freight rates. In keelboat days the rate between New Orleans and Louisville was $5 per hundred pounds. By 1820 it had fallen to $2 and within twenty years to 20¢ per hundred pounds.[58]

The steamboat, however, failed to solve the marketing problem of the booming frontier. It was unable to accommodate the interior expanses and it was limited in navigation to the high-water periods that accompanied the spring and fall floods. The result was that in one part of the year goods glutted the markets and brought ruinous low prices, while in another part they spoiled before they could reach the south on the crest of the spring floods.[59]

No more adequate were the few and bumpy roads. Even the Old National Road—now Route 40—which started at Cumberland, Maryland, in 1811, reached Wheeling, in present West Virginia, in 1818 and pushed on to Columbus and Indianapolis in the next two decades—could carry only a small portion of frontier trade. In 1825 its total traffic amounted to only forty thousand tons. At the same time steamboats carried to the South more than one million five hundred thousand bushels of wheat and corn.[60]

Some other means of transportation must be devised, and devised quickly, to accommodate frontier prosperity. In 1825 Governor De Witt Clinton of New York furnished a solution to frontier trade when he completed the Erie Canal from Albany to Buffalo. It reduced the time of conveyance between Buffalo and New York City from twenty to eight days. It lowered freight charges from $100 a ton to $25 and then to $15. All along its route it revived business and raised the value of property. Eventually it made New York City the greatest commercial center of the United States.[61]

In this new means of transportation Ohio as well as other regions of the Great Lakes Frontier found the solution to their commercial problem. The merchants and farmers of Ohio hailed the Erie Canal with wild enthusiasm; they demanded canals of their own. Bowing to their wishes, the state legislature in February 1825 authorized two canals: the Ohio and Erie from Portsmouth on the Ohio to

Cleveland by way of the Scioto, Muskingum and Cuyahoga rivers; and the Miami and Erie Canal from Cincinnati to Toledo by way of the Great Miami, Auglaize and Maumee rivers. On July 4, Ohio's twenty-first birthday, Governor De Witt Clinton and Governor Jeremiah Morrow of Ohio met at Cleveland and journeyed to near Newark, where, before a concourse of ten thousand people and amid martial music and marching troops and rhapsodic oratory, each of the two officials dug a spade of earth. And the great ditch began to yawn before mule teams straining with scoop buckets and tireless Irish crews with mattocks and shovels. Three weeks later the governors repeated the ceremony at Middletown, in western Ohio, as they inaugurated construction of the Miami and Erie Canal. Soon the canal fever spread to Indiana, Illinois and Wisconsin, summoning construction crews that cut the familiar forty-foot ditches, edged with berm and towpath, through swamps, forests and prairies of those regions.[62]

The Erie and Ohio Canal opened in 1833 and the Erie and Miami in 1845. By this time canals were bowing out and railroads were bowing in. In the same year that the Erie and Ohio Canal was completed, Michigan Territory chartered the first railroad in the Great Lakes Frontier. Its route started at Toledo, which was then believed to lie in Michigan Territory, and ran for thirty-three miles to the market town of Adrian. Horses drew its cars on oak rails until 1837. Then the famous "No. 80" of the Baldwin Locomotive Works, thundering on rails capped with strap iron, created a national sensation by pulling three cars at the incredible speed of twenty miles an hour! In the same year the railroad inaugurated its passenger coach or "Pleasure Car," which contained a lower middle compartment for freight and two end compartments, each of which could seat eight persons. Its benches ran along each side and its door opened, often impulsively, to the ground. Being top heavy, it was as much off the rails as on. This luxurious conveyance imposed on the railroad a heavy expense which it attempted to defray by increasing its fare for the trip from $1.50 to $2.25.[63]

In time coaches became higher and longer. The next decade saw double-decker cars. The seats of the upper deck were reserved for women and were covered with sheepskin to soften the jars and jerks and jolts of their journey. Twenty-horsepower engines manned by a fireman and an engineer usually pulled a half dozen freight cars, each of which could hold about two tons of merchandise. At intervals of five or six miles the train would stop to replenish its wood supply from the forest and its water supply from the ditches.[64]

At this time Ohio, Indiana, Illinois and Michigan chartered a number of railroads. Some of them never progressed beyond the paper stage; only about a half dozen had any considerable mileage at the time of the admission of Wisconsin, which closes this book. Of these perhaps the most ambitious was the railroad that the merchants of Sandusky planned to build from Lake Erie to the Ohio River. Surveyors laid the right of way and grading crews built up the roadbeds and laid the tracks from Sandusky to Bellevue, a distance of sixteen miles. This segment of the railroad, known as the Mad River and Lake Erie Line, was hailed in eastern business and financial circles as a major economic project; famous people such as Ralph Waldo Emerson eagerly invested in it. In 1839 it made its first run with four cars carrying one hundred fifty "ladies and gentlemen" at such speed—twenty to fifty miles an hour—that the animals along the way fled in terror. The speed of the railroad, however, was somewhat more spectacular than that of the train. It took another nine years to advance to Springfield on the Mad River. This bold railroad was not bold enough; like all north-south railroads of that period, it lost money because it was regarded as an adjunct to waterborne commerce and built its line to connect water routes. Not until the next decade, when railroads began to run independently of water routes in an east-west direction, did they grow rich and powerful.[65]

7

The Great Lakes Frontier was the logical ground for the propagation of the religions that were first nurtured in the older Appalachian Frontier across the Ohio. Here the Methodists and Baptists continued the revivals introduced by the Presbyterians. These three were the most important Protestant denominations in the Great Lakes Frontier. The Methodists were the most numerous and the Presbyterians the most active in financing missions and fostering education. The latter early established churches in Cincinnati, Chillicothe, Dayton, Springfield and Columbus. In 1801 they increased greatly their prestige in the Great Lakes Frontier by adopting the Plan of Union, which joined them to the Congregationalists for the purpose of promoting "mutual forbearance, and a spirit of accommodation." The Plan, introduced in the previous year by Jonathan Edwards the Younger in the Connecticut General Association, afforded an opportunity to Congregationalist and Presbyterian settlers of a new community to form a single congregation under a pastor belonging to either denomination. It also enabled a predominantly Congregationalist or a predominantly Presbyterian congregation to form a church discipline in accordance with its wishes, regardless of the religion of its pastor. Any disagreements between pastor and congregation were to be referred to the presbytery or association of which the pastor was a member, or, if more agreeable, to a committee composed of an equal number of Congregationalists and Presbyterians.[66]

The Plan enabled the two groups to adopt a strong missionary program. While the Congregationalist ministers worked among the Indians, the Presbyterian ministers tried with difficulty to bring sinful or indifferent frontiersmen back to Christian living. The renumeration for their indefatigable labors sustained their souls more than their bodies. One minister's salary was $150, of which, however, he received just $17 in cash; another spent $100 more than his promised salary in discharging his ministerial duties; still another was grateful that he ate well and slept comfortably but complained that he received "not a dollar in money." Many Presbyterian ministers remained with their congregations only because they were married to frontier women.[67]

The most successful religion in the Great Lakes Frontier was Methodism. The democratic nature of its government, its doctrine of free will and free grace as opposed to that of limited grace and predestination practiced by Calvinistic Presbyterians and its stress on the close relationship between God and man provided great comfort to such people as the pioneers, who lived remote from human contacts and who prized individual responsibility above all earthly possessions. The circuit riders never overlooked these preachments, even amid the screaming, yapping and jerking of the camp meetings.[68]

The Methodist Church owed part of its success to the fact that its ministers came from the same class as their flocks. They understood better than did the preachers of other faiths the habits, feelings and prejudices of the pioneers. In one of his interminable sermons that prince of Indiana preachers, John Strange, disdained the eloquence taught in seminaries:

My Alma Mater was Brush College, more ancient, though less pretentious, than Yale, Harvard, or Princeton. Here I graduated, and I love her memory still. Her academic groves are the boundless forests and prairies of these Western wilds; her Pierian springs are the gushing fountains from the rocks and mountain fastnesses; her

Arcadian groves and Orphic songs are the wildwoods, and the birds of every color and every song, relieved now and then with the bass hootings of the night owl and the weird treble of the whippoorwill; her curriculum is the philosophy of nature and the mysteries of redemption; her library is the word of God, the Discipline, the hymn book, supplemented with trees and brooks and stones, all of which are full of wisdom and sermons and speeches; and her parchments of literary honors are the horse and the saddlebags.[69]

The Baptist minister, too, disdained seminary learning. He was usually a simple farmer who worked on his land nearly every day in the week, for he believed that as an agent of God he should come from the people and should, like them, pursue some secular occupation. God, he believed, called him to preach His word; his church then gave him an opportunity to "exercise his gifts," which, if acceptable, enabled him to become a licensed preacher. At first he usually had no congregation; he traveled hither and yon, preaching in the cabins of the settlers until he received a congregation and took an examination before a council of brethren, which ordained him "by prayer and the laying on of the hands of the eldership."[70]

The first Baptists in the Great Lakes Frontier came from New York and New Jersey and settled in Cincinnati, where they organized the Miami Association in 1797. In the next fifteen years these zealous champions of separation of church and state organized three more associations in Ohio with some sixty churches and twenty-four hundred members. By this time their influence had spread to Indiana and Illinois.[71]

The Baptist ministers were no sycophants; they practiced what they preached. Their record show that they assiduously and successfully policed the morals of their congregations. Malicious gossiping, cheating, lying, fighting, drinking, gambling, whoring and horse racing—all were punished with severe penalties. The Baptists, like the Quakers, despised slavery; their influence in Indiana resulted in her admission as a free state. The "Hardshell" or Antimission Baptists frowned on missionary work and found justification for their stand in the Bible. They argued that God as the author of mankind needed no assistance to bring the faithful to the fold. The faithful were already saved, while the faithless were doomed to eternal damnation regardless of preaching. The "Two-Seed" Baptists were the followers of Daniel Parker, who preached that Adam and Eve were created from the good seed, or the divine spirit, but that the serpent, after it caused the fall of man, had planted its seed in every woman. Those born of the original or good seed were children of God and would, after their death, dwell blissfully in celestial mansions; those born of the second seed were children of the serpent or the devil and would descend into hell. No amount of preaching or missionary work could save them.[72]

An interesting sect that flourished for a time in the Great Lakes Frontier were the Shakers, who called themselves the United Society of Believers. This communistic sect originated in England in the middle of the eighteenth century. In 1774 Ann Lee, or "Mother Ann," as she was called by her followers, brought it to New York, where she formed several small communities. Among converts from Presbyterianism were Richard McNemar, John Dunlavy and Matthew Houston who became leaders of Shakerism in Kentucky and Ohio. About 1805 Malcolm Worley founded the main Shaker settlement at Union Village, near Lebanon, Ohio, whence the sect spread to Shaker Heights, Ohio, and to Busseron Creek, a few miles above Vincennes, Indiana.[73]

The Shakers derived their name from the wiggling, hand clapping and marching that characterized their religious ceremonies. Inspired by passages in Jeremiah and in Psalms, they believed that dancing was the original mode of worship of God's ancient people and that, therefore, they were fulfilling ancient prophecies by restoring it. They eschewed pork as unwholesome and rejected politics, military service, learning, literature and amusement. They held that God is dual—male and female, father and mother—and that this principle is manifest in the vegetable as well as in the animal kingdom. They found justification for this belief in the Book of Genesis: "So God created man in His own image; in the image of God created He him; male and female created He them." God's first appearance on earth as a man was in the form of Jesus; as a woman, in the form of Ann Lee, founder of the Shaker faith. Mankind was composed of two orders: the rudimental or Adamic order, which included all married people, and the spiritual order, which consisted of people required to keep the "higher law" of living in strict celibacy. In the Adamic order the sexual act should be devoid of loveplay, be as short as possible and be performed only to produce offsprings. The Shakers clearly regarded marriage, not as a Christian institution, but as a civil right; they abstained from it in imitation of Christ and his Apostles. This shortsighted creed spelled their utter decline: in the Great Lakes Frontier they never counted their members above two thousand.[74]

The Shakers in Indiana maintained peaceful relations with the

Indians under the Prophet. They sent the Shawnee high priest a grindstone "which will be of help to you in sharpening your axes and hoes, that you may work easier, and we have sent you fifty bushels of wheat and Rye, three bushels of Salt and some meat." They assured the Indians that "we love you because the work of the good spirit which is among you & among us is all one—to make us all one good people—children of the good spirit—All brothers of one family, united to the good spirit above." Having suffered persecution at the hands of their fellow Christians, they could well sympathize with the ideals of the Prophet and his followers: "Brothers, we do not think strange if some people call the work of the good spirit which is among you foolishness and nonsense—it is because they do not understand it."[75]

The democratic atmosphere of the Great Lakes Frontier proved congenial spawning ground for a number of American creeds, some of which proved ephemeral and some of which took firm root and prospered. Among the latter were the Disciples of Christ. The founder of this faith was Thomas Campbell, who had served as a minister of the Scotch-Irish Anti-Burgher or ultra-conservative group of Presbyterians and had conducted a school in County Armagh, Ireland. Leaving his brilliant son Alexander in charge of the school, in 1807 Thomas Campbell migrated to America in search of his health. At Philadelphia, where he landed, the Anti-Burgher Synod admitted him and sent him to the Presbytery of Chartiers at the village of Washington, in western Pennsylvania. There he could not subscribe to the narrow ruling of the Philadelphia synod that prohibited "occasional communion"; that is, communion with other groups of Christians. Believing in the unity of Christ's followers and finding this view especially applicable to frontier conditions of western Pennsylvania, Campbell delivered a sermon in which he lamented existing divisions among Christians and, resolving to practice what he preached, invited everyone of his hearers, irrespective of his or her religious affiliation, to enjoy the approaching privilege of the Lord's Supper. This offended his colleagues; they became his enemies; despite his willingness to submit to their wishes, they misrepresented and calumniated him in their endeavor to discredit him in the eyes of his congregation. At last he could tolerate bigotry and tyranny no longer. He left the Anti-Burgher group of Presbyterians and became an independent preacher.[76]

In barns, groves and houses he gathered those few who had placed themselves under his spiritual care. Under his commanding personality and spiritual warmth his followers soon grew so numerous that he deemed the time ripe for a declaration of his religious platform. He called a special meeting at an old farmhouse in the neighborhood and there read to his followers his famous principle: "Where the Scriptures speak, we speak; where they are silent, we are silent." This became the watchword of the Disciples of Christ.[77]

In September 1809 "the Christian Association of Washington," as Campbell's followers called themselves, adopted his "Declaration and Address," which embodied their religious principles. This declared that they took "the Divine Word alone for our rule; the Holy Spirit for our teacher and guide, to lead us into all truth; and Christ alone, as exhibited in the Word, for our salvation; that by so doing, we may be at peace among ourselves, follow peace with all men, and holiness, without which no man shall see the Lord."[78]

Yet Campbell had no desire to form a new religion. He still hoped that all Christians might unite on the broad platform of the Scriptures. Supported by his son Alexander, who had just arrived in America, he applied for admission to the Presbyterian Synod of Pittsburgh, which promptly refused it. Forthwith Campbell organized the Christian Association into the Brush Run Church in which he served as elder and his son as preacher. The new church soon decided that infant baptism conflicted with its principles; instead it adopted immersion as the only form of baptism described in the Scriptures. This greatly pleased the Redstone Baptist Association, which invited the Brush Run Church to join it. Though Campbell pointed out to the Baptists that his church did not see eye to eye with their views in regard to the Lord's Supper and baptism, he eventually united with them.[79]

For the next seventeen years the Disciples of Christ were nominally Baptists. During this time Alexander Campbell, who had been spending much of his time establishing and conducting Buffalo Seminary at Bethany, in present West Virginia, gradually assumed leadership of the sect as his father grew older and more infirm. Now Alexander became increasingly active in propagating his views, especially among the Baptists. His followers, who called themselves "Reformers," advocated the restoration of Christianity to its pristine purity. In 1823 he founded a journal, *The Christian Baptist*, whose purpose, he wrote, was "the eviction of truth and the exposure of error." He became a master of ornate prose. He characterized Christianity as "the perfection of that divine philanthropy which was gradually developing itself for four thousand years. It is the bright effulgence of every divine attribute, mingling and harmonizing, as the different colors in the rainbow, in the bright shining after rain, into one complete system of perfection—the perfection of GLORY to God in the highest heaven, the perfection of PEACE on earth, and the perfection of GOOD WILL among men."[80]

He traveled in western Pennsylvania, Ohio and Kentucky, preaching and debating and attacking Sunday schools, missionary societies, synods, conferences, bishops and reverends—anything which he believed had no Scriptural basis or authorization. His forceful and convincing arguments rewarded him with thousands of followers; his Reformers influenced many Baptists congregations in the Great Lakes Frontier. By 1826 they began to separate themselves from the Baptists and to form congregations of their own. Campbell found new followers among the Republic Methodists—a group that opposed centralization and that had withdrawn under James O'Kelley—and among the "New Lights" under Barton W. Stone, a disaffected Presbyterian minister who objected to the orthodox tenets on election and predestination. In addition, many Baptist congregations, especially in western Kentucky, joined Campbell. Soon his faith spread to Ohio, Indiana and Illinois, where it became increasingly powerful. The movement that aimed at uniting all Christians had succeeded only in adding another to their number.[81]

The earliest Christians in the Great Lakes Frontier were, of course, Roman Catholics. They had explored the region, colonized it, endowed it with Christian civilization and introduced Indians to Christ. The mother church in the Great Lakes Frontier was St. Anne's Chapel built by Father de L'Halle of the Recollect Order. At the same time Catholic missions, largely Jesuit, spread all over the Great Lakes Frontier save Ohio. In the latter part of the eighteenth century Catholic activity waned as the Illinois County declined in importance. In 1789 the Holy See placed the region under John Carroll, the great bishop of the Baltimore diocese. Three years later Bishop Carroll sent Father Benedict Joseph Flaget to Vincennes, then known as the Old Post. He found the French settlers living in a state of semibarbarism. He reported "a poor log building, open to the weather and almost tottering. The congregation, if possible, in a still more miserable condition. Out of seven hundred souls, only twelve could be induced to approach holy communion during the Christmas festivities." Bishop Carroll wasted no time in taking steps to change matters. A born fisherman of men, he sent enterprising priests to Kaskaskia, Cahokia and Detroit. In 1804 Detroit incorporated a parish that contained three thousand persons.[82]

By 1808 the Catholic population had grown so rapidly that the

Holy See saw fit to establish the first frontier see at Bardstown, Kentucky, a settlement of Catholics from Virginia, Maryland and the Carolinas, with Father Flaget as bishop. Five years later, during his first inspection of his diocese, which included Kentucky, Tennessee and all of the Great Lake Frontier, Father Flaget expressed keen disappointment with Catholic activity north of the Ohio. "Twenty years more without priests," he wrote, "and they will have forgotten even the sign of the cross." He began to travel extensively in his diocese, settling local troubles, reconciling dissensions and encouraging the building of new churches. At last success blessed his crusading efforts. In 1815 he reported fifty Catholic families in Ohio and three Catholic parishes in Illinois with a hundred twenty families. Thenceforth the Catholic population in Ohio, augmented by German and Irish canal workers, grew so large that in 1821 the Holy See established the diocese of Cincinnati with Edward Fenwick as bishop. Within twelve years his successor, Bishop John B. Purcell, estimated thirty thousand Catholics in Ohio, though they had only nine brick and eight wooden churches. At about the same time the Holy See established two more dioceses: one at Detroit with Father Frederic Résé, and the other at Vincennes with Father Simon Bruté de Rémur. By 1830 Indiana counted thirty thousand Catholics.[83]

12

Americanization of Michigan and Wisconsin

THE SPRING OF 1815 BROUGHT PEACE TO MICHIGAN TERRITORY. BUT peace spelled destitution. No longer supplied by the English, bands of hungry Indians swooped down on farmhouses of French settlers, their former friends, burning fences, stealing fruit from orchards, and killing cattle. At the same time the homeless and starving settlers of River Raisin hovered around Detroit, expecting the territorial officials to turn the stones in the streets into bread. Governor Cass distributed what little food remained in the territory, but starvation was so widespread that he had to petition the Federal Government for help. At President Madison's request Congress voted the territory a special appropriation.[1]

Lewis Cass, who had succeeded William Hull in 1813, worked diligently to alleviate the general suffering as quickly as possible. Though born and schooled in comfort at Exeter, New Hampshire, and though young in years—he was only thirty-two—he was a veteran in his knowledge of pioneer vicissitudes. When he was seventeen years old he journeyed on foot over the Allegheny Mountains to seek his fortune in the Great Lakes Frontier. In Marietta, Ohio, he studied law and at the age of twenty was admitted to the bar. Four years later he was elected to the legislature of Ohio, where he originated a bill that inaugurated the movement that led to the defeat of Burr's conspiracy. In 1807 President Jefferson appointed him United States marshal of Ohio, a post which he held until the outbreak of the War of 1812. In appreciation of his brilliant record in that conflict, President Madison promoted him to civil governor of Michigan Territory.[2]

With the assistance of the territorial secretary, William Woodbridge, a scholarly and retiring gentleman who, like Cass, had migrated to Ohio from New England, the governor undertook the great task of converting the lackadaisical French settlements to active American communities. He must make them prosperous and progressive in peace and able to defend themselves in case the British attacked them. He must advertise the strategic value and the physical charms of the territory; he must attract the tide of immigration until it carried "the schoolhouse and the newspaper into the farthest corner of the land, where the Jesuit had, a century before, planted his cross and sang his *ave*."[3]

In May, 1815, the War Department authorized Cass to distribute $1,500 among the poor of the territory. This was indeed a paltry sum; but at the end of the war the government was in no financial position to "do more than dribble out its dollars." The money in the form of flour brought temporary relief to the settlers of River Raisin; it hardly ameliorated the condition of the territory. No occasional alms could bring prosperity to settlers who insisted on using primitive methods of farming. Those living in and around Detroit were better off and were content with their big orchards; but the poorer ones, relieved for the present from want, made no effort to clear the unbroken forest that hemmed them in to the riverbanks. Cass felt that American aggressiveness alone could cure Gallic lethargy. Good old Yankee stock—from which he himself had sprung—that was the tonic Michigan needed to grow and prosper! He was amazed to discover that the French settlers were ignorant of the spinning wheel and the loom, that they drew their manure over the ice in the winter in order to dump it into the lake in the spring, that they threw away their sheep wool, and that they looked on soap-making as an experiment from which few cared to profit. The governor favored direct measures to change this situation, but he soon realized that indirect methods would be more efficacious. If he could offer Eastern farmers land for sale in unlimited quantity, if he could convince them of its value, would they not flock to the territory in large numbers? Would not the Americanization of Michigan then be assured? He bent all his efforts to obtaining the answers to these questions.[4]

At the beginning of the war Congress had passed an act in which it offered volunteers two million acres of land in Michigan. To attract settlers to the territory as quickly as possible, Cass requested Edward Tiffin, Surveyor General of the United States, to have it platted. The surveyors duly appeared in early winter and began to work in the southeastern part of the territory, between the Maumee and the Raisin rivers. Cass had communicated with the Indians and had obtained from them a promise that the surveyors would not be molested. But the chain men and axmen soon returned home with a gloomy tale of the territory. Either wet weather or hardships or fatigue or dread of attack had so perverted their judgment that they described the interior of Michigan to Tiffin as an endless swamp unworthy of their efforts. They may have been influenced by the unfavorable report which Monroe had made for President Jefferson before the Northwest Territory was organized. After reconnoitering in scattered sections of the territory, Monroe had written Jefferson that most of it was "miserably poor, especially that near the Lakes Michigan and Erie. . . . The district, therefore, within which these fall will never contain a sufficient number of inhabitants to entitle them to membership in the confederacy."[5]

Tiffin swallowed the surveyors' report wholesale and spewed it to Josiah Meigs, Superintendent of the General Land Office. At about the same time Tiffin declared in his official report to the Federal Government that the two million acres reserved for the volunteers "will not contain anything like one hundred part of that quantity or is worth the expense of surveying it." He described Michigan as a territory of swamps and lakes with intermediate spaces of sandhills on which grew no vegetation save very small scrubby oaks. Meigs hastened to assure President Madison that scarcely one acre in a thousand was fit for cultivation. The president believed him and advised Congress in February 1816 that the quota of bounty lands assigned to Michigan should be transferred to Illinois and Missouri.[6]

Cass read a copy of the official report with undisguised anger. His pen raced across the paper in a protest to Meigs: "The quality of the land in this Territory has been grossly misrepresented." He added that Tiffin's description was based on incorrect information; but the newspapers emphasized the doings of Congress and naturally accepted its version of the controversy. So did the geographer Jedediah Morse, who in his widely used *Traveller's Guide* represented the sandhills of Michigan as "extending into the interior as far as the dividing ridge . . . some times crowned with a few stunted trees, and a scanty vegetation, but generally bare, and thrown by the wind into a thousand fantastic shapes."[7]

Cass lost a battle but he was determined to win the war. He began to bombard Meigs with long letters, reminding him that the surveyors had come to Michigan in the wettest season the territory had ever known and that they had run the line along a dividing ridge between waters running east and waters running west. No wonder they got their feet wet! Furthermore, two of the surveyors had by no means agreed with the others in disparaging the territory; on the contrary, they had praised it in glowing terms! He continued this verbal siege for several months while he instructed Meigs on the proper method of conducting the surveys, boasted that he had many potential land buyers, and predicted that the territory would be quickly settled. At last Meigs surrendered. In the summer of 1816 he wrote Cass that he had instructed Tiffin to resume the surveys and that, as soon as they were completed, he would issue in Detroit a proclamation that the Michigan lands were open for sale. By the end of September Tiffin's crew was at work in the Michigan woods.[8]

2

In addition to his office as civil governor of Michigan Territory, Cass was also Superintendent of Indian Affairs, not only for Michigan but for most of the Great Lakes Frontier, with jurisdiction over the subagencies in Ohio, Indiana and Illinois. He devoted about half of his time to his work with the Indians. His dealing with them often took him away from Detroit, his seat of government, for weeks and sometimes for months, during which time he experienced hardships of wilderness travel that often taxed even his iron constitution. He became acquainted with every Indian village in the territory, with every stream big enough to float a birch canoe, with every tribe south of Canada and east of Minnesota. He believed that the Indians should be treated with respect. He deplored the use of force without justification and he strongly urged a liberal compensation for every cession of land they made. He advised them that, since the cultivated lands were pressing more and more on their hunting grounds and since they were unwilling to adjust to the institutions of the whites, they would do well if they migrated across the Mississippi, where each of them should be encouraged to occupy and own a piece of land; but that their land and other property should be protected if they preferred to remain on their original territory, where they should be subject, like the Americans, to wise and just laws. He praised the American system of continuing annuities as far superior to the British system of immediate presents as full and final payment. This, in brief, was his Indian policy. He never deviated from it during the eighteen years he was governor of Michigan Territory.[9]

His humanitarian views brought him easy success in his treaties with the regional tribes. In September 1817 he journeyed with his old comrade-in-arms, General Duncan McArthur of Ohio, to Fort Meigs, where he and the representatives of most of the regional tribes signed a treaty by which they ceded a small block of land north of the line drawn by the Treaty of Greenville. This removed the "forbidden" southern strip which Hull had reserved for the tribes in his treaty of 1807 and which had separated the territory from the United States. The *Detroit Gazette* exulted that the treaty precluded the possibility of any future Indian confederacy and that, therefore, it brought security to the territory.[10]

In the next two years Cass signed two even more important treaties with the Indians. In 1818 at St. Marys, Ohio, the governor with Jonathan Jennings and Benjamin Parke of Indiana received from the Potowatomi an area north of the Wabash between the Tippecanoe and Vermilion rivers, and from the Wea an area south of the Vermilion. The other treaty, which Cass in the following year signed with the Chippewa on the present site of Saginaw, Michigan, increased the public domain by six million acres of the world's finest timberland running in a northeasternly direction from the Kalamazoo River to Thunder Bay River. Early in 1819 John Calhoun, Secretary of War, instructed Cass to try to persuade the Chippewa to give up their lands and migrate across the Mississippi. When he arrived at the treaty ground, however, he quickly observed that the tribe was living up to its reputation of hostility to Americans. Overlooking his instructions, he signed with them a treaty on his own responsibility. The treaty granted them $1,000 in cash and agreed that the United States should pay them an additional sum of whatever it thought they ought to receive and in such a manner as would do them the most good. The federal government also promised to furnish them with the services of a blacksmith and with a supply of livestock, farming implements and teachers to instruct them in agriculture.[11]

At this time Michigan Territory included the present states of Michigan, Wisconsin and a part of Minnesota. Though Cass was already acquainted with much of this vast expanse of land over which he governed, he determined to increase his knowledge of it. On November 18, 1819, he wrote to Secretary of War Calhoun asking for permission to undertake an extensive exploratory tour of the territory. He said he wanted to investigate the moral, economic, and social condition of the Indians and of their feelings toward the United States, to secure new land cessions from them, and to explain to them "the views of the Government respecting their intercourse with the British authorities at Malden, and distinctly to announce to them that their visits must be discontinued." In addition he hoped to examine the country for the possibility of establishing a military post at Sault Ste. Marie and to ascertain the existence of rich deposits of copper, iron, silver and gypsum, for which private interests were already clamoring. "All that will be required," he wrote, "is an ordinary birch canoe, and permission to employ a competent number of Canadian boatmen." He suggested that "an additional canoe, to be manned with active soldiers, and commanded by an intelligent officer, would not increase the expense, and would give greater effect to any representations which might be made to the Indians." The voyage, he concluded, would have added value if it included an intelligent officer who could make correct maps for the government and a person who knew the minerals as well as the flora and fauna of the region.[12]

The government zealously endorsed the expedition. And Cass busied himself during the winter and spring of 1820 making preparations for it. He had the Chippewa, whom he considered master craftsmen, build three canoes at Saginaw Bay; he enlisted the services of ten soldiers under Lieutenant Eneas Mackay; he persuaded ten Indians to join him as guides and hunters under the supervision of two experienced interpreters. The War Department chose Captain D. B. Douglas, professor of engineering at West Point, to serve as chief topographer and Charles C. Trowbridge, a young Detroiter, as assistant topographer of the expedition. Its physician was Alexander Woolcott, Indian agent at Chicago, and its geologist Henry Rowe Schoolcraft, who had once been a glass blower. Cass chose Major Robert A. Forsyth as his personal secretary and James Duane Doty as secretary of the expedition.[13]

At least, on May 24, the voyagers were ready to depart. The excited people thronged along the shore of Lake St. Clair and cheered wildly as the Canadian boatmen, occupying two of the three canoes and singing a merry song, raced with the Indians past large orchards and windmills upstream. The Canadians were winning the race when a gale nearly capsized the canoes and drove them ashore, where their occupants stayed for the next forty-eight hours.[14]

The next start was more auspicious. Covering about seventy miles a day, they entered stormy Lake Huron, toiled across treacherous Saginaw Bay, and skirted the eastern shore of the Michigan peninsula until, on June 6, they reached Mackinac Island. The commander of the fort on the bluff, Captain Benjamin K. Pierce, whose brother Franklin later became president of the United States, had his men salute the voyagers with a running fire of twenty guns.[15]

Here they spent six days. Schoolcraft marveled at the beauty of the island and described it with the simplicity and vividness of a literary master:

It is a mass of calcereous rock, rising from the bed of Lake Huron, and reaching an elevation of more than three hundred feet above the water. The waters around are purity itself. Some of its cliffs shoot up perpendicularly, and tower in pinnacles like ruinous Gothic steeples. It is cavernous in some places; and in these caverns the ancient Indians, like those of India, have placed their dead. . . . The harbor, at its south end, is a little gem. Vessels anchor in it, and find good holding. The little old-fashioned French town nestles around it in a very primitive style. The fort frowns above it, like another Alhambra, its white walls gleaming in the sun. The whole area of the island is one labyrinth of curious little glens and valleys. Old green fields appear, in some spots, which have been formerly cultivated by the Indians. In some of these there are circles of gathered-up stones, as if the Druids themselves had dwelt here.[16]

After rambling around the island and making themselves acquainted with its features and inhabitants, the voyagers, feeling fully rested, journeyed to Sault Ste. Marie, where Cass summoned the Chippewa to persuade them to build a fort on the spot. Dressed in neat and decorated buckskins and adorned with British medals, the representatives of the tribe sat in a semi-circle in front of the governor's marquee, where he had spread a tempting array of gifts, and waited for him to express his wishes. After they smoked the pipe with the Americans, the governor, through his half-breed interpreter, John Riley, asked for permission to build and garrison a fort. He reminded them that their forefathers had given the land to the French, that the French had lost it to the British, that the British, in turn, had lost it to the Americans, and that the Indians had recognized the American rights by the Treaty of Greenville. One of the chiefs replied that he favored confirmation of the grant but that he disapproved of the proposed fort because he feared his young men might kill the garrison's cattle. Cass assured him that this should cause the Indians no uneasiness, for the Americans could take care of themselves. Just as sure as the sun rose and set, he added, so sure would Americans garrison that point, with or without permission. At these words Sassaba, who had fought with Tecumseh at the Thames and lost a brother in that engagement, jumped up in a rage and strode up to the governor. He was a tall, imposing man painted in vermillion and indigo and wearing a British military coat with two enormous epaulettes and a large silver medal. He hated Americans, he thundered; he hated the Great White Father in Washington; he hated Cass and his soldiers; they must leave, or they would be killed. So saying, he drove his war lance into the ground at the governor's feet. Then he turned and strode from the conference, kicking the presents out of his way. The other chiefs rose silently and followed him to the Indian camp, which lay on a small hill a few hundred yards from that of the Americans. Over his lodge he raised a British flag while the chiefs armed their braves. This challenge infuriated Cass. Ordering his soldiers to hold their ground and waving away Schoolcraft's offer of assistance, he walked with John Riley to Sassaba's lodge and, in the face of threatening braves, yanked down the British flag. Then he entered the lodge and told Sassaba calmly but firmly that his act was an indignity he would not tolerate. He added that they stood on American soil over which no flag other than the Stars and Stripes could fly in peace or in war. He warned the chief that repetition of his act would bring the strong foot of the United States down on his neck. And he strode from the lodge, carrying the captured flag to his tent. In so dealing with the Chippewa Cass showed rare knowledge of Indian character.[17]

The Americans, seeing the infuriated Indians sending their women and children out of camp, momentarily expected to hear the war whoop. It never came. The daughter of one of the chiefs, Mrs. John Johnston, called the chiefs together in the absence of her husband and warned them that resistance was madness and that Cass was a man great enough to carry his flag through Chippewa country. When she counseled peace, two of the more reasonable chiefs supported her and persuaded the others to resume the conference. Whereupon Sassaba and one or two of his friends left their lodges in a huff, clearing the air for more conciliatory negotiations. Within two hours the Indians signed a treaty in which they ceded to the United States a piece of land ten miles square in return for a quantity of goods and perpetual fishing rights.[18]

Two days later the Americans resumed their journey along the southern shore of Lake Superior. Soon they reached Pictured Rocks, which inspired Schoolcraft's deft pen:

This coast, which extends twelve miles, consists of a grey sandstone, forming a series of perpenducular façades, which have been fretted, by the action of the waves, into the rude architecture of pillared masses, and open, cavernous arches. These caverns present their dark mouths to observation as the voyager passes. At one spot called the Doric Rock, near the commencement of these picturesque precipices, a vast entablature rests on two immense rude pillars of the water-worn mass. At a point called La Portail, the vast wall of rock had been so completely excavated and undermined by the lake, that a series of heavy strata of rock rested solely on a single pillar standing in the lake.[19]

Schoolcraft and the others almost held their breath in passing the coast; and when, at night, they compared their observations around the campfire, nobody could recall such a scene of simple novelty and grandeur in any other part of the world. They all agreed that, if a storm had overtaken them while they were passing, their deaths would have been inevitable.[20]

Westward they paddled to Keweenaw Bay, where they encountered squalls that almost upset their canoes. Tired and drenched to the skin, they entered Portage River, crossed Portage Lake, and trudged breathlessly under their canoes and supplies to the western shore of Keweenaw Peninsula. On June 27 they reached a Chippewa village on the mouth of the Ontonagon River where Chief Plover received them "in a most friendly manner." When they expressed interest in copper deposits he furnished them with guides, who led them thirty miles to a huge nugget lying partly in the water. Schoolcraft observed that its face "is almost purely metallic, and more splendent than appears to consist with its being purely metallic copper. There is no appearance of oxidation. Its size, roughly measured, is three feet four inches, by three feet eight inches, and about twelve or fourteen inches thick in the thickest part." He thought it weighed as much as a ton or a ton and a half. Earlier travelers had "cut freely from it," and Schoolcraft himself "obtained adequate specimens, but found my chisels too highly tempered, and my hammer not heavy enough to separate large masses." He tried to locate other ore deposits, but the Indians had only vague knowledge of them and never succeeded in leading him to them.[21]

By now they had traveled nine hundred and fifty miles from Detroit and had been gone more than forty days. On the morning of July 11 they passed the western tip of Lake Superior and entered the St. Louis River, a serpentine stream that, leaping and foaming from crag to crag, relieved their drudgery and peril with adventure. "Everything around us," wrote Schoolcraft, "wore the aspect of remoteness. Dark forests, swampy grounds, rocky precipices and the distant roaring of the river as it leapt from rock to rock, would have sufficiently impressed the mind without heavy rains, miry paths and the train of wild and picturesque Indians, who constituted a part of our carriers." They found wild rice growing in streams; they scared up flocks of eagles, buzzards, kingfishers and herons; they discovered to their amazement a Negro living with his Indian wife and their half-breed children in a Chippewa village. A hundred miles more of such episodes brought them to Savanna Portage by which they reached Sandy Lake and, on July 17, the Mississippi River. Following it northward to the lake region of present Minnesota, they arrived on the shores of Red Cedar Lake, which they renamed Cassina or Cass Lake in honor of their intrepid leader. Anxious to discover the source of the river, Cass ascended it for more than three hundred fifty miles. Then, finding navigation more and more difficult and the summer waning, he turned homeward. Encouraged by the descending river and the prospect of seeing their loved ones, the voyagers made rapid progress to the falls of St. Anthony, on the sites of present Minneapolis and St. Paul, where they warmly shook hands with Colonel Henry Leavenworth, who was establishing a military camp on the spot and who invited them to a banquet that included such rare dishes as corn on the cob, peas, beans, cucumbers, beets, radishes and lettuce. After supper they amused themselves in Leavenworth's "luxurious kitchen gardens" by trapping a gopher, which to these Yankees was a curious animal whose skin they carefully preserved.[22]

The last leg of their journey, which began on August 2, took them to Prairie du Chien, up the Wisconsin, across a portage to the Fox, and northward to Green Bay—a distance of about three hundred miles which they covered in just eighteen days! And how delighted they were to find a party of American soldiers digging the foundations of a sawmill! Schoolcraft vividly recalled the scene: "Our appearance must have been somewhat rusty at this time, for these sons of Mars did not recognize their superior officers in Capt. Douglas and Lt. Mackay; glibly saying, in a jolly way, as they handed them a drink of water, 'After me, sir, is manners;' and drinking off the first cup." The garrison of the fort saluted Cass and congratulated him and his men for passing among so many savages without losing their scalps.[23]

Here Cass reorganized the expedition. He sent Trowbridge with three men including James Duane Doty and John Riley, the interpreter, to trace the western and northern shore of Green Bay and the northern shore of Lake Michigan, while he with the remaining men paddled down the western shore of Lake Michigan to Chicago, whence they continued to Detroit on horseback over the old Sauk Trail, now U.S. Route 112. The people accorded them a thunderous welcome, which Trowbridge and his exploratory party, alack, missed by ten days.[24]

The expedition had significant results. By speeches and articles, some of which appeared in the *North American Review*, Cass made great progress in his endeavor to Americanize the territory he had visited. At about the same time Schoolcraft's eminently readable *Summary Narrative of an Exploratory Expedition to the Sources of the Mississippi River in 1820*—published in bright green buckram with gold lettering—stimulated not only scientific study of the tribes in the Lake Superior country but also widespread interest in the region as one of fabulous mineral deposits. Thus these two men may be credited with starting Wisconsin and, to some extent, Minnesota on their road to statehood.[25]

In his determination to clear more of Michigan Territory for American settlement Cass negotiated another Indian treaty shortly after his return to Detroit. He met the tribes in Chicago and purchased from them the region south of the Grand and north of the St. Joseph rivers. Now no unceded land remained in the Lower Peninsula save that north of the Grand River and north and west of the head of Thunder Bay River. The governor had prepared the way for the great migration that was about to begin.[26]

At about the same time the federal government sent Colonel Hugh Brady with a body of troops to build at Sault Ste. Marie a stockaded fort to which he gave his name. The new Indian agent of the region was none other than Henry Rowe Schoolcraft, who soon married Jane Johnston, the beautiful and talented daughter of John Johnston, an educated Irishman, perhaps of noble ancestry, who had wandered to the Great Lakes Frontier and there married a Chippewa woman of great charm and intelligence. Jane, who showed no features indicative of her Indian blood save high cheek bones and lustrous black eyes, diligently assisted her husband in collecting Chippewa lore and in translating Chippewa poetry into English. His compilations were eventually published and furnished Henry Wadsworth Longfellow with material for his epic, *Hiawatha*.[27]

Most of the Chippewa, however, preferred the arts of war. In

1822 the federal government decided to control them by building at the present site of Saginaw a fort under Major Daniel Baker. Unfortunately, malaria struck the fort in the following year and brought down all but one of its occupants, which included one hundred twenty civilians and sixty enlisted men. Though the surgeon in charge, Dr. Zina Pitcher, was the sickest of all, he made the rounds of his patients every day on a mattress carried by men well enough to move around or lift something. Major Baker caught the infection and vowed he would leave the fort if he recovered. He was able to keep his vow, reporting to the government that only Indians, muskrats, and bull frogs could live in Saginaw. The disease gave the fort as bad a reputation as the Tiffin report had given to the entire territory. The *Detroit Gazette* attributed the malaria to the heavy rains of the preceding summer, which had caused the Saginaw River to flood surrounding wooded lands, making them stagnant and "loading the atmosphere with poisonous vapors." The Federal Government saw fit to abandon the post.[28]

3

By this time Michigan Territory had made significant political, economic and social progress. In 1818 Cass offered its inhabitants, who numbered about eight thousand, the privilege of the second stage of territorial government, which would provide them with a local legislature and a delegate to Congress. He was confident that such a measure of self-government would appeal to most of them and would, moreover, encourage migration to the territory. He was mistaken. Most of the voters were Frenchmen who were too ignorant to assume the responsibilities of popular government, too impoverished to pay taxes, and too fond of Cass to accept privileges at the expense of his power.[29]

Undaunted, the governor then encouraged the American settlers of newly organized Macomb County to petition Congress to permit them to elect a delegate to that body. When Congress granted their request, they elected William Woodbridge, who, however, resigned his office because unsuccessful candidates protested that he retained his position as secretary of the territory and collector of customs. The next delegate, Solomon Sibley, lost his office when he sided with unsuccessful politicians in Washington. In 1823 Michigan entered the second stage of territorial government when it organized a Legislative Council of the nine men whom the President had chosen from the eighteen elected by the voters. Two years later, when the population of the territory reached thirty thousand, Congress increased the membership of the Legislative Council to thirteen members. In 1827 Congress gave the people of the territory permission to choose councillors without presidential selection.[30]

Sibley's successor as delegate to Congress was Father Gabriel Richard, one of Michigan's greatest sons. This venerable Sulpician, whom Woodbridge regarded as one of the most learned men in the United States, was the only priest ever elected to Congress. In 1798 Bishop John Carroll of Baltimore had sent him to Detroit to serve as assistant to Father Michel Levadoux, with whom he had fled from France during the French Revolution. His tall and sepulchral figure combined piety with elegant learning and rare common sense. A spotless Christian, he knew no prejudice; he loved all men regardless of race or creed. He opened in Detroit a preparatory school for boys whom he planned to send to St. Mary's Seminary in Baltimore, but unluckily a great fire in the following year destroyed both the school and the church. Father Richard quickly rebuilt St. Anne's and became its pastor. In the ensuing years he built at Springwells a school for both white and Indian children in which he taught the boys carpentry, farming, printing and bookbinding, and the girls carding, spinning, sewing and weaving.

In 1808 he journeyed to Washington, where he interested President Jefferson in his educational plans, though he never received the funds he was promised to carry them out. Returning to Detroit with a printing press—the first one in the territory—he published a small gazette which he called the *Michigan Essay* or *Impartial Observer*. At the same time he printed a number of religious and educational pamphlets and an anthology of his favorite French writers. When the War of 1812 broke out, he immediately championed the American cause and won General Procter's enmity—together with a short imprisonment—for denouncing his tyranny. The crowning point of his academic achievement came in 1817, when Governor Cass appointed him vice president of the newly established and tax-supported Catholepistemiad or University of Michigania, which consisted of an elementary school, an academy or preparatory school, and a college—all in one small building. Father Richard and the president, John Montieth, a Presbyterian minister, served as its only administrative officers as well as its faculty. Montieth held seven and Father Richard six professorships, for each of which they received $12.50 a year. These picayunish salaries became enviable sinecures when the Catholepistemiad failed to attract any students. Good Father Richard hastened to donate his salary to the church. The Catholepistemiad continued its bleak existence until 1821, when its awesome or awful name was changed to that of the University of Michigan.[31]

Father Richard used his influence as delegate to Congress to have a bill passed for the construction of a road from Detroit to Chicago. It connected these two military posts by the old Sauk Trail over which Indians journeyed annually to receive presents from the British at Fort Malden. Authorized in 1825, the Chicago Road ran southwestward through Ypsilanti, Tecumseh, Hillsdale, Coldwater and White Pigeon. A little south of Niles it crossed the St. Joseph River and the Indiana line as it pursued its destination. The government neglected the road until after the Black Hawk War, though it received enough attention from stage companies to get their coaches by perilous places.

In 1836 the English author, Harriet Martineau, traveled on the segment of the road between Detroit and Ypsilanti and thought that Juggernaut's car would have been demolished on it. She found having to dismount and walk no less bewildering: "such hopping and jumping; such slipping and sliding; such looks of despair from the middle of a pond; such shifting of logs, and carrying of planks, and handing along the fallen trunks of trees!"

A Detroit newspaper agreed with her: "The road from this point to Ypsilanti looks at certain times as if it had been the route of a retreating army, so great is the number of wrecks of different kinds which it exhibits." Eventually the Chicago Road was improved, and it contributed to the Americanization of Michigan Territory, as did the Territorial or "Upper" Road, which was authorized in 1829 and which ran from Detroit to the St. Joseph River.[32]

But what immediately stimulated emigration to the territory was the improvement of navigation on the Great Lakes. On August 27, 1818—the year in which Michigan's public lands were open to settlement—the first steamboat on the upper lakes, the *Walk-in-the-Water*, named perhaps for the Wyandot chief who vainly offered his services to the Americans in the War if 1812, reached Detroit from Buffalo. The Indians along its route had been told that a great ship drawn by sturgeons was about to make her appearance in the Detroit River. Curiously they thronged the banks around Malden and, seeing the *Walk-in-the-Water* move majestically and rapidly against the strong current without the assistance of sails or oars, greeted her with shouts of surprise and ejaculations of wonder. Soon she joined other steamboats in making regular nine-day schedules between Buffalo and Detroit.[33]

Even more significant to the development of Michigan Territory was the opening of the Erie Canal in 1825. It changed the direction of western migration from the Ohio Valley to the route of the canal and the Great Lakes. Thousands of settlers from New England and New York who had originally intended to go farther west were content to take advantage of the cheap transportation on the canal and settle in Michigan which, after the completion of Tiffin's surveys, was no longer regarded as an interminable swamp. The Erie Canal was a kind of assembling basin for those pioneers who were about to weave their destinies in the future states of Michigan and Wisconsin.[34]

The Federal Government realized that the territory, regardless of its political, economic, and social growth, would never enjoy the stability it needed for statehood so long as the tribes waged boundary wars. Early in 1827 James Barbour, Secretary of War, sent Lewis Cass and Colonel Thomas L. McKenney as commissioners to negotiate an agreement in which the boundaries of the Sioux, Chippewa, Sauk and Foxes, Winnebagos, Menominee and Potawatomi would be clarified. With a sizable staff including Schoolcraft and Robert Forsyth, the two commissioners journeyed by steamer to Green Bay, where the regional tribes assembled to meet them. The commissioners discovered that the Winnebagos, instead of sending representatives to the council, had withdrawn to Fort Crawford, at Prairie du Chien, which the Americans had abandoned in 1821, and had organized under Red Bird. Resenting American encroachment on his lands around the Fever River in northern Illinois, this young and handsome chief—the American poet William Ellery Leonard described him as "an extraordinary fellow . . . sculptured as if by some ancient Greek artist out of brown-red stone"—killed several settlers at Prairie du Chien, attacked soldiers canoeing down the Mississippi from Fort Snelling, and threatened thousands of lead miners at Galena, Illinois.[35]

Cass handled the situation with his usual promptitude. With Forsyth, fifteen canoemen, and an interpreter he dashed up the Fox and down the Wisconsin rivers. Though Indians everywhere warned him to turn back, he sped on until he came to a Winnebago village, where he landed and remonstrated with several chiefs on the consequences of their conduct. As the governor turned to leave, a young brave leveled at his heart and pulled the trigger. The rifle missed fire. The Indian was ready to try again when the chiefs, realizing what terrible retribution awaited them should the governor be killed, disarmed and upbraided him.

The shaken governor raced to Prairie du Chien, where he discovered the sad plight of the settlers and encouraged them by organizing them into a force as best he could. Then he hurried for help to Colonel Josiah Snelling at the Falls of St. Anthony, while he sent to the Winnebago messengers offering them the choice of attending the council at Green Bay or of swift and terrible punishment. Doubting that Snelling could come to his assistance, he pushed for St. Louis, where the nearest soldiers were stationed. At Dubuque he persuaded friendly Foxes to go to the assistance of the settlers; at Galena he comforted the panicky and unarmed lead miners. Though Galena lay in Illinois and therefore outside his jurisdiction, he organized a body of volunteers under Henry Dodge, commandeered weapons for them from Rock Island, and raced to St. Louis, which he reached on July 10.

William Clark, Governor of Missouri, immediately sent against Red Bird a force of five hundred regulars under General Henry Atkinson, while Major William Whistler moved against the chief with another force of regulars from Fort Howard at Green Bay. Caught between Atkinson's regulars and Dodge's volunteers on one side and Whistler's regulars on the other, Red Bird wisely raised a white flag. He was imprisoned in Fort Howard, where later he died. Near the spot where he surrendered, the United States built Fort Winnebago, which was soon to figure prominently in the Black Hawk War. As for Cass, he returned to Green Bay, where on August 11 he signed with the assembled Indians, including the chastised Winnebagos, a treaty by which they agreed to permit the United States to settle what boundary disputes might arise among them.[36]

4

Early in July 1831 President Jackson appointed Lewis Cass his Secretary of War. Inasmuch as no new governor had as yet been appointed, the executive authority of the territory passed to the secretary, John T. Mason, a Virginian who in recent years had been living at Ashland, Kentucky. Mason cared nothing for politics. He owed his position to his need of providing a livelihood for his large family. The commission house in Cincinnati that handled his pig iron defaulted in its payments, leaving him in straitened circumstances. He appealed to his friend, President Jackson, who appointed him secretary of Michigan Territory. No sooner did Mason arrive at his post than he decided to look after some land claims he had inherited in Texas. In the summer of 1831 he and his son, Stevens Thomson Mason, who was nineteen years old, journeyed to Washington and visited Jackson. The father resigned his office and requested that his son be appointed in his place. Jackson was so impressed with the boy's handsome features and discerning mentality that he granted the request.

News of his appointment preceded him to Detroit and gave its leading Whigs—Jackson's political enemies—an opportunity to organize a committee to interview the "stripling" in the hope of ascertaining disqualifications by which they could obtain his removal. They doubtless were supporters of the cherished delusion that gray on the head means gray matter in the head.

Young Mason received the committee courteously, admitting that he was only nineteen years old but emphasizing that he had withheld from the president no information bearing on his qualifications for his office. Nevertheless, the Whigs addressed the president a memorial containing one hundred and sixty-two signatures and asking the secretary's removal on the ground of his minority and lack of the freehold qualifications required by the statute that created the office he held. At the same time the Whig newspapers of the territory assaulted Mason and Jackson with a barrage of ridicule and abuse. News of the incident soon spread and aroused much comment in many newspapers throughout the country. A few of them defended the propriety of the appointment. The Washington *Globe*, which served Jackson as his official organ, contended that Mason had been duly appointed and that, therefore, he could be removed only for actual misconduct.[37]

During this war of words young Mason quietly mapped wise strategy. Realizing that his Whig enemies would waste no time in dispatching their memorial, he mailed to the president a letter in which he pointed out that the opposition to him was political and invidious, and asking for his support. At about the same time he published in the *Free Press* a statement in which he admitted his inexperience as well as the higher qualifications of many men in the territory.

"Is there any difficulty," he asked, "of getting the advice of wiser and abler men? The oldest ask advice; and no man in that respect is independent of the society in which he lives. The difference is, youth yields to advice; but age, seldom or never."

His arguments were as irrefutable as his language was moderate and free of arrogance—discretions which enabled him to go "far towards turning the feelings of opposition to kindly sympathy." In time, as he showed more and more that political acumen and sound judgment are no respecters of age, all opposition toward him collapsed. No man complained when, at the end of July, Lewis Cass administered to Mason the oath of office in the little brick building that served as the territorial capitol.

The governor attended a farewell dinner which the citizens of the town arranged in his honor and then, on August 1, departed for Washington to assume his new post. His successor at Detroit was George B. Porter, an affluent lawyer from Lancaster, Pennsylvania, who recently had been appointed United States marshal of the eastern part of Pennsylvania. Shortly after his arrival in Detroit business recalled him to Lancaster, where he remained for several months. During this period Mason was acting governor.[38]

While the territory seethed with the controversy over Mason it learned of an Indian uprising in northern Illinois. There the Sauk and Foxes dwelled in a large village that for a century had been their principal seat and burying ground. In 1804 they had ceded their vast domain east of the Mississippi—some fifty million acres for an annuity of $1,000—to the United States which, however, had permitted them to continue to live and hunt on it as long as it remained under federal control. The American lead miners around the Fever River soon coveted the region. They began to build fences and to beat squaws who climbed over them; they sent cattle into cornfields; they plowed up graves; they set fire to the village while its inhabitants were away on a hunting trip.

The Sauk and Foxes were powerless to stop the intruders. Their supreme chief, Keokuk, had grown amiable and peaceful in his old age. Furthermore, he realized the futility of trying to resist the whites; acting on the advice of the Indian agent, Robert Forsyth, he persuaded most of them to migrate to their lands across the Mississippi. Only one of his headmen, Black Hawk, refused to move from their ruined village. He, too, was an old man, but he retained much of the fighting zeal of his youth. His face was a piece of crumpled yellow parchment; his numerous scars were trophies of his temerity. He had bloodied himself at Fort Malden, at River Raisin, and at the Thames under the great Tecumseh. Now he vowed to show no mercy in driving the whites from the region. His men paid them back in kind. They threw down fences, sent their horses into cornfields, stole potatoes, and even rolled out a barrel of whiskey and destroyed it. The frightened miners appealed to Governor John Reynolds, who gathered six hundred volunteers at Beardstown and then sent them under General Edmund P. Gaines against Black Hawk and his warriors in the village. They found it abandoned. During the night of June 25, 1831, Black Hawk with his braves, learning that the whites were approaching with an army superior in numbers to his own, slipped away to the safety of the Iowa shore.[39]

The people of Michigan Territory read reports of these events in adjacent Illinois with mingled wonder and alarm. Might not the uprising spread to their own region? With excited eyes they read their newspapers for new reports of the stirring drama. Having reached the Iowa country too late to plant corn or build huts for shelter, Black Hawk with his little band spent the winter in great misery. As he shivered and starved, he planned to cross the river in the spring, march to the Winnebagos, who had declared themselves his friends, and plant a crop of corn. He felt that the Americans would let him alone as long as he showed no belligerency and refrained from returning to his old village. For a year he would be peaceful, while he recovered his strength with rest and good food; then, assisted by the British, Winnebagos, Ottawas, Chippewa and Potawatomi—a roseate picture formed from reports brought him by Indian runners—he would take the warpath against the hated Americans and repay them for the humiliation and injustice they had inflicted on his people. Persuading himself that his present pacific inclinations were as genuine as his future warlike intentions, on April 6, 1832, he and his four hundred warriors took their squaws and children—they counted about a thousand in all—and crossed the Mississippi in full view of Fort Armstrong at the Yellow Banks below the mouth of the Rock River.[40]

To the pioneers his return was like fire before a gale. The word "Injun" was whispered into a kind of black magic which conjured up an image of a half-naked devil who, yipping and yelping, galloped furiously on a painted pony against a defenseless cabin to bloody his hands on innocent women and children. Once more Governor Reynolds called for volunteers. In reply, settlers left their spring plowing, grabbed their rifles, and rode away to form themselves into companies at the nearest crossroads. They voted for their captains as boys form for a tug of war—each man standing in line behind the man of his choice.

Among the successful candidates was an awkward and angular young man named Abraham Lincoln, who had just come up with fellows from Clark's Grove, where he managed Offutt's store in the prolonged absence of its proprietor. The boys in each company, like those in Lincoln's, whooped, yelled and fired their rifles as they rushed off to war. They all gathered sixteen hundred strong at Beardstown, where Reynolds divided them into four regiments, a spy battalion, and two odd battalions and placed them under Brigadier General Samuel Whiteside. This officer hurried with mounted recruits to Fort Armstrong and thence up the east bank of the Rock River in search of Indians, leaving General Henry Atkinson with four hundred regular infantry and three hundred volunteer infantry to follow in boats. On May 12 Whiteside arrived at Dixon's Ferry, where he found two independent raw militia battalions under Majors Isaiah Stillman and David Bailey. Itching for adventure, Stillman and Bailey obtained from Whiteside permission to advance and spy out the land farther up the Rock River. Two days later they encamped in a small grove of scrub oak surrounded by undulating prairie near the mouth of Sycamore Creek.[41]

They were unaware that Black Hawk was nearby. For a week he had been conferring with the Winnebagos, from whom he learned that neither they nor any other tribe nor the British had any intention of joining him. He could count only on a few Potawatomi hotheads. Utterly dejected, he was on the point of relinquishing his military plans and of returning to the Iowa country to plant corn, when he learned that the force under Stillman and Bailey was only eight miles away. Thinking that it had come to summon him to return to the west bank of the Mississippi, he decided to surrender. He sent out eight of his braves on horseback. Three of them under a flag of truce were to arrange a council while their remaining comrades were to observe the proceedings from a distance.

Toward sunset the Americans saw the trucebearers approaching about a mile away. Some of them instantly jumped onto their horses and ran the Indians in amid yells and deprecations. The wild excitement of the Americans mounted to pandemonium when they discovered the five observers on a knoll less than a mile away. Ten, twenty, fifty of them dashed down the prairie toward the Indians who, seeing them approach, wheeled and rode away. The Americans shot two of them. Their comrades back in camp heard the sputtering of rifles and construed it as the beginning of hostilities. One of them grabbed his gun and shot down one of the trucebearers before his officer could stop him. The officers tried in vain to restore order. Soldiers trickled out of camp and, amid the threats and curses of their officers, eventually formed a meandering swift stream over the darkening prairie.[42]

Meanwhile the three Indian observers had returned to Black Hawk with news of what had occurred. The chief shed his gloom

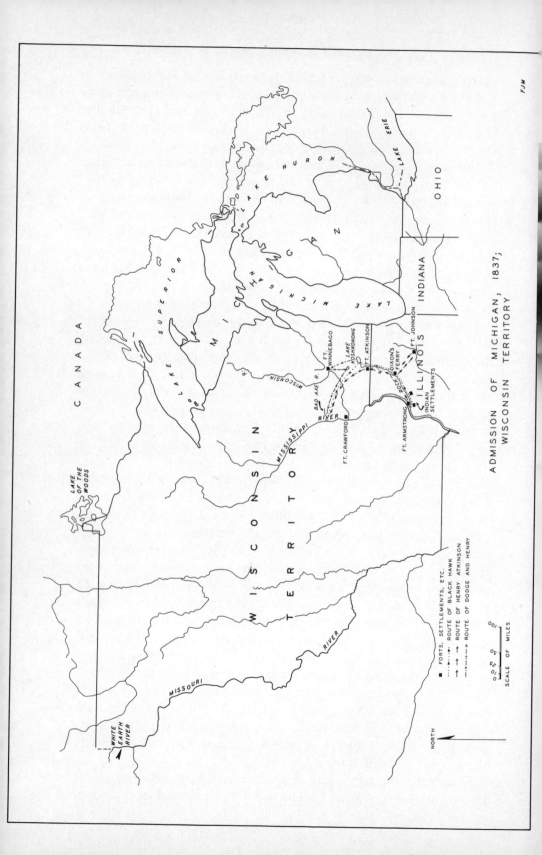

ADMISSION OF MICHIGAN, 1837;
WISCONSIN TERRITORY

like a cloak. Repudiating his peaceful intentions, he resolved to retrieve his slipping influence with one swift victory. Though he had only forty warriors, he took measures to encourage the Americans in their illusion that he had many times that number. Appealing to his men with burning words to avenge the death of their comrades, he formed them behind a clump of chaparral and waited for the Americans to approach. Then, whooping, yelling and firing their guns, they popped from their hiding place, mowing down their reckless enemies by the score. In the madness of sudden fear the rest imagined just what Black Hawk had conjured up for them: a forest full of blood-thirsty savages! "Injuns! Injuns!" they yelled as they stampeded in the darkness back to camp.[43]

They ran so fast that Black Hawk's warriors were unable to catch them. And they kept on running all night and all day past camp and into Dixon's Ferry, where they told Atkinson, who had recently arrived with his boats, how Black Hawk had deployed fifteen hundred—no, two thousand—of his savages against their paltry numbers! Some of Stillman's men stopped only long enough to catch their breath; then, ignoring Atkinson's admonitions, they started running again—this time toward home and safety.[44]

Black Hawk was more astonished than elated by the accident that had brought him overwhelming victory. He found himself in possession of blankets, saddlebags, rifles, ammunition and food with which to carry on the war, which he knew would now begin in earnest. But he determined to avoid an encounter until he was fully prepared; he hoped his recent victory would win him the allies he needed. Guided by a few friendly Winnebagos, he removed his women and children to the swampy wilderness around Lake Koshkonong near the headwaters of the Rock River, now in southern Wisconsin. So now what the people of Michigan Territory had feared and seen approaching came to pass: the Black Hawk War raged at their very thresholds! They soon learned that on May 15 Governor Reynolds had issued another call to arms, stating his opinion that the Winnebagos and the Potawatomi had joined Black Hawk to overrun the entire Great Lakes Frontier. Immediately General Hugh Brady, commander at Detroit, marched with a small force to join Atkinson, while Acting Governor Mason ordered General John R. Williams, commander of the territorial militia, to raise a force of volunteers to protect the settlements in the Lower Peninsula. All this mustering and marching proved needless. No sooner had Williams departed for Jonesville, on the Chicago Road, where he was to assist Brigadier General Joseph Brown, than

Mason received word that Atkinson had more men than he needed to handle Black Hawk. Williams and his men were recalled.[45]

Meanwhile Atkinson with thirty-two hundred men pressed northward against Black Hawk. To obtain supplies for the forthcoming showdown, he sent three of his highest officers—General Milton K. Alexander, General James D. Henry, and Colonel Henry Dodge—with their men to Fort Winnebago, eighty miles away, while he himself with his regulars retired to Lake Koshkonong to await their return. On arriving at Fort Winnebago they learned that Black Hawk was encamped about thirty miles north of Atkinson's headquarters. Elated at the prospect of winning the laurels of the war for themselves, they agreed to disobey orders and to march directly against Black Hawk. Alexander's men refused to go, and Henry's men threatened to mutiny; but eventually Henry and Dodge with their men began to march over the swampy ground, while they sent messengers to apprise Atkinson of their doings and whereabouts. When the messengers had traveled twenty miles they discovered unmistakable evidences of Black Hawk's trail and dashed back to inform their leaders. Though their men were exhausted, Henry and Dodge led them through a terrific rain storm with nothing in their stomachs save raw meat and a little flour-and-water dough. This army marched, not on its stomach but on its determination to take Black Hawk before other troops arrived. The abandoned pots and kettles and blankets they kicked out of their way as they advanced told them that the Indians were in precipitous flight. The guides thought that Black Hawk could not be more than two or three miles away.[46]

At that time the Indians had come to within a mile and a half of the Wisconsin River. To protect his followers as they crossed, Black Hawk stationed fifty of his braves on the bluffs nearby. The Americans dismounted as they came up and with terrifying yells and heavy fire drove the braves toward the river. The fear that disaster might overtake him in the darkness over the marshy ground, however, prevented Henry from following up his advantage.[47]

Just before dawn on the following morning the Americans heard an Indian delivering an oration in shrill, eager tones from a hill near the river. Nobody in camp understood the oration. Was it addressed to a war party? The faces of Henry's men clouded with fear. To reassure them he extolled their courage while he denounced the wickedness of their enemies; if they stood their ground they would be successful again. Later they learned that Black Hawk's aide, Ne-a-pope, had delivered the oration "in which he confessed their starving condition, their inability to fight when encumbered with women and children, and their anxiety to be permitted peaceably to pass over the Mississippi."[48]

The defeat of the Indians at the bluffs of the Wisconsin impelled a sizable group of their women, children, and old men to beg canoes and rafts from the Winnebago and float down the river. Eventually they would have crossed the Mississippi to Iowa had not the garrison at Prairie du Chien detected them and captured or shot most of them. Some of the rest were drowned, others succeeded in landing, only to perish of hunger or be hunted down in the woods by Menominee under white officers.[49]

That afternoon Black Hawk saw approaching an army transport steamer, the *Warrior*, under John Throckmorton. He hailed the boat with a white flag and, when it landed, called out to Throckmorton in Winnebago to send a canoe that he might come aboard and surrender. Throckmorton pretended that the white flag was a ruse. Later he reported with fiendish glee that after allowing the women and children fifteen minutes to get out of the way, he "let slip a six-pounder, loaded with canister, followed by a severe fire of musketry; and if ever you saw straight blankets, you would have seen them there. . . . We fought them for about an hour or more until our wood began to fail. . . . This little fight cost them twenty-three killed, and of course a great many wounded. We never lost a man. . . ."[50]

In need of provisions, Henry and Dodge, after their engagement with the Indians on the bluffs of the Wisconsin, fell back and joined Atkinson. They wasted no time pursuing Black Hawk, who sent twenty-five of his braves to retard them in their camp while he made his escape with his followers. The braves attacked the Americans and then gave ground, while Henry, bringing up the rear with his baggage, discovered the main Indian trail leading to the river. Ordering his three hundred men to dismount, he sent them against the Indians, who fought bravely from tree to tree while the women, "with their children clinging around their necks, plunged desperately into the river to be almost instantly drowned or picked off by sharpshooters." The *Warrior* returned and participated in the pandemonium and slaughter by raking with canister the islands which some of the women, children and old men had reached. A participant, John A. Wakefield, professed that his heart ached at the sight of "little children . . . suffering the most excruciating pain," though he hastened to assuage his guilty feelings by rationalizing that "the Ruler of the Universe, He who takes vengeance on the guilty, did not design those guilty wretches to escape His vengeance for the horrid deeds they had done, which were of the most appalling nature."[51]

Black Hawk himself saw little of the massacre. With a small party of warriors and thirty-five squaws and children he took refuge in the secluded rocky valleys of the Wisconsin until, on the following day, his guilty conscience impelled him to return to the bluffs above the mouth of the Bad Axe, where he witnessed the last long agonizing hour of the butchery below him. By that time one hundred and fifty of his men had been killed and as many more had drowned. The Americans counted twelve killed and about twelve wounded.

Black Hawk returned in a daze to his place of refuge, where two Winnebagos captured him and his son and a few of his friends and delivered them up to Joseph M. Street, the Indian agent at Prairie du Chien. There they remained until the spring of 1833, when they were taken to Washington. In June they were released and taken on a tour of eastern cities, where they attended theaters and museums and attracted large crowds, which showered them with attention and gifts. Later Black Hawk returned to Iowa, where Keokuk eventually welcomed him back like a prodigal son. He fades from our view with a nostalgic appeal to his conquerors: "Rock River was a beautiful country. I loved my towns, my cornfields, and the home of my people. I fought for it. It is now yours. Keep it as we did."[52]

5

The American losses in the Black Hawk War were trifling compared to those inflicted at the same time by a more deadly and insidious enemy—an enemy that struck down soldiers, old men, women and children with equal savagery and passed on only to return in the following year with replenished virulence. This was Asiatic cholera. For years it had been creeping westward from India, leaving terror and death in its path. It lengthened itself across Asia to Turkey, Moscow, Germany and then England and Ireland, until in 1831 it boarded an emigrant ship and struck down the passengers before they landed in Quebec. Then it ascended the St. Lawrence River to Montreal, whence it traveled to Albany and New York and Philadelphia and Pittsburgh and Erie. It never varied or softened its characteristics: intolerable queasiness, inward burnings, craving for cold drink, vomiting, unbearable stomach spasms, diarrhea, slow circulation, bleary and sunken eyes, cold and discolored skin, and then—death.[53]

In July 1832 it reached Detroit. Earlier that summer President Jackson sent General Winfield Scott with nine companies to end the Black Hawk War as quickly as possible. They came in four steamers, one of which, the *Henry Clay*, arrived in Detroit just as the people were celebrating Independence Day. The cholera attacked two soldiers, one of whom it killed before nightfall. The army surgeon was so terrified that he pretended illness and fled to a hotel. Two Detroit doctors who hastened to the succor of the afflicted found sixteen new cases of the disease. Under their direction the townsfolk turned a dockside warehouse into a hospital and removed the sick men to it. That night eleven of them died. In the morning the corpses were ranged side by side just outside the hospital for the benefit of those who cared to see them.[54]

By this time the *Henry Clay* had proceeded on her way, only to land again near Fort Gratiot, on Lake St. Clair, to care for her stricken passengers. The ship had become a floating charnel house. The cholera became so violent and caused so much alarm that no discipline could be maintained; insubordination increased with each passing day. As soon as the steamer docked, the soldiers jumped to shore, hoping to escape from the terrifying and appalling scene. Some fled to the fields, some to the woods. Some lay down in the streets and died, unwept and alone, under cover of the riverbanks. Others sought the forest, only to die of the disease or to be killed by wild animals.[55]

The cholera soon attacked the townsfolk. Acting Governor Mason turned the unused top floor of his office building into another hospital, but many of its patients died before nurses and doctors could be found to attend them. The fear of contagion alienated neighbors, separated relatives, and broke up families. The bells tolled dolefully for the dead hour after hour, while billows of smoke rose from pitch pine knots that burned on street corners as a preventative of contagion. Through the streets rumbled heavy wooden carts driven by wardens who rang bells as they chanted: "Bring out the dead! Bring out the dead!" And doors would fling open and distressed or weeping persons would emerge with the bodies of their beloved and dump them on the cart. The dread specter entered Mason's household and struck down Granny Peg, his old and kindly colored nurse. Mason's sister, Emily bravely went out into the street and hailed down a death-cart.[56]

The few doctors in the Great Lakes Frontier vied with one

another in speculating on the causes of the disease and in prescribing their cures for it. Some of them blamed bad air, chemical exhalations from the center of the earth, drastic changes in atmospheric conditions and comets. The famous Dr. Daniel Drake of Cincinnati—by now the cholera had reached his city—theorized that the disease was caused by "animals too small to see" that bred in outhouses, barns and on unclean persons. He prescribed large quantities of whisky, a peaceful mind and a flannel shirt over the upper part of the body. In desperate cases he recommended copious bleeding from the jugular vein.[57]

The people of neighboring villages caught the infection of terror and closed their public houses. Then, thinking this precaution inadequate, they tore up bridges, barricaded all their roads, quarantined themselves and posted militiamen to stop any travelers from Detroit. On July 10 the Detroit stagecoach with passengers attempted to pass the quarantine in Ypsilanti. The militiamen stopped the coach and one of them fired at its lead horse when its driver argued that he carried not only the mail but also important dispatches for General Scott in Chicago. The horse was frightened but not injured; and the coachman, after wasting precious time in angry expostulations with the militiamen, was allowed to resume his journey.[58]

A few days late Mason came galloping along the Chicago Road toward Mottville, where he hoped to distribute emergency proclamations for the southern counties. Wishing to avoid Ypsilanti because of its quarantine, he sought out Samuel Pettibone, who knew the region well, to guide him by a circuitous route to a point a little beyond Mottville. The favor fell abortive when a tough-looking deputy, Eliphalet Turner, on a faster horse, overtook Mason, ignored his explanations and conducted him to Sheriff Withington. Livid with rage, Mason identified himself to the satisfaction of the sheriff and continued to Mottville. At Mason's request, Governor Porter, who had returned to the territory in the previous month, removed Turner as well as Sheriff Withington from office.[59]

Meanwhile in Detroit the cholera continued unabated. The warden, as he passed in his death-cart, was no longer allowed to ring his bell; it only intensified the panic. On July 19 most of the townsfolk, in response to the Detroit Presbytery, joined in a special prayer that God "would avert the pestilence from our land and, in the midst of deserving wrath, remember mercy." The prevailing misery inspired many heroic deeds. Young men organized them-

selves into a nursing corps. Dr. Marshall Chapin for weeks gave his
services to the poor and the dissipated without remuneration of any
kind. At the end of July the disease abated; but it had yet to claim
its most illustrious victim. Father Gabriel Richard had worked day
and night among suffering and death. In September he went to a
shack to administer extreme unction to a man who had asked for
him. Weakened by his unresting ministrations, he easily succumbed
to the disease. The people could not stop to mourn; they raised
their heads and worked harder to eradicate the misery that surrounded them. Father Richard would have blessed their decision.[60]

6

Despite war and pestilence the stream of migration continued to
pour into the territory. Most of the settlers came from New England, New York and Ohio, where they had been accustomed to
self-government. They naturally favored statehood. In addition
to the privilege of choosing their own officers and making their
own laws, they championed statehood as the only means of obtaining canals and railroads. In their newspapers they repeatedly
pointed out that the population of the territory was already fifty
thousand and that it was rapidly approaching the number required
for statehood. In the fall of 1832 the Legislative Council permitted
them to vote on the issue. They showed they favored statehood by
a large majority. Whereupon the Legislative Council petitioned
Congress to pass an enabling act which would permit the people to
elect deputies to a convention that would draw up a state constitution.

This action precipitated a boundary dispute between Michigan
and Ohio. The Ordinance of 1787 declared that not fewer than
three and not more than five states should be formed from the
Northwest Territory. It also fixed the boundaries of what later
became the states of Ohio, Indiana and Illinois. But Congress anticipated the establishment of two more states in that part of the Northwest Territory lying "north of an east and west line drawn through
the southernly bend or extreme of Lake Michigan."

Unfortunately, the vague geographical knowledge on contemporary maps rendered impossible any equitable distribution of lake
frontage. Small wonder that the constitutional convention of Ohio,
aiming to secure as favorable a boundary as possible, described the
northern boundary of the new state as either that given in the
Ordinance or, should it strike Lake Erie below Maumee Bay, one

running from the southern extremity of Lake Michigan to the most northernly cape of the bay. Congress admitted Ohio with this uncertain boundary, though in 1805 it established Michigan Territory with its southern boundary as that described in the Ordinance.[61]

To prevent possible friction between the state of Ohio and Michigan Territory and to enable them to reach a permanent agreement, Congress in 1812 ordered a survey that would agree with the boundaries of the Ordinance. War postponed the survey until 1817, when Edward Tiffin, Surveyor General of the United States, ordered William Harris to run the line described in the Ohio constitution.[62]

Governor Cass protested the Harris line to Congress and, through a committee, to President Monroe, who ordered another survey to agree with the boundaries of the Ordinance. This took the name of the surveyor, John A. Fulton. Between the Harris line and the Fulton line lay the "Toledo Strip," a tapering piece of land five to eight miles wide and containing about four hundred sixty-eight square miles.[63]

For the next thirteen years the Toledo Strip was governed in accordance with the laws of Michigan Territory. Then Congress, learning that the Fulton line was inaccurate, ordered Captain Tallcott of the United States Army to make another survey, which practically coincided with the Fulton line. The Tallcott line only intensified the boundary dispute. The people of Ohio had promoted the village of Toledo, which they hoped to make the northern terminus of the Miami Canal; they had no intention of surrendering it to the forthcoming state of Michigan. On their part, the people of the territory insisted on their "ancient rights" of drawing the southern boundary in accordance with the Ordinance.[64]

So matters stood when the territorial legislature began to petition Congress for an enabling act. Instead of replying, Congress, for the purpose of establishing temporary government, greatly enlarged the territory, attaching to it all the land north of the state of Missouri and west of the Mississippi to the Missouri River—an enormous region that encompassed present Michigan, Wisconsin, Minnesota, Iowa and the eastern half of North Dakota and South Dakota.

A few days later, on July 6, 1834, Governor Porter suddenly died of an undiagnosed illness and Mason once more found himself Acting Governor. Three weeks later the cholera struck the territory with greater virulence than before, though it was of shorter duration. No sooner had it vanished than Mason called the Legislative Council in special session to accept the recent acquisition of territory and to discuss the boundary dispute. Though he expressed confidence in the speedy admission of Michigan he advised the delegates to abstain from legislating on the boundary dispute, a matter which he believed should be settled by Ohio and Michigan as soon as the latter became a state. He then recommended a census of the territory east of the Mississippi to ascertain its readiness for statehood.[65]

The census showed a population of 85,856—a number almost a third greater than that required for statehood and much larger than that of any other state in the Great Lakes Frontier at the time of its admission. Mason wasted no time reconvening the Council and reminding it of the words of the Ordinance: "Such State *shall*"— he emphasized the word—"be admitted by its delegates into the Congress of the United States on an equal footing with the original States, in all respects whatever, and *shall* be at liberty to form a permanent Constitution and State government." Accordingly, and without awaiting congressional authorization, on January 26, 1835, the Council drew up a bill calling for a constitutional convention for the ensuing May.[66]

Governor Robert Lucas of Ohio countered this move by having permanent markers placed along the Harris line. To this threat Mason replied with legislation that provided a fine of $1,000 or five years' imprisonment for anybody save territorial or federal officers who would accept office or exercise official functions in the disputed strip. Undaunted, Lucas proceeded to organize the area into a new county, which he named for himself and for which he appointed a sheriff and a judge to hold court in defiance of Mason. This only spurred Mason to more drastic measures: he mobilized the militia, called for volunteers and placed himself at the head of both forces to direct military operations.[67]

News of possible armed collision between the state and the territory spread far and wide and eventually reached President Jackson in Washington. He consulted the Attorney General, who, after careful examination of the problem, sympathized with Mason; he denied the right of Ohio to exercise jurisdiction in the Toledo Strip without congressional approval.

Though Jackson concurred in this decision, he was unwilling to act. He feared the loss of Ohio, which possibly held the balance of power in the next presidential election; and he was unwilling to to displease Indiana and Illinois, both of which sided with Ohio. On one side were three great states with considerable votes in the electoral college; on the other, a territory with no votes at all. Jack-

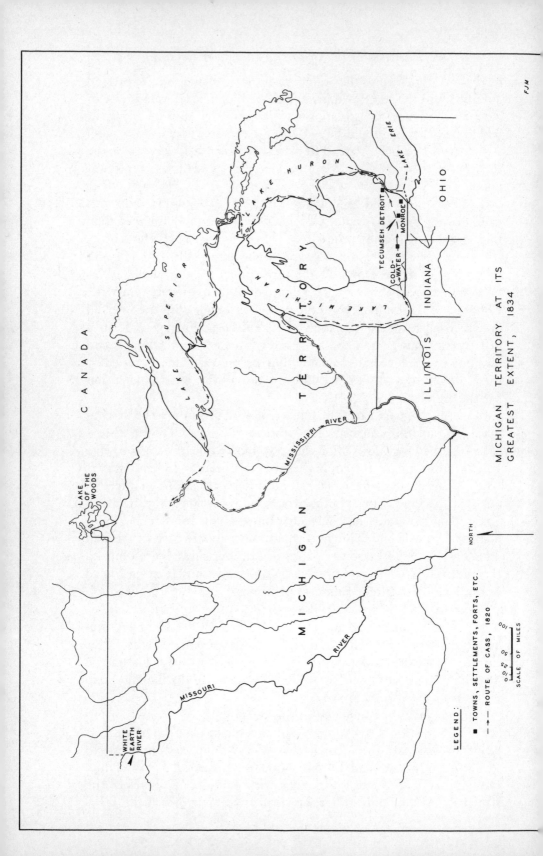

LEGEND:
■ TOWNS, SETTLEMENTS, FORTS, ETC.
→ ROUTE OF CASS, 1820

MICHIGAN TERRITORY AT ITS
GREATEST EXTENT, 1834

SCALE OF MILES
0 25 50 100

son extricated himself from his dilemma by appointing two commissioners to attempt to settle the difficulty. Early in April the commissioners arrived in Detroit and interviewed Mason, who agreed to refrain from using force as long as Lucas stayed out of the Toledo Strip. The commissioners, however, found Lucas less cooperative; he was unwilling to accept their suggestions to take no further action and to leave the matter to Congress. The commissioners then were constrained to return to Mason and deliver Jackson's personal message: on pain of being removed from office, he must refrain from enforcing the law that contained heavy penalties for Ohioans who accepted offices or attempted to exercise official functions in the Toledo Strip. Mason stuck to his guns. He denounced the power of removal for enforcement of law as "an act of executive usurpation and tyranny which would place every department of the government within the despotic control of a single officer."[68]

On May 11 the constitutional convention met in Detroit. While the delegates deliberated, Mason led his militia and volunteers to the Toledo Strip and marched to jail any Ohio officials who refused to leave at a specified time. At the head of a sizable posse one of Mason's deputy sheriffs, William McNair, permitted the Ohio surveyors who were remarking the Harris line to get well within the strip and then arrested nine of them and lugged them off to the town of Tecumseh to answer charges. The other surveyors escaped, while one of Mason's men increased their speed by firing his gun high above their heads. They soon arrived in Perrysburg, where they told a tale of hair-breadth escape that aroused immense indignation.

Lucas tattletaled to President Jackson, who ordered McNair to submit a report of the incident. A man of humor, McNair laughed off his exploit as a mere bagatelle; he wrote that the escaped surveyors had made incredibly fast time on foot through a cottonwood swamp and had arrived next morning in Perrysburg "with nothing more serious than the loss of hats, and their clothing, like Governor Morey's breeches, without the patch." Of the arrested men, two were discharged, six were admitted to bail, and one, a Colonel Fletcher, was jailed when he refused to put up bail. By this time the arrests had swelled with numerous tellings into a murderous attack. News of it confounded the slow means of transportation and spread like a forest fire all over the country. Lucas, seeing that Mason was in earnest, now backed down; he expressed willingness to remove his surveyors from the Harris line. Then he called a special session of the Ohio assembly, which voted to accept the suggestions of Jackson's commissioners on condition that they could persuade Mason to do likewise. At the same time it took the precaution of appropriating $300,000 to enforce the jurisdiction of Ohio up to the Harris line, and passed a law which carried a penalty of from three to seven years' imprisonment for anybody found guilty of "abducting" Ohioans. To which the constitutional convention in Detroit replied that it would recognize no authority in the Toledo Strip save that of the United States. The Legislative Council outdid the Ohio assembly by meeting the emergency with an appropriation of $315,000.[69]

Now matters between the state and the territory grew progressively worse. The leader of Mason's militia, General Joseph W. Brown, arrested B. F. Stickney, an ardent Ohioan who imagined himself a military man with the rank of major, and had him tied to his horse and taken to Monroe for trial. Stickney's sons had numbers rather than names. His oldest born, One Stickney, was a peaceful man; but Two Stickney was a bully who seriously injured a Michigan sheriff with a penknife and then fled. Mason offered a reward of $500 for Two's capture; but Lucas refused to extradite him. From early spring to late summer each party charged the other with outrages and insults. Mason's supporters tore down a flag of Ohio which had been raised in Toledo. In reporting the incident a Michigan paper referred to the desecrated flag as "the disgraceful badge of treason" and stated that patriotic citizens dragged it through the streets and finally burned it "with suitable demonstrations of contempt." The Ohio newspapers offered an entirely different version of the incident: Brown had the flag taken down and tied to the tails of several horses in his troop. Carl Wittke says that Toledo produced its own Barbara Fritchie, who unfurled the dishonored flag or another like it. The legend, however, is only partially retold. General Brown was too hard a man to emulate Stonewall Jackson by threatening to shoot like a dog any man who dared to harm a hair on her head. Loyal Ohioans in Toledo deluged the newspapers of their state with stories of outrages committed by "bloodthirsty Michiganders." They charged them with burglaries, kidnappings and abuse of women, who were "dragged off in false pretenses to Monroe." To which a Michigan newspaper retorted that the alleged insulted and abased women were of the kind who "would suffer themselves to be much harder dealt with, under other circumstances, without a murmur."[70]

Meanwhile the constitutional convention had completed its work. The constitution, signed on June 24, provided that it should be submitted to the people for ratification or rejection on October 5, that an election for state officers should be held on the following day, and that the state legislature should assemble for the first time on November 1, 1835. The constitution was a simple and brief document which provided for a bicameral legislature, a governor with veto power over the acts of the legislature, and a judiciary consisting of a supreme court and other courts. It contained a bill of rights, forbade slavery or involuntary servitude, and granted suffrage to every white male inhabitant over twenty-one years old. It stressed the importance of education by providing for a superintendent of public instruction to be named by the governor with the consent of the legislature. It also created a system of common schools, with one school in each district "at least three months in every year." It promised that, as soon as circumstances permitted, a library would be established in each township, and that land and funds would be granted for the support of a university.[71]

The next three months produced events that proved the most memorable in Mason's life. In August he accepted the nomination of the governorship from a Democratic convention assembled in the village of Ann Arbor. At about the same time John Forsyth, Secretary of State, sent him a letter apprising him of his dismissal as secretary of Michigan Territory for failing to preserve the "spirit of moderation and forbearance" which President Jackson deemed "necessary for the preservation of public peace." Forsyth sent a copy of this letter to Governor Lucas, who derived from it a hint by which he saw the possibility of winning the Toledo war. He would claim jurisdiction over Lucas County by requesting the judges of the state to hold court in it! He sent Colonel Mathais Van Fleet with twenty sharpshooters to escort the judiciary from Miami to Toledo. The judges, knowing that eleven hundred "Michiganders" were in and around the village, trembled at the governor's request; but Van Fleet restored their sense of dignity and honor with a martial reprimand: "If you are women, go home; if you are men, do your duty as judges of the court. I will do mine." At midnight on September 6 Van Fleet escorted the judge of Lucas County, his bailiff, the reporter, the sheriff and various witnesses to the schoolhouse in Toledo. They carefully blacked out the windows, lit a tallow dip, hastily wrote the proceedings on loose paper, and deposited them in the clerk's hat.

When the court adjourned, they all went to a nearby tavern, registered their names, and had a drink all around. They were about to refill their glasses when the village wag ran into the tavern shouting that a strong force under General Brown was coming to arrest them. Dropping their glasses, they sprang for their horses and sped toward Miami by the river route. When they reached the top of a hill they halted for a few minutes to rest. Then and there the clerk recovered enough of his breath to discover that he had lost his hat with the papers containing the proceedings of the court. He vaguely remembered that the hat—an elongated stovepipe that carried everything from a spare collar and dickey to court papers—had caught the overhanging branch of a tree with such violence that, despite his precaution of steadying it on his head with his left hand as he rode, it had plopped to the ground. The papers furnished Governor Lucas with jurisdiction over the disputed area: they must be recovered at all cost!

Nerving themselves to the possibility of encountering a superior force of Michiganders, they searched every inch of ground in the teeming darkness as they retraced their steps. Their courage and perseverance were eventually rewarded. There, by the side of the road, was the lost hat, with some of the documents still in it and some strewn all around in the mud! Their joy at recovering the precious papers was so great that Colonel Van Fleet ordered two salutes to be fired on the spot. He knew that he was near the Ohio line and that, if Michiganders pursued him, he would reach safety before he could be overtaken. Down the road they ambled, bragging of their prowess like so many boys marching to school. They reached home about dawn.[72]

Three days later a messenger found Mason during a dress parade of his troops and handed him Forsyth's letter of dismissal. The acting governor read it, called for attention, and announced to his men that he was no longer their leader. General Brown immediately disbanded his troops. That ended the Toledo War, whose "onpleasantness," says a witty frontier writer, "had resulted in the destruction of many lives of chickens and honey bees, and occasionally a turkey."[73]

Mason's successor, John Scott Horner, who arrived in Detroit on September 19, had the misfortune to be cast among the people of Michigan under circumstances that gave each a prejudiced opinion of the other. They naturally regarded him as a puppet of Washington politicians and therefore the embodiment of a policy opposed to that which they had embraced. His corpulence, his sour expression, and his raspy voice only intensified the contempt they felt toward him. And when he began to free all the Ohio trespassers from Michigan jails in obedience to the orders of his superiors, they were certain that his purpose was to help Lucas gain his objective.

In this conviction they were correct, for Horner kept the governor of Ohio informed on circumstances in the territory and hinted that they should redound to the satisfaction of the state. Such a man should not have been surprised that nobody in Detroit, Monroe and Ypsilanti would carry out his orders. Yet Horner was so ignorant of frontier life that he regarded the people as "rebellious," and openly said so. They naturally greeted his appearance in public with boos and clods of dirt. Once, when he attempted to speak on the steps of the courthouse in Monroe, they waved him off as a Judas. They dubbed him "Little Jack Horner," and composed ribald verses about him in imitation of that nursery rhyme. Eventually he left Detroit in disgust. But in Ypsilanti, where he took refuge, he found himself in even greater danger. The rough element of the village, learning that he had freed Lucas' supporters, gathered angrily beneath his window and aroused him from sleep with a bombardment of curses, stones and blobs of horse dung. Terrified, he returned to Detroit, where he remained until May 1836 when he moved to Wisconsin Territory, which Congress had recently established and of which President Jackson had appointed him secretary.[74]

Meanwhile, in the previous October, the people of Michigan had elected Mason governor, Edward Mundy lieutenant governor, and Isaac E. Crary representative in Congress. Mason was not present to receive the congratulations and applause of the people. Soon after his dismissal he had departed for the East to work for the admission of Michigan. Three weeks after his election the Michigan legislature met for the first time and elected Lucius Lyon and John Norvell to the United States Senate.[75]

The two senators and the representative journeyed to Washington to take their seats in the Twenty-fourth Congress; but it would admit them only as spectators. In March 1836 Thomas Hart Benton proposed that the Harris line be made the southern boundary and the Menominee and Montreal rivers the western boundary, of Michigan. Benton also proposed that the western portion of the Upper Peninsula be attached to Michigan as indemnity for her loss of the Toledo Strip. About a month later Congress created Wisconsin Territory from the remnant of Michigan Territory. In June, after heated debates, one of which lasted twenty-five hours, Congress passed bills for the admission of Michigan and Arkansas. To keep an equal balance in the senate, Arkansas was asking for admission as a slave state. But Michigan, having refused to adjust her boundary line to the satisfaction of the government, remained "a sovereign state out of the Union." And her status could not be changed until her inhabitants accepted the conditions expressed in the admission bill.

On September 26, in obedience to the wishes of Congress, the Michigan legislature assembled at Ann Arbor a convention of assent, which rejected the conditions "as an unconstitutional interference with the rights of the state." The people had forecast this decision long before the convention was assembled. In March a committee of citizens had drawn up a resolution stating that the people of Michigan had given "no man or body of men authority to alter by bargain or compromise the boundaries to which they have uniformly asserted a right."

The resolution dismissed the Upper Peninsula as a "sterile region on the shores of Lake Superior, destined by soil and climate to remain forever a wilderness." To Sheldon McKnight, editor of the *Free Press*, the Upper Peninsula was a "region of perpetual snows— the ultima Thule of our national domain in the North." Senator Lyon reflected with charming sarcasm that the region could furnish the people of Michigan with Indians for all time and now and then with a little bear meat for a delicacy. Then, suddenly, criticism stopped. Word reached Michigan that the Federal government was about to distribute the surplus of the United States Treasury among the states and that it would refuse Michigan her share of nearly $400,000 unless she entered the Union. That changed matters entirely. The critics of the Upper Peninsula now became its most ardent supporters. Now Senator Lyon predicted that the Upper Peninsula in twenty years would be worth more "than forty million of dollars, and that even after ten years the State would not think of selling it for that sum." And Sheldon McKnight thought that "the white fish of Lake Superior might be a fair offset for the lost bull frog pastures of the Maumee." Even Stevens Thomson Mason, who had sacrificed his territorial office and Jackson's friendship to proud determination, now advised the people to accept the conditions in the admission act for the sake of national harmony. In December a self-appointed committee called for a second convention of assent. This was known as "the frost-bitten convention" because it met on December 24 in extremely bitter weather. It consented to the boundaries with a promptitude that almost besmirched its dignity. The deputies hustled their report to President Jackson, who in turn hustled it to Congress with a recommendation that it be accepted.

After some debate on the propriety or validity of the frost-bitten convention, Congress approved the admission act. Jackson signed it, and at long last, on January 26, 1837, Michigan added a new star to the American flag.[76]

7

Of all the territories in the Great Lakes Frontier, only the last, Wisconsin, started its separate existence with a legislature and a delegate to Congress. The federal government considered that Wisconsin had passed through the first stage of territorial government when it was a part of Michigan. Its first governor was Henry Dodge, who owed his office principally to the dash and bravery he had exhibited during the Black Hawk War. On July 4, 1836, Dodge and Horner took their oaths of office at Mineral Point, which at that time was the largest settlement in Wisconsin.[77]

Toward the end of October the Wisconsin legislature assembled at Belmont in a frame building that had been built for the purpose. The delegates almost immediately began to fight among themselves over the selection of a territorial capital. They considered a dozen places, some of which existed only on paper, before one of the territorial judges, James Duane Doty, declared for the present site of Madison, a virgin forest which he owned. The supporters of the rejected sites whispered that Doty realized his aim by distributing choice lands among the members of the legislature. Be that as it may, Doty advanced sound arguments for his choice: the site of Madison was beautiful and healthful; it represented a compromise in the rivalry between Green Bay and the lead mining region in the south; and, lying between the settlements of Lake Michigan and the Mississippi, it would help immeasurably in developing the unsettled interior. The temporary capital of the territory was Burlington, which is now in Iowa.[78]

The surveyors arrived on the site of Madison, named for President Madison, in February 1837 while the ground was still blanketed with snow, and began to plot the town. In the center of the site they laid out a park from which the streets, named in honor of the signers of the constitution, emanated in imitation of Washington. A month later Even Peck, a tavern keeper from Blue Mound Mine, thirty miles westward, sent two Frenchmen to build for him a log tavern to serve the workmen who were building the town. Later that spring his wife, Roseline, with their two-year-old son arrived in Madison to become the town's first permanent settlers.[79]

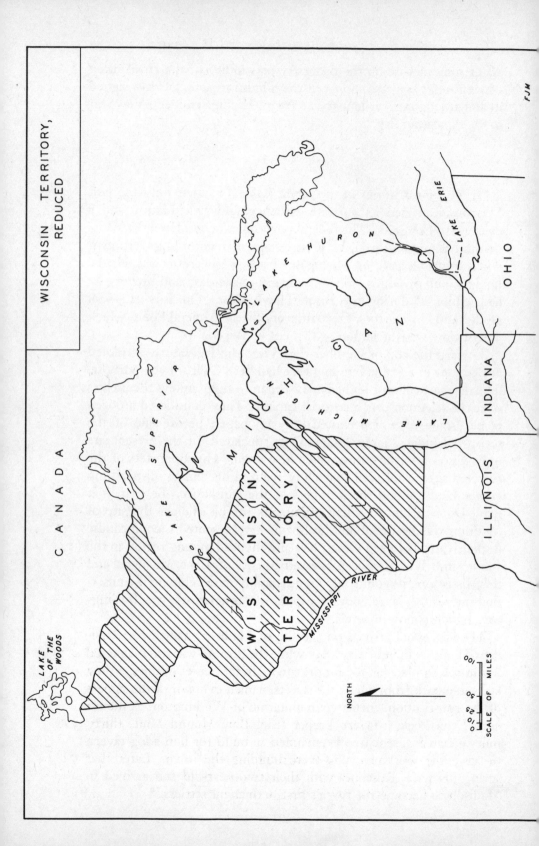

The statehouse, which rose slowly in the center of town, was made of logs that the building commissioner, Augustus A. Bird of Milwaukee, had brought from the surrounding forest and cut at his own sawmill, which he had brought from the East by steamboat. That November, before the statehouse was completed, the legislature returned to Madison, only to find that the town could accommodate no more than fifty boarders. The legislature adjourned until January 26, 1839, when it hoped enough of the town would be completed to board all the officials of the territorial government.[80]

Meanwhile the territory had diminished. On June 12, 1838, Congress passed a law which, effective July 3, established Iowa Territory from that portion of Wisconsin Territory lying west of the Mississippi and a line drawn due north from its headwaters. The congressional law specified that, after July 3, the legislature should disband and a new legislature be elected in its stead. It requested Governor Dodge to reapportion the seats in the new legislature.[81]

The legislature of Wisconsin, like that of Michigan, waged a war of words with Congress over loss of territory to a neighboring state. We will recall that when Illinois became a state in 1818 she obtained a strip of land along Lake Michigan north of the east and west line which the Ordinance designated as the boundary of future states in the Northwest Territory. This strip of land, sixty-one miles wide and containing eighty-five hundred square miles, developed into a rich agricultural and mining region on which were planted the cities of Chicago, Evanston, Elgin, and Galena. Governor Dodge claimed with justification that Congress, if it had observed the Ordinance, would have awarded this area to Wisconsin. He induced the territorial legislature to adopt a vigorous memorial to Congress. After thirteen months passed without a reply, the legislature again memorialized Congress that Illinois held a large and valuable area "contrary to the manifest right and consent of the people of the territory."

The memorial or resolution, as it was called, created an uproar on both sides of the line. Oddly enough, the people of Wisconsin, realizing that Dodge had induced the boundary dispute to hurry Wisconsin into statehood, opposed the memorial more than did those of Illinois. Dodge knew his plan would fail unless he could count on the large population in the disputed area. The small population of the territory were as yet unwilling to assume the added taxes and civil and social responsibilities that attended statehood.[82]

The Whig victory of 1840 deprived Dodge, an ardent Democrat,

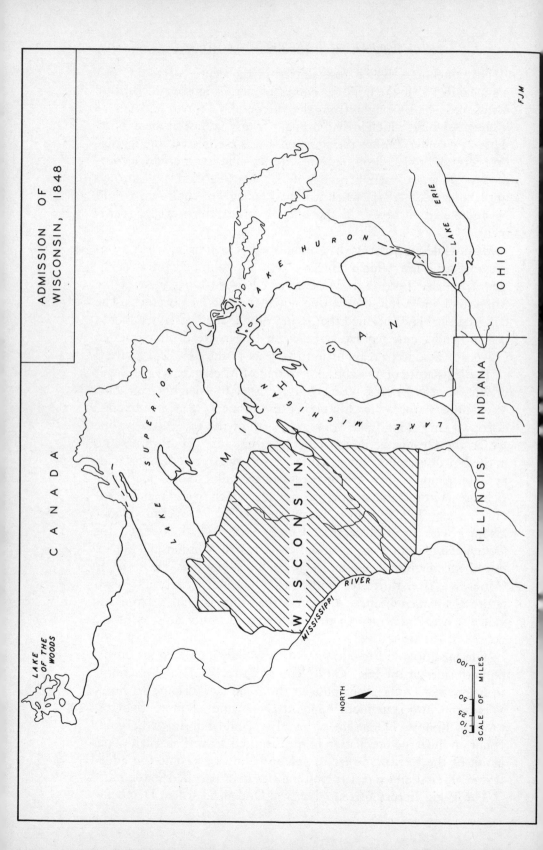

ADMISSION OF
WISCONSIN, 1848

FJM

CANADA

LAKE
OF THE
WOODS

LAKE SUPERIOR

WISCONSIN

MISSISSIPPI RIVER

M I C H I G A N

LAKE HURON

LAKE MICHIGAN

LAKE ERIE

OHIO

INDIANA

ILLINOIS

NORTH

SCALE OF MILES
0 10 25 50 100

of his office. His successor, a strong Harrison and Tyler man, was James Duane Doty, who soon resumed the boundary war with Illinois. He ousted from the disputed area some Illinois land commissioners and informed the governor of the state that he was exercising authority over a body of people who should be citizens of Wisconsin.[83]

Late in 1843 he induced the legislature to draw up a report in which it asked Congress to grant Wisconsin such compensation as Michigan had obtained for her loss of her southern border. The report suggested that the compensation be made in the form of a congressional appropriation for such internal improvements as a railroad between Lake Michigan and the Mississippi, a canal between the Fox and Rock rivers, and harbors at several ports on Lake Michigan. The report threatened that, if Congress refused these reasonable suggestions, Wisconsin would, like Michigan, become a sovereign state outside the Union. The report appealed for justice while it warned that the people of Wisconsin could show the world that they lacked neither the disposition nor the ability to protect their interests. The belligerent tone of the report aroused heated debates between the conservative and liberal members of the legislature. The conservatives washed their hands of the report as a declaration of war against Illinois and the United States. Nevertheless, it passed by a close vote and reached Congress, where it died an ignominious death. Wisconsin, unlike Michigan, never succeeded in solving her boundary dispute. On the contrary, she lost some more land when, in 1848, she entered the Union. Congress deprived her of the region between the St. Croix River and the upper Mississippi and bestowed it graciously on Minnesota.[84]

In the autumn of 1844 President Tyler removed the trouble-making Doty from office. But his successor, Nathaniel P. Tallmadge, enjoyed his post barely eight months. When Polk became president on March 4, 1845, he restored the faithful fellow Democrat Dodge, who kept his office until Wisconsin became a state. Dodge, of course, immediately resumed agitation for statehood. His chances of success were now considerably better. The territory counted one hundred fifty-five thousand people, a large percentage of whom saw the advantages of statehood and were willing to assume the responsibilities it entailed. Dodge induced the legislature to put the question of statehood before qualified voters, who in April 1846 overwhelmingly responded in the affirmative. Meanwhile the territorial delegate, Morgan L. Martin, had introduced an enabling act in Congress, which passed it.

Assured that President Polk would approve it, Dodge and the legislature called a constitutional convention which in December 1846 produced an ably written constitution. Unfortunately, it contained provisions that displeased the majority of the people. The provision chiefly responsible for its defeat denied power to the legislature to establish any institution or corporation with any kind of banking privileges. Its sponsor was E. G. Ryan, a brilliant lawyer from Racine who had lost heavily in recent bank failures and who had become an uncompromising opponent of banks of issue. The Democrats objected to the provision that married women might own property, either real or personal, separate from her husband. The Whigs disliked the provision that granted suffrage to Negroes and that made them eligible for office.[85]

In November 1847 the legislature called for the election of delegates to a second constitutional convention. It assembled in the following month and drew up a constitution that carefully avoided the pitfalls of the defeated one. This time a banking provision gave the legislature power to submit the question "bank or no bank" to the people at any general election and to grant bank charters or pass a general banking law. The friends of Negro suffrage made a strong but vain appeal. The provision about married women and property was deleted. Then all went swimmingly. The people adopted the constitution on March 13, 1848, and Congress approved it in the following May. Meanwhile the people had elected Nelson Dewey, the Democratic candidate, as the first governor of the sovereign state of Wisconsin. At the end of May President Polk signed the congressional bill which admitted Wisconsin in the sisterhood of states.[86]

A hundred seventy-five years had passed since that fair May day in 1673 when Louis Jolliet and Father Jacques Marquette had paddled down Green Bay, crossed Lake Winnebago, and drifted toward the village of the Mascouten and Miami on the lower Fox River in the present state of Wisconsin. Since that day the epic of the Old Northwest had made a complete circle and had ended at about its starting point.

Notes

CHAPTER I

1. Louise Phelps Kellogg, ed., *Early Narratives of the Northwest*, p. 237. Francis Parkman, *La Salle and the Discovery of the Great West*, pp. 64-65 (hereafter Parkman, *La Salle*). Francis Borgia Steck, *The Jolliet-Marquette Expedition, 1673*, presents strong arguments in support of his view that Father Claude Dablon and not Father Marquette wrote the narrative of the first expedition from a copy of Jolliet's lost narrative, from Jolliet's recollections and from Marquette's notes.
2. Parkman, *La Salle*, pp. 49-53.
3. *See* Earnest Gagnon, *Louis Jolliet*, p. 10 ff.
4. Clarence W. Alvord, *The Illinois Country*, pp. 55-56. Kellogg, ed., p. 227.
5. Parkman, *La Salle*, p. 60. Kellogg, ed., p. 228.
6. Parkman, *La Salle*, pp. 40-60.
7. Kellogg, ed., p. 234.
8. *Ibid.*, p. 236. Reuben Gold Thwaites, ed., *The Jesuit Relations and Allied Documents*, LIX, 107 (hereafter Thwaites, ed., *Jesuit Relations*).
9. Kellogg, ed., p. 239.
10. Parkman, *La Salle*, p. 68. Kellogg, ed., pp. 238-249.
11. *Ibid.*, p. 250.
12. Parkman, *La Salle*, p. 71.
13. Kellogg, ed., p. 253.
14. *Ibid.*, p. 254.
15. *Ibid.*, p. 256.
16. Parkman, *La Salle*, p. 74.
17. *Ibid.*, pp. 75-76 n.
18. *Ibid.*, pp. 77-78.
19. Alvord, *The Illinois Country*, p. 67. Parkman, *La Salle*, p. 79. Kellogg, ed., p. 265.
20. *Ibid.*, p. 275. Thwaites, *Jesuit Relations*, LIX, 199.
21. Quoted in Parkman, *La Salle*, p. 339.
22. *Ibid.*, pp. 146-148.
23. *Ibid.*, p. 161.
24. *Ibid.*, p. 162.
25. *Ibid.*, pp. 127-128.
26. *Ibid.*, p. 163. Francis Gaither, *The Fatal River: The Life and Death of La Salle*, p. 119.
27. Parkman, *La Salle*, p. 166. John Bartlet Brebner, *The Explorers of North America*, p. 252.
28. *Ibid.*, p. 171.
29. Pierre Margry, ed., *Découvertes et Établissements des Français dans l'Ouest et dans le Sud de l'Amérique Septentionale, 1614-1698, mémoires et documents inédits*, I, 580-582.
30. Parkman, *La Salle*, pp. 180-181.

31. *Ibid.*, Gaither, pp. 124-125.

32. Parkman, *La Salle*, pp. 190-191.

33. *Ibid.*, p. 192. Brebner, p. 253.

34. Gaither, pp. 139-146.

35. Parkman, *La Salle*, p. 194.

36. *Ibid.*, p. 199.

37. *Ibid.*, pp. 200-201.

38. Gaither, pp. 158-159. Parkman, *La Salle*, pp. 206-207. Alvord, *The Illinois Country*, p. 83.

39. I. J. Cox, ed., *The Journeys of Réné Robert Cavelier, Sieur de la Salle*, I, 120-122. Parkman, *La Salle*, p. 211. Gaither, p. 161.

40. Parkman, *La Salle*, p. 212.

41. *Ibid.*, p. 213.

42. Cox, I, 126 ff.

43. Parkman, *La Salle*, pp. 217-218.

44. Kellogg, ed., pp. 291-296.

45. Margry, ed., I, 510-515, 525 ff.

46. *Ibid.*, II, 186-189. Brebner, p. 255.

47. James A. James, *The Life of George Rogers Clark*, pp. 69-73 (hereafter James, *Life of Clark*). Clarence W. Alvord, *The Old Kaskaskia Records*, pp. 35-37.

48. Alvord, *The Illinois Country*, p. 138.

49. James, *Life of Clark*, p. 70.

50. Alvord, *The Illinois Country*, pp. 192-193.

51. *Ibid.*, pp. 154-156, 198-200.

52. *Ibid.*, pp. 202-203.

53. *Ibid.*

54. Clarence W. Alvord and Clarence E. Carter, eds., *The Critical Period, 1763-1765*, p. 126.

55. Constantin Francois Chasseboeuf, Comte de Volney, *View of the Climate and Soil of the United States . . .* , p. 372.

56. *Ibid.*, pp. 332-337.

57. Alvord, *The Illinois Country*, p. 218.

58. *Ibid.*

59. *Ibid.*, p. 219.

60. *Ibid.*, p. 208.

61. *Ibid.*

62. *Wisconsin Historical Collections*, XVI, 437. Alvord, *The Illinois Country*, p. 210.

63. Margry, ed., VI, 455-459.

64. Alvord, *The Illinois Country*, pp. 212-213.

65. *Ibid.*

66. Albert T. Volwiler, *George Croghan and the Westward Movement, 1741-1782*, pp. 34-38.

67. *Ibid.*, p. 105. Villiers du Terrage, Marc, Baron de, *Les Dernieres Années de la Louisiane Française; le Chevalier de Kerlérec, d'Abbadie Aubry Laussat*, p. 85.

68. *See* Aubry's Memoir in *Illinois Historical Collections*, I, 166-170.

69. Francis Parkman, *The Conspiracy of Pontiac*, I, 309-312.

70. Volwiler, pp. 167-175. Nicholas B. Wainwright, *George Croghan, Wilderness Diplomat*, pp. 197-199.

71. Volwiler, pp. 187-188. Wainwright, pp. 201-238.

72. Volwiler, pp. 227-229. Alvord, *The Illinois Country*, pp. 262-264.

73. *Ibid.*, p. 266.

CHAPTER 2

1. Draper MSS, 3J30, 41. James A. James, ed., *George Rogers Clark Papers, 1771-1781*, VIII, 218 (hereafter James, ed., *Clark Papers*).

2. Draper MSS, 3J42.

3. Draper MSS, 3J43.

4. Draper MSS, 3J43. Clark's Diary, in James, ed., *Clark Papers*, VIII, 46.

5. Draper MSS, 48J12.

6. Draper MSS, 3J43.

7. Draper MSS, 3J43.

8. Draper MSS, 3J45.

9. Draper MSS, 3J45-46. George Rogers Clark to George Mason, in James, ed., *Clark Papers*, VIII, 116.

10. Draper MSS, 3J44. Clark to Mason, in James, ed., *Clark Papers*, VIII, 34, 36.

11. Draper MSS, 1J124.

12. Draper MSS, 1J126.

13. Draper MSS, 1J128.

14. Draper MSS, 3J4.

15. Draper MSS, 3J6-8.

16. John Anthony Caruso, *The Appalachian Frontier*, pp. 179-180.

17. Draper MSS, 1J127.

18. Draper MSS, 3J46.

19. Draper MSS, 3J47.

20. Draper MSS, 3J48, 48J18. James, ed., *Clark Papers*, VIII, 18.

21. Draper MSS, 3J50.

22. Draper MSS, 3J52, 18J83-84.

23. James, *Life of Clark*, p. 118.

24. Draper MSS, 3J53-54. James, *Life of Clark*, p. 118. Temple Bodley, *George Rogers Clark*, pp. 62-63.

25. Draper MSS, 3J55-56. Alvord, *Old Kaskaskia Records*, p. 176.

26. Draper MSS, 3J56.

27. Draper MSS, 3J57. *See* Jacob Piatt Dunn, "Father Gibault: The Patriot Priest of the Northwest," in Illinois State Historical Society *Transactions*, X (1906), 15-34.

28. Draper MSS, 3J58. James, ed., *Clark Papers*, VIII, 120-121.

29. Draper MSS, 18J80. Theodore Roosevelt, *The Winning of the West*, II, 106.

30. James, *Life of Clark*, p. 119. Bodley, pp. 64, 74.

31. Draper MSS, 18J80-83.

32. Draper MSS, 3J61.

33. Jean Henri Antoine Doniol, *Histoire de la Participation de le France a l'Établissement des États-Unis d'Amérique, correspondance diplomatique et documents*, II, 293.

34. Draper MSS, 3J64-65. James A. James, *Oliver Pollock*, p. 139.

35. James C. Randall, "George Rogers Clark's Service of Supply," in *Mississippi Valley Historical Review* (hereafter *M.V.H.R.*), VIII (1922), 257.

36. Quoted in James, *Oliver Pollock*, p. 1.

37. *Ibid.*, p. 65.

38. James, ed., *Clark Papers*, VIII, 55. Randall, VIII, 253.

39. Quoted in James, *Oliver Pollock*, pp. 144-145.

40. *Ibid.*, p. 143.

41. *Ibid.*

42. *Ibid.*, p. 145.

43. James, ed., *Clark Papers*, VIII, 125.

44. Clark to Mason, in *Ibid*.

45. Draper MSS, 3J72 (newspaper excerpts).

46. Draper MSS, 3J74.

47. Draper MSS, 3J76.

48. Draper MSS, 3J94-95.

49. Quoted in Bodley, p. 93.

50. Roosevelt, II, 231.

51. James, ed., *Clark Papers*, VIII, 89.

52. *See* John Bakeless, *Background to Glory: The Life of George Rogers Clark*, pp. 132-135, for a vivid account of Helm's surrender.

53. James, ed., *Clark Papers*, VIII, 97. Alvord, *The Illinois Country*, p. 332.

54. Draper MSS, 3J83.

55. Draper MSS, 3J95-98.

56. Draper MSS, 3J99.

57. Draper MSS, 3J100.

58. Draper MSS, 3J102. George Rogers Clark to John Rogers, Kaskaskias, Virginia, February 20, 1779, in Draper MSS, 3J103.

59. Roosevelt, II, 268.

60. Draper MSS, 3J105-108.

61. Draper MSS, 3J106-111, 7J62-65.

62. Draper MSS, 3J111-112, 7J66.

63. Draper MSS, 7J68.

64. Draper MSS, 3J113.

65. Draper MSS, 3J114.

66. "Bowman's Journal," in James, ed., *Clark Papers*, VIII, 159.

67. Draper MSS, 3J115.

68. Draper MSS, 3J116-120.

69. Draper MSS, 3J121.

70. Draper MSS, 3J122.

71. Draper MSS, 3J125.

72. *See* terms of capitulation in Draper MSS, 3J126. Bakless, pp. 188-210, describes in detail the events leading up to the recapture of Vincennes.

73. Draper MSS, 3J132.

74. Draper MSS, 20J106, 3J143.

75. James, ed., *Clark Papers*, VIII, 159-160.

76. *Ibid.*, VIII, 161.

77. Clarence W. Alvord, ed., *Cahokia Records, 1778-1790*, pp. 614, 615.

78. *Ibid.*, p. 616.

79. James, *Life of Clark*, pp. 166-168.

80. Draper MSS, 6J133. James, ed., *Clark Papers*, VIII, 146.

81. Bodley, p. 143.

82. Draper MSS, 49J52.

83. *Michigan Pioneer and Historical Collections*, XIX (1892), 539.

84. Draper MSS, 8J136. *Maryland Journal*, October 17, 1780. Newspaper clippings in Draper MSS, 6J209.

85. *See* Clark to Thomas Jefferson, in Draper MSS, 8J138.

86. *Kentucky Gazette*, August 20, 1780.

87. Draper MSS, 8J118, 126.

88. Draper MSS, 8J127. Milo Milton Quaife, "The Ohio Campaigns of 1782," in *M.V.H.R.*, XVII (1931), 528.

89. Claude H. Van Tyne, *The American Revolution*, p. 284.

90. Clarence W. Alvord, "Virginia and the West," in *M.V.H.R.*, III (1916), 196.

91. Samuel Flagg Bemis, *Diplomacy of the American Revolution*, p. 219 n.
92. Alvord, *The Illinois Country*, p. 356.

CHAPTER 3

1. "Narrative of John Brickell's Captivity Among the Delaware Indians," in *The American Pioneer*, II (1842), 46. Timothy Pickering Papers.
2. *Pennsylvania Archives*, Series 1, X, 554.
3. Francis Whiting Halsey, *The Old New York Frontier*, p. 157.
4. *Ibid.*, p. 166.
5. *Ibid.*, p. 190.
6. E. F. Bliss, ed., *Diary of David Zeisberger*, pp. 10-18. Consul W. Butterfield, *History of the Girtys*, pp. 132-133. Boyd Cumrine, *History of Washington County, Pennsylvania*, pp. 102-108. "The Moravians and Their Missions," in *M.V.H.R.*, XIX (1930), 356-358.
7. Consul W. Butterfield, *Historical Account of the Expedition Against Sandusky Under Colonel William Crawford in 1782*, p. 33 (hereafter Butterfield, *Crawford*).
8. Consul W. Butterfield, *Washington-Irvine Correspondence*, pp. 99-100.
9. *Ibid.*, pp. 9, 38.
10. *Ibid.*, pp. 173-174.
11. *Ibid.*, p. 168.
12. *Ibid.*, pp. 121, 125, 128.
13. Butterfield, *Crawford*, pp. 343-369.
14. Henry S. Manley, *The Treaty of Fort Stanwix, 1784*, p. 19. See the Ordinance of 1783 in the U.S. Continental Congress *Journals . . . 1774-1789*, XXV, 681-693. Randolph C. Downes, *Council Fires on the Upper Ohio*, p. 284 (hereafter Downes, *Council Fires*).
15. *Ibid.*, pp. 284-286.
16. Manley, pp. 24-56. *Penn. Archives*, Series 1, X, 88.
17. *Ibid.*
18. *Ibid.*
19. Downes, *Council Fires*, p. 292. Draper MSS, 23U (no pagination).
20. Draper MSS, 1W26, 27. Memorandum of the proceedings at the Treaty of Fort McIntosh, in Timothy Pickering Papers. *American State Papers, Indian Affairs*, I, 11.
21. *Ibid.*
22. *Ibid.*
23. *Ibid.*
24. Burke A. Hinsdale, *The Old Northwest*, pp. 189-246.
25. *Ibid.*
26. Beverley W. Bond, *The Foundations of Ohio*, pp. 258-265.
27. *Ibid.*, pp. 248, 260-261.
28. Draper MSS, 1W39-44.
29. Draper MSS, 3U186, 304.
30. Ebenezer Denny, "Military Journal of Major Ebenezer Denny" in *Historical Society of Pennsylvania Publications*, VII, 278.
31. Draper MSS, 3U186.
32. Draper MSS, 3U186-187.
33. Denny, VII, 278-280.
34. *Ibid.*
35. Draper MSS, 3U394. "Butler's Journal," in *Olden Time*, II, 522.

36. Draper MSS, 3U394. "Butler's Journal," II, 523.
37. *Ibid.*, II, 523-524.
38. Denny, VII, 285. "Butler's Journal," II, 530-531.
39. W. H. Smith, ed., *St. Clair Papers*, II, 19.
40. William L. Stone, *Life of Joseph Brant*, II, 248.
41. Draper MSS, 23U45.
42. Downes, *Council Fires*, pp. 300-301.
43. A. B. Hulbert, ed., *Records of the Ohio Company*, I, xxvi-xxviii.
44. Rowena Buell, ed., *Memoirs of Rufus Putnam*, pp. 101-102.
45. Hulbert, ed., *Records of the Ohio Company*, I, 4-13. *See* "Origin of the Ohio Company," in Ohio Archaeological and Historical Society (hereafter O. A. & H. S.) *Quarterly*, I (1887), 37-46.
46. A. B. Hulbert, ed., *Ohio in the Time of Confederation*, pp. 114-120. Hulbert, ed., *Records of the Ohio Company*, I, li-liii.
47. William Parker Cutler and Julia Perkins Cutler, eds., *Life and Journals and Correspondence of Manasseh Cutler*, I, 6 *passim*.
48. *Ibid.*, I, 203-252.
49. *Ibid.*, I, 295.
50. *Ibid.*, I, 298-305.
51. *Ibid.*
52. Hinsdale, pp. 255-269. Cutler and Cutler, eds., I, 335-373.
53. Theodore Pease, "The Ordinance of 1787," in *M.V.H.R.*, XXV (1929), 167-180. *See also* William Parker Cutler, "The Ordinance of July 13, 1787," in O. A. & H. S. *Quarterly*, I (1887), 10-37.
54. Bond, *Foundations of Ohio*, p. 267.
55. Hinsdale, p. 264.
56. *Ibid.*

CHAPTER 4

1. Journal of Rufus Putnam, in Rufus Putnam Papers.
2. Thomas J. Summers, *History of Marietta*, pp. 53-54.
3. "Christopher Gist's Journal," in J. Stoddard Johnston, ed., *First Explorations in Kentucky*, p. 158.
4. Summers, p. 54.
5. *Ibid.*
6. *Ibid.*, p. 45. Journal of Rufus Putnam, in Rufus Putnam Papers.
7. Memoirs of Rufus Putnam, in Rufus Putnam Papers, pp. 14-22. Memorandum Book of Rufus Putnam, in Rufus Putnam Papers.
8. Memoirs of Rufus Putnam, in Rufus Putnam Papers, p. 133.
9. Memoirs of Rufus Putnam, in Rufus Putnam Papers, p. 134.
10. Bond, *Foundations of Ohio*, p. 281. Samuel P. Hildreth, *Pioneer History of the Ohio Valley*, p. 205 (hereafter Hildreth, *Pioneer History*).
11. Memoirs of Rufus Putnam, in Rufus Putnam Papers, p. 135.
12. Hildreth, *Pioneer History*, pp. 160, 207. Memoirs of Rufus Putnam, in Rufus Putnam Papers, pp. 135-137.
13. Hildreth, *Pioneer History*, p. 207.
14. *Ibid.*, p. 208.
15. Summers, p. 72.
16. Cutler and Cutler, eds., I, 379-380.
17. Bond, *Foundations of Ohio*, pp. 282, 283. Hildreth, *Pioneer History*, pp. 213-214.

18. *Ibid.*, p. 215.

19. "Varnum's Oration," in *ibid.*, pp. 505-508. *See* biographical sketch of Judge Varnum in Samuel P. Hildreth, *Biographical and Historical Memoirs of the Early Settlers of Ohio, with the Narratives of the Incidental Occurrences in 1775*, pp. 165-185 (hereafter Hildreth, *Biographical Memoirs*).

20. "Order of Celebration, July 4, 1788, at Marietta," in Hildreth, *Pioneer History*, p. 509.

21. "St. Clair's Address," in *ibid.*, pp. 510-512.

22. "A Contemporary Account of Some Events," in *ibid.*, p. 513.

23. *Ibid.*, pp. 214-215. Clarence Edwin Carter, ed., *The Territorial Papers of the United States*, III, 278-289.

24. "A Contemporary Account of Some Events," in Hildreth, *Pioneer History*, p. 513.

25. *Ibid.*, pp. 222-223.

26. Cutler and Cutler, eds., I. 413-420.

27. Hildreth, *Biographical Memoirs*, pp. 230-240. Lewis Alexander Leonard, ed., *Greater Cincinnati and Its People*, I, 43.

28. Cutler and Cutler, eds., I, 418.

29. Carter, ed., III, 289-290.

30. Hildreth, *Pioneer History*, pp. 263-264.

31. *Ibid.*, pp. 264-266.

32. *Ibid.*

33. *Ibid.*

34. *Ibid.*, p. 442.

35. *Ibid.*, p. 388.

36. Thomas Carlyle to Ralph Waldo Emerson, quoted in W. H. Venable, *Footprints of the Pioneers in the Ohio Valley*, p. 46.

37. C. T. Greve, *History of Cincinnati*, I, 44.

38. Beverley W. Bond, ed., *The Correspondence of John Cleves Symmes*, pp. 7, 280 (hereafter Bond, *Symmes Correspondence*).

39. *Ibid.*, p. 280.

40. Bond, *Foundations of Ohio*, p. 291.

41. *Brunswick* [N. J.] *Gazette and Weekly Monitor*, January 8 and 22, 1788.

42. Cutler and Cutler, eds., I, 403-404.

43. John Cleves Symmes to Jonathan Dayton, Pittsburgh, August 21, 1788, in Bond, ed., *Symmes Correspondence*, pp. 36-44.

44. *Ibid.*

45. Quoted in Greve, I, 160-161.

46. Symmes to Dayton, Northbend, May 18-20, 1789, in Bond, ed., *Symmes Correspondence*, pp. 53-55.

47. Greve, I, 175.

48. *Ibid.*, I, 177-178.

49. *Ibid.*, I, 161.

50. *Cist Miscellany*, II, 61. Greve, I, 196-197.

51. Symmes to Dayton, Northbend, May 18-20, 1789, in Bend, ed., *Symmes Correspondence*, p. 63.

52. Dr. Daniel Drake's Memoir of the Miamis Country, 1779-1794, in Draper MSS, 1O125; printed in Historical and Philosophical Society of Ohio *Quarterly Publications*, XVIII (1923), 70-71.

53. Bond, *Foundations of Ohio*, p. 297.

54. Greve, I, 209, 213.

55. A well-known legend in Cincinnati.

56. Drake's Memoir, Draper MSS, 1O129.

57. Symmes to Dayton, Northbend, June 19, 1791, in Bond, ed., *Symmes Correspondence*, p. 142.

58. Greve, I, 339-340.

59. Theodore Thomas Belote, "The Scioto Speculation and the French Settlement of Gallipolis," in *Cincinnati University Studies*, III, Sec. 2 (1907), pp. 22-29.

60. *Ibid.*, III, 29-32. Daniel J. Ryan, "The Scioto Company and Its Purchase," in O. A. & H. S. *Publications*, III, 109-134.

61. Ryan, III, 110.

62. Belote, III, 26-28.

63. *Ibid.*, III, 47-48. Gallipolis Papers, I, 135.

64. Belote, III, 52-53. Memoirs of Rufus Putnam, in Rufus Putnam Papers, p. 141.

65. Belote, III, 46. *The American Pioneer*, II, 182.

66. Memoirs of Rufus Putnam, in Rufus Putnam Papers, p. 143. La Croix MSS, in Gallipolis Papers.

67. John L. Vance, "The French Settlement and Settlers of Gallipolis," in O. A. & H. S. *Publications*, III (1890), 51.

68. John Heckewelder, *Journal*, June 24, 1792. Gallipolis Papers, II, 161.

69. H. M. Breckenridge, *Recollections of Persons and Places in the West*, pp. 23-41.

70. *Ibid.* N. P. Dandridge, "Antoine Francois Saugrain," *Ohio Archaeological Quarterly*, XV (1906), pp. 192-206.

71. Breckinridge, p. 53.

72. *Ibid.*

73. J. A. Caldwell, *History of Belmont and Jefferson Counties, Ohio*, pp. 138, 462-463.

74. Alfred E. Lee, *History of the City of Columbus*, I, *passim*.

75. R. W. and M. D. Steele, *Early Dayton*, pp. 20-82.

76. P. P. Cherry, *The Western Reserve and Early Ohio*, p. 59.

77. Harlan Hatcher, *The Western Reserve*, pp. 25, 27, 28. Charles Whittlesey, *Early History of Cleveland*, Ohio, pp. 181-184.

78. *Ibid.*

79. *Ibid.*, p. 184.

80. "Holley's Journal," in *ibid.*, pp. 192-202.

81. Hatcher, p. 45.

82. *Ibid.*, p. 46

83. *Ibid.*, p. 47.

84. Quoted in Bond, *Foundations of Ohio*, p. 366.

CHAPTER 5

1. Draper MSS, 23U95-135.

2. Randolph C. Downes, *Frontier Ohio, 1788-1803*, p. 7.

3. *Ibid.*

4. Smith, ed., II, 95-96.

5. St. Clair to Henry Knox, January 27, 1788, in St. Clair MSS.

6. Miscellaneous Memorandum, in Timothy Pickering Papers.

7. Draper MSS, 23U79.

8. Draper MSS, 23U104-106.

9. Draper MSS, 23U107.

10. Draper MSS, 23U116-119.

11. Draper MSS, 23U120-122.

12. Draper MSS, 23U124-126.

13. Draper MSS, 23U140.

14. Walter Lowrie and Mathew St. Clair Clarke, eds., *American State Papers, Indian Affairs*, I, 5-7. Draper MSS, 23U144-154.

15. Draper MSS, 23U142.

16. Smith, ed., II, 113.

17. Harmar to Knox, Fort Harmar, November 24, 1787, in Smith, ed., II, 30-33.

18. *Ibid.*, II, 89. Downes, *Frontier Ohio*, p. 18.

19. Quoted in *ibid.*, p. 20.

20. Downes, *Council Fires*, p. 313.

21. Jacob Burnet, *Notes on the Early Settlement of the North-Western Territory*, p. 86.

22. Draper MSS, 2W148-150, 187-190, 200, 268-273.

23. St. Clair to Knox, Fort Steuben, Ohio, January 26, 1790, in Smith, ed., II, 132.

24. St. Clair to Knox, New York, August 23, 1790, in *American State Papers, Indian Affairs*, I, 92-93.

25. Gamelin's Journal, in *ibid.*, I, 93-94.

26. *Ibid.*

27. *Ibid.*

28. *Ibid.*

29. *Ibid.*

30. *Ibid.*

31. *Ibid.*

32. *Ibid.*

33. Smith, ed., II, 155-162.

34. *American State Papers, Indian Affairs*, I, 94, 102.

35. St. Clair to Major Murray, an officer commanding the British troops at Detroit, Marietta, September 19, 1790, in Smith, ed., II, 186-187.

36. Denny, VII, 345-350.

37. *Ibid.*, VII, 345-349.

38. *Ibid.*

39. *Ibid.*

40. *Ibid.*

41. *Ibid.*

42. *Ibid.*

43. *Ibid.*

44. Ibid., VII, 351-352.

45. Edgar S. Maclay, *Journal of William Maclay*, pp. 350, 395.

46. Downes, *Frontier Ohio*, p. 25.

47. *Ibid.*, p. 26.

48. *American State Papers, Indian Affairs*, I, 172.

49. *See* General Knox to General Butler, June 9, 1791, in Smith, ed., II, 216-217.

50. *American State Papers, Indian Affairs*, I, 139-140.

51. *Ibid.*, I, 147, 164.

52. General Scott's instructions and his reports are given in *ibid.*, I, 129. Smith, ed., II, 207.

53. Logan B. Esarey, *A History of Indiana*, I, 128.

54. *Ibid.*

55. *American State Papers, Indian Affairs*, I, 133.

56. *Ibid.*, I, 133-135.

57. Denny, VII, 356-374.

58. *Ibid.*

59. Arthur St. Clair, *A Narrative of the Manner in Which the Campaign Against the Indians in 1791 Was Conducted*, pp. 12, 21, 42, 87.

60. B. S. Bartlow and others, eds., *Centennial History of Butler County, Ohio*, pp. 88-89.

61. Bond, *Foundations of Ohio*, p. 326.

62. Denny, VII, 375.

63. *Ibid.*

64. *Ibid.*, VII, 374-375.

65. *Ibid.*

66. *Ibid.*

67. Beverley W. Bond, ed., "Memoirs of Benjamin Van Cleve," in Historical and Philosophical Society of Ohio *Quarterly Publications*, XXII (1922), 25-28.

68. Denny, VII, 377. Draper MSS, 6J128.

69. Bond, ed., "Memoirs of Benjamin Van Cleve," XXII, 26.

70. *Ibid. See* Kermit Cook, "Military Defenses of the Frontier in the Northwest Territory," in *West Virginia History*, X (1948), 47-52.

71. Bond, ed., "Memoirs of Benjamin Van Cleve," XXII, 28.

72. Smith ed., I, 181. Fraser Ellis Wilson, *The Peace of Mad Anthony*, pp. 72-75.

73. Fraser Ellis Wilson, *Arthur St. Clair*, pp. 97-99.

74. Bond, *Foundations of Ohio*, pp. 328-329.

75. *Ibid.*, p. 331.

76. *American State Papers, Indian Affairs*, I, 229-230, 234-235.

77. Ernest A. Cruikshank, ed., *The Correspondence of Lieutenant Governor John Graves Simcoe*, I, 177, 188, 190, 201, 207.

78. Hendrick to Timothy Pickering, December 11, 1792, in Timothy Pickering Papers.

79. *American State Papers, Indian Affairs*, I, 323-324.

80. *Ibid.*, I, 340-341.

81. Bond, *Foundations of Ohio*, pp. 340-341.

82. *American State Papers, Indian Affairs*, I, 340-342.

83. *Ibid.*, I, 352-353.

84. *Ibid.*, I, 356.

84. *Ibid.*, I, 357.

86. Harry Emerson Wildes, *Anthony Wayne, passim.*

87. Bond, *Foundations of Ohio*, pp. 342-343.

88. Wildes, pp. 399, 408.

89. *Ibid.*, pp. 414-415.

90. *Ibid.*, p. 415.

91. Roosevelt, IV.

92. "William Clark's Journal of General Wayne's Campaign," in *M.V.H.R.*, I, 419-430. *See* Lieutenant Boyer, "A Journal of Wayne's Campaign," in J. J. Jacob, *Life of Cresap.*

93. *American State Papers, Indian Affairs*, I, 492. Drayer MSS, 1U16.

94. Draper MSS, 1U16.

95. J. Burnet, pp. 187-205. *American State Papers, Indian Affairs*, I, 527. Roosevelt, IV, 118.

96. Wayne to Knox, Headquarters, Greenville, December 23, 1794, in *American State Papers, Indian Affairs*, I, 547-548.

97. *Ibid.*, I, 575, 577. J. Burnet, p. 222.

98. *American State Papers, Indian Affairs*, I, 573.

99. Treaty of Greenville, in *ibid.*, I, 562-563.

CHAPTER 6

1. Wilson, *Arthur St. Clair*, pp. 1-39.
2. *The Centinel of the Northwestern Territory*, November 8 and 23, 1793; September 20, 1794, (hereafter *Centinel*).
3. *Ibid.*, January 31, 1795.
4. *Ibid.*, February 7, 1795.
5. *Ibid.*, May 6, 1795.
6. Bond, *Foundations of Ohio*, p. 418.
7. *Centinel*, October 24, 1795.
8. Arthur St. Clair to James Ross, January 21, 1790, in St. Clair Papers.
9. *Centinel*, September 20 and 27, 1794.
10. *Ibid.*, January 31, 1795.
11. St. Clair to John Jay, December 13, 1788, in Carter, ed., II, 168.
12. St. Clair to Thomas FitzSimons, March 10, 1787, in J. Burnet, VIII, 553.
13. *Centinel*, July 12, 1794.
14. Downes, *Frontier Ohio*, pp. 192-193.
15. *Ibid.*, p. 182.
16. St. Clair to Robert McClure, June 14, 1798, in St. Clair Papers.
17. Downes, *Frontier Ohio*, p. 186.
18. Smith, ed., I, 208. Bond, *Foundations of Ohio*, p. 437.
19. *Ibid.*, p. 437.
20. *Ibid.*
21. Alfred Byron Sears, *Thomas Worthington*, p. 16. F. D. Cole, "Thomas Worthington," in O. A. & H. S. *Quarterly*, XII, 339-374.
22. Sears, *Thomas Worthington*, pp. 3-4.
23. J. Burnet, pp. 301-302. Bond, *Foundations of Ohio*, p. 447. Sears, *Thomas Worthington*, p. 50.
24. Smith, ed., II, 474-480.
25. Worthington to Albert Gallatin, August 13, 1801, in Letter-Book, pp. 67-69, Worthington MSS.
26. St. Clair to James Ross, n.d., in Smith, ed., II, 482. Ruhl Jacob Bartlett, "The Struggle for Statehood in Ohio," in *Ohio Historical Quarterly*, XXXII (1923), 480.
27. Bond, *Foundations of Ohio*, p. 457.
28. Downes, *Frontier Ohio*, pp. 196-197. Albert Douglas, "Major-General Arthur St. Clair," in O. A. & H. S. *Quarterly*, XVI, 470.
29. Bond, *Foundations of Ohio*, p. 458.
30. *Ibid.*
31. J. Burnet, p. 316.
32. Bond, *Foundations of Ohio*, p. 461.
33. Ross to St. Clair, Washington, February 3, 1801, in Smith, ed., II, 529. McMillan to St. Clair, January 1, 1801, in St. Clair MSS.
34. James B. Finley, *Sketches of Western Methodism*, p. 273.
35. Sears, *Thomas Worthington*, p. 64. Bond, *Foundations of Ohio*, p. 464.
36. Sears, *Thomas Worthington*, pp. 65-66. Worthington to Baldwin, November 30, 1801, Letter-Book of Thomas Worthington, Worthington MSS, pp. 98-100.
37. Sears, *Thomas Worthington*, p. 69.
38. *See* description of brawl in *Scioto Gazette*, January 2, 1802. Sears, *Thomas Worthington*, pp. 69-70.
39. *Ibid.*
40. *Ibid.*, p. 71.

41. *Ibid.*, p. 74. Randolph C. Downes, "The Statehood Movement in Ohio," *M.V.H.R.*, XVIII (1932), 167.

42. Sears, *Thomas Worthington*, p. 75.

43. *Annals of Congress*, 7 *Cong. 1 Sess.*, pp. 465-466. Jacob Burnet to Paul Fearing, February 2, 1802, in Paul Fearing MSS.

44. John Cleves Symmes to Thomas Jefferson, Washington, January 23, 1802, in Carter, ed., III, 205-207.

45. Thomas Worthington to Thomas Jefferson, Washington, January 30, 1802, in Smith, ed., II, 565-570.

46. St. Clair to Thomas Jefferson, Cincinnati, February 13, 1802, in *ibid.*, II, 573-574.

47. *Annals of Congress*, 7 *Cong. 1 Sess.*, pp. 268 ff. Paul Fearing to St. Clair, May 1, 1802, in Paul Fearing MSS.

48. Worthington to William Giles, November 17, 1802, in Carter, III, 257.

49. Remarks of Governor St. Clair before the Constitutional Convention, in Smith, ed., II, 592-597.

50. *Ibid.* Alfred B. Sears, "The Political Philosophy of Arthur St. Clair," in *O.A. & H.S. Quarterly*, XLIX (1940), 54-55.

51. Downes, *Frontier Ohio*, pp. 233-234.

52. Gallatin to Jefferson, November 20, 1802, in Carter, III, 259.

53. James Madison to Arthur St. Clair, Washington, November 22, 1802, in *ibid.*, III, 260.

54. Madison to Byrd, Washington, November 22, 1802, in *ibid.*, III, 259. Randolph C. Downes, "Thomas Jefferson and the Removal of Governor St. Clair in 1802," in Ohio Historical *Quarterly*, XXXVI, 74.

55. St. Clair to Madison, Cincinnati, December 21, 1802, in Smith, II, 559-601.

56. Sears, *Thomas Worthington*, p. 98.

57. *Annals of Congress*, 7 *Cong. 1 Sess.*, Appendix, pp. 1349-1351. *See* Rush R. Sloane, "When Did Ohio in Fact Become a Sovereign State of the Union?" in *O. A. & H. S. Publications*, IX (1900-1901), 278-302.

CHAPTER 7

1. Freeman Cleaves, *Old Tippecanoe: William Henry Harrison and His Time*, pp. 33-34.

2. *Ibid.*, pp. 6-8. Homer J. Webster, "William Henry Harrison's Administration of Indiana Territory," in Indiana Historical Society *Publications*, IV (1907), 183-185.

3. *Ibid.*

4. Cleaves, p. 25.

5. Charles S. Todd and Benjamin Drake, *William Henry Harrison*, p. 18. *See also* Benson J. Lossing, *Pictorial Field Book of the War of 1812*, p. 572.

6. Cleaves, p. 31.

7. *Ibid.*, pp. 29-30.

8. Jacob Piatt Dunn, *Indiana*, pp. 295-296.

9. Jacob Piatt Dunn, ed., "Slavery Petitions and Papers" in Indiana Historical Society *Publications*, II (1894), 456-457.

10. *Ibid.*, II, 457-458.

11. *Annals of Congress*, 6 *Cong.*, p. 735.

12. Dunn, *Indiana*, p. 303.

13. Dunn, ed., "Slavery Petitions and Papers," II, 462-463.

14. *American State Papers, Public Lands,* I, 146.

15. *Ibid., Misc.,* I, 387. Dunn, *Indiana,* p. 309.

16. Cleaves, pp. 43-44.

17. Webster, IV, 204.

18. *Ibid.,* IV, 205.

19. *Ibid.,* IV, 211. Dunn, *Indiana,* p. 330.

20. Dunn, ed., "Slavery Petitions and Papers," II, 485.

21. *Ibid.,* II, 485-486.

22. *Ibid.,* II, 487.

23. *Ibid.,* II, 497.

24. *Ibid.*

25. *Ibid.,* II, 510-511.

26. Webster, IV, 222-223.

27. Dunn, *Indiana,* p. 392. *See also* Bernhard Knollenberg, *Pioneer Sketches of the Upper Whitewater Valley,* pp. 18-26, 116-119.

28. Dorothy Riker, "Jonathan Jennings," in *Indiana Magazine of History,* XXVIII (1932), 223-226. Jonathan Jennings to David G. Mitchell, Vincennes, June 27, 1807, in William H. English Collection; printed in Dorothy Riker, ed., "Unedited Letters of Jonathan Jennings," in Indiana Historical Society *Publications,* X (1932), 161.

29. Riker, "Jonathan Jennings," XXVIII, 226-227.

30. Dunn, *Indiana,* pp. 390-391. Esarey, *A History of Indiana,* I, 243.

31. Dunn, *Indiana,* p. 392.

32. *Ibid.,* p. 393.

33. *Ibid.,* pp. 392-395.

34. *Ibid.,* p. 396.

35. William Wesley Woolen, *Biographical and Historical Sketches of Early Indiana,* p. 394.

36. *Western Sun,* June 10 and 24, 1809. Dunn, *Indiana,* p. 400.

37. *Western Sun,* July 8, 1809.

38. *Ibid.,* November 1, 1809.

39. Dunn, *Indiana,* p. 403.

40. *Ibid.,* p. 404.

41. *Ibid.,* p. 408.

42. Mabel Morrison, *Ann Gilmore Hay,* pp. 12ff.

43. Jennings to Ann Jennings Mitchell, Jeffersonville, August 15, 1811, in William H. English Collection.

44. *Annals of Congress, 1811-1812,* p. 1248.

45. Dunn, *Indiana,* p. 418.

46. *Annals of Congress, 14 Cong.,* p. 1273. *Western Sun,* April 20, 1816. *Niles Weekly Register,* December 14, 1815.

47. *Western Sun,* April 20, 1816.

48. *Ibid.,* February 10, 1816.

49. *Ibid.,* February 24, 1816.

50. Indiana Constitution of 1816, Article 2, Sec. 7.

CHAPTER 8

1. Moses Dawson, *A Historical Narrative of the Civil and Military Services of Major-General William H. Harrison,* p. 11.

2. Harrison to Henry Dearborn, July 15, 1801, in Logan B. Esarey, ed.,

The Messages and Letters of William Henry Harrison, I, 25-31 (hereafter Esarey, ed., *Messages and Letters*).

3. Glenn Tucker, *Tecumseh*, pp. 36-37.

4. *Ibid.*, pp. 76-80. Cleaves, p. 52.

5. J. Wesley Whickar, "Shabonee's Account of Tippecanoe," in *Indiana Magazine of History*, XVII (1921), 356.

6. Benjamin Drake, *The Life of Tecumseh and His Brother the Prophet* (microcard), pp. 228-230 (hereafter B. Drake, *Tecumseh*).

7. Tucker, p. 89.

8. *Ibid.*, pp. 91-92.

9. B. Drake, *Tecumseh*, p. 87.

10. *Ibid.*, pp. 88-89. Arthur W. Brady, "The Moravian Mission in Indiana," in Mississippi Valley Historical Association *Proceedings*, 1919-1920, pp. 286-297.

11. Harrison to the Delawares, early in 1806, in Esarey, ed., *Messages and Letters*, I, 182-183.

12. Edward Eggleston and Lillie Eggleston Seelye, *Tecumseh and the Shawnee Prophet*, p. 121.

13. Dawson, p. 81.

14. William Wells to Harrison, August 20, 1807, in Esarey, ed., *Messages and Letters*, I, 239.

15. Cleaves, p. 57.

16. Harrison to Eustis, Vincennes, May 18, 1808, in Esarey, ed., *Messages and Letters*, I, 290-291.

17. Tucker, pp. 123-131.

18. The Prophet to Harrison, August [1], 1808, in Esarey, ed., *Messages and Letters*, I, 299-300.

19. Harrison to Dearborn, Vincennes, September 1, 1808, in *ibid.*, I, 302.

20. Same to same, Vincennes, November 9, 1808, in *ibid.*, I, 321-322.

21. Henry Adams, *History of the United States*, VI, 74.

22. Tucker, p. 145.

23. Adams, VI, 75.

24. Eustis to Harrison, July 15, 1809, in Esarey, ed., *Messages and Letters*, I, 356-357.

25. B. J. Griswold, *The Pictorial History of Fort Wayne, Indiana*, p. 183-188.

26. Journal of the proceedings of the treaty at Fort Wayne and Vincennes, in Esarey, ed., *Messages and Letters*, I, 362-378.

27. *Ibid.*

28. *Ibid.*

29. *Ibid.* Elmore Barce, "Governor Harrison and the Treaty of Fort Wayne, 1809," in *Indiana Magazine of History*, XI (1915), 358-367.

30. Elmore Barce, "Tecumseh's Confederacy," in *Indiana Magazine of History*, XII (1916), 161-166.

31. Harrison to Eustis, June 15, 1810, in Esarey, ed., *Messages and Letters*, I, 424-425, 433.

32. Cleaves, p. 71.

33. Harrison to Eustis, June 26, 1810, in Esarey, ed., *Messages and Letters*, I, 434.

34. Harrison to the Prophet, July 19, 1810, in *ibid.*, 447-448.

35. *Ibid.*

36. Harrison to Eustis, Vincennes, August 6, 1810, in *ibid.*, I, 457.

37. Tucker, pp. 160-161. B. Drake, *Tecumseh*, p. 126.

38. Tecumseh's speech to Governor Harrison, in Esarey, ed., *Messages and Letters*, I, 463-469.

39. *Ibid.*

40. B. Drake, *Tecumseh*, pp. 126-127. Cleaves, p. 74.

41. *Ibid.*, pp. 74-75.

42. Tucker, p. 166.

43. Tecumseh's speech to Harrison, in Esarey, ed., *Messages and Letters*, I, 463-467.

44. *Ibid.*

45. Elmore Barce, "The Old Chicago Trail," in *Indiana Magazine of History*, XV (1919), 7.

46. Harrison to Eustis, August 7, 1811, in Esarey, ed., *Messages and Letters*, I, 549.

47. Tucker, p. 190.

48. Harrison to Eustis, June 19, 1811, in Esarey, ed., *Messages and Letters*, I, 520.

49. Harrison to Tecumseh, June 24, 1811, in Dawson, p. 179. Esarey, ed., *Messages and Letters*, I, 522-524.

50. Eustis to Harrison, July 17, 1811, in *ibid.*, I, 535-536.

51. *Ibid.*

52. Eustis to Harrison, July 20, 1811, in Esarey, ed., *Messages and Letters*, I, 536-537.

53. Adams, VI, 94.

54. Tucker, p. 192.

55. Harrison to Eustis, Vincennes, August 6, 1811, in Esarey, ed., *Messages and Letters*, I, 542-546.

56. *Ibid.*

57. *Ibid.*

58. *Ibid.*

59. Harrison to Eustis, October 13, 1811, in Esarey, ed., *Messages and Letters*, I, 599-600.

60. Dawson, p. 196.

61. *Ibid.*, 196-200.

62. Harrison to Eustis, camp near the Vermillion River, November 2, 1811, in Esarey, ed., *Messages and Letters*, I, 606-608.

63. Harrison to Eustis, November 18, 1811, in *ibid.*, I, 621.

64. Tucker, p. 222.

65. Cleaves, p. 98.

66. Walker's Journal, in Esarey, ed., *Messages and Letters*, I, 703.

67. Harrison to Dr. Scott, in *ibid.*, I, 691.

68. Woollen, p. 189. Cleaves, p. 101.

69. *Ibid.*

70. Tucker, p. 227.

71. *Ibid.*, p. 230.

72. *Ibid.*, p. 229.

CHAPTER 9

1. Louis Morton Hacker, "The West and the War of 1812," in *M.V.H.R.*, X (1924), 389.

2. Julius W. Pratt, "Western Aims in the War of 1812," in *M.V.H.R.*, XII (1925), 49.

3. Hacker, X, 372-375.

4. Pratt, "Western Aims in the War of 1812," XII, 40.

5. James Parton, *Life of Andrew Jackson*, I, 140.

6. Christopher B. Coleman, "The Ohio Valley in the Preliminaries of the War of 1812," in *M.V.H.R.*, XII (1920), 43.

7. Andrew W. Young, *History of Wayne County, Indiana* . . . , p. 66.

8. Ray Allen Billington, *The Westward Movement*, p. 269.

9. *Ibid.*

10. Adams, VI, 122.

11. *Annals of Congress, 12 Cong.*, I, 416.

12. *Ibid.*, I, 426. Quoted in Julius W. Pratt, *Expansionists of 1812*, p. 51.

13. *American State Papers, Indian Affairs*, I, 805.

14. Quoted in Pratt, *Expansionists of 1812*, p. 55. *Muskingum Messenger*, April 12, 1812. *Lexington Reporter*, June 6, 1812.

15. Pratt, *Expansionists of 1812*, p. 58.

16. Jefferson to Kosciusko, June 28, 1812, in H. A. Washington, ed., *Writings of Thomas Jefferson*, VI, 67.

17. Quoted in Pratt, *Expanionists of 1812*, pp. 154-155.

18. Adams, VI, 294-295.

19. *Ibid.*

20. Eustis to Hull, June 24, 1812, in *Michigan Pioneer and Historical Collections*, XV (1890), 397. Draper MSS, 22U11.

21. *Annals of Congress, 12 Cong.*, I, 1397.

22. Adams, VI, 303-305.

23. *Ibid.*, VI, 319.

24. John C. Parish, ed., *The Robert Lucas Journal of the War of 1812*, pp. 36-39.

25. Alec R. Gilpin, *The War of 1812 in the old Northwest*, pp. 92-93.

26. *Ibid.*, p. 91. Thomas B. Van Horne to John S. Gano, July 28, 1812, in "Gano Papers," *Historical and Philosophical Society of Ohio*, XV (1920), 80-81.

27. James G. Forbes, *Trial of Brig. General William Hull*, pp. 155-157.

28. Milo Milton Quaife, ed., *War on the Detroit* . . . , pp. 89-90. Harrison to Eustis, Cincinnati, August 29, 1812, in Richard C. Knopf, ed., *William Henry Harrison and the War of 1812*, I, 25 (hereafter Knopf, ed., *Harrison*).

29. Tucker, pp. 254-255.

30. Gilpin, pp. 98-99. Lewis Cass to John S. Gano, Detroit, August 12, 1812, in "Gano Papers," XV, 85.

31. Quaife, ed., *War on the Detroit*, p. 284.

32. Cass to Eustis, Washington, September 10, 1812, in *Michigan Pioneer and Historical Collections*, XV (1890), 480.

33. Tucker, pp. 261-262.

34. *Ibid.*, pp. 263-264.

35. William Wood, ed., *Select British Documents of the Canadian War of 1812*, I, 461.

36. *Ibid.*

37. Lossing, p. 287.

38. *Ibid.*

39. Forbes, pp. 40, 91.

40. Gilpin, pp. 118-119.

41. *Ibid.*, p. 119.

42. Lossing, pp. 303-304. Extract of letter from Fort Wayne, August 19, 1812, in Knopf, ed., *The National Intelligencer Reports The War of 1812 in the Northwest*, V, Part 1, 147 (hereafter Knopf, ed., *National Intelligencer*).

43. Gilpin, pp. 232-233.

44. Lossing, pp. 404-411.

45. Adams, VI, 345-347.

46. Harrison to Eustis, St. Mary's, September 21, 1812, in Esarey, ed., *Messages and Letters*, II, 145. Same to same, Headquarters, Piqua, September 24, 1812, in Knopf, ed., *Harrison*, I, 33.

47. Same to same, St. Mary's, September 21, 1812, in Esarey, ed., *Messages and Letters*, II, 145.

48. Same to same, Headquarters, Franklinton, Ohio, October 15, 1812, in Knopf, ed., *Harrison*, I, 38-41.

49. Quoted in Lossing, p. 339.

50. Gilpin, p. 158.

51. Harrison to Monroe, Headquarters, N.W. Army, Franklinton, January 6, 1813, in Knopf, ed., *Harrison*, I, 69-73.

52. Lossing, p. 351.

53. Lewis to Winchester, Frenchtown, January 20, 1813, in Esarey, ed., *Messages and Letters*, II, 321.

54. Major McClanahan to Harrison, Portage River, January 26, 1813, in *ibid.*, II, 339.

55. Elias Darnell, *Journal of the Kentucky Volunteers*, p. 38.

56. Harrison to——, Headquarters, Portage River, 15 miles from Miami Rapids, January 24, 1813, in Knopf, ed., *Harrison*, I, 77-79.

57. John K. S. F. Richardson, *War of 1812*, p. 140.

58. Darnell, pp. 60-63. B. F. H. Witherell, "Reminiscences" in *Wisconsin Historical Collections*, III, 307-308.

59. Harrison to McKeehan, January 31, 1813, in Esarey, ed., *Messages and Letters*, II, 346.

60. Gilpin, pp. 174-175.

61. Harrison to John Armstrong, February 24, 1813, in Esarey, ed., *Messages and Letters*, II, 368.

62. Gilpin, pp. 179-184.

63. Cleaves, p. 167.

64. Lossing, p. 485.

65. Cleaves, pp. 168-169. Lossing, p. 486. Extract of a letter from a member of the Chillicothe guards, Sandusky, May 8, 1813, in Knopf, ed., *National Intelligencer*, V, Part 2, 104-105.

66. Tucker, pp. 292-294.

67. Gilpin, pp. 189-190.

68. *Ibid.*

69. Harrison to John Armstrong, Headquarters, Lower Sandusky, May 13, 1813, in Knopf, ed., *National Intelligencer*, V, Part 2, 109-110.

70. Tucker, p. 295.

71. Lossing, p. 499.

72. *Ibid.*, pp. 500-502. *See also* siege of Fort Meigs in Knopf, ed., *National Intelligencer*, V, Part 2, 127-130.

73. Lossing, pp. 503-504.

74. *Ibid.*

75. *Ibid.*

76. *Ibid.*, p. 508.

77. Alexander Slidell MacKenzie, *Life of Commodore Oliver Hazard Perry*, I, 175-182.

78. Lossing, pp. 513-514.

79. *Ibid.*, pp. 514-515.

80. Cleaves, p. 185.

81. Gilpin, p. 211.

82. Lossing, pp. 519-523.

83. *Ibid.*, pp. 526-528.

84. *Ibid.*, p. 528. *See* Barclay to Yeo, His Majesty's late Ship *Detroit*, Put in Bay, September 12, 1813, in Richard C. Knopf, ed., *Anecdotes of the Lake Erie Area War of 1812*, pp. 42-45.

85. *Ibid.*, p. 530. Perry to William Jones, September 22, 1813, in Knopf, ed., *National Intelligencer*, V, Part 2, 189.

86. Quoted in Lossing, p. 544.

87. Tucker, pp. 302-303.

88. Gilpin, p. 219.

89. Harrison to Armstrong, Sandwich, Canada, September 30, 1813, in Esarey, ed., *Messages and Letters*, II, 555.

90. Cleaves, pp. 195-196.

91. Tucker, pp. 305-307.

92. *Ibid.*

93. Lossing, p. 549.

94. Tucker, p. 307.

95. Lossing, pp. 552-553.

96. Harrison to Armstrong, October 9, 1813, in Esarey, ed., *Messages and Letters*, II, 502.

97. Tucker, p. 316.

98. *Ibid.*, pp. 316-317.

99. Black Hawk's account in *Scioto Gazette* (Chillicothe), November 29, 1836. Tucker, p. 318. Gilpin, p. 226.

100. Lossing, pp. 555-558.

CHAPTER 10

1. Ninian W. Edwards, *History of Illinois From 1778-1833 and Life and Times of Ninian Edwards*, p. 14.

2. *Ibid.*, p. 15.

3. *Ibid.*, p. 18.

4. Solon J. Buck, *Illinois in 1818*, p. 146. Beverley W. Bond, *The Civilization of the Old Northwest*, pp. 192-193 (hereafter Bond, *Old Northwest*).

5. *Ibid.*, p. 195.

6. See Edwards' message referring to the territorial judiciary system, in Edwards, pp. 85-92, 155-158.

7. *Ibid.*, pp. 158-164.

8. *Ibid.*, p. 184.

9. *Ibid.*, pp. 93-100.

10. Buck, p. 196.

11. *Ibid.*, p. 197.

12. E. B. Washburne, ed., *The Edwards Papers*, pp. 103-110.

13. *Ibid.*

14. *Western Intelligencer*, July 9, 1816.

15. John Reynolds, *The Pioneer History of Illinois*, p. 370.

16. *Western Intelligencer*, December 11, 1816.

17. Quoted in Buck, pp. 207-208.

18. *Western Intelligencer*, August 21, 1816.

19. Reynolds, pp. 395-399.

20. Daniel Pope Cook to Ninian Edwards, Washington, September 25, 1817, in Washburne, ed., p. 137, 138.

21. *Western Intelligencer*, November 20, 1817.
22. *Ibid.*
23. *Ibid.*
24. *Ibid.*
25. *Ibid.*, December 4, 1817.
26. *Ibid.*
27. *Ibid.*, December 11, 1817.
28. Buck, p. 215.
29. *Western Intelligencer*, December 23, 1817.
30. *Ibid.*, January 13, 1818.
31. Arthur Clinton Boggess, *The Settlement of Illinois, 1778-1830*, p. 115.
32. *Western Intelligencer*, April 15, 1818.
33. *Annals of Congress, 15 Cong., 1 Sess.*, II, 1670-1681.
34. *Western Intelligencer*, April 22, 1818. *Illinois Intelligencer* (same paper), May 8 and 24, 1818.
35. *Western Intelligencer*, April 23, 1818.
36. *Illinois Intelligencer*, June 10, 1818.
37. *Ibid.*, July 1, 1818.
38. *See* "Journal of the Convention" in Illinois State Historical Society *Journal*, VI (1894), 355-424.

Chapter 11

1. Benjamin S. Parker, "Pioneer Life," in *Indiana Magazine of History*, III (1907), 126-128.
2. *Ibid.*, III, 129.
3. *Ibid.*, III, 129-130.
4. *Ibid.*
5. *Ibid.*, III, 130.
6. Cherry, p. 79.
7. Parker, III, 182-183.
8. *Ibid.*, III, 183. R. Carlyle Buley, *The Old Northwest*, I, 206.
9. Parker, III, 184.
10. *Ibid.*
11. *Ibid.*, III, 185.
12. William Faux, *Memorable Days in America . . .*, pp. 248-249.
13. "Reminiscences of Judge Finch," in *Indiana Magazine of History*, VII (1911), 161.
14. Buley, I, 154. Cherry, p. 142.
15. Buley, I, 172-173. A. C. Glidden, "Pioneer Farming," in *Michigan Pioneer and Historical Collections*, XVIII (1891), 418-420.
16. Glidden, XVIII, 421-422.
17. Buley, I, 1885-1886.
18. Parker, III, 2-3.
19. *Ibid.*
20. *Ibid.*
21. *Ibid.*, III, 3-4.
22. *Ibid.*
23. *Ibid.*
24. *Ibid.*, III, 5.
25. A. D. P. Van Buren, "The Frolics of Forty-Five Years Ago," in *Michigan Pioneer and Historical Collections*, V (1882), 307.
26. *Ibid.*, V, 308. Jackson Wolford, "The Play Party in Indiana," *Indiana*

Historical Collection, IV (1916), contains many ballads of the pioneer period. *See* one version of "Weevely Wheat Song" in John Lomax and Alan Lomax, *American Ballads and Folk Songs*, p. 290.

27. Quoted in Buley, I, 328.

28. Robert Carlton Hall, *The New Purchase*, p. 132.

29. Buley, I, 330.

30. Caruso, p. 72. Quoted in Buley, I, 330.

31. Hall, pp. 154-156.

32. *Ibid.*

33. These expressions are still widely used in the Great Lakes Frontier. *See* Thomas Low Nichols, *Forty Years of American Life*, pp. 60-70.

34. Otto Juettner, *Daniel Drake and His Followers*, pp. 80-93.

35. A. D. P. Van Buren, "The Fever and Ague—'Mosquito Rash'—Mosquitos and Old Pioneers' Foes," in *Michigan Pioneer and Historical Collections*, V, 301. *Western Monthly Magazine*, I (1833), 304.

36. Quoted in Buley, I, 293.

37. *Ibid.*, I, 247-248.

38. *Ibid.*, I, 248.

39. *Ibid.*, I, 258. Caruso, p. 219.

40. Buley, I, 259-260.

41. Quoted in *ibid.*, I, 234.

42. Parker, III, 188. Buley, I, 265-268.

43. Quoted in *ibid.*, II, 327. Logan B. Esarey, "The Pioneer Aristocracy," in *Indiana Magazine of History*, XIII (1917), 273.

44. Cherry, p. 100. D. D. Banta, "The Early Schools of Indiana," in *Indiana Magazine of History*, II (1906), 47.

45. *Ibid.*, II, 47.

46. *Ibid.*, II, 81-83.

47. *Ibid.*, II, 84. A. D. P. Van Buren, "The Log Schoolhouse Era," in *Michigan Pioneer and Historical Collections*, XIV (1887), 316.

48. *See* B. O. Williams, "My Recollections of Early Schools in Detroit," in *Michigan Pioneer and Historical Collections*, V (1882), 547. Cherry, p. 102.

49. Banta, II, 85-88.

50. *Ibid.*, II, 136-137.

51. *Ibid.*, II, 137-138.

52. *Ibid.*, II, 131.

53. *Ibid.*, II, 132.

54. *Ibid.*

55. Buley, II, 383.

56. Walter Hawinghurst, *Land of Promise*, p. 215 *passim*. Leland Baldwin, *The Keelboat Age*, pp. 159-174.

57. William J. Petersen, *Steamboating on the Upper Mississippi*, pp. 48-67. Charles H. Ambler, *Transportation in the Ohio Valley*, pp. 113-116.

58. Peterson, pp. 68-74. For an interesting picture of life on the Ohio and Mississippi rivers, see Wilson Daniels, "Memoirs," in *Indiana Magazine of History*, II (1915), 99-127.

59. Billington, pp. 334-335.

60. *See* A. B. Hulbert, "The Old National Road—the Historic Highway of America," in O. A. & H. S. *Publications*, IX (1901), 405 *passim*.

61. Billington, pp. 301-302.

62. George White Dial, "Construction of the Ohio Canals," in O. A. & H. S. *Publications*, XIII (1904), 460-481. Ambler, pp. 81-102.

63. Clarence Frost, "The Early Railroads of Southern Michigan," in *Michi-*

gan Pioneer and Historical Collections, XXXVIII (1912), 500. Hawinghurst, pp. 294-295.

64. *Ibid.*, p. 295.

65. *Ibid.*, p. 295 *passim.*

66. William Warren Sweet, *The Story of Religions in America*, pp. 306-309.

67. William Warren Sweet, ed., *The Presbyterians*, p. 105.

68. For a fuller discussion of Methodism and camp meetings, *see* Caruso, pp. 225-226, 228-231. *See also* John E. Iglehart, "Methodism in Southwestern Indiana," *Indiana Magazine of History*, XVII (1921), 117-149.

69. Quoted in William Warren Sweet, ed., *The Rise of Methodism in the West*, pp. 54-55.

70. William Warren Sweet, ed., *The Baptists*, p. 36.

71. *Ibid.*, pp. 22, 55, 82.

72. *Ibid.*, pp. 69, 75.

73. J. P. Maclean, "The Society of Shakers," in O. A. & H. S. *Publications*, IX (1901), 35-39. Sweet, *The Story of Religions in America*, pp. 339-340.

74. Maclean, "The Society of Shakers," IX, 72-75. Maclean presents a fuller discussion of the Shakers in *Shakers of Ohio . . .*

75. Shakers to Indian friends, Turtle Creek, September 1, 1807, in Shaker Papers.

76. Winfred Ernest Garrison and Alfred T. DeGroot, *The Disciples of Christ*, pp. 124-135.

77. Morrison Meade Davis, *How the Disciples Began and Grew . . .*, p. 48 *passim.*

78. *See* Campbell's Declaration, in Garrison and DeGroot, p. 146.

79. *Ibid.*, pp. 153-158. Sweet, *The Story of Religions in America*, pp. 342-343.

80. *The Christian Baptist*, I (1823), Preface and 1.

81. Alonzo Willard Fortune, *The Disciples in Kentucky*, pp. 48-64. Henry K. Shaw, *Buckeye Disciples*, pp. 62-77.

82. Sweet, *The Story of Religions in America*, p. 320. Jean Dilhet, *État de l'Église Catholique ou Diocèse des États-Unis . . .*, pp. 81-130. Martin J. Spalding, *Sketches of the Life, Times, and Character of the Rt. Rev. Benedict Joseph Flaget . . .*, pp. 18-63. J. Herman Schauinger, *Cathedrals in the Wilderness*, pp. 39 f, 60-61.

83. Thomas T. McAvoy, *The Catholic Church in Indiana*, p. 169.

CHAPTER 12

1. Andrew C. McLaughlin, *Lewis Cass*, pp. 89-90.

2. Frank B. Woodford, *Lewis Cass*, p. 74.

3. McLaughlin, p. 95.

4. *Ibid.* Woodford, p. 98.

5. James Monroe, *Writings*, I, 117.

6. Edward Tiffin to Josiah Meigs, November 30, 1815, in *Michigan Pioneer and Historical Collections*, XVIII (1891), 660. *American State Papers, Public Lands*, III, 164-165.

7. Jedediah Morse, *Traveller's Guide*, p. 169.

8. Woodford, p. 113.

9. Elizabeth Gasper Brown, "Lewis Cass and the American Indian," in *Michigan History*, XXXVII (1953), 286-298. Lewis Cass, "Indians of North America," in *North American Review*, XX (1826), 53.

10. Detroit *Gazette*, September 28, 1817.

11. Woodford, pp. 124-135.

12. Lewis Cass to John C. Calhoun, Detroit, November 18, 1819, in Henry Rowe Schoolcraft, *Summary Narrative of an Exploring Expedition to the Sources of the Mississippi River in 1820*, pp. 27-31.

13. *Ibid.*, p. 43.

14. *Ibid.*, p. 48.

15. *Ibid.*, pp. 57-58.

16. *Ibid.*, p. 59.

17. *Ibid.*, pp. 79-80.

18. *Ibid.*, pp. 80-81.

19. *Ibid.*, p. 86.

20. *Ibid.*, p. 87.

21. *Ibid.*, p. 97.

22. *Ibid.*, pp. 110 ff.

23. *Ibid.*, pp. 178-185.

24. *Ibid.*, pp. 210-220.

25. Woodford, p. 138.

26. James V. Campbell, *Outline of the Political History of Michigan*, p. 406.

27. C. H. Chapman, "The Historic Johnston Family of the 'Soo,'" in *Michigan Pioneer and Historical Collections*, XXXII (1903), 305-353, includes many Chippewa legends translated by Mrs. Schoolcraft.

28. *Detroit Gazette*, September 6 and October 17, 1822.

29. Woodford, p. 153.

30. McLaughlin, p. 123-124.

31. Campbell, pp. 204, 255. Bayrd Spill, "The University of Michigan: Beginnings," in *Michigan History Magazine*, XII, 652-654.

32. Harriet Martineau, *Society in America*, I, 318-326. Detroit *Daily Advertiser*, December 24, 1836. Martineau, II, 2. For a fuller discussion of the roads, see Elmore Barce, "The Old Chicago Road" in *Indiana Magazine of History*, XV (1919), 1-14.

33. Milo Milton Quaife, *Chicago's Highways*, p. 36.

34. George N. Fuller, "Settlement of Michigan Territory," in *M.V.H.R.*, II, 41. George N. Fuller, *Economic and Social Beginnings of Michigan*, p. 72.

35. *Detroit Gazette*, August 28, 1827.

36. Woodford, pp. 140-142. McLaughlin, pp. 127-129.

37. Lawton T. Hemans, *Life and Times of Steven Thomson Mason*, p. 59.

38. Quoted in *ibid.*, pp. 62-63.

39. Theodore Calvin Pease, *The Frontier State*, pp. 154-155, 158.

40. Henry Little, "A History of the Black Hawk War of 1812," in *Michigan Pioneer and Historical Collections*, V (1882), 152-159.

41. Carl Sandburg, *Abraham Lincoln*, p. 28. John Allen Wakefield, *History of the Black Hawk War*, p. 154.

42. Frank E. Stevens, *The Black Hawk War . . .* , pp. 132-133.

43. *Ibid.*, p. 134.

44. *Sangamo Journal*, May 24, 1832.

45. Hemans, pp. 74-75.

46. Wakefield, pp. 109-110. E. Buckner, "A Brief History of the War with the Sac and Fox Indians . . . ," in *Michigan Pioneer and Historical Collections*, XII (1887), 429.

47. *Ibid.*, XII, p. 111.

48. Pease, *The Frontier State*, pp. 168-169.

49. Black Hawk, *Autobiography*, p. 132.

50. Quoted in Benjamin Drake, *The Life and Adventure of Black Hawk*, pp. 153-154.

51. Quoted in Wakefield, pp. 132-133. Buckner, XII, 432.

52. Milo Milton Quaife, *Chicago and the Old Northwest*, p. 337. Reuben Gold Thwaites, "Story of the Black Hawk War," in *Wisconsin Historical Collections*, XII, 264-265.

53. Buley, I, 254.

54. Hemans, pp. 80-81.

55. *Ibid*. Kent Sagendorph, *Stevens Thomson Mason*, p. 164.

56. *See* C. M. Burton, "Detroit in the Year 1832," in *Michigan Pioneer and Historical Collections*, XVIII (1897-1898), 168-170.

57. Daniel Drake, "Epidemic Cholera—Its Pathology and Treatment," in *Western Journal of the Medical and Physical Sciences*, V (1832), 612.

58. Hemans, p. 82.

59. *Ibid*., p. 83. Sagendorph, p. 168.

60. *Ibid*., p. 166. Hemans, pp. 83-84.

61. Thomas McIntyre Cooley, *Michigan*, p. 214.

62. Buley, II, 192.

63. *Ibid*.

64. Hemans, pp. 113-114.

65. Campbell, p. 440. Hemans, p. 125.

66. Hemans, pp. 131-132.

67. Buley, II, 195.

68. Hemans, p. 146.

69. Buley, II, 197.

70. Carl Wittke, "The Ohio-Michigan Boundary Dispute Re-Examined," in O. A. & H. S. *Quarterly*, XLV (1936), 307.

71. Hemans, pp. 152 ff.

72. Tod B. Galloway, "The Ohio-Michigan Boundary Line Dispute," in O. A. & H. S. *Publications*, IV (1895), 225-228.

73. R. C. Crawford, "Reminiscences," in *Michigan Pioneer and Historical Collections*, IV (1881), 41-53.

74. Sagendorph, pp. 207-211.

75. Hemans, pp. 183-188.

76. Wittke, XLV, 318. Hemans, pp. 196-199. For a detailed discussion on the admission of Michigan, see Clark F. Norton, "Michigan Statehood: 1835, 1836, or 1837," in *Michigan History*, XXXVI (1952), 321-350.

77. Joseph Schafer, *The Wisconsin Lead Region*, p. 50. Reuben Gold Thwaites, *Wisconsin*, p. 239.

78. *Ibid*., p. 243.

79. William Francis Raney, *Wisconsin*, p. 100. Thwaites, *Wisconsin*, pp. 244-245.

80. *Ibid*., p. 245.

81. Ellis Baker Usher, *Wisconsin*, I, 99.

82. Thwaites, *Wisconsin*, p. 273.

83. Raney, *Wisconsin*, p. 99.

84. Thwaites, *Wisconsin*, p. 275.

85. Usher, *Wisconsin*, pp. 102-103, 104-107. Bayrd Still, "State-Making in Wisconsin, 1846-48," in *Wisconsin Magazine of History*, XX (1936), 34-59.

86. *Ibid*.

Selected Bibliography

PRIMARY WORKS

MANUSCRIPTS

Lyman C. Draper Collection, Wisconsin State Historical Society, Madison, Wisc.:

Series J	George Rogers Clark Papers
Series O	Drake Papers
Series U	Frontier Wars
Series W	Harmar Papers

English, William H., Collection, Indiana Historical Society Library, Indianapolis, Ind.

Fearing, Paul, MSS, Marietta College Library, Marietta, O.

Gallipolis Papers, Historical and Philosophical Society of Ohio, Columbus, O.

Pickering, Timothy, Papers, Massachusetts Historical Society, Boston, Mass.

Putnam, Rufus, Papers, Marietta College Library, Marietta, O.

St. Clair, Arthur, MSS, Ohio State Library, Columbus, O.

Shaker Papers, Western Reserve Historical Society, Cleveland, O.

Worthington MSS, Library of Congress, Washington, D.C.

PRINTED SOURCES
NEWSPAPERS AND JOURNALS

Brunswick [N.J.] *Gazette and Weekly Monitor*, 1788.
Centinel of the Northwestern Territory, 1793-1795.
Christian Baptist, 1823.
Detroit Gazette, 1817-1827.
Detroit Daily Advertiser, 1836.
Kaskaskia *Western Intelligencer* (*Illinois Intelligencer* after 1818), 1816-1818.
Kentucky Gazette, 1780.
Lexington Reporter, 1812.
Maryland Journal, 1780.
Muskingum Messenger, 1812.
Olden Time Magazine, 1848.
Sangamo Journal, 1832-1833.
Scioto Gazette, 1802-1836.
Vincennes *Western Sun*, 1809-1816.

Books

Alvord, Clarence W., ed. *Cahokia Records, 1778-1790* (Springfield, 1907).

Alvord, Clarence W., and Carter, Clarence E., eds. *The Critical Period, 1763-1765* (Springfield, 1915).

American State Papers, Indian Affairs (Washington, 1832-1861).

Annals of Congress, 1789-1817 (Washington, 1834-1855).

Black Hawk. *Autobiography* (New York, 1836).

Bliss, E. F., ed. *Dairy of David Zeisberger* (Cincinnati, 1885).

Bond, Beverley W., ed. *The Correspondence of John Cleves Symmes* (New York, 1926).

Breckenridge, H. M., *Recollections of Persons and Places in the West*.

Buell, Rowena, ed. *Memoirs of Rufus Putnam* (New York and Boston, 1903).

Burnet, Jacob. *Notes on the Early Settlement of the Northwest Territory* (Cincinnati, 1847).

Burnett, Edmund Cody, ed. *Letters of Members of the Continental Congress* (Washington, 1921-1943).

Carter, Clarence E., ed. *Territorial Papers of the United States* (17 vols., Washington, 1934-1950).

Cox, I. J., ed. *The Journeys of Réné Robert Cavelier, sieur de la Salle* (2 vols., New York, 1905).

Cruikshank, Ernest A., ed. *The Correspondence of Lieutenant Governor John Graves Simcoe* (5 vols., Toronto, 1923).

Cutler, William Parker, and Cutler, Julia Perkins, eds. *The Life, Journals, and Correspondence of Manassah Cutler* (2 vols., Cincinnati, 1888).

Darnell, Elias. *Journal of the Kentucky Volunteers* (New York, 1854).

Denny, Ebenezer. *Military Journal* (Philadelphia, 1860).

Doniol, Henri. *Histoire de la Participation de la France a l'Établissement des États-Unis d'Amérique, correspondance diplomatique et documents* (5 vols., Paris, 1886-1892).

Esarey, Logan B., ed. *The Messages and Letters of William Henry Harrison* (2 vols., Indianapolis, 1922).

Faux, William. *Memorable Days in America . . .* (London, 1823).

Forbes, James G. *The Trial of Brigadier General William Hull* (New York, 1814).

Hall, Robert Carlton. *The New Purchase* (2 vols., New York, 1843).

Heckewelder, John. *Journal* (Cincinnati, 1840).

Hulbert, A. B., ed. *Ohio in the Time of the Confederation* (Marietta, O., 1918).

——, ed. *Records of the Ohio Company* (2 vols., Marietta, O., 1917).

Jacob, J. J. *Life of Cresap*. (New York, 1841).

James, James A., ed. *George Rogers Clark Papers* (Springfield, 1912).

Johnston, J. Stoddard, ed. *First Explorations in Kentucky* (Louisville, 1898).

Kellogg, Louise Phelps, ed. *Early Narratives of the Northwest* (New York, 1917).

Knopf, Richard C., ed. *Anecdotes of the Lake Erie Area. War of 1812.* (Columbus, 1957).

——, ed. *The National Intelligencer Reports the War of 1812 in the Northwest* (Columbus, 1958).

——, ed. *William Henry Harrison and the War of 1812* (Columbus, 1957).

Maclay, Edgar S., ed. *Journal of William Maclay* (New York, 1890).

Margry, Pierre, ed. *Découvertes et Établissements des Français dans l'Ouest et dans le Sud de l'Amérique Septentionale, 1614-1698 mémoires et documents inédits* (6 vols., Paris, 1879).

Martineau, Harriet. *Society in America* (3 vols., London, 1837).
Parish, John C., ed. *The Robert Lucas Journal of the War of 1812* (New York, 1906).
Pennsylvania Archives. First Series (12 vols., Philadelphia, 1852-1856).
St. Clair, Arthur. *A Narrative of the Manner in Which the Campaign Against the Indians in 1791 Was Conducted* (Philadelphia, 1812).
Schoolcraft, Henry Rowe. *Summary Narrative of an Exploring Expedition to the Sources of the Mississippi River in 1820* (Philadelphia, 1855).
Smith, W. H., ed. *St. Clair Papers* (2 vols., Cincinnati, 1882).
Sweet, William Warren, ed. *The Baptists* (New York, 1931).
———, ed. *The Presbyterians* (Chicago, c. 1936).
———, ed. *The Rise of Methodism in the West* (New York, 1920).
Thwaites, Reuben Gold, ed. *The Jesuit Relations and Allied Documents* (73 vols., Cleveland, 1904).
United States Continental Congress *Journals . . . 1774-1789.*
Volney, Constantin François Chasseboeuf, Comte de. *View of the Climate and Soil of the United States . . .* (London, 1804).
Wakefield, John Allen. *History of the War Between the United States and the Sac and Fox Nations of Indians . . .* (Jacksonville, Ill., 1834).
Washburne, E. B., ed. *The Edwards Papers* (Chicago, 1884).
Washington, H. A., ed., *Writings of Thomas Jefferson* (8 vols., Washington, D.C., 1853-1854).
Wood, William, ed. *Select British Documents of the Canadian War of 1812* (New York, 1920-1923).

Magazines

Bond, Beverley W., ed. "Memoirs of Benjamin Van Cleve," in Historical and Philosophical Society of Ohio *Quarterly Publications*, XXII (1922).
"Butler's Journal," in *Olden Time*, II (Pittsburgh, 1848).
Butterfield, Consul W., ed. *Washington-Irvine Correspondence* (Madison, 1882).
Cass, Lewis. "Indians of North America," in *North American Review*, XXII (1826).
Cist Miscellany (microcard, 2 vols., Cincinnati, 1845-1846).
"William Clark's Journal of General Wayne's Campaign," in *Mississippi Valley Historical Review*, I.
Crawford, R. C. "Reminiscences" in *Michigan Pioneer and Historical Collection*, IV (1881).
Drake, Daniel. "Epidemic Cholera—Its Pathology and Treatment," in *Western Journal of the Medical and Physical Sciences*, V (1832).
Dunn, J. P., ed. "Slavery Petitions and Papers," in Indiana Historical Society *Publications*, II (1894).
"Gano Papers," in Historical and Philosophical Society of Ohio *Quarterly Publication*, XV (1920).
Illinois Historical Collections (32 vols., Springfield, 1903-1945).
Little, Henry. "A History of the Black Hawk War of 1832," in *Michigan Pioneer and Historical Collections*, V (1882).
"Narrative of John Brickell's Captivity Among the Delaware Indians," in *American Pioneer*, II (1842).
Riker, Dorothy, ed. "Unedited Letters of Jonathan Jennings," in Indiana Historical Society *Publications*, X (1932).
Whickar, J. Wesley, "Shabonee's Account of Tippecanoe," in *Indiana Magazine of History*, XVII (1921).

SECONDARY WORKS

Books

Adams, Henry. *History of the United States* (9 vols., 1890-1891).

Alvord, Clarence W. *The Illinois Country* (Springfield, Ill., 1920).

———. *Old Kaskaskia Records* (Springfield, Ill., 1909).

Ambler, Charles H. *Transportation in the Ohio Valley* (Glendale, Calif., 1936).

Bakeless, John. *Background to Glory* (Philadelphia, 1957).

Baldwin, Leland. *The Keelboat Age* (Pittsburgh, 1941).

Bartlow, B. S., and others, eds. *Centennial History of Butler County, Ohio* (Indianapolis, 1905).

Bemis, Samuel Flagg. *Diplomacy of the American Revolution* (New York, 1935).

Billington, Ray Allen. *The Westward Movement* (New York, 1950).

Bodley, Temple. *George Rogers Clark* (New York, 1926).

Boggess, Arthur Clinton. *The Settlement of Illinois, 1778-1830* (Chicago, 1908).

Bond, Beverley W. *The Civilization of the Old Northwest* (New York, 1934).

———. *The Foundations of Ohio* (Columbus, 1941).

Brebner, John Bartlet. *The Explorers of North America* (New York, 1955).

Buck, Solon J. *Illinois in 1818* (Springfield, Ill., 1917).

Buley, R. Carlyle. *The Old Northwest* (Bloomington, Ind., 1951).

Butterfield, Consul W. *Historical Account of the Expedition Against Sandusky under Colonel William Crawford in 1782* (Cincinnati, 1873).

———. *History of the Girtys* (Cincinnati, 1890).

Caldwell, J. A. *History of Belmont and Jefferson Counties, Ohio* (Wheeling, W.Va., 1880).

Campbell, James V. *Outlines of the Political History of Michigan* (Detroit, 1876).

Caruso, John Anthony. *The Appalachian Frontier* (Indianapolis and New York, 1959).

Cherry, P. P. *The Western Reserve and Early Ohio* (Akron, 1921).

Cleaves, Freeman. *Old Tippecanoe* (New York, 1939).

Cooley, Thomas McIntyre. *Michigan* (Boston, 1886).

Cumrine, Boyd. *History of Washington County, Pennsylvania* (Philadelphia, 1882).

Dandridge, N. P. *Antoine François Saugrain: The First Scientist of the Mississippi Valley.*

Davis, Morrison Meade. *How the Disciples Began and Grew . . .* (Cincinnati, 1915).

Dawson, Moses. *A Historical Narrative of the Civil and Military Services of Major-General William H. Harrison* (Cincinnati, 1824).

Dilhet, Jean. *État de l'Église Catholique ou Diocèse des États-Unis . . .* (Washington, 1922).

Downes, Randolph C. *Council Fires on the Upper Ohio* (Pittsburgh, 1940).

———. *Frontier Ohio, 1788-1803* (Columbus, 1935).

Drake, Benjamin. *The Life and Adventures of Black Hawk.* (Cincinnati, 1838).

———. *The Life of Tecumseh and His Brother the Prophet* (Cincinnati, 1841).

Dunn, Jacob P. *Indiana* (New York and Boston, 1896).

Edwards, Ninian W. *History of Illinois From 1778-1883* and *Life and Times of Ninian Edwards* (Springfield, Ill., 1870).

Eggleston, Edward, and Seeyle, Lillie Eggleston. *Tecumseh and the Shawnee Prophet* (New York, 1878).

Esarey, Logan B. *A History of Indiana* (2 vols., Indianapolis, 1918).

Finley, James B. *Sketches of Western Methodism* (Cincinnati, 1856).

Fortune, Alonzo Willard. *The Disciples in Kentucky* (n.p., 1932).

Fuller, George N. *Economic and Social Beginnings of Michigan* (Lansing, 1916).

Gagnon, Earnest. *Louis Jolliet* (Montreal, 1913).

Gaither, Francis. *The Fatal River: The Life and Death of La Salle* (New York, 1931).

Garrison, Winfred Ernest, and DeGroot, Alfred T. *The Disciples of Christ* (St. Louis, 1958).

Gilpin, Alec R. *The War of 1812 in the Old Northwest* (East Lansing, Mich., 1958).

Greve, C. T. *History of Cincinnati* (2 vols., Chicago, 1904).

Halsey, Francis Whiting. *The Old New York Frontier* (New York, 1901).

Hatcher, Harlan. *The Western Reserve* (Indianapolis, 1949).

Hawinghurst, Walter. *Land of Promise* (New York, 1946).

Hemans, Lawton T. *Life and Times of Stevens Thomson Mason* (Lansing, 1920).

Hildreth, Samuel P. *Biographical and Historical Memoirs of the Early Settlers of Ohio* (Cincinnati, 1852).

———. *Pioneer History of the Ohio Valley* (Cincinnati, 1848).

Hinsdale, Burke A. *The Old Northwest* (New York, 1899).

James, James A. *The Life of George Rogers Clark* (Chicago, 1928).

———. *Oliver Pollock* (New York, 1937).

Juettner, Otto. *Daniel Drake and His Followers* (Cincinnati, 1909).

Knollenburg, Bernhard. *Pioneer Sketches of the Upper Whitewater Valley* (Indianapolis, 1945).

Lee, Alfred E. *History of the City of Columbus* (New York and Chicago, 1892).

Lossing, Benson J. *Pictorial Field Book of the War of 1812* (New York, 1869).

McAvoy, Thomas T. *The Catholic Church in Indiana* (New York, 1940).

MacKenzie, Alexander Slidell. *Life of Commodore Oliver Hazard Perry* (New York, 1840).

McLaughlin, Andrew C. *Lewis Cass* (Boston and New York, 1899).

Maclean, J. P. *Shakers of Ohio . . .* (Columbus, 1907).

Manley, Henry S. *The Treaty of Fort Stanwix, 1784* (Rome, N.Y., 1932).

Morrison, Mabel. *Ann Gilmore Hay* (n.p., 1925).

Morse, Jedediah. *Traveller's Guide* (New Haven, 1826).

Nichols, Thomas Low. *Forty Years of American Life* (New York, 1937).

Parkman, Francis. *La Salle and the Discovery of the Great West* (Boston, 1919).

Parton, James. *Life of Andrew Jackson* (New York, 1859-1860).

Pease, Theodore Calvin. *The Frontier State* (Springfield, 1918).

Petersen, William J. *Steamboating on the Upper Mississippi* (Iowa City, Iowa, 1937).

Pratt, Julius W. *Expansionists of 1812* (New York, 1949).

Quaife, Milo Milton. *Chicago and the Old Northwest* (Chicago, 1913).

———, ed. *War on the Detroit . . .* (Chicago, 1940).

Raney, Francis William. *Wisconsin* (New York, 1940).

Richardson, John. *The War of 1812* (Toronto, 1902).

Roosevelt, Theodore. *The Winning of the West* (4 vols., New York, 1904).

Sagendorph, Kent. *Stevens Thomson Mason* (New York, 1947).

Sandburg, Carl. *Abraham Lincoln* (New York, 1954).

Schafer, Joseph. *The Wisconsin Lead Region* (Madison, Wisc., 1932).

Schauinger, J. Herman. *Cathedrals in the Wilderness* (Milwaukee, 1952).

Sears, Alfred Byron. *Thomas Worthington* (Columbus, 1958).

Spalding, Martin J. *Sketches of the Life, Times, and Character of the Rt. Rev. Benedict Joseph Flaget . . .* (Louisville, 1852).

Steck, Francis Borgia. *The Jolliet-Marquette Expedition, 1673* (Quincy, 1928).

Steele, R. W., and Steele, M. D. *Early Dayton* (Dayton, 1896).

Stevens, Frank E. *The Black Hawk War* (Chicago, 1903).

Stone, William L. *Life of Joseph Brant* (2 vols., New York, 1864).

Sweet, William Warren. *The Story of Religions in America* (New York, 1930).

Thwaites, Reuben Gold. *Wsiconsin* (Boston and New York, 1908).

Todd, Charles S., and Drake, Benjamin. *William Henry Harrison* (New York, 1847).

Tucker, Glenn. *Tecumseh* (Indianapolis, 1956).

Usher, Ellis Baker. *History of Wisconsin* (10 vols., Chicago, 1914).

Van Tyne, Claude H. *The American Revolution* (New York, 1905).

Venable, W. H. *Footprints of the Pioneers in the Ohio Valley* (Cincinnati, 1888).

Villiers du Terrage, Marc, Baron de. *Les Derniers Années de la Louisiane Française; le Chevalier de Kerlérec, d'Abbadie Aubry, Laussat* (Paris, 1904).

Volwiler, Albert T. *George Croghan and the Westward Movement, 1741-1782* (Cleveland, 1926).

Wainwright, Nicholas B. *George Croghan, Wilderness Diplomat* (Chapel Hill, N.C., 1959).

Whittlesey, Charles. *Early History of Cleveland, Ohio* (Cleveland, 1867).

Wildes, Harry Emerson. *Anthony Wayne.*

Wilson, Fraser Ellis. *Arthur St. Clair* (Richmond, 1934).

———. *The Peace of Mad Anthony* (Greenville, O., 1909).

Woodford, Frank B. *Lewis Cass* (New Brunswick, N.J., 1950).

Woolen, William Wesley. *Biographical and Historical Sketches of Early Indiana* (Indianapolis, 1883).

Young, Andrew W. *History of Wayne County, Indiana . . .* (Indianapolis, 1882).

Magazine Articles

Alvord, Clarence W. "Virginia and the West," in *Mississippi Valley Historical Review*, III (1916).

Banta, D. D. "The Early School of Indiana," in *Indiana Magazine of History*, II (1906).

Barce, Elmore. "The Old Chicago Trail," in *Indiana Magazine of History*, XV (1919).

Bartlett, Ruhl Jacob. "The Struggle for Statehood in Ohio," in Ohio Archaeological and Historical Society *Quarterly*, XXXII, (1923).

Belote, Theodore Thomas. "The Scioto Speculation and the French Settlement of Gallipolis," in *Cincinnati University Studies*, III (1907).

Brady, Arthur W. "The Moravian Missions in Indiana," in Mississippi Valley Historical Association *Proceedings* (1919-1920).

Brown, Elizabeth Gasper. "Lewis Cass and the American Indians," in *Michigan History*, XXXVII (1953).

Burton, C. W. "Detroit in the Year 1832," in *Michigan Pioneer and Historical Collections*, XVIII (1897-1898).

Chapman, C. H. "The Historic Johnston Family of the 'Soo'," in *Michigan Pioneer and Historical Collections*, XXXII (1903).

Coleman, Christopher. "The Ohio Valley in the Preliminaries of the War of 1812," in *Mississippi Valley Historical Review*, XII (1920).

Cook, Kermit. "Military Defenses of the Frontier in the Northwest Territory," in *West Virginia History*, X (1948).

Cutler, William Parker. "The Ordinance of July 13, 1787," in Ohio Archaeological and Historical Society *Quarterly*, I (1887).

Dandridge, N. P. "Antoine François Saugrain," in *Ohio Archaeological Quarterly*, XV (1906).

Daniels, Wilson. "Memoirs," in *Indiana Magazine of History*, II (1915).

Davies, W. C. "The Beginnings of the Ohio Company," in Ohio Archaeological and Historical Society *Publications*, IV (1895).

Dial, George White. "Construction of the Ohio Canals," in Ohio Archaeological and Historical Society *Publications*, XIII (1904).

Douglas, Albert. "Major General Arthur St. Clair," in Ohio Archoeological and Historical *Quarterly*, XVI (1907).

Downes, Randolph C. "Thomas Jefferson and the Removal of Governor St. Clair in 1802," Ohio Archaeological and Historical Society *Quarterly*, XXXVI (1926).

Dunn, Jacob P. "Father Gibault: The Patriot Priest of the Northwest," in Illinois State Historical Society *Transactions*, X (1906).

Esarey, Logan B. "The Pioneer Aristocracy," in *Indiana Magazine of History*, XIII (1917).

Finch, John. "Reminiscences," in *Indiana Magazine of History*, VII (1911).

Frost, Clarence. "The Early Railroads of Southern Michigan," in *Michigan Pioneer and Historical Collections*, XXXVIII (1912).

Fuller, George N. "Settlement of Michigan Territory," in *Mississippi Valley Historical Review*, II (1915).

Galloway, Tod B. "The Ohio-Michigan Boundary Line Dispute," in Ohio Archaeological and Historical Society *Publications*, IV (1895).

George, John J. "The Miami Canal," in Ohio Archaeological and Historical Society *Quarterly*, XXXVI (1927).

Glidden, A. C. "Pioneer Farming," in *Michigan Pioneer and Historical Collections*, XVIII (1891).

Hacker, Louis Morton. "The West and the War of 1812," in *Mississippi Valley Historical Review*, X (1924).

Hulbert, A. B. "The Old National Road—the Historic Highway of America," in Ohio Archaeological and Historical Society *Publications*, IX (1901).

Iglehart, John E. "Methodism in Southern Indiana," in *Indiana Magazine of History*, XVII (1921).

Illinois State Historical Society, "Journal of the Convention," VI, No. 3 (1913).

Maclean, J. P. "The Society of Shakers," in Ohio Archaeological and Historical Society *Publications*, IX (1901).

Parker, Benjamin S. "Pioneer Life," in *Indiana Magazine of History*, III (1907).

Pease, Theodore. "The Ordinance of 1787," in *Mississippi Valley Historical Review*, XXV (1929).

Pratt, Julius W. "Western Aims in the War of 1812," in *Mississippi Valley Historical Review*, XII (1925).

Quaife, Milo Milton. "The Ohio Campaigns of 1782," in *Mississippi Valley Historical Review*, XVIII (1931).

Randall, James G. "George Rogers Clark's Service of Supply," in *Mississippi Valley Historical Review*, VIII (1922).

Riker, Dorothy, "Jonathan Jennings," in *Indiana Magazine of History*, XXVIII (1932).

Ryan, Daniel J. "The Scioto Company and Its Purchase," in Ohio Archaeological and Historical Society *Publications*, III (1894).

Sears, Alfred B. "The Political Philosophy of Arthur St. Clair," in Ohio Archaeological and Historical Society *Quarterly*, XLIX (1940).

Sloane, Rush R. "When Did Ohio in Fact Become a Sovereign State of the Union?" in Ohio Archaeological and Historical Society *Publications*, IX (1900-1901).

Spill, Bayrd. "State-Making in Wisconsin, 1846-1848," in *Wisconsin Magazine of History*, XX (1936).

———. "The University of Michigan: Beginnings," in *Michigan History Magazine*, XII (1925).

Thwaites, Reuben Gold. "Story of the Black Hawk War," in *Wisconsin Historical Collections*, XII (1892).

Van Buren, A. D. P. "The Fever and Ague—'Mosquito Rash'—Mosquitos and Old Pioneers' Foes," in *Michigan Pioneer and Historical Collections*, V (1882).

———. "The Frolics of Forty-Five Years Ago," in *Michigan Pioneer and Historical Collections*, V (1882).

———. "The Log Schoolhouse Era," in *Michigan Pioneer and Historical Collections*, XIV (1887).

Vance, John L. "The French Settlement and Settlers of Gallipolis," in Ohio Archaeological and Historical Society *Publications*, III (1890).

Webster, Homer J. "William Henry Harrison's Administration of Indiana Territory," in Indiana Historical Society *Publications*, IV (1907).

Williams, B. O. "My Recollections of Early Schools in Detroit," in *Michigan Pioneers and Historical Collections*, V (1882).

Wittke, Carl. "The Ohio-Michigan Boundary Dispute Re-Examined," in Ohio State Archaeological and Historical Society *Quarterly*, XLV (1936).

Acknowledgments

This second volume of my projected six-volume history of the American Frontier would scarcely have been completed in such good time without the experience, knowledge and patience of many persons. For all kinds of help I am grateful to the staffs of the following institutions: the Ohio County Library, Wheeling, West Virginia; the Carnegie Library of Parkersburg, West Virginia; the Library of West Virginia University; the Marietta College Library, Marietta, Ohio; the Carnegie Library of Pittsburgh; the Library of the University of Chicago; the Detroit Public Library; the New York City Public Library; the Indianapolis Public Library; the Boston Public Library; the Library of Ohio State University; the Library of Indiana University; the Cincinnati Public Library; the Library of Ohio University; the Library of Congress; the Wisconsin State Historical Society; the Massachusetts Historical Society, Boston; the Ohio State Library, Columbus; the Indiana Historical Society Library, Indianapolis; and the Historical and Philosophical Society of Ohio. My special thanks go to Virginia Perry, Virginia Ebeling, Naomi Otto, Lois Hiebel, Michael Reynolds, Charles Shetler and Agnes Patton.

I owe a debt of gratitude to that steadfast friend of creative scholars, Robert F. Munn, Director of Libraries, West Virginia University, for obtaining for me microfilm of several indispensable historical collections. His gracious assistance in my behalf precluded the necessity of extensive travel and added expense and permitted a full measure of time for research and writing.

I am indebted to George Blazier, Archivist of Marietta College, for permission to use the Rufus Putnam Papers and the Paul Fearing Papers, which figure so prominently in the chapters on the early settlements and government of Ohio. I want to express my thanks to F. Gerald Ham, Associate Curator, West Virginia University, for graciously placing at my disposal microfilm of the Shakers Letters as well as photostatic material pertaining to this interesting sect, on which he is writing a dissertation.

I am grateful to my good wife, Marie, for her patience and forbearance while this work inched toward completion, and to Ruel Foster and Ernie McCue for lightening my literary burden with cheerful words on difficult or fruitless days. Last but not least, I acknowledge my appreciation of the wise editorial guidance and encouragement given by Harry Platt, former editor of Bobbs-Merrill, and by my present editors, Monroe Stearns and Andrée Fé Coers.

JOHN ANTHONY CARUSO
Morgantown, West Virginia

Index

Current boundary lines have been observed in locating towns, villages, forts, etc., within states and provinces.